WENDY LEBLANC grew up in Sydney. After 15 years of a highly successful career in the Australian financial markets, she married Rick and became mother to Daniel. With no desire to return to her career, Wendy and her family moved to the Northern Tablelands in New South Wales where she discovered another yet more challenging job—motherhood. The lessons of motherhood set her on a course of both personal revelation and academic investigation into how families and communities work, and what is causing them to break down.

Wendy now works as a freelance conflict consultant offering mediation and conflict resolution services in situations as diverse as families in distress and industrial disputes throughout rural and regional New South Wales. She has coordinated and taught intensive courses for women and children escaping domestic violence, and has been president of the district's Women's Centre and Child Sexual Assault Service. She has been involved in lobbying for increased support for sole parents and their children and is currently campaigning to introduce the Hope for the Children Foundation to Armidale.

At forty-five, Wendy has just completed her PhD thesis at Macquarie University, entitled *Paradigm conflict: A study in broad spectrum conflict generated by the onset of motherhood*. *Naked Motherhood* is based on the research undertaken for her thesis and inspired by the hundreds of mothers she has met, interviewed and taught over the past ten years.

Wendy will donate 5% of the income she receives from *Naked Motherhood* after its publication to the Hope for the Children Foundation. 'Hope' is a Rotary sponsored project which is run primarily by volunteers who have successfully raised their own children, who have enjoyed the process, and who understand the vital role community plays in the early parenting years. They are trained to non-judgementally support and assist families who are stressed or distressed by the changes parenthood has brought to their lives.

NAKED MOTHERHOOD

SHATTERING ILLUSIONS AND SHARING TRUTHS

WENDY LeBlanc

RANDOM HOUSE

Random House Australia Pty Ltd
20 Alfred Street, Milsons Point, NSW 2061
http://www.randomhouse.com.au

Sydney New York Toronto
London Auckland Johannesburg
and agencies throughout the world

First published 1999

Copyright © Wendy LeBlanc 1999

All rights reserved. No part of this publication may be reproduced,
stored in a retrieval system, or transmitted in any form or by any means,
electronic, mechanical, photocopying, recording or otherwise, without the
prior written permission of the Publisher.

National Library of Australia
Cataloguing-in-Publication Data

LeBlanc, Wendy.
    Naked motherhood : shattering illusions and sharing truths.

    Bibliography.
    Includes index.
    ISBN 0 091 83991 2.

1. Motherhood. 2. Mother and child. I. Title.

306.8743

Design by Gayna Murphy
Typeset by Asset Typesetting Pty Ltd, Sydney
Printed by Griffin Press, a division of PMP Communications, Adelaide

10 9 8 7 6 5 4 3 2 1

This book contains non-specific, general advice and should not be relied on as a substitute for personal
or family counselling or medical consultation. The author and the publisher cannot accept responsibility
for any consequence arising out of any negligent misstatement or other error contained within this book
or any failure of a reader to obtain appropriate professional medical advice.

*To my mother, Annette Swain,
in honour of her remarkable ability to endure
and rise above the difficulties of motherhood.
Thank you for all the years of love and support.*

DO NOT LAUGH AT THE PRINCESS
CHANGED TO A FROG
SPLAYED GLASS-BELLIED
ON THE WINDOW TO YOUR KINGDOM
—SHE IS YOUR MOTHER

E.A. HORNE

CONTENTS

Acknowledgements xii
Note to the Reader xiv
Introduction 1

ONE: THE FIRST SHOCKS 12
Rites of Passage 13
When Pregnancy is Special 15
When Pregnancy is Less Than Special 16
Birth 19
When Bonding Works 22
When Bonding is Difficult 24
Time to Adjust 31
Exhaustion 32
Some Babies Sleep—Others Do Not 36
Breastfeeding 38
When the Mind Lets You Down 41
The Horror Hours 43
Help for Hanging in There 44

TWO: REALITY SETS IN 49
Instinct 50
Abandonment 53
The Loss of Freedom and Spontaneity 56
Loneliness and Isolation 59
Interruptions to Personal Interests 62
Crying 64
Immersion, Obsession and Mania—a Continuum 65
Trapped 68
Achievement 71
Recognition and Acclaim 73
Time Out 75
Asking for Help 78
The Conspiracy of Silence 79
Help for Hanging in There 84

THREE: THE CHANGING SELF-IMAGE 93
Physical Changes 94
General Health and Fitness 100
Self-perception 103
The Health of the Baby 105
Identity 107
Self-esteem 109
Conversation 112
Sex Appeal 114

Status 116
Judgementalism 118
Failure 124
Society 127
Help for Hanging in There 131

FOUR: THE EMOTIONAL ROLLER-COASTER 138
Control and Coping 138
Emotionalism 142
Joy 143
Frustration 143
Anger and Rage 144
Guilt 146
Responsibility 147
Fear 148
Empathy 152
Childhood Issues Revisited 155
Grief 160
Blues, Stress and Depression 161
Post Traumatic Stress 167
Love 168
Help for Hanging in There 170

FIVE: A MOTHER'S RELATIONSHIP WITH HER PARTNER 179
Women Change 181
Security 182
Dependency 183
Men Change 187
Selfishness 189
Lack of Empathy 190
Communication 192
Intimacy 194
Sex 195
Equality 198
Power 199
Roles 201
Envy 202
Raising the Children 204
The Brady Bunch 205
Breakdown of Coping Mechanisms 206
Violence Against Women 209
Violence Against Men 213
Help for Hanging in There 215

SIX: MOTHERS WITHOUT PARTNERS 229
Celebrating Birth 230
Blame 232
No Relief in Sight 233
Poverty and Humiliation 237
Decisions and Responsibility 241
Guilt 243
The Ex-Partner—The Father 245

CONTENTS

The Fantasy and the Reality 250
The Schedule 252
Social Life 255
Other Men 258
Intensity of Mother–Child Relationships 262
You and Me Against the World 264
No Regrets 269
Help for Hanging in There 272

SEVEN: A MOTHER'S RELATIONSHIPS WITH THE GREATER WORLD 277
The Relationship with One's Own Mother 278
The Rest of the First Family 283
Friends 285
Other Mothers 286
The Lost Tribes 290
Child Care 298
Relaxation and Holidays 304
Feeling Left Behind 306
Women Who Don't Work ... and Those Who Do 307
Help for Hanging in There 324

EIGHT: REMARKABLE REWARDS 333
Motherhood Refreshes 335
Physicality and Sensuality Rediscovered 335
There is No Better Excuse 337
Appreciation of Other Women 337
Friendships Become More Meaningful 338
Humility 339
Motherhood is Connectedness 340
Mothers Are Tough 342
Mothers Are Resourceful 342
Necessity is the Mother of Invention 343
Courage 344
The Privilege of Motherhood 345
Assertiveness Grows 346
Confidence Rises 347
Emotional and Personal Growth 347
A Person Complete 348
The Daily Hero 349
Faith and Spirituality 350
The Love is Unbelievable 350

Epilogue 352
Appendices 357
Who to Call for Help 363
Bibliography 373
Index 380

ACKNOWLEDGEMENTS

As always, it is not possible to list everyone who deserves my thanks so I will pick out those who have been most present in their support. First must come my husband, Rick, who willingly supported me financially while I researched and wrote a book from which there was no guarantee of income. His endless patience with my lack of computer skills and his lack of expectation that I should do 'wifely' things around the house while this book was being born are deeply appreciated.

I cannot thank my son, Daniel, enough for the support and encouragement he offered me as my back turned to him and my face to the computer. His understanding is well beyond his tender years.

Then there is my Mum, Annette Swain. Her belief in my ability to finish this work and get it out into the public arena has been unwavering. Her editorial suggestions have been invaluable. Our relationship has grown closer as we have discussed the issues contained in this book and that, by itself, has been a bonus which has made all the effort worthwhile.

My dear friend Kelesi Woodhouse believed in me when my own faith in myself wavered. Time and again she set me back on my path with a support which boosted my courage and commitment. She also, in the midst of post-natal depression and early motherhood, coordinated the discussion forum I held on motherhood in the Blue Mountains.

My thanks go to Marion Cutting who coordinated the forum held in Sydney and to the NSW Nursing Mothers Association who assisted by distributing invitations to these forums for me.

ACKNOWLEDGEMENTS

Through the efforts of Narelle George I have questionnaires and letters from New Zealand which confirmed my suspicion that the conflicts women are experiencing during their transition to motherhood are not merely an Australian phenomenon. Narelle's intense honesty in sharing her own experiences has contributed invaluable depth to this work.

Without the remarkable intuition of Jenny Halliday I would never have met Barbara Holborow, who introduced me to her publisher, now mine. I cannot thank Barbara enough. Without Mary-Ann Scott, Liz Horne, Marta Hum, Nancy Crozier and Salvina Sjøholm I could not have presented my manuscript with such confidence. Nor would I have survived the ups and downs of publishing my first book without Robert Hindmarch's tireless counsel. Kym Kilpatrick has been a stalwart sounding board on the issues of domestic violence, abuse and post traumatic stress disorder. She also has provided wonderful editorial support.

To those family members and friends who have listened to me talk endlessly about the issues contained in this book, from the bottom of my heart, I thank you for your patience and your support. And then there is everyone else; women who attended discussion forums; all the women who took the time to fill out my long and difficult questionnaire; others who have written to or phoned me to tell me their stories; students in my classes and women in the street who have taken the time to trust me with their intimate lives.

Thank you, all of you. This book is for you, in honour of all you have given and all you will continue to give to mothering your children.

NOTE TO THE READER

My research into the contemporary status of motherhood and how it is affecting women, men and children is ongoing. I am certain that the issues contained in *Naked Motherhood* are but the tip of the iceberg. If you would like to share your story, particularly if motherhood has affected you in a manner not covered in this book, and you have devised ways of coping that work for you that you believe may help others, please write to:

>Wendy LeBlanc
>PO Box 964
>Armidale NSW 2350

or e-mail me on:

>wendyl@northnet.com.au

INTRODUCTION

OUR MOTHERS WALK NAKED

This is not a book full of advice on how you can be a better mother. It is the distilled experiences of how hundreds of Australian and New Zealand women have experienced and coped with their transition from independent woman to 'mother'. It is about what it means to a woman to become a mother; what motherhood does to her life, identity, priorities, relationships and future. It is about all the things nobody tells you until afterwards and the things nobody talks about even then. It is about the side of motherhood that is buried beneath a conspiracy of silence which clouds any debate about the changes it brings to a woman's life at this time, in this society.

It is not an emperor who is walking naked through our streets, it is our mothers. All of us collude with the conspiracy by pretending we can see her fully clothed in all her mythological finery. We fear we will look foolish and inadequate if we admit we find motherhood difficult or cry out for help when we feel we can cope no longer on our own. Our mothers walk naked—and they do walk alone.

Too many of us come to motherhood expecting our lives to be disrupted for only a matter of a few months. However, once the effects of pregnancy and birth have worn off, a significant number of women awaken to a very different world from the one they expected. Amongst some of the more shocking aspects of motherhood are chronic exhaustion, prolonged depression, ill-health, an inability to bond with the baby, a breakdown in relationships, plummeting self-worth and self-esteem, anger (and rage), and gyrating emotions.

There have been a few things said to me in the course of researching this book which have been said so often they are worth repeating here:

- But nobody ever tells you that!
- Why didn't somebody tell me the truth???
- But I am (or my experience is) probably a bit different from most other people you have talked to.

After listening to the stories of all these women I find that everyone *does* have a different tale to tell. However, their underlying experiences of shock and confusion are extraordinarily similar. When I realised this I set out to catalogue the potential side effects of motherhood and how they may impact on a woman's psyche, identity, emotions, self-image, relationships, place in our society and life focus. My primary purpose in writing it has been to put a name to those effects about which many women feel they must not speak for fear of being called 'crazy'. Until a problem has a name and is recognised it cannot be debated, nor can it be resolved—it cannot even be seen. Until it is acknowledged, nobody understands that they are not alone with their difficulties of adjustment to what is supposed to be a natural occupation—that of motherhood.

In spite of the outpouring of hurt and dismay, helplessness and regret I encountered amongst mothers from all walks of life regarding these issues, I also discovered that there is almost universal agreement (even amongst those who would choose not to be mothers if they had their time over) that motherhood has made them:

- More compassionate and empathic
- Able to love more deeply
- Stronger, tougher, more determined
- More complete as a person
- More acutely aware of the value of life, relationships and time!

Many people have asked me what I think is so different for mothers today that they are stressed and depressed in numbers indicative of a silent epidemic. Why are we women finding the most basic biological desire to reproduce our species so hard to fulfil? Several reasons are glaringly obvious, others are more subtle. The following have emerged as core problems.

The Age of First-time Mothers

The average age at which a woman becomes a mother is now over twenty-eight, which means many of us are well into our thirties and even our forties when we make the transformation into 'mother'. Although a woman in her thirties may not feel any older than a twenty-year-old, her body does not bounce back quite so readily and she tires more easily. The demands of pregnancy, childbirth and mothering put her under a degree of physical stress she has most likely never before encountered. Unfortunately, the myth remains that her life will return to normal within a matter of weeks, at the most three months. Because there is no hint that it may take years, she is quite unprepared for the rigours of motherhood.

Our Mobile Society

Our society is more mobile now than at any other time in human history. Our family sizes are shrinking. The chances of a woman bearing her first baby surrounded by the community in which she grew up are minimal. What is more likely is that she may become a mother with little or no family and perhaps no close friends within hundreds of kilometres who can help and guide her. Her isolation is often profound and her loneliness escalates as she craves adult company with whom to share her joys and the difficulties of becoming a mother.

There Are Losses

By the time many women become mothers they have had jobs, careers, possessions, independence, autonomy, freedom and the time and space to be self-focussed for ten or more years. They have grown accustomed to directing their own lives and to receiving positive feedback for their achievements out there in the world. When they become mothers it often feels as though the door has been slammed shut on that life forever. That is a huge shock.

Lack of Equality

For thirty years women's liberation has fought for equal rights to equal work for equal pay. Even though only 3%[1] of the corporate boardroom is filled by

---

1 Horan, Wall and Walker, 'Statistics: Facts of the Matter' in *Good Weekend*, the *Sydney Morning Herald*, 6.3.1993

women and only 10% of our politicians are women; even though women still only earn 65% of the male wage and do 70% of all unpaid work, the majority of child care and occupy the majority of the low-paid, part-time jobs,[2] we nevertheless have come to *expect* equality. While we are child-free, no matter where we are in the paid-working or academic hierarchy we *expect* to be treated with equal respect and value as anyone else. We have been lulled into thinking that equality is possible if only we work hard enough for it.

The truly astonishing shock for independent, self-determining women when they bear their babies is that they awaken to a world where there is such a thing as a female paradigm. Over time, and with disbelief in their hearts and minds, they learn that it is denigrated and devalued. Eventually they begin to realise that the only equality we ever had a hope of attaining was on the male playing field where 'doing' and 'achieving' and earning dollars are the only yardsticks of a successful life. A woman is not considered to have led a meaningful, worthwhile, fulfilling, rewarding or successful life anymore if 'all she ever did' was raise her children well. This is depressing.

Economic Imperative

Economic times have made it essential for many families to have access to two incomes, so women who do not necessarily wish to be there are being drawn back into the workforce in ever increasing numbers. Alternatively, because mothering is so devalued, many mothers feel paid work is essential to their mental health. They may love the work they did before they became mothers and find they prefer it to mothering, or may feel the need to regain their lost identity and self-worth by doing something which is valued by the society. Whether they choose or are forced to re-enter the paid workforce, mothers are being asked to fit two jobs into one lifetime and feel as though they are being torn apart by the demands being made on them.

Those mothers who choose full-time motherhood are often made to feel less worthy than those who have returned to paid employment as though they were 'wasting time'. This comes at a time when their economic status is likely to have declined significantly—especially if they need to obtain paid work but are unable to do so, or if they are single. Adding insult to injury, a new mother is often shocked to discover that she also suffers an insidious decline in economic power within her relationship as her partner assumes more than his fair share of

---

2 NSW Women's Advisory Council, *Women and Work: An Overview*, Sydney, 1991.

control over the family's finances because he is the one 'earning' it and she is at 'leisure'.

Without exception, every woman I interviewed for this book said she thought mothering her children was the hardest job she had ever done and expressed her wrath at her society's inability to value it. The majority also said it was the most rewarding—but by no means all of them.

MY STORY

My story, too, is different from others I have recorded. Thoughts about motherhood, for me, began thirty years ago when I was thirteen. My mother was then quite sure I would leave school, get a job, find a man and settle down to raise babies by the time I was in my early twenties. I used to tell her, all those years ago, that if I had not found 'magic man number one' by the time I was twenty-seven or twenty-eight I would begin looking for him then. I knew I would only ever have one child of my own and that I would not be a mother until I was into my thirties—both unusual expectations at that time. At eighteen I suddenly knew, with absolute certainty, that my child would be a boy and I would call him Daniel.

I set out to find a career and essentially coincidence steered me into the world of merchant banks and the commodities and financial markets. I bought a unit. I bought a house. Then I bought a German shepherd pup. I made a conscious decision that, if I was considering bringing a baby into my life, I had better make sure I could love another being enough to care for it. I thought it was better to find out with a dog than a child. As it turned out, anyone who knew me for the next fourteen years also knew Karla.

I began to attend personal growth workshops to find out who I really was. I wanted nothing less than to scour myself clean of as many of my destructive issues as I could before I became a mother so that I would not pass them along to my son. I realise now that these classes were but a game compared with the level of personal growth a baby brings to a woman's life. But I did not know that then.

One morning I woke up and I was twenty-eight. It was time to find magic man number one. It took me two years to find him but one day he stood up in a crowded room and the same inner voice which had told me I would become a mother in my thirties to a boy called Daniel now told me, 'That is the man you are going to marry.' And it was. We moved in together and I gave up smoking.

In 1985 the merchant bank for which I worked promoted two women to the level of associate director. The bank I worked for was only the second in the entire financial market to lift the glass ceiling. Both women had worked for the company longer than I had but were of my own age and held approximately equivalent positions. I found myself feeling uncomfortable in their presence and dissatisfied with myself. Realising that we women tend to be our own worst enemies I questioned why I could not be happy for them. The answer that came back to me was that I now had the opportunity to make real career choices. With the doorway to 'real success' opened wide I knew, if I was to continue this career, I had to become upwardly mobile. When I asked myself whether I wanted to do that I saw, in my mind's eye, years stretching into the distance being consumed by the making of money. Everything inside me recoiled in horror and screamed a reverberating 'NO!!!'

Six weeks later I was pregnant. Eight weeks after that Rick and I married and six months after that, when I was thirty-two years old, Daniel came into our lives. Not once, not even for a tiny moment, have I ever regretted my career choice. This, and all my fulfilled prophecies of the twenty years prior, however, say nothing about how easy—or not so easy—I found the process of adjustment to motherhood.

What I never expected was that I would become a completely different person from the moment Daniel was born. I did not realise that everyone else would suddenly treat me as though I had no value, no contribution to make and no valid opinions anymore. I had not understood how closely my identity was bound up with being a person with a 'significant' job. Certainly my expectations of babies were way off beam and nothing, *nothing* had prepared me for the exhaustion, the fear of not mothering him perfectly and the overwhelming love I had for him—nor many of the other issues contained in this book.

THE STUDY

As I began to realise that motherhood was fraught with unexpected pitfalls for me I wondered how women coped whose lives were less blessed than mine. I had a car and I could escape the house whenever I needed to. I owned a home with a beautiful water view. I had enough money to buy the occasional diversion. My husband was supportive and a loving, involved father. I had

INTRODUCTION

achieved a certain degree of credibility in the workforce and thought I knew what I was capable of doing and who I was as a person. (HA!)

How, I still wonder, do women cope who are stuck in high rise rented flats with no money, no car, no space to get away from their children, no partner—or a destructive one? How do they hold onto their self-esteem if it had no solid base to begin with? How do women cope if they cannot speak English, or if they do not have any social supports at all? If I in my privileged position found this hard, how hard is it for them?

Initially out of curiosity I developed a questionnaire asking a diverse group of women to rate their experiences of 69 possible changes motherhood may bring to a woman's life and relationships. The questionnaire is divided into four categories. They are:

- Whether the change was expected
- What effect it had on her ability to cope
- What effect it had on her sense of inner conflict (intrapersonal conflict)
- What effect it had on her conflicts with others (interpersonal conflict)

I asked them to rank their experiences from:

- '1' if the change was completely expected and had no effect or a positive effect on her life, through to
- '5' if the change was totally unexpected, caused her extreme difficulty in coping, or maximum intra- or interpersonal conflict

Many of the surveys returned with accompanying letters which are poignant and express both the heartache and pride of being a mother.

Once I saw the degree of passion and pain with which these women were experiencing motherhood I undertook a series of discussion forums and followed these up with individual interviews. During each of these, mothers discussed what their expectations of motherhood had been prior to the birth of their first babies and how becoming a mother had affected them as people. They talked about the changes motherhood brought to their relationships, identity, ambitions, view of the world, and the altered expectations they now had of themselves and their society. The ages of the women who contributed to this research were from twenty-two to forty-two years of age at the time of the birth of their first babies and the average was twenty-nine years of age, which is just over the national average for all first-time mothers in Australia. The forums were held in cities and in regional and rural areas; in wealthy, middle-class and depressed neighbourhoods. They were full of laughter and genuine anguish at the way our society relates to motherhood and to our children.

Of the women who contributed to this work, 95% still had pre-teen first children so their memories of early motherhood had not yet been clouded by the rigours of teenhood. They are 'average' women who have not attained public acclaim or notoriety—yet. Some are highly educated and qualified and have achieved at high levels in their chosen fields. Others are undereducated and have worked in less powerful positions. Some have been full-time mothers since their first child was born; others went back to paid work a.s.a.p. Some are wealthy, some comfortable; others suffer enormous financial stresses and deprivation. They are married, divorced, single; they have happy relationships and unhappy ones and some have lived through horrific domestic violence. Some aspire to do great things with their lives; others are content to take life as it comes. Some live over one hundred kilometres from the nearest town, others next door to the local shopping centre. For reasons of privacy and confidentiality I have changed the name of every woman, partner and child quoted or referred to in this book.

In spite of their diversity, at the heart of every mother's story I have recorded is a profound sense of being undervalued. Each feels negated by politicians and business, by advertisers and television script writers; and perhaps also by other women, by their sisters and brothers, by their own mothers and mothers-in-law, or by their spouses. Many feel cheated—robbed of the right to revel in this most unique of human experiences by a culture which tends to view motherhood as the doing of nothing. Somewhere in the last twenty years, mothering has subtly become categorised as a leisure activity and therefore, especially when practised full-time or at the cost of 'real work', as an indication of subnormal ambition, an act of laziness or self-indulgence.

Nevertheless, if a mother finds the institution of motherhood stifling or unrewarding as a full-time occupation and goes back to the paid workforce, it is she who will be accused of not nurturing enough, of selfishness. It is she who will be blamed if her child does not thrive in school, has emotional or psychological problems, does not develop into a model citizen. And she will feel guilty.

INTRODUCTION

Women today find themselves in a no-win situation. They have choices their foremothers never had, it is true, but this is a two-edged sword. None of these choices are fully acceptable to a society which still wants its women to shoulder the responsibility of mothering *and* wants to draw on their other talents *but* does not want to participate in the nurturing of their children.

One of the most obvious effects of relegating mothers to this no-man's land is the significant increase in their experiences of postnatal stress (PNS) and postnatal depression (PND). These 'diseases' affect up to 88% and 30–50% of first-time mothers respectively.[3] These statistics are frightening. If they related to a new virus which specifically attacked one sector of the population you could guarantee that millions—nay, billions—of dollars would be thrown into research to discover its cause and its cure.

Unfortunately this is not a virus in the accepted sense. But it is an epidemic and it is affecting all but 12% of new mothers. Its effects can be truly debilitating with consequences that are so long-term as to hold the potential to affect future generations. The hidden costs of not acknowledging, researching and treating this epidemic are inestimable in terms of its ability to destroy physical and emotional health, to undermine human potential and to create destructive relationships.

These injustices, and the many more I uncovered as my research unfolded, spurred me into writing this book.

IT IS TIME TO RETHINK WHAT EQUALITY MEANS

At the turn of the last century the suffragettes fought for the right to vote. In the middle of this century the fight began, and continues, for the right to gain equal work at equal pay with equal opportunities for advancement. It is time to move on from this most valuable base which we and our foremothers established. As the next century begins it is time to start the fight for the equality of male and female paradigms and values.

Rather than polarise the debate between men and women further by using terms like male and female paradigms, I have created some new terms of my own. The first is the 'doing' paradigm which describes the predominantly

---

3 NSW Women's Consultative Committee, *If Motherhood is Bliss, why do I feel so awful?* NSW Ministry for the Status and Advancement of Women, Recommendation 5.1.2.4, p.9.. Sydney, 1994, p.19. This committee was convened by the NSW Ministry for the Status and Advancement of Women. It surveyed 882 women across NSW and cross-culturally to ascertain the degree to which women were experiencing postnatal stress and depression.

male world of material achievement and success; the second is the 'relating' paradigm which describes the predominantly female world which is concerned with the achievements and successes of relationships. Many women today, of course, operate in the doing paradigm with a diminished concern for relationships just as many men have become more concerned with relational issues. Perhaps in the next century we will find balance between these paradigms, but as it stands now, the doing paradigm dominates.

According to the doing paradigm the things which matter are: balance sheets, budget deficits, expanding economies and eternally escalating consumerism; jobs today and user pays; power, political expediency and short-term thinking—economic rationalism and productivity.

In the relating paradigm the things which matter are: our children and their safety, education and opportunities; the ability to parent in ways that are rewarding; meaningful work and promotion; relationships with partners and friends; the ability to care for the elderly and the weak; the long-term future of the planet—quality of life.

It is easy to see why the doing paradigm is dominant. A woman who does not work, children, poor folks, old folks and those who cannot keep up with the rapid speed of change of the late twentieth century are 'not productive'. And if you are not productive in the doing paradigm you are a cost and a liability— you are on the negative side of the balance sheet no matter how much you contribute to the collective quality of life. You are the bit which gets cut back when times are tough.

Who defines what productivity means? Productivity is not objective, it is subjective. It all depends on the way you look at the world, what you value and therefore include on the balance sheet. Did you know that if women's unpaid domestic work had been included in the calculations of Australia's gross domestic product (GDP) in 1994 the GDP would have risen by $228 billion or by 58%?[4] This is a pretty significant slice of the country's productivity to ignore, isn't it?

Whether the doing paradigm includes women's labour in the productivity calculations or not, the majority of women consider that giving birth to their babies is the most incredible act of productivity of which any human being is capable. There is no creation on earth as miraculous as the birth of a baby and no labour as valuable as the raising of that baby in an environment of

---

4 Peter Cook, *Early Childcare: Infants & Nations at Risk*, Melbourne, 1996, p.42

INTRODUCTION

unconditional love. Mothers are, after all, physically producing the next generation. What computer chip could possibly be worth more than the people who will one day use the blessed things!

True equality will only be ours when the relating paradigm is seen to be worth as much as the doing paradigm. It is time we acknowledged that the institution of motherhood, in its currently devalued form, is not serving the needs of women any longer. Neither, therefore, is it serving the needs of our children, our relationships or our society. Little is written to prepare a prospective mother for the potentially difficult consequences she may encounter after she enters motherhood. There is no public reassurance that, if those consequences come upon her, she is far from inadequate; and that she is a normal woman experiencing normal manifestations of the transition to motherhood in this not so normal social structure—a structure that not only fails to facilitate this transition but ignores it altogether.

What follows is an exposé of the issues, their symptoms and consequences, that are causing an epidemic of postnatal stress, depression and conflict amongst women who are attempting to live by the values of the relating paradigm in a world dominated by the paradigm of material achievement. If you have encountered any of the experiences contained in this book know, *absolutely*, that you are not alone.

My most heartfelt wish for this book is that it will encourage women, whether they have chosen to be mothers or not, whether they have chosen full-time motherhood or motherhood combined with paid work, to talk about the reality of their lives—warts and all. The current social structure, based on an imbalanced worship of the paradigm of material achievement, *is* undermining our ability to comfortably fulfil the mothering role and in many cases it is destroying that ability. Only when we collectively acknowledge the conflict of interest between the parenting population and those who would have us believe that economic growth and escalating consumption are all-important, will we begin to realise the magnitude of its impact on us, our relationships, our children and our society. Only when we speak out collectively will there be any possibility of change.

ONE
THE FIRST SHOCKS

We all know that motherhood begins with pregnancy and childbirth. That much is obvious. What is far less obvious is what these processes will mean for the woman involved; how they will affect her physically, psychologically and emotionally. Nobody can accurately predict who amongst us will be blessed with the text-book painless birth and wondrous experience of motherhood, and who will feel as though they have been taken to their limits and beyond. The myth is that if a woman attends the right childbirth classes, does her pelvic floor exercises, practises yoga and meditation, is fit and healthy she can expect a 'reasonable' and manageable birth experience which will naturally progress to blissful motherhood. For some women this is the case. For others the process is so far removed from this it strands them in a seemingly foreign land.

When a woman gives birth to her first baby she usually feels, and rightly so, that she has accomplished and survived the most remarkable feat of creation and endurance she is ever likely to achieve in her lifetime. Some report experiencing a sense of exhilaration for days after the birth greater than that which the best drug on earth is able to provide. When that high begins to wear off and the new mother looks around for support to help integrate this life-changing experience, she finds no-one who is willing or able to understand what is going on inside her. All she has to help her is her creation, a mysterious being who now consumes her every minute, who demands everything of her and who, in its earliest days, is able to give so little in return. Everybody else goes back to their lives as though nothing in the world has altered when, in her world, absolutely everything has changed.

The reality of raising a baby ever so slowly begins to seep into her consciousness and more often than not there is a yawning gulf between her expectations and the actual experience. To a large degree women themselves are responsible for these unacceptable gaps in our knowledge. We do not honestly tell our younger women before they become pregnant about our experiences and so do not pass on our wisdom. Subsequently a new mother comes to birth and the institution of motherhood desperately ignorant of what it will mean to her, as a person, to make such a life-transforming decision as bringing a baby into her world.

I have given birth once. Two years later I was the official photographer at the birth of one of my nieces. These are the two truly miraculous moments in my life. No less remarkable is the enormous transformation the woman undergoes as she, in an instant, becomes a mother. I am left all these years later profoundly in awe of the power, the pain and the passion of this process.

RITES OF PASSAGE

In our tribal days women gathered together around the birth of a child, recognising the 'important biological and social transition'[5] the new mother was undergoing. It was women's business and men deferred to their expertise. Those who had passed before into motherhood prepared the mother-to-be for the birth and educated her. Her girlfriends, not yet mothers, bid her farewell knowing she was leaving their world and entering that of mothers. She in turn bid farewell to her girlhood with ceremony and guidance. Even when the process of birth went awry and the outcome was not ideal, the new mother derived security from the collective involvement and wisdom of her female community; and there was a collective sense of awe in the processes of life. Celebration.

A woman used to bear her child amidst her family, her network of support. In many cultures around the world the new mother is still expected to stay in

---

[5] Stanislav Grof, 'Healing Potential of Non-Ordinary States of Consciousness: Observations from Psychedelic Therapy and Holotropic Breathwork', paper presented at Portiuncula Centre for Spiritual Development, Toowoomba, February, 1996, p.2

her own home for thirty and even forty days after she gives birth.[6] There she begins her earliest days of mothering surrounded by care and assistance—and rejoicing. When she doesn't know what to do with a screaming babe an experienced aunt whisks the child away, calming the baby's nerves as well as those of the new mother. If her baby coughs her grandmother is there to soothe the mother's fears and to prescribe those things she used to give her own children. Should exhaustion ever overcome the new mother then her sister is at hand to help. Her own mother is there if she feels ill.

Today we attend impersonal classes, we give birth amongst strangers, we relinquish our power to give birth to (mostly) male obstetricians—and then we go home, often alone. We give ourselves no time to become mothers. One day we are not. The next day we are. And that is about as much ritual and training as any one of us undertakes when we commit ourselves to the awesome responsibility of the role of mother. I can think of no other role a person can play which is of such extreme value to the human race and which requires no training to win the job, no apprenticeship, no assistance, no guidelines against which to measure success or failure and practically no way to be sacked or quit if we find we hate the job or are no good at it.

We study today only the lead-up to motherhood. If a woman is conscientious and pleased about becoming a mother she eats well, exercises, does yoga, deep breathing, meditates, listens to beautiful music, ceases smoking and drinking alcohol and coffee. She goes to the antenatal classes with her partner. She reads books about her feelings, looks at pictures of what is happening inside her belly at every stage of foetal development, reads books that tell her what to expect of baby week by week. But there is nothing to prepare a woman for the change she may experience in herself after she has crossed the threshold of motherhood.

Where are our rites of passage that acknowledge the value, the achievement, the triumph of birth? Where are our ceremonies that pay homage to mother and child? The Western world's most honoured mother is Mary. A new star was born to celebrate her son's birth. Great men and poor walked days and nights to venerate mother and child. Even the animals knew this was a blessed event. Without wishing to denigrate the historical and spiritual value of the virgin birth, nevertheless, the birth of any baby can be no less spectacular an event for any mother and she deserves to be honoured for her achievement.

---

6 Gabrielle Carey, 'Prenatal Depression, Postmodern World', in ed. Debra Adelaide, *Mother Love*, Milsons Point, 1996, p.180

WHEN PREGNANCY IS SPECIAL

Pregnancy, particularly for the older mother, can bring some special rewards. When we have deliberately waited or been forced to wait through infertility, not having found an appropriate partner or having temporarily put career ahead of children, we encounter pregnancy as an honour, a privilege, a choice. It is not easily taken for granted and there is often a sense of having earned this baby.

Women bloom when they are pregnant and the older we are, the nicer that feeling of glowing may be. Our skin improves, our hair grows thicker, our breasts burst forth, we look younger as fluid builds up in our bodies, smoothing out the little lines on our faces, rounding all our features.

Above all, a pregnant woman is special—the original mother-to-be. She gradually becomes self-absorbed, self-focussed and feels the world's eyes are turned to gaze upon her. Increasingly, throughout the nine months of anticipation, a mother-to-be becomes the centre of the universe. Once-important careers fade gradually into insignificance and little things emerge instead—tiny singlets and jumpsuits that this kicking, squirming being inside her body will wear one day soon. She holds those garments against her tummy and wonders and marvels that so much baby could be packed in there. She spring cleans and paints furniture, she sews and knits—she dozes off in the afternoon at her desk.

If she is lucky, her partner has joined her on this journey and treated her gently, with awe at the process unfolding before his eyes. He grows ever more nervous about the birth as the big day approaches. He goes into responsibility overdrive as it dawns upon him that a new life is about to come into the world. He and her friends and relations treat her as though she is a special being—she holds court as her belly swells.

I had felt just like that, I remember, when a glimmer of reality suddenly filtered through my self-absorption. I was only a couple of weeks away from birth day, seated in a friend's kitchen drinking juice while she sipped champagne. Her three children aged between two and eight were tearing through the house with assorted friends and dogs hot on their heels. The TV was blaring. So was the stereo. The phone rang and my friend, oblivious to the noise, abandoned me to the cacophony. An uneasy thought entered the recesses of my mind that probably the state of pregnancy bore no relation to the state of motherhood other than that one preceded the other. I did not realise then how right I was.

WHEN PREGNANCY IS LESS THAN SPECIAL

It is almost heresy for a woman to admit that she hates being pregnant, yet many women report that that is how they felt. Pregnancy and birth are worshipped the world over so when a woman dares to say that she does not like the condition, she is seen to be undermining one of our greatest icons and feels there must be something wrong with her. There are, however, some good reasons for feeling less than overjoyed.

Impaired Health

Health is the obvious and probably the most socially acceptable reason. Most books on pregnancy talk about morning sickness and assure the pregnant woman this will pass by the end of the first trimester. Some women, unfortunately, experience illness day and night throughout their pregnancy. It is thought that hyperemesis, as this sort of prolonged sickness is termed medically, may be brought about by stress. Often, if the pregnant woman is able to distance herself from the situation or person causing this unbalance, the illness will fade.[7] Perhaps Yvonne was experiencing this kind of stress-induced illness when, in her fifth month of pregnancy with her third child, she said:

> I can't eat. I can't even cook dinner for the kids or I throw up. I'm not putting on weight. I've got to get help, but where do I go?

Whatever the cause, though, feeling unwell, nauseous or actually vomiting daily is not conducive to enjoying pregnancy and can obviously cause a woman to become concerned about the health of her unborn baby.

As pregnancy progresses, a woman may discover that she has back, hip, leg problems of which she was previously unaware or which worsen dramatically. Varicose veins may appear on her legs and she may also develop them in her vagina or in her rectum (haemorrhoids). As she puts on weight and the baby bears down upon her pelvic floor these problems can be magnified. Simply being unable to move about in as agile a manner as she used to can cause her to loathe the condition of pregnancy.

Women do not go into pregnancy expecting to have their lives severely disrupted until the final stages, if then. If the pregnancy develops worrying

---

7 Sheila Kitzinger, *Pregnancy and Childbirth*, Lane Cove, 1982, p.118

symptoms, either in the foetus or within the woman's body, the mother-to-be may find her fears for her baby and the changes she must make to her lifestyle outweigh the pleasures. For example, vaginal bleeding may herald miscarriage and require prolonged periods of hospitalisation and bed rest. A woman normally used to good health and mobility may find this causes deep anxiety and irritation.

Similarly, high blood pressure needs to be treated with more rest than that which a woman may find comfortable. Without proper treatment it can develop into toxaemia which affects 5–10% of all pregnant women.[8] The symptoms of toxaemia are high blood pressure in conjunction with high fluid retention and a build-up of uric acid in the blood. If it is not treated, the woman's body begins to excrete too much protein and the placenta fails, triggering premature labour. It can also cause the mother to fall into a coma and so is not to be taken lightly. Such conditions can be successfully treated, but it goes without saying that a pregnancy fraught with worries about the survival of the baby and mother is a less than wondrous experience.

A pregnant woman is also more prone to minor complaints like constipation, bladder and urinary infections and thrush. She is likely to lose some control over her bladder. Whilst these symptoms of pregnancy are less debilitating than others, they can serve to take the gloss off the experience. And, if any of them are combined with other negative side effects, they may serve as the last straw in a woman's ability to revel in the creation and carrying of new life.

An Unsupportive Partner

The pleasure in being pregnant can be totally destroyed by a partner who does not want the child or who cannot tolerate the change in his partner's body and who spends the nine months making sure the mother-to-be is in no doubt about his feelings. Robyn, whose children are now adults, remembered clearly what that was like. Twenty-one years later her indignation was still evident:

> When I was eight-and-a-half months pregnant, feeling fat and ugly like a whale, I was standing in the bathroom doorway, naked after having a shower. My husband looked at me with disgust and just said, 'Yuk,' as he walked away.

[8] Sheila Kitzinger, *ibid*, p.121

Under these circumstances a woman, who may otherwise have basked in the glow of pregnancy, may do everything in her power to deny, conceal or disassociate from her condition.

An Unplanned Pregnancy

Similarly, if a woman is not yet ready to become a mother and does not want to alter her lifestyle or interrupt her career, she may rankle at her pregnant state and the baby growing inside her. She may see it as the agent by which her hopes and dreams for the future are being destroyed and so find the nine months are a matter of endurance rather than a time of fulfilment.

An Alien Inside

A small percentage of both men and women said they felt quite strange about another life form taking over its mother's body. They likened it to an alien invasion. The baby inside seems to be a parasite consuming the body in which it lives, growing at her expense. Some people are merely uncomfortable with this feeling or bemused by it. Others feel a powerful sense of revulsion. They experience the baby's movements as an exceedingly unpleasant reminder that the alien is developing in the woman's swelling womb, readying itself for the final takeover; and that this is an experience over which they have no control.

Rosemary's pregnancy came after many years of infertility, and after she had turned forty. She and her partner had put more effort, physically, financially and emotionally, into becoming pregnant than most couples. Their commitment to being parents had been well thought through and certainly this did not happen to them on a whim or by accident. Yet Rosemary was six months pregnant when she admitted her real feelings:

> I haven't dared to tell anybody that I feel like this. I mean, being pregnant is supposed to be all beautiful and glowy, isn't it? I am afraid that if I talk about how I really feel, other women will think there is something wrong with me. But I do feel as though my body has been invaded by an alien being. I hope that changes.

Because she felt so uncomfortable with the process of pregnancy, Rosemary experienced an underlying anxiety about her ability to relate to her child when he was born and how well she might or might not adjust to motherhood.

THE FIRST SHOCKS

BIRTH

Giving birth to one's first child is a life-changing experience the magnitude of which simply cannot be duplicated anywhere else. But because we no longer live communally and our families are so much smaller than they used to be and because the majority of babies are no longer delivered at home, a modern day woman absorbs almost no understanding of the process of birth during her youth. Thus, although a great deal is written about birth, women continue to experience the process with shock and dismay. Sally told:

> With the onset of labour my overwhelming mind-scream was, 'YOU HAVE GOT TO BE KIDDING!!!!!'

Other women, with remnants of their original disbelief still in their voices, described their initial reactions to labour:

- How am I going to handle this!
- I begged for pain relief.
- Shock.
- It was pretty horrific.

When my first labour pain overtook my body and mind I could not believe that *this* was the pain about which I had read and talked so much and yet had been told so little. The only honest comment made to me prior to giving birth to my son was by a mother of three, Ellen, who said:

> Wendy, when you are in labour you won't care if the Queen of England herself walks in the door.

However, Ellen did not finish the story. She did not tell me that I would not care because I would not be able to find a single cell in my brain that was not fully devoted to coping with the pain. I felt totally cheated of the opportunity to prepare mentally for such an onslaught to my body. Once I was in it I had no hope of carving enough brain space to understand it or to get beyond it. It took every single resource I could muster (and then some) to remain remotely intact as a human being.

Marilyn gave birth to her first child by caesarean section because he was a large baby and presenting in the breech position. Feeling she had failed in some way as a woman, she determined to give birth naturally when she became pregnant with her second child. All did not go well with this second birth. The baby became wedged and her delivery was again by caesarean. Interestingly, any thought that the first birth had been a failure vanished with the onset of her labour pains. Her evaluation of the two processes was unequivocal:

> Now I know what all you ladies have been through. Oh no. That is ridiculous. Give me a caesar any day!

I relate this story for its comparative value and am in no way advocating medical interference in childbirth unless it is absolutely necessary. Noni also gave birth to her first baby by caesarean section. She said:

> I felt like a freak and a failure. I knew everybody out on the street could see that I had failed as though I had it tattooed across my forehead.

Other women who experienced a caesarean birth have described it as Vanessa did:

> I felt as though there had not been a birth.

She went on to say that the midwife who had attended the birth of her first baby informed her that delivering caesarean babies was her 'penance' for her past sins, leaving Vanessa feeling as though it was she who had sinned.

An epidural administered during birth can have a similar effect on a woman's sense of having given birth. Sandra wrote:

> In my first birth the epidural spelled the end of it being my labour. After that it was all under the control of the hospital staff and I didn't feel that I had given birth, the obstetrician had given birth instead.

It took Sandra five years and a second, unassisted birth to recover from her first.

Christine, a midwife for more than twenty years, told that she believes a straightforward delivery to be a shock to a woman—let alone a difficult delivery. Another midwife, Linda, told how the hospital system simply takes over so that a woman feels she has no say in what is happening to her. She pointed out that when a woman has not given her informed and provisional consent to the use of drugs, instruments or surgery prior to the birth of her baby she is usually in no fit mental or emotional state during the birth to consider these difficult decisions, resist medical pressure or advocate for alternatives. Linda will no longer work in the maternity ward because she cannot tolerate the insensitivity and interference of the medical staff nor the way the system undermines a woman's power, her instinct to give birth and her desire to nurture. These sentiments are echoed over and over again by homebirth midwives, hospital midwives and mothers. Linda said:

> So many of labour's experiences taint a woman's experience of motherhood. It is wrong that we allow the medical system to do so much harm.

So the moment of birth can be either magic or devastating. If a woman has had a long, difficult, complicated birth her reaction may be anything but that described in many pregnancy and birth books. Maureen, who had had:

> the whole disaster, you know, tears and forceps and 42 hours' labour,

said that when the hospital staff handed her her son she did not want to know about him. All she wanted to do was sleep, to forget the days of torture she had endured. 'Take him away,' was all she could say.

Unfortunately, such enormous emphasis is placed upon having the perfect birth experience that most women go into labour hoping and believing they will do it 'right'. If things do not go exactly as planned a woman is in no fit state of mind to begin asking meaningful questions and to make rational, balanced decisions when she is in extreme pain. There simply is not enough mind space left for her to evaluate her situation and that is how she falls to the mercy of the medical profession.

In keeping with the conspiracy of silence, women share their less than perfect experiences of childbirth only with other mothers. They do not tell non-mothers or pregnant women their truths. They seem to do this out of a misguided sense of not wanting to unnecessarily frighten a woman who is already pregnant or for fear of turning a prospective mother away. They may also do it because they are afraid of appearing inadequate themselves, especially if the woman to whom they're speaking proves to be one who does have a pain-free birth.

Which, of course, some women do. Childbirth is not always excruciatingly painful and a small percentage of women I interviewed said that they enjoyed the process, that they found it empowering, uplifting and not particularly painful. They all said they would happily go through it again. It has to be said that these women do appear to be in the minority. Notably, nearly all of them had given birth at home, and none had suffered any complications at all.

Giving birth is our introduction to motherhood. If the experience is honest, if we remain in control and understand all that is happening to us then we are far more likely to enter motherhood feeling positive about our ability to cope. If our experience suddenly takes a negative turn, if others take over the control and do not explain what they're doing to us and our babies, we may begin our mothering career doubting the value and efficacy of our natural instincts. Women need to know about all possible aspects of the birth experience so they are able to base their choices and expectations upon the widest range of reality available to them. To present them with only the ideal is dishonest at best. At worst it prevents a woman from preparing herself for all eventualities and the opportunity to take charge of the birth of her first child. The resulting disappointment, regret or guilt may linger for years, affecting how she feels about herself and the way she subsequently treats and relates to her child.

WHEN BONDING WORKS

- 60% of women interviewed said they felt they bonded immediately or within the first few days with their first babies

The overwhelming love many women feel for their babies the instant they are born is staggering. It is all-consuming and wonderful beyond belief. For me, if everything in the world had ended then and there I could not have cared less because the only thing that there was in my world was my son. Nothing anybody could have said or done would have changed how I felt about him and I do not suppose I will ever experience such a moment of magic again in my life.

The change in a bonded mother's life orientation can be instantaneous and dramatic. Suddenly she no longer sees the world through her own eyes but through her baby's. Nothing and no-one holds any significance for her unless

THE FIRST SHOCKS

they honour and enhance his world. Her absorption in her baby is total. In my journal, two days after Daniel's arrival, I wrote:

> Once again I spend the entire day doing almost nothing but being with Danny. I cannot believe how utterly absorbed I am with his existence, his every facial expression, his tiny hands and nails, the lines on his palms, his hair and ears. Right now I need nothing else to keep me satisfied. I sometimes am gazing at him in my arms and clear emotion wells up inside me, washes through to my throat and my eyes spill over.

However, women have reported that the hospital where they gave birth apparently did not understand the new mother's powerful need to be with her newborn baby. My own experience was not uncommon. The hospital staff thought they were indulging me, a slightly neurotic older mother, in allowing us to hold Daniel for the first hour of his life. Then the nurses insisted on taking him to check him over, promising to look after my infinitely fragile and precious baby and to return him to me in no more than half an hour.

Time passed. Daniel was not brought back to us. I began to fret. I insisted Rick go and find out how long he would be. He came back saying it would be a while yet. The nurses were busy. Seven babies had been born that day and seventeen were in the nursery. I should not make waves. More time passed and my level of fretting grew. I insisted we go to the nursery since I could not bear to think of my baby lying alone, perhaps crying alone. Daniel was crying when we arrived as were half the babies in the nursery and no-one was holding them. This was my first experience of the doing paradigm taking precedence over the relating paradigm.

We stood by our baby holding his tiny hand for over an hour during which time no hospital official came near us or him. I began to feel faint and returned to my bed. Still nobody brought my baby to me. I can remember the effort it took to control my feelings of panic and distress. I grew increasingly desperate in my powerlessness to protect and nurture my baby.

Finally, three-and-a-half hours after they had taken him, the nurses returned my baby to me. I cannot begin to describe the relief I felt. In the next four days I did not once allow the system to take my son away from me again. Nor did I leave him with anyone, including his father, for more than half an hour for over a year, so powerful was the effect of losing him at the very beginning of his life.

Fortunately for us the hospital's interference did no other long-term damage to our relationship.

Unfortunately, some women told me they were not able to see their babies for a full day after birth, with the hospital staff variously telling them that they were very busy, that the doctors had yet to check the baby, that the new mother needed to rest. All considered that the explanations they were given were inadequate. The majority experienced this separation as having had a profoundly damaging effect on their relationships with their babies. Sometimes the effects were felt for years to come.

I, and others like me, experienced the first hours and days of our babies' lives in a whirl of love and passion incomparable with any other life experience. And we take those precious memories, preserved for all time in pristine clarity, with us to our graves. How any medical system can be so out of touch with this powerful life force that it intentionally comes between a mother and her newborn baby is quite beyond explanation or justification.

WHEN BONDING IS DIFFICULT

- 30% of women interviewed said it took a few weeks to a few months to bond
- 5% said it took longer than three months
- 5% said it took two or more years

It is expected that because a woman gives birth to a baby she will naturally bond with it. *The Macquarie Dictionary* defines the 'bonding process' thus:

> The process occurring in the *first hours* and days after birth, which establishes through *physical contact* the *instinctive relationship* between parent, *esp. mother*, and child.[9] [emphasis added]

What does this say of the woman who does not bond with her baby perhaps for years? It suggests she is less than normal, unable to respond to a genetically programmed instinct. Therefore at the deepest level of her being she feels flawed. It implies that physical contact with her baby will inevitably and instantly lead to bonding and that touch is all that is required. By logical

9 *The Macquarie Concise Dictionary*, 2nd ed., North Ryde, 1982, p.100

THE FIRST SHOCKS

deduction the definition implies that if bonding does not happen there must either be something wrong with the woman herself or that she is doing something wrong. This definition also implies that bonding can only occur in those first few days. You either come up to scratch as a normal mother then or you have blown it for all time.

When bonding does not happen, the mother is more dismayed than any other person could ever be. She is usually at a loss to explain it and afraid to admit it has not happened—even to herself. Normally there is no-one in her immediate environment who understands and so she has no-one with whom she can safely share her problems and feelings. She automatically feels isolated, alone and vulnerable. Because she was ill-prepared for the possibility, there is little she can say in her own defence. Thus she tends to accept other people's negative judgements of her at a time when her self-esteem is already at a seriously low ebb.

The anguish and guilt all these women feel, their deep and abiding sense of inadequacy and their self-deprecation is profound. At a time when they are in deep emotional pain they feel there is no-one to whom they can turn for understanding and support for fear they may be judged inadequate or even evil. So they keep it to themselves, sometimes taking it out on their babies behind closed doors, imagining that every other mother is ever-adoring of her baby. Each felt that she had been cheated of the opportunity to enjoy her baby's first years. Every one of them felt deep guilt for having given her baby a less than perfect start to life.

Women who had not bonded with their babies reported that their experiences included:

- Not loving her baby or feeling repulsed by it
- Feeling afraid of the baby
- Feeling trapped by the baby
- Feeling cheated of a carefree or meaningful life
- Feeling her individuality had been taken from her forever
- Exhaustion and ill-health turned caring for her baby into an endurance test of physical, emotional and psychological torture
- Feeling afraid for her very survival as a coherent, meaningful human being
- Feeling incapable of putting her infant's needs ahead of her own, for fear that she may not cope

- Being afraid that naming these fears would cause them to overtake her completely

When a mother who does not instantly enter the peculiar symbiosis that bonding is sees another mother who appears to be bonded she feels as though she is missing something huge. She assumes there is something wrong with her. Typically she reads the popular books on mothers and babies, everywhere receiving the message that bonding is normal, natural and that, even for the most dysfunctional of mothers, it happens within the first three months. So she waits for the three months to come and go, hoping that any day now this bonding thing will happen for her. For many, of course, it does and the few awful months are soon overtaken by the joys and pleasures of loving a baby. Even so, the guilt often hangs on.

But what of those women for whom bonding does not happen at six months or twelve—or longer? How does she feel when she realises there may be no light at the end of the tunnel, only eighteen years of being tied to this squalling, demanding baby? Sometimes angry, even enraged. Trapped. Occasionally violent. Sometimes depressed to the core. Sometimes the lot. Only when she grows quite unable to contain the internal pressure does she speak out and seek help. Listening to mothers who did not bond with their babies was heartbreaking. It took courage for Madelaine to admit:

> I didn't want my baby around. If he'd died of SIDS I'd have been relieved.

As shocking as this may seem to mothers who have had the privilege of bonding with their babies, this is not an uncommon admission. This mother was twenty-five when she accidentally and prematurely conceived her first child. Her career in the hospitality industry was beginning to take off and she loved the fullness of life it offered, the socialising, the organising, the challenges. She also loved her husband and felt they were developing a relationship which would embrace children in time, when she was in her thirties, when she felt ready. At twenty-five Madelaine was not ready but felt compelled to 'do the right thing' by her baby and so gave up work to become a full-time mother. Immediately it seemed she had been cheated out of her career but more than that, she felt as though her life had ended. It took her two years to feel she loved her baby.

THE FIRST SHOCKS

Rhonda quit work to be with her baby full-time without realising she was giving up her entire social network. Once her social support structures were removed she found herself resenting her newborn baby for enforcing her aloneness. She found it quite impossible to recreate herself every single day of the week. She said:

> I lost my identity when I had this baby—I just drowned in looking after this baby, this house. I had to stay home all the time so that the baby could sleep.

Rhonda did not bond with her baby until a year later and then only when she went back to work part-time.

Pam had twin girls at the age of forty and they are now in school. The constant demands of raising two babies at once meant there were double the interruptions to her thought processes and sleep, and her ability to achieve even the simplest of tasks was severely compromised. This woman, once the manager of a small business, found it preferable to be emotionally distanced from her children than to attach to them closely, knowing she was unable to fulfil their every need. During a discussion group she admitted:

> I still look at them sometimes and think they can't be mine. I suppose I feel they are mine more now but I don't really feel connected to them.

Christine spent 43 hours in labour so that when her son was finally born she was exhausted and incensed at the ordeal she had undergone. She had third-degree tears to her vagina and serious haemorrhoids. She did not want to hold him after he was born, nor feed him. She only wanted to sleep in order to escape the memory of the birth and to recover. She continued to begrudge his demands on her body, feeling that she would never recover her health or her energy and saw him as literally trying to kill her. She said:

> I did not love my little boy until he was two years old. I hated him. He took away my life, he wrecked my marriage, he ruined my health.

From what these women told me, bonding can be affected by a long list of contingencies. The following is a list of their combined experiences:

- **A Difficult Pregnancy:** it can be hard to love a squalling baby when that same baby made a woman feel ill for nine whole months and cheated her of the ability to enjoy pregnancy.
- **A Brush With Death:** if a woman's life was threatened during childbirth she may find herself unable to trust her baby, unable to forgive it for causing her close brush with death and may even be afraid of it.
- **Health:** if her health was seriously compromised during pregnancy or birth she may not recover sufficiently or fast enough for her to raise the energy to bond.
- **Disappointed Expectations:** if the birth went disastrously awry of her expectations she may feel her failure every time she looks at her baby.
- **Medical Staff:** if hospital staff were judgemental and unsupportive of her during the birth she may see her baby as the agent of her powerlessness.
- **Premature Birth:** if the baby is born prematurely and looks more like a 'tiny frog' than a pink and glowing little person, the new mother may secretly feel she has produced a less than perfect baby. She may also be afraid to bond with the baby in case it does not survive and, of course, may not have the chance to hold her baby for days, weeks or even months.
- **Handicaps:** if the baby is born with any obvious handicap, birth marks or its head is pulled out of shape by the birth the mother may find she blames herself and/or is offended that she has given birth to an imperfect child.
- **Separation After Birth:** if a woman does not get to hold her baby for hours or even days after birth she may feel that the baby does not belong to her.
- **Unresolved Losses:** if the new mother has previously miscarried, had an ectopic pregnancy or given a child up for adoption she may now realise fully what it is she lost and be afraid to bond with this baby for fear of losing it or because of lingering guilt.
- **Past Parenting Influences:** if, in her own family, the children were treated badly she may be afraid she will repeat negative parenting patterns passed down for generations and so distance herself from her baby.

THE FIRST SHOCKS

- **Premature or Accidental Conception:** if she conceives accidentally at a time when she is not yet ready to become a mother she may feel the cost of giving up her former life to be too high a price to pay.
- **Interrupted Career:** if a woman's identity is closely tied to her career and she feels compelled, for whatever reason, to give it up in order to mother her baby, she may feel her life has come to a grinding halt. Her baby may be seen to be the barrier preventing her from resuming the career she mourns and her estrangement from her baby can grow as she sees others forging ahead and herself falling ever further behind.
- **Social Life:** if she is an extroverted, social woman who is suddenly isolated at home she may see her baby as the destroyer of her social interconnectedness.
- **The Wrong Sex:** if the pregnant woman believes she knows the sex of her baby and her belief proves incorrect the new mother may feel that she has not been relating to the child she has carried for the past nine months. If the sex of the child is one with which she feels uncomfortable or if the baby is of the sex not wanted by herself, her partner, her family or his, she may internalise that disappointment, feel she has failed to produce the goods required and relate to the child with antagonism.
- **Displeased Spouse or Family:** if her spouse is less than pleased by the birth of her baby a mother may be afraid to show her true feelings towards it for fear of displeasing him further or feel she has to choose between them.
- **A Less Than Adequate Relationship:** if the baby is born into an already troubled relationship the additional stresses of exhaustion and diminished communication will almost certainly make it worse. A new mother may feel that it is the baby's fault she is handcuffed to her man and therefore distance herself from the baby in an attempt to put distance between herself and her partner.
- **The Baby Does Not Bond:** if the baby itself does not bond, does not instinctively suckle, does not sleep, has severe colic or reflux problems, these alone may not cause the rift in the bonding process, but bonding may be delayed or even destroyed by the persistent tendency of the medical profession, and people generally, to lay the blame for these problems squarely at the new mother's feet.

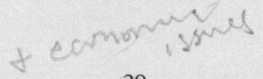

Few of these 'what ifs' appear in the pregnancy and birth books, antenatal classes, or parenting books. Nor are they often discussed in mothers' groups and playgroups. Certainly they never surface in the obstetrician's office. The first time a woman is likely to hear non-bonding acknowledged is after the event and only then if she encounters a sensitive nurse or clinic sister or joins a postnatal depression support group. Then she will learn that she is not alone with her apparent failure to bond, that external factors can and do have a significant effect on the process, that there are steps she can take to alleviate and work through her fears and that, in the majority of instances, this feeling of distance, separation and rejection of her baby will pass—in time. It will, however, pass all the more quickly if the new mother is able to access relevant information, support and help. Generally speaking the bonding process will start to unfold when her circumstances begin to meet her needs: when she feels appreciated by others, when she feels rested, when the baby comes out of the humidicrib, when any abnormalities have been defined and a course of action planned, when her health returns or when she returns to work. It may take months and even years.

Above all women need to know that this could happen to them. Too many books on motherhood gloss over non-bonding, assuring the new mother it will happen for her within a matter of weeks or a few months at most. Acknowledging the possibility that bonding may not happen, sometimes for years, and assessing the indicators prior to conception and birth may forewarn a woman. Kylie, a psychologist, wrote:

> I didn't bond with my son straightaway at all but because I had an awareness of the bonding process and how it can go wrong I was less harsh on myself and on him. I was more able to surmount the 'hump'.

Preventative measures need to be taken before a woman finds herself up to her neck in motherhood, frantically trying not to drown in it. With little or no spare physical, mental or emotional energy to work her way through such a deeply painful experience, a new mother may find it difficult to stand back and gain an unbiased perspective on her situation. Women who do bond with their babies need to know that non-bonding does happen to hundreds and hundreds of women in the Western world. They also need to know that non-bonding does not necessarily make a woman a 'bad' mother.

THE FIRST SHOCKS

TIME TO ADJUST

During the first four days of Daniel's life, time ceased to exist for me. I had the strangest sensation that the world outside the hospital had vanished. All that existed were my baby and me. The people who came to see us were but apparitions who appeared and disappeared through the walls. Because current convention offers no rites of passage I believed this to be a temporary phenomenon and expected that when I returned home my life would return to 'normal'. The entry in my journal, written the day I left the hospital, expresses the sense of discontinuity I experienced in my transition to the outer world:

> How strange the world looks. I have seen it through the hospital windows as though I were looking at a movie and not reality. The only reality has been that hospital and Daniel. Now I am surprised by how normal everything looks—nothing has changed. Don't they all know that my son was born? I come home and I find food in the fridge that was there when I left—I have been gone a lifetime and yet it has not yet perished. Programs which were advertised on TV are still being advertised —they haven't even been shown yet. I have been in a strange time warp.

The majority of the women who participated in this study admitted that a few days in hospital are not long enough to adjust to the new role of mother. Most agreed that if they could have had a month during which time someone else cooked, cleaned and washed and their only task was to continue to be with their babies, getting to know them and rearranging their own identities then they might have been less shocked by motherhood. On the other hand others said that even when help was offered they had difficulty in accepting it. This appears to be largely because women today have been conditioned to believe that motherhood is no big deal, that it is something they ought to be able to take in their stride. If they need help they feel incompetent.

In our modern day world we are encouraged to spend as little time as possible 'malingering' over the interruption to our lives that is the birth of our children. If we are to be seen as good mothers we must pick up the reins again—fast—and continue with our lives as though nothing but a baby has happened. Everyone has babies. There is nothing special about being the mother of one of them. Our mothers did it. Our grandmothers, too. Friends. Women for all time have been mothers. It is just part of life. Time to adjust is but a waste of time, which is, in part, why so many new mothers become exhausted within the first year of parenting.

EXHAUSTION

- 43% of mothers surveyed expected to be exhausted during the first twelve months of their first baby's life
- only one woman reported having had no experience of it
- 90% reported an impact on coping; 63% in the severe to extreme range
- 64% experienced intrapersonal conflict; 38% severe to extreme
- 81% engaged in interpersonal conflict; 49% severe to extreme

Exhaustion is simply not acknowledged as part of the process of the first year or years of parenting. There is little in the literature to forewarn a new mother and when it is mentioned it is glossed over as a short-term aberration. It is seen to be part of the adjustment to parenthood which women are expected to take in their stride while getting on with the rest of their lives. The following advice was published in 1994:

> As the baby starts to nap at regular times, and to sleep six or seven hours through the night, the mother can recover from sleep deprivation. This process can take *several weeks*, but then the new mother *feels like herself again*.[10] [emphasis added]

As an expectant mother reads these words she could be forgiven for feeling assured that once her baby is born her sleep will be disrupted for a mere 'several weeks'. With advice like this abounding, women enter motherhood confident they can cope with this short-term disruption to their lives. When the new mother finds herself still experiencing broken nights' sleep twelve months later (or five years later), far from 'feeling like herself again' she feels shattered as a human being. If she does not feel like her 'old self', certainly within three months, she begins to feel there must be something wrong with her. The truth is she will never be her old self again. *She will never be a non-mother ever again in her life.*

10 Ann Dunnewold and Dianne G. Sanford, *Postpartum Survival Guide*, Oakland, 1994, p.20

THE FIRST SHOCKS

Before baby it is easy to pin-point when and why a person is tired because it is usually brought about by a specific event or series of events such as late nights, physical exertion, a period of sustained hard work or study. After the addition of a baby to the household exhaustion does not arrive on any given day. Rather, it steadily creeps into every nerve in a mother's body over weeks and months of broken sleep. It sneaks into her brain and muddles her thinking and her memory. It snakes around her emotions and squeezes at inopportune moments causing her to cry or to explode in inappropriate circumstances and company. Adelle said:

> I was exhausted—totally—off my brain. You think you are OK at the time but how can you tell? I thought I was drowning in it. I thought it would always be like that.

Exhaustion sneaks up on a mother so she never really sees it happening until one day she wonders if life always felt this bad. There seems to be no end in sight. It often seems preferable to deny its existence than it is to face the appalling thought that it may never go away. Sally groaned:

> Every day. Day after day. Week after week. I didn't realise I was totally exhausted until almost two years had passed. The process was so steady that the wearing away of my reserves happened just like a dripping tap eventually wears away concrete. I did not notice it happening because there never was a day when I could say—'now I am exhausted'.

What follows is a selection of spontaneous comments made by the women in this study who have suffered from exhaustion.

> *Maureen*: I did not expect exhaustion. I thought, 'I'll sleep when the baby does.' I expected the baby to eat and sleep and sleep for four hours at a stretch. He never did.

> *Carol*: The worst thing for me was the sleep deprivation.

> *Rhonda*: It was like starting a new job that I couldn't quit. It seemed endless. I wanted to take her back to the Target refund counter.

Nikki: Even Mary Poppins gets every second Tuesday off—and gets paid for it—and leaves when the wind changes! Today is the first time I have slept in since I became a mother three years ago.

Margaret: He was screaming with colic, awake every two hours, day and night. I didn't expect this to happen.

Sarah: I never thought I would be that tired that I would have to hold my eyelids up because they wouldn't automatically open.

Nancy: I did not know how tired I was until I was untired.

Pam: I have had six years of broken nights' sleep. Some days I will just literally walk around in circles.

Denise: I never went out because I was so exhausted. It is just that it is endless is what makes it so exhausting. The interruptions. No change. No end in sight. Too tired to understand that it will eventually end.

Anna: I was in shock. I had four walls around me. David fed every three hours, day and night, crying, crying. I did not want anyone to visit I was so exhausted. All I could think was, 'I'm just dying. Go away.' Three years. I was so tired for three years and everyone was asking me, 'Why are you always sick?'

Within a week volunteers in sleep clinics who are woken regularly throughout their sleep cycle begin to become disoriented, muddled in their thinking.[11] They cannot concentrate well, are unable to remember easily. Their moods can swing wildly and they may say or do things they would not dream of doing under normal circumstances. They may rage at the slightest frustration when, with enough sleep, they are able to pursue long and arduous tasks to their conclusion. They have uncontrolled crying fits for minor reasons. They report that they feel they are going mad. Reasoning is impaired which may cause them to follow people and advice they would otherwise question or reject. Personality begins to break down.

---

11 Wallace B. Mendelson, *Human Sleep: Research and Clinical Care*, New York, 1987, p.16

THE FIRST SHOCKS

> When wakefulness is enforced, no bodily functions go seriously awry except those of the brain. Apparently, extended wakefulness affects the coordination of various parts of the nervous system, and there is the onset of hallucinations and other symptoms of mental disturbance ... *Lack of sleep will kill more quickly than lack of food.*[12]
> [emphasis added]

Many of the women who contributed to this book compared their exhaustion directly with 'torture' and, half-jokingly, pointed to their babies as the 'little terrorists' who perpetrated it. Amongst these women there was a common sense of feeling as though their very survival had been in jeopardy as sleep deprivation steadily took its toll.

Exhaustion, like torture, is an efficient means of restructuring a victim's mental processes. It causes a person to doubt herself to the extent of not even knowing who she is anymore, making her vulnerable to suggestions about her worth, abilities and value to the world. It is why so many mothers feel stupid, worthless, brainless, empty-headed, emotional. A woman only has to make a few wrong decisions, believe and follow some wrong advice, forget something her partner told her in the last hour to begin to doubt herself. If additionally she lives with a less than supportive spouse (let alone one who is actively destructive) it does not take long for the negative reprogramming to begin to convince her that she is at best, inadequate and at worst, a worthless burden upon the world.

General exhaustion was rated as the most common cause of conflict with other adults, usually the woman's partner, as well as the most difficult aspect of motherhood with which a new mother must learn to cope. Nikki said:

> I was trying to recover, my body was exhausted, trying to survive on sleep that was interrupted every one-and-a-half to two hours. My husband still insisted on going off every day and I, more fool me, accepted the situation! Why did I buy that shit? It's just totally unfair. I still feel very, very angry about it.

Tracey returned to part-time work as welfare officer when her son was six months old. In her letter to me she wrote:

12 Isaac Asimov, *The Human Brain*, New York, 1965, p.193

> My husband slept through the night when our son was six weeks old. I didn't. Our son woke up and I responded up to five times per night. I nearly went mad with sleep deprivation. But my real breakdown came last year when Peter was three ... I felt that I was doing more and more and others were doing less and less ... I started to have anxiety attacks, everything was too much.

The only woman I interviewed who said that exhaustion was never a problem for her was Caroline who lived on a commune in outback NSW at the time of the birth of her first child. She said:

> We had no sleep problems because the baby slept in the same bed between his mother and father. When he woke for a feed I just fed him and went back to sleep—I presume he eventually dropped off the breast and slept too. That part was never a bother for me. There was not much crying, no interrupted sleep.

Comparing the words of the majority of women with those of Caroline, I am caused to wonder whether the current, accepted structure of motherhood is the best model for our mothers or our children. Within the paid working world it is illegal to employ anyone in a job which demands they be on call 24 hours per day, 365 days per year. No other job requires that an employee only ever sleep for two to three hours at any one time and a total of no more than five or six hours in any one day. When a woman is employed she may enjoy morning and afternoon tea breaks, lunch breaks, four weeks per year holiday, sick leave, superannuation—oh, yes—and a wage or salary. Mothers get none of these benefits and bear all the costs and responsibilities.

SOME BABIES SLEEP — OTHERS DO NOT

- 67% of women surveyed expected their sleep to be interrupted by their first babies
- 84% reported an impact on coping; 63% severe to extreme
- 60% experienced intrapersonal conflict; 26% severe to extreme
- 66% engaged in interpersonal conflict; 38% severe to extreme
- almost no-one expected these interruptions to go on for more than three months

THE FIRST SHOCKS

- all expected their babies would sleep for long periods of time throughout the day

The truth is that some babies sleep a great deal while others sleep very little, day or night. Some are awake only long enough to feed while others sleep for twenty minutes and are awake for hours on end. Some, placed in their bassinets while still awake, will lull themselves off to sleep—others require rocking or feeding until they doze off. Sometimes a baby will sleep through the night from six weeks of age, others may require some form of physical contact during the night for up to five or six years. This is definitely outside the realms of common expectation.

Part of that expectation is that a baby will willingly sleep alone in her own crib. In a respectable family, it seems, there must be separation and distance between the parents' bed or bedroom and the children's no matter how much distress this causes all members of the family. If we think about it, a baby has spent the whole of its life tucked up warmly in its mother's womb. Here there is constant motion, constant sensations of its skin being massaged, constant sound. To take a baby from the womb and plunk it in a silent, motionless crib where the only skin-touch sensations come from the baby's own movements must seem to the baby as though his world has ceased.[13] It has been recognised that:

> Falling asleep [is] rendered more difficult for the infant who is kept strictly separated from the mother's body warmth.[14]

Often a baby will begin to sleep through the night, whether at six weeks or six months, and her parents will sigh with relief, assuming the battle for sleep is over. Just as they begin to take their rest for granted their peace is shattered and broken nights return full force. Their baby may begin to react to noises which never bothered her before. The household may have experienced a change in its routines which now disturb her. Guests may alert a toddler to 'stranger danger' and cause her to feel less secure and therefore to settle less easily. Illness can throw the best sleeping habits into chaos. Nikki bemoaned:

---

13 Ashley Montagu, *Touching: The Human Significance of the Skin*, New York, 1986, p.154
14 A. Montagu, *ibid*, p.196

Every time we think we have this sleep thing beaten, he gets sick and
we have to start all over again.

When the sleep routine is broken after a period of stability the return to sleepless nights can be devastating to the parents. This is all the more so because they were lulled into a false sense of security, had grown accustomed to getting enough rest and now find they are back at the starting post.

BREASTFEEDING

Breastfeeding is considered one of the most natural occupations for a mother, and one she is supposed not only to want to do but to find enjoyable from the start. And, for many women, they do and it is. Breastfeeding is the best excuse in the world to sit down, have a drink of something refreshing, relax, think whole thoughts, read, doze. It can be a time of blissful closeness with her baby; a time to gaze lovingly into her eyes, to stroke her head, her face, to hold her tiny hands. To bond. To play. Some women love to breastfeed because of this close contact with their babies, because their instinct to nurture is strong and because they wholeheartedly believe mother's milk to be the best start in life they can offer their babies. They also enjoy it because they encounter none of the possible difficulties with which breastfeeding can be fraught.

However, like all other aspects of motherhood it can have its downside as well. The non-bonded mother may feel that her baby is draining her, demanding too much of her physical body. She may feel that sitting still for great lengths of time unable to do anything for herself during these periods is intolerable, especially if her baby is a less than efficient or fussy feeder. Kaye, an accountant who gave birth to her first baby when she was in her late twenties, said to me with more than a little shock evident in her voice:

Wendy, she wanted to feed every two hours! Oh no! That is no way to
run a life!!! I put her on the bottle.

At the time Kaye's daughter was three months old. She was truly stunned that a baby was going to occupy her undivided attention for half an hour every two hours and there was no way she could come to terms with this disruption to her normally ordered life.

THE FIRST SHOCKS

Women's breasts produce milk in vastly different quantities and of differing qualities. Breast size is no indicator of how successfully a woman will be able to feed her baby. The new mother may find she produces so much milk which flows so fast she must lie down when she feeds in order to slow it. If she does not recognise this need she may find her baby is taking in too much milk, too fast, which causes him to overfeed and feel uncomfortable, to become colicky or to throw the whole lot up minutes later. Lisa wrote:

> Once, when my oldest child was only two months old, I had a horrible day. All she wanted was to be held. She kept throwing up all day and I, thinking I had to keep the fluids up to her, kept feeding her. Both of us cried off and on all day. Then, when my husband came home we decided to take her to the hospital. When we arrived and she was examined she had stopped crying and throwing up. The doctor kindly suggested we not worry as the only reason she was throwing up was that she was overfed. We wished the floor would open and swallow us up. The embarrassment of it all!!!

On the other hand, a mother may be producing too little milk or milk which is not of a quality able to satisfy the baby's hunger. She may find herself constantly feeding a baby who never seems to be satisfied. Not only will the baby, therefore, settle and sleep less but when her mother finds that she has been wanting for enough food she may feel extremely guilty, as though she were deliberately trying to starve her newborn babe.

When a woman's milk first comes in a few days after her baby is born, her breasts may become so distended and painful she finds she is unable to move without them hurting. Attaching a baby to such a breast ultimately relieves the pressure but in the first few minutes the pain can be excruciating. Sally told me:

> My breasts felt as though they were packed to bursting with jagged rocks. It only lasted a few days but they were so painful they kept me awake. I was scared of putting my baby to my breasts because it hurt so much. That was horrible.

Similarly, nipples can crack and can become so sore that feeding the baby one more time is a source of real dread. Ducts can become blocked causing mastitis—a painful inflammation of the breast which can make a woman feel quite ill. These problems require attention or medical treatment which can make a woman feel as though breastfeeding is just not worth the pain. Carol spoke to me of her daughter's suffering with mastitis:

> It was cruel to see her in so much pain and so ill and still trying to feed her baby.

Babies bring their own agenda to feeding too. Some fuss and fidget taking forever to drink an adequate amount of sustenance. Others guzzle so fast that they become colicky and cranky or throw up. Some do not attach to the breast well while others latch on like the proverbial leech. Some babies do want to feed every two hours, day and night. Some settle easily after a feed, making the effort doubly rewarding; others do not.

Then there are babies who do not attach to the breast at all or they bite rather than suck. A mother must make the choice as to whether to bottle feed or to express her milk. Melanie, after agonising weeks, realised her baby could not suck properly and decided to take the latter route. She explained:

> I had a double electric breast pump draining off my milk. I felt like a cow. In between showering and feeding myself I seemed always to be sterilising bottles. The disappointed expectations! Prior to this I had made unkind judgements about women who only breastfed their babies for a short time.

If a woman has expectations of enjoying and being able to breastfeed easily she often suffers a sense of let-down, disappointment and failure if these are not fulfilled.

When to wean a baby is fraught with judgements. It is considered acceptable to feed a baby up until it is walking or around one year old. Increasingly thereafter, people in our society feel uncomfortable being around a mother who is still breastfeeding her toddler. It becomes quite unacceptable to continue feeding after the child is able to walk up to its mother, lift her jumper, pull down her bra and begin suckling. Two years really does seem to be the socially acceptable limit. Yet, in most of the world's remaining 'natural' societies, it is accepted that a mother may feed a child for up to five years.

On the other hand, negative judgements are often made of the woman who finds that breastfeeding is not pleasurable but irritating or painful or who finds that the drain on her is too high. Breastfeeding is physically more demanding than is generally acknowledged and ought not to be underestimated. When a woman chooses to wean her baby at a few weeks or months of age she is often made to feel as though she has failed as a mother in denying her baby its rightful place at her breast and has disadvantaged him physically, emotionally and psychologically. It is often felt there must be something wrong with her as a woman.

Weaning itself can be a testing time. As prolactin levels fall so, too, do the endorphin levels in the brain, leaving the mother experiencing 'withdrawal' symptoms. Estrogen and progesterone gradually return to normal as does the menstrual cycle.[15] A woman may mourn or deeply grieve the loss of the special and close contact she had with her baby. Likewise, her child may take a little time to accept the new state of affairs, tugging at his mother's heart strings because he wants to suckle longer than she feels comfortable breastfeeding. Within a week or so, however, most mothers, breasts and toddlers do accept the situation and settle into the new stage of their relationship.

WHEN THE MIND LETS YOU DOWN

- only 16% of women surveyed said they expected their thinking process to be affected by the birth of their first baby
- 71% reported an impact on coping; 29% severe to extreme
- 53% experienced intrapersonal conflict; 26% severe to extreme
- 51% engaged in interpersonal conflict; 23% severe to extreme

As pregnancy progresses the new mother-to-be becomes more self-absorbed and less interested in the day-to-day dealings of the world around her. Her thinking may become a little scatty and her memory for things that do not directly affect her may wander. This is seen to be a benign side effect of the hormonal changes she is undergoing as a result of pregnancy and is smiled upon in an understanding sort of way by most people. Nearly everybody expects this will cease once the baby is born.

However, as long as a woman is breastfeeding, the natural opiate levels in her brain will remain higher than normal. These cloud her thinking processes.

---

15 A. Dunnewold & D.G. Sanford, *op.cit.*, p.62

Added to this are the side effects of exhaustion which diminish a person's ability to think, reason and remember. Sometimes dramatically. Many women said that people who were not exhausted who lived with or near them often did not realise or understand what they were going through. Because of this lack of understanding others grew frustrated with the new mother and judged and criticised her. In the worst cases they told her how to run her life and, if she did not comply, grew cross with her, blaming her for every little thing that went wrong.

The fact is that an exhausted person's brain aches. Thinking actually hurts. Trying to reason even a relatively simple idea through to its natural conclusion can be a monumental effort when the brain refuses to focus, too overloaded to think in straight lines. A tired brain does not remember trivia very well, either. Thus when a spouse asks that his suit be picked up from the dry cleaners her brain may lose the request in the fog of exhaustion long before it is parked in the short-term memory bank. Before her partner turns away the new mother may have forgotten that he even spoke to her. Later, when he goes to his wardrobe expecting to find his clean suit and becomes irritated—or worse—she, desperately scanning her brain, can find no trace memory of the request. The seeds of self-doubt are sown.

Although exhaustion may not appear to affect a woman externally, internally she feels as though she is dying. If a woman is living with a partner who cannot or will not understand her predicament she rapidly begins to doubt, not only her ability to direct her own life, but her very sanity. On this subject Sandra wrote from New Zealand:

> I felt stoned from lack of sleep. I got very depressed and thought
> I was no good as a mother. He [her husband] seemed to criticise every
> little decision I made concerning the baby, and in my state of
> vulnerability I assumed he was right and my decisions were wrong.
> I thought about suicide a lot during that time, rather than thinking
> about leaving the marriage. I truly believed that I could not take care
> of Bettina on my own.

Later in her letter Sandra said that after reaching out for help in the form of counselling she realised she actually coped better with their daughter when her husband was not around. Yet her initial reaction to his criticism was to accept it as truth because her normally clear, logical and intelligent mind was subsumed by exhaustion. She was quite unable to view her life situation in a rational manner, unable to weigh up the legitimacy of her husband's criticism against the reality of her ability to parent—to the extent she seriously considered killing herself. It should be said that Sandra is a general practitioner, well used to dealing with crises and making vital decisions.

THE HORROR HOURS

It has been found that 60% of parents believe their babies have colic and nearly 30% consider the complaint to be moderate or severe.[16] Studies have shown that the average baby cries for three hours per day, the majority of which occurs between the hours of 6 p.m. and 9 p.m. These are the 'horror hours'.

At this end of the day the mother is tired too. She may have been on duty for twelve hours already. Still there are hours stretching ahead filled with walking and consoling and feeding and cajoling before she can sit down and relax—or sink into blissful sleep herself. By five in the afternoon a mother may feel she has given every inch of herself throughout the day and now has not a drop of giving left in her. Yet, somehow, she must go on giving of herself until either her partner arrives home to relieve her or her baby sleeps. Sarah said:

> At the end of the day I am so tired I can hardly keep my eyes open.

Of course, a baby absorbs its mother's emotions and responds to her rising levels of irritation at the demands being made on her and her desperation to stop having to give. This only adds to the baby's already tired and unsettled behaviour, exacerbating mother and baby's rub against each other. Jackie said:

> I get to the end of the day and all I can think about is getting through the next minute. If I tried to think about the next three hours I'd go crazy!

---

16 Justine Ferrari, 'Don't cry mum, it's just part of growing up', the *Weekend Australian*, 9–10.3.1996

HELP FOR HANGING IN THERE

Before You Become a Mother

While you are pregnant, or earlier, it may be useful to begin a journal. In the first pages write a list of everything you have achieved in your adult life of which you are justly proud. Write down every attribute you possess that enabled you to accomplish them. After your baby is born, if the going gets tough and you begin to doubt yourself, come back to these pages, read them and realise that the gifts you once expressed so easily have not vanished. They are still there inside you awaiting the day you find the time and space to reclaim them.

Create Your Own Rituals and Give Yourself Time

In the absence of social ritual, create your own. One that is being resurrected is to ceremonially bury the placenta in an appropriate place and plant a tree over it. As the tree grows stronger year by year it will remind you, symbolically, of your own growing inner strength. Create time and space to talk about your birth experience until it finds a comfortable place in your consciousness. If it was traumatic seek professional counselling as soon as possible so you can lay to rest any residual fear, guilt or sense of having been victimised.

The most precious gift you can give yourself after becoming a mother is time to adjust to the role. In an ideal world, at the very least, every mother would have someone come in and take care of the house, shopping, cooking, washing for a month after the birth of her babies. This would give her time to learn to relate to her baby, to understand what this new personality needs and to grow gently into her new life role.

Unfortunately the world is not perfect. If you can afford to pay for such help, do so. Do not feel you must now fill up your day with tasks that are important in the doing paradigm in order to make up for having the assistance you deserve. Not only will you benefit but so will your baby and your partner. For those who cannot afford paid help, do not feel guilty about accepting it when it is offered and, whatever you do, accept it every time. You do not have to do this alone to prove you are able to cope with motherhood.

Expect the Best, Prepare for the Worst

Giving birth to your first child is a momentous event in your life and you will never get the opportunity to do it again. You have a right to expect the very best in care and information. You must ask the questions or you will not get the answers you require and you can only ask the right questions if you have first educated yourself. Read. Ask friends who are already mothers what it is you need to know about birth.

Do not be afraid to ask what can go wrong. Too much knowledge cannot hurt; too little can be disastrous. Remember, to give birth to a child was once a potentially deadly pastime. The complications still happen. The difference is that medical science has found ways of managing them so that women do not actually die in childbirth very often anymore.

You need to know what your doctor will do and how you want her or him to respond if any of the 'what ifs' of childbirth happen to you. If your doctor cannot, or will not, discuss your concerns with you to your satisfaction consider finding another. There are still too many obstetricians who do not seem to understand that childbirth has meaning for the mother, father and baby which reaches far beyond a strictly satisfactory medical outcome.

Your partner needs to know your contingency plans as well, if not better than you. It will be he who will have to advocate for you if the birth does not go as you both hoped. At the time he may be emotionally exhausted or feel helpless and overwhelmed seeing you in pain. This is no time for him to be making spontaneous decisions which will affect the wellbeing of his partner and his child.

If it is possible, have an assertive friend who is already a mother attend the birth as your advocate. This is especially important if you do not have a partner or your partner does not wish to be involved with the birth. Your friend will have a good idea of whether you are receiving appropriate medical help and can support and reassure you.

Bonding Happens—In Time

Look at the list of warning signs for non-bonding. If during pregnancy you feel significantly ambivalent about or afraid of becoming a mother you need to begin talking about it now. Find someone who will take you seriously and who will allow you to express your fears without trying to explain or rationalise them away. They are real for you and they will not necessarily go away just because you give birth to your baby. In fact they may grow.

There are many things which can be done to help after the baby is born. The more you touch, stroke and cuddle your baby the more likely you are to begin to have compassionate feelings for her. Eye contact is vitally important. Spend time every time she is awake looking into her eyes and smiling whether you feel like doing it or not. Soon she will begin to respond to your approaches. Positive feedback is a strong knitter of bonds between a baby and her mother. Try taking baths or showers together. The body contact and the warmth may soothe your baby and you, giving you the opportunity to grow closer.

When you hear your mind-talk telling you your baby is rejecting you, force yourself to objectively question whether this is fact or only your low opinion of yourself and your situation. Step back from your baby and whatever you were trying to achieve for a moment. Think back over the last twenty-four hours and consciously make a note of at least three positive interactions you have had, no matter how small they may have been. Dwell on them. Ask yourself what was good about them. Remember the feelings. Now go back to your baby and try to recreate those actions, that mood, those feelings.

Above all know that no mother is, or can be, eternally patient with her new baby. None of us give unconditionally every moment of every day. It is not physically possible. All of us get crabby, upset and many of us wonder how we ever thought we could be mothers.

Do not try to cope with non-bonding alone. It is asking too much of yourself. The books all say that bonding happens within days, three months at the most. This is not necessarily so. Get help before you and your baby suffer any further. Join a postnatal depression support group, see a counsellor, see a therapist.

Exhaustion is an Unacceptable Reality

Exhaustion after birth is considered normal—yet it should not be so. If you find you are exhausted you are certainly not alone and it is not proof that you are incompetent. Sleep or rest whenever your baby sleeps—every book on mothering says this. Why do so few of us heed this advice? Mostly because we are desperate to feel as though we have achieved something which seems to be worthwhile and so we use up baby's sleeping time trying to *do* something. Sometimes we refuse to sleep because we are equally desperate to have some time to ourselves unfettered by our baby's demands. Learn to do less. This means you will achieve less. So what? Accept this and understand it will only last for the first year or so of your baby's life.

Explain to your partner how you feel. Understand that he, too, is likely to be very much more tired than usual. Be aware that exhaustion causes short tempers and agree to give each other some extra latitude.

Should you reach the point of feeling you cannot cope any longer, whatever it takes, get help from relatives, friends, neighbours or one of the agencies listed at the end of this book. Even a couple of hours each day for a week will make a difference. It is not reasonable to expect one woman to tend to the needs of a baby to the extent that she feels she will die if she does not get some sleep.

Sleep Patterns Can Be Helped

The mistake many new mothers make is to think their baby will soon begin to sleep through the night and so they go on struggling with the problem, sometimes for years. The time to get help is in the beginning.

Start by realising that most babies settle better if they are kept to a routine with predictable rituals performed before regular sleep times. Play soothing music before and while he is sleeping. In a Pavlovian response many babies will grow sleepy as soon as they hear the familiar sounds. If your baby has difficulty settling and staying asleep you may find that if you lie next to him he will drift off more easily and sleep longer. This may mean that you and your partner occupy separate beds for a time, or that you share your bed with your baby. Do not let social prejudice prevent you from taking whatever action you find necessary to rise above exhaustion. Do not try to get back to a 'normal' life. Your irritation at being unable to do as you used to do will be passed onto your baby and will unsettle him.

Breastfeeding: Trust Yourself

When it comes to feeding a baby your own instincts are often the best guide. There is no point in forcing yourself to breastfeed if it is not working for both you and your baby. Although you may be disappointed, putting your baby onto a bottle will not harm her as much as struggling to breastfeed when this is distressing for both of you. If your baby is one who sucks for comfort do not be embarrassed if a dummy is what solves the problem.

Nursing Mothers Association of Australia's breastfeeding counsellors can advise you on most feeding problems and many a mother has told me they would not have survived had she not contacted one of them. The clinic sisters are another source of support and information.

Only you can know when to wean your baby. Whether that is shortly after the birth or in three years time, try not to let our narrow social attitudes to breastfeeding influence you into feeding longer than you are comfortable, or weaning earlier than you want.

The Brain Does Clear
Your foggy brain will return to its once-sharp state when you are less stressed. Until then, explain to your partner what it feels like to be inside your head. Tell him that you do not deliberately forget his requests, it is rather that you are exhausted and unable to think as clearly as you used to. Both of you need to know that this is a temporary phenomenon, that you have not suddenly turned into a half-baked idiot. Get your partner to write down anything he'd like you to do, and keep a list of the things you need to do and buy.

Keep your journal handy and regularly read the pages in which you recorded your achievements prior to motherhood. Make sure you tell yourself that you could not have done these things if you had been stupid. You are not stupid. Just very, very tired.

Share the Horror Hours
It seems to be a fact that babies are more unsettled late in the day when everyone else around them is tired also. If your baby is one of these you and your partner need to negotiate a way of being able to share this load. For the first year of your baby's life it will help you all if he can come home earlier than usual—not later.

Keep dinners simple so you are not struggling to cook whilst trying to pacify a fractious baby. Your diet may be boring for a while but it will not last forever. Make it clear to other family members and friends that interruptions at this end of the day are not helpful unless they are there to lend a hand. Discourage phone calls during the arsenic hours. Leave those activities you know your baby enjoys, such as baths, until late in the day.

TWO
REALITY SETS IN

Women today are raised to believe they are equal members of our society, that we can aspire to achieve anything a man can. We are taught that we may eventually enter the exalted halls of power in any profession if we are willing to spend our lives single-mindedly focussed on so doing.

What a young girl is not told is that equality is only extended to her when her endeavours are in those fields which are valued according to the yardstick of the doing paradigm. The only way a woman can hope to receive equal pay for equal hours worked in equally difficult professions is to ensure that those professions are the ones valued by the male of the species. Since men cannot give birth to babies and cannot physically nourish them once they are born, this field of endeavour is not measured by their yardstick. Anyone performing well or even outstandingly at these tasks is, therefore, not valued.

Those areas of achievement which do not rate as worthy of value are not worthy only within the doing paradigm. If our yardstick for achievement were drawn from the relating paradigm then the creation of life, quality nurturing and the ability to sustain meaningful relationships and mutually supportive communities would be of paramount importance. These qualities, unfortunately, are deemed to be less worthwhile pursuits than the creation of material wealth and the economic rationalism which has a planet-wide stranglehold on our thinking right now.

Because the feminist cry for thirty years has so loudly demanded that we be treated as equals in the male world we have overlooked those areas of endeavour and concern which are essential to feminine (and, coincidentally, to society's) wellbeing. In so doing we have unwittingly contributed to their devaluation. We truly have thrown the baby out with the bath water.

Thus, it is not until a woman first becomes a mother that she realises that the strictly feminine pursuits of birth and mothering are considered to be worth very little in a world which equates value with sale price potential alone. The new mother soon comes to realise that her society which once led her to believe she was equal to any man now abandons her, treating her as a person who is 'economically inactive'.[17]

INSTINCT

Underpinning many of the unbidden reactions to motherhood is a woman's often unexpectedly strong inner drive to protect and nurture her new baby. There is, however, a physiological and practical basis for this.

Hormones secreted by a woman's body during pregnancy increase her responsiveness to babies and small children and, during her early days of mothering, they increase her ability to behave in a nurturing manner.[18] After birth the hormone oxytocin triggers nipple erection in preparation for the following milk let-down response.[19] In the early months of feeding and nursing, when her baby cries a mother's milk begins to flow whether the baby suckles immediately or not. Some mothers find they are so attuned to their baby's needs that their milk regularly begins to flow moments before the baby cries to be fed. These are instinctive responses.

These reactions can come as quite a surprise to the new mother who may have never before been interested in small children. It stands to reason, however, that an infant born as helpless as a human baby could not survive a week unless some adult felt compelled, at the deepest level, to feed and shelter it. That compulsion has to be strong enough to overcome sleep deprivation, loss of freedom and every other drawback of motherhood detailed in this book, or the babies would die and we, as a species, would quickly become extinct.

In the charge to make women and men equal, the sometimes powerful draw

---

17 Marilyn Waring, *Counting for Nothing*, North Sydney, 1990, p.37
18 Jean Stockard & Miriam M. Johnson, *Sex Role Development*, Englewood Cliffs, 1980, p.136
19 Anne Moir & David Jessel, *BrainSex*, London, 1991, p.144

to nurture has been demoted from being a matter of instinct to one of cultural preference and now, to one of individual choice. Thus women, especially those who have never cared for a baby and who had no interest in children prior to the birth of their own, enter motherhood unaware that they may be one of the many women who are passionately driven to nurture and protect at all costs. When Glenda admitted:

> I really hated kids before Sonya but then I developed a liking for them afterwards,

she was not alone. Over 50% of the women surveyed said they had had no interest in children until they had their own. Because of the demotion of nurturing behaviour from instinct to choice a woman will often feel silly, foolish or even guilty that she wants to, and does, succumb to the insistent and persistent call of her deepest self. When a woman *does* discover she has a nurturing instinct which she did not suspect was there, plans she made prior to the birth of the baby to return to work or to work from home may suddenly seem irrelevant or impossible. Sandra wrote:

> I had unrealistic expectations of what I could achieve in addition to being a new mum. I thought I wanted to continue to work full-time, but surely we should have been organising things so that I had the option of stopping work if everything didn't go as planned.

In a country where paid work is valued above parenting many women do not expect to experience so 'illogical' a response as to want to nurture and become absorbed in their baby's world rather than return to the workforce. If plans were made before the birth that cannot be rescinded, a woman may find herself torn apart internally when she has to hand her six-week-old baby or her twelve-month-old crawler or toddler to a day care centre and go back to paid work.

A new mother who does return to the workforce against her deep need to nurture may find herself riddled with guilt and a sense of loss that she cannot articulate. Because the wrench away from her baby can be so painful a woman may justify her actions, rationalising that 'quality time' is better than 'quantity time'. She may deny that she or her children have missed anything. Sometimes she also becomes judgemental of those women who do elect to stay home, treating them as though their lives are a waste for having made such a limiting decision. And these feelings can be even more intense if a woman has been compelled to return to the workforce through financial need as opposed to choice.

Whether the scientific community can prove it conclusively or not women report being very surprised at the difference having a baby made to the way they behave and specifically use the word 'instinct'. Adelle is still in awe of her response:

> The one true thing my mother said to me before I had the boys was, 'You will kill for your baby.' I did not know what she was talking about at the time but that protective instinct is so strong.

And Sarah's admission is typical of every mother to whom I have spoken:

> It's like a lioness with her cubs—you would defend them from anything. I could not believe it, as soon as he was born this natural instinct took over.

This instinct to protect her children from all real or imagined threats has taken on a whole new meaning in today's world. It is not considered safe to let young children play in the yard of a block of units, in the local park or remain in the car unattended while their mother goes about her own business even for a short period of time. Nor is it safe to leave a baby in a pram outside a shop. With the ever present spectre of child abuse, not only physical and sexual but emotional as well, many mothers are reluctant to leave their young children with any other adult. This reluctance may extend to their own mothers if the new mother feels she, herself, was raised in a destructive manner. Only a handful of women said they had comfortably been able to let others take care of their children during the first year or two of their lives and only two said they had been away with their spouses, alone, within the first four or five years of parenthood. Many had not done so after ten years or more.

All of which means that a mother must and wants to be within sight of her children at all times and all of her activities must necessarily consider and include her children. Even the mothers who had not bonded with their babies and those who admitted to having been less than gentle with them when they reached breaking point still said that their instinct to protect their children was paramount. The majority also agreed that their unexpected need to be with their babies had contributed to their sense of abandonment by the rest of the adult world.

ABANDONMENT

After the specialness of pregnancy, the lack of specialness of motherhood can be an anticlimax and sometimes an overwhelming let-down. Often there seems to be nobody to whom the new mother can turn for affirmation of herself as a woman or a mother. Denise lamented:

> I expected to be more special after I became a mother, but instead I became a nobody. That was a shock.

There it is. Motherhood. Whole days of it that used to be filled with 'important things to do' ... and adults. Now they are full of baby and nappies and chores that seem never ending. Maureen recognised this dilemma when she said:

> Motherhood is beautiful but there are two sides to it and nobody ever tells you about the other side.

One aspect of the 'other side' of motherhood is that many new mothers feel abandoned. During pregnancy all attention is focussed on the woman and how she is going to give birth to her baby. Her feelings are important. Her health is important. However, after the birth and after ascertaining that the new mother has physically survived there is little interest in how she is coping, feeling, thinking—or even behaving. She becomes an extension of the baby, its lifeline, and she seems to have importance only in this context. Roger noticed this in his sister and told me:

> I had not seen my sister for fifteen years and in the meantime she'd had three kids. When I asked her how it had been she told me that she loved being pregnant because she was the centre of attention but she hated it after her baby was born because she just felt so unimportant.

The new mother is, of course, delighted that everyone ooo's and aaaah's over her baby, her greatest creation. Perhaps, basking in the pride of her achievement, she does not realise for a time that she, as a person, has apparently ceased to exist. It may take her days, weeks or even months to see that her needs are going unacknowledged or being treated as secondary to the baby's (and often her spouse's). Sarah told:

> I found the hardest thing to adjust to was that people talked to me differently because I was a mother. How's the baby? Everything related to the child. Once I went out of the workforce I became a nobody.

Kylie agreed:

> This was one of my biggest shocks, too. It was one of the reasons I loved going back to work.

Over and over again women expressed their shock at plummeting from the heights of the egocentricity of pregnancy and the feelings of worthfulness as a paid worker to the depths of abandonment once they became mothers.

In the past, the months after the birth of a baby were seen to be special for the mother. It was a time for adjusting to her new status, getting to know her baby and bonding with it. It was a time in which to physically recover, to sift through the life-changing experience of childbirth and make sense of it. As mentioned earlier, in many cultures a woman used not to leave her home for a specified period after birth, until she and her baby were strong enough to face the world. Family and community members took care of the mother and the day-to-day concerns of living. The new mother was only expected to become a mother. Remnants of these traditional extended family support systems exist in pockets within our society, particularly within our migrant communities, but they are diminishing.

All too commonly today, because the extended family and sense of community have crumbled, a new mother will find herself at home alone with her baby and not a single person in the world to support her. Family are unable to help since they are working or living at too great a distance. Friends rarely call for they are home handling their own mothering or are working. Partners and workmates return to their jobs sometimes within a week of the new mother giving birth. Often there seems to be no-one to whom she can turn to meet her own needs. Worse still, since there is a pervasive feeling that staying home to look after a baby or child is 'doing nothing', when friends do visit they often seem to expect the mother to cater to *their* needs rather than considering that she may appreciate a little help or nurturing herself. As Anna said, the attitude is:

> that an 'at home' mother can be on tap at all times. Therefore friends and relations expect that the mother is there to provide for them when they visit.

Even her own family may turn out to be less than helpful. They may be absent, constantly critical, interfering or judgemental. They may resent the fact that they are no longer of central concern to the new mother and have been usurped by this baby. As a result they behave in ways which are undermining to the mother at a time when she is trying to adjust to a whole new way of being in a whole new world. Cathy lamented:

> I just wanted someone to show that I was worth something and worth helping. Instead, my mother-in-law expected to be waited on whenever she came to visit.

As the new mother looks around for support she may find that she knows nobody with a small baby. If she is in her thirties or forties when she first gives birth, seek though she might, she may find it difficult to find anyone of her own age in a similar situation—let alone anyone who is her 'kind of person'.

Not only does a woman often feel as though she has been abandoned by friends and family but by society itself. It does not take very long for her to realise that unless she is in paid work her needs, concerns, fears, hopes, dreams, her love for her baby, her pride in becoming a mother all count for nothing—as Rosemary discovered. She was a PhD student until she gave birth to her baby at the age of forty. Her services had been in demand all over the world for years. After her son was born he suffered health problems which kept him at such a level of pain that he did not sleep day or night and screamed much of the time he was awake. At her wits' end with the medical profession, Rosemary vented her frustration:

> I am so sick of the medical profession treating me as though I am an hysterical, ignorant mother. I know there is something wrong with my baby but they will not take me seriously. Why do they have to treat me as though I no longer have a brain in my head?

The sixty-four thousand dollar question. After the glory and creativity of pregnancy is it any wonder that so many women feel abandoned once they have given birth to their babies?

Where once a woman had time to grow into her new role of mother, today she gives birth to her baby and a week later is out doing the shopping, running the house, caring for a partner—and learning how to be a mother. She takes her brand new, prize-winning baby home and shuts the door. Nine months she spent growing this baby, anticipating its arrival, revelling in the joy of creation. If she is lucky she will have one week in which to reap the rewards of glorified motherhood and then it is over. Suddenly she is just another pram pushing, exhausted mother haunting the supermarkets and parks of our nation desperately surviving another day of loneliness; and facing the alarming deterioration in both her looks and her mental processes and plummeting self-esteem that go hand in hand with exhaustion and isolation.

This is why the opening scene in the film *The Lion King* is so poignant and touches the heart as deeply as it does. The proud parents watch as their new born cub is held up high for all the world to see and every animal bows down to honour his birth. We all ache to be so honoured for the achievement of giving birth—especially to our first child.

THE LOSS OF FREEDOM AND SPONTANEITY

- 59% of women surveyed expected their freedom to be curbed after the birth of their first child
- 76% reported an impact on coping; 51% severe to extreme
- 67% experienced intrapersonal conflict; 46% severe to extreme
- 72% engaged in interpersonal conflict; 51% severe to extreme

Because many women breeze through pregnancy, experiencing it not as an illness or medical condition to be treated but, as Natalie said, 'just a phase in my wellbeing', they do not expect having a baby to so dramatically alter their lives. Margaret admitted:

> I did not expect this to happen. I just thought I would get this beautiful baby wrapped up in a bunny rug ... like a little pet, really. That was a shock.

REALITY SETS IN

Martha's comment echoed the expectations of most new mothers:

> I never thought life would change very much. No-one tells you the truth.

However, childbirth educators report that women do not want to know about the difficulties of motherhood once they are pregnant and so their classes only focus on her life up to the birth of the baby. The time for education is, undoubtedly, before pregnancy. Adelle admitted, as did many a mother, that she did not even think beyond the birth.

Yet life does change more dramatically than most women expect after the birth of their first baby. Instead of being able to decide to leave the house on a whim they must take into account the baby's every need and often this means giving up activities she once took for granted. Sharon, an outspoken, self-assured woman who was used to being an equal partner on her family's farm said:

> Why, I couldn't get onto a horse anymore and help with the cattle. I had to stay home and let the men do it all.

No longer does she simply pick up the reins or her purse and the keys to the car when she wants to go out. Now she must change and feed (and change again) her baby and possibly herself. She must come and go according to the baby's sleep patterns. If the baby routinely sleeps at predictable times she is able to plan her comings and goings. More often than not, though, babies are unpredictable and throw the best laid plans into chaos.

When I have asked women what was the hardest thing for them to adjust to when they first became mothers the most consistent initial reply has been a resounding, 'lack of freedom'. Women lament, sometimes for years, this inability to direct their own life in a manner they once considered normal, if they considered it at all. No longer are they free to pursue their most cherished interests since the baby's needs must always come first and, after the daily rounds of caring, cleaning and cooking, there is little energy or enthusiasm left to pursue those interests. As Cathy said:

> I used to love sewing. I can't remember the last time I had the machine out.

and Marilyn:

> Once I used to read a book every week. Now I keep only magazines because there is a better chance I will get to the end of a two page article than a 500 page novel.

To transform, literally overnight, from being a woman who takes for granted her ability to spontaneously come and go as she pleases into one who is anchored for unpredictable lengths of time within the four walls of her home, is a shock for which most of us are not prepared. Added to this, when already exhausted, the mere thought of having to pack the baby's bag with rattles and teething rings, bibs and nappies, changes of clothes, bottles, nappy liners, bottom wipes becomes too much to contemplate. As the months wear on some mothers begin to hide out at home filling their day with excuses not to emerge into the greater world. Adelle told me:

> I found it backbreaking. I can remember not wanting to go to a BBQ because they had a zillion steps and I could see myself running up and down them all afternoon. So we did not go.

The need to be able to plan ahead becomes paramount if life is to continue with any semblance of organisation or predictability. Even those once trivial and irritating tasks like hanging out the washing have to be scheduled or the household is likely to wake up one morning and find itself devoid of socks or underwear or worse still, nappies. Women adjust more or less easily to this need to plan every task, including sleep and relaxation. For those who are able to make this adjustment to their thinking patterns life maintains some sort of order. Often, however, this is at cost to her ability to enjoy the present moment since she is forever, mentally, projecting into the future. Those who adjust less well find they tend to live a life of crisis management and are, therefore, in a perpetual state of anxiety. This woman also loses the enjoyment of the moment, feeling as though she should be doing something towards averting some unnamed future disaster.

Always living in the future is not spontaneous and it is stressful. The slightest change in this moment of now can mean all future plans collapse into chaos and have to be made all over again. Yet living only in the now most assuredly means not living up to the expectations which are placed upon mothers and which mothers, themselves, take on board. This is a dilemma which some women never resolve.

How can one small being so dramatically impact on a woman's freedom? In part it is because women today have far greater expectations of their ability to achieve and to be mobile. They do not expect that motherhood might mean staying home endlessly with a baby in order to allow it to develop a sleeping routine. They do not expect that the decision to do something as simple as shop may require detailed planning around the baby's likely waking and feeding times. No longer is a woman free to swim in the surf because it would mean leaving her baby unattended on the beach. She cannot guarantee that she will be able to complete a game of tennis. She cannot attend an educational course or a movie with any certainty she will see it through to the end. She ceases having late nights because they only add to her sleep deprivation and ruin her for the following day.

For many women there is little opportunity to leave a baby with a trusted family or community member while she exercises her freedom to do something which pleases her or which needs to be accomplished without the fettering of a baby. There also seems to be an underlying attitude that if a woman is not the 100% full-time carer of her babies but is, instead, out 'enjoying' herself, she is shirking her responsibilities, being self-indulgent—even selfish and lazy. New mothers often feel as though their freedom has been taken from them forever.

LONELINESS AND ISOLATION

- 42% of women surveyed expected to be lonely, but only 29% expected to be isolated
- 76% reported an impact on coping; 66% severe to extreme
- 72% experienced intrapersonal conflict; 66% severe to extreme
- 65% engaged in interpersonal conflict; 52% severe to extreme

One of the most immediate effects of motherhood can be the realisation that one is lonely and alone. Some of us escape from the house every day whether it be to a park (even though our baby is only twelve weeks old and unable to use or appreciate the equipment) or to the local shopping complex in which to stroll with the other mothers who are also escaping from home. We walk the beaches, the by-ways and the highways of our nation. Anywhere we can go to avoid being locked into those four walls—anywhere that will not cost too much, where it will not matter if our babies holler, throw up, poo in their pants or otherwise act in an unsociable manner.

Heidi was twenty-five when she had her first child. As is not uncommon, she and her husband moved to a new neighbourhood just before the baby was born. Here she knew no-one but here they thought their lifestyle could be more family oriented. She said:

> The isolation. This was just the worst thing because it was so unexpected. My self-esteem hit the bottom. If somebody had warned me I could have prepared for it but I had no chance.

Some new mothers cope by never going out into the world of other mothers because they fear they may be judged incompetent. These women experience their baby's crying in public as a display of their inability to control even an infant. They are convinced that every other mother out there has the game under control and can do it all perfectly while she does not feel as though she can cope at all. Marilyn was one of them.

> I did not take Josh for a walk in the pram in case he cried and someone would think I was a bad mother.

Because women are having their children at later ages many have been in the paid workforce or the academic world for ten years or more before transforming into a mother. In most cases these careers are undertaken at a distance from the family's home and friendships are formed on the basis of common work and social interests. If a woman then elects to have a baby and to stay home with it she often finds herself not only completely isolated from the local community but from her former work community, since they no longer have anything in common. Marilyn continued:

> When you have a three-week-old baby and all your friends are at work it is hard to find a group to fit into.

The need to search for new friends can be unexpected and the search itself can be daunting. For some women the task is so overwhelming they do not even try. Instead they withdraw into their own homes with only their baby for company and solace. Years can pass before they connect with companion mothers. Even those who are perhaps more outgoing can find their confidence shattered by a series of attempts to find friendship amongst other mothers which do not work well. These failures to find support only serve to confirm her isolation.

Mandy was thirty-two and an advertising director when she gave birth to her first baby. When she left work she discovered that she knew nobody in her neighbourhood and certainly nobody her own age with a new baby. Mandy explained:

> Loneliness was the worst thing, really. I loved pregnancy. I had a great birth. But after I was totally isolated. Quite often I called my husband and said, 'Please come home.'

Some women, like Charmaine, do find a like-minded group immediately:

> I found a wonderful mothers' group through the Baby Health Clinic. Only one did not enjoy the first six months and couldn't wait to go back to work. But I could not have got through motherhood without champagne. We drank champagne at lunch every week.

Others are not so lucky and as a result stay home believing, as Catrina did, that everyone else is occupied and that they alone are condemned to a lifetime of loneliness:

> I was stuck in my own little box and did not realise how many people nearby were stuck in theirs. There is no way to meet them.

Those women from rural Australia who were interviewed for this book said they felt their city counterparts would not experience this sense of isolation as much as they did. They all felt that in the city it would be easier to obtain work, simpler to travel to the shopping centres, that a city mother 'could look forward to brighter times sooner'. Yet one mother who lived in a city said:

> Loneliness equals Power-Less-Ness in capital letters—no matter where you live.

For the urban mother the sense of isolation is often intensified by the very knowledge that she is surrounded by people with whom she has no means of contact. Her loneliness can be magnified by her sense that, with so many people close by, she should be able to find like-minded friends and her inability to do so must indicate there is something wrong with her. Marilyn recalled:

> I remember the first Melbourne Cup Day after Josh was born. I had nowhere to go for the first time in my adult life. I rang everybody and they were all out and I knew they were all at lunches and I was stuck at home.

As later investigation proved, each one of Marilyn's friends and acquaintances was feeling the same sense of invisibility. All had gone to a shopping centre, beach or park, in an attempt to silence their own feelings of isolation and an uncomfortable feeling that they had somehow ceased to exist.

The belief that it is a mother's duty to stay at home so her baby can sleep, her duty not to inconvenience other members of her community with a crying baby, her duty to not need any help with being a mother all contribute to her feelings of loneliness, isolation and powerlessness.

INTERRUPTIONS TO PERSONAL INTERESTS

- 39% of women surveyed expected their personal interests to be disrupted
- 76% reported an impact on coping; 43% severe to extreme
- 55% experienced intrapersonal conflict; 40% severe to extreme
- 59% engaged in interpersonal conflict; 30% severe to extreme

Just as women tend to believe that their lives will return to normal within about three months of having a baby, they also tend to believe that when that happens they will have more time to focus on their hobbies and interests or will be able to work from home. To find they have not only less time than when they were working, but in many cases no time, is a contingency for which few make plans. Nikki, when pregnant, could not hear her friends' warnings. She admitted that she used to say:

> Well maybe I'll be lucky and get a good one who sleeps. I know I will have to stop teaching for the first six weeks, and maybe twelve, but after that, hopefully, the baby can sleep while I teach.

REALITY SETS IN

In truth, she had included the 'hopefully' only to appease her mothering friends who had been trying to tell her that she might not find it so easy to continue her career as a teacher with the baby present. As it turned out Nikki did not return to teaching for four years, and then only sporadically.

Since so few women expect a baby to overtake their lives as completely as they do, they tend to daydream about all the reading, gardening, creating, renovating, sport playing, you-name-iting for which they will have time when they have been released from paid work to have a baby. However, a baby's interruptions are loud, insistent and compelling. Trying to complete a task before attending to his needs can cause a new mother's stress levels to rise. This causes her to think less clearly, become increasingly less able to focus and irritable with her baby for calling her away. Often it is easier to delete the activity from the agenda than it is to persist. Denise quietly reminisced:

> I used to imagine myself sewing gorgeous little clothes for my baby while he slept peacefully in his cradle. I haven't made him a thing yet and he's in school already!

One of the most difficult aspects of a baby's interruption to tasks is the unpredictability of when they will occur. Pam eloquently expressed how much this impacted on her ability to converse with other adults:

> I hang onto the moments of adult interactions so when interruptions come, that equals anger!

Clearly it is easier to organise one's day around regular, rhythmic breaks in concentration because one can plan for them. A baby does not work to clockwork.

As a baby becomes increasingly mobile he is better equipped to interrupt his mother's every task. He can go to her. He can tug on her clothes, wrap himself around her legs, stick his face in between hers and whomever or whatever currently holds her attention. The toilet and the telephone signal to the toddler (and many an older child) that mother is about to stay in one place for a period of time and is unlikely to get up and run away. Toilet and telephone time are clearly made for the toddler to have mother's undivided attention. As are those times when she sits, hoping to talk with a friend, read a book, take a nap. A sitting mother is a sitting target for a child to grab her face space. Early on in their mothering careers most women learn that if anything is ever to be accomplished, they must never be still. It is a habit many of us will take to our graves.

Because there are not enough hours in the day to meet every expectation we now place on mothers, it goes without saying that any time she gives to herself must be time in which she is not meeting those expectations. If her partner is of the view that mothering is a leisure activity her guilt will be compounded by his attitude that she has time to meet all the needs of the household before she ever thinks about herself. Penny admitted:

> My husband makes me feel so bad if I spend any time doing what I want to do for me, that I either don't do it or I hide it from him.

There is some myth afoot that a woman must not have any personally enjoyable or fulfilling times while she is mothering. What other job does not schedule in breaks of some kind during which time a worker may do as she pleases—including enjoying and indulging herself? Unless a woman has built a support system around her, is willing to ask for and expects to be given time out from her mothering role she will find her personal interests being shelved, sometimes for years. Being forewarned she may consider putting into place contingency plans before she becomes alienated from her dreams.

CRYING

- 62% of women surveyed did not expect the noise of their baby's crying and their inability to halt it to affect them
- 67% reported an impact coping; 41% severe to extreme
- 63% experienced intrapersonal conflict; 44% severe to extreme
- 66% engaged in interpersonal conflict; 47% severe to extreme

All new mothers expect their baby to cry at times. What is less well known is that sometimes the crying can go on for a very long time, occur frequently and has the power to turn a once-proud woman into a heap of failure and misery.

The cry of one's own baby can be remarkably distressing to the new mother and many find they can focus on nothing else from the moment their baby begins to howl. The sound seems overwhelming, completely dominates her mind and can even be physically painful to the mother herself. A woman will do almost anything to make her baby stop crying. Whatever task she was in the middle of doing, whatever conversation she was enjoying ceases to have any meaning for her until the crying ceases.

If it does not stop but goes on for any length of time, a mother may find herself passing rapidly through a range of emotions from helplessness, powerlessness, worthlessness and failure to anger and rage. She, herself, may be reduced to tears or forced to leave her baby to cry alone for fear of hurting it—and she may hurt it in an attempt to halt the noise.

Most mothers recall a day or night (or days and nights) when they walked, holding a screaming baby, for hours on end until they themselves were reduced to emotional wreckage. Nothing cuts to the core of a sense of failure faster than an inability to meet a baby's needs so that it will stop crying. Heidi recalled:

> One day my daughter cried for seven hours nonstop. The emotions scared me. I tried everything. Feeding, playing, burping, bouncing, walking, talking. I begged her to stop. I screamed at her. I cried. I imagined throwing her over the balcony. Then I knew I needed help. I threw her onto our bed, slammed the door shut and phoned my husband. I begged him to come home. It was two hours before he did.

When Heidi's partner arrived it was to find his wife a shattered shell of her former self, racked with guilt and remorse for having treated her baby with such callous roughness, for having thought such dreadful thoughts ... for having been unable to cope.

Nobody tells you there will be days like this so a new mother does not know that it is normal and likely to happen, at least once. And she does not know that it is OK to seek help—before she breaks.

IMMERSION, OBSESSION AND MANIA—A CONTINUUM

- Almost half the mothers surveyed were surprised by their powerful need to be with their babies
- 51% reported an impact on coping; 29% severe to extreme

- 43% experienced intrapersonal conflict; 28% severe to extreme
- 49% engaged in interpersonal conflict; 19% severe to extreme

Some women feel they know their babies intimately long before they are born. Many of us think we know them after the first day, the first week, the first month. We often make the mistake of thinking that now that baby has reached this stage of cuteness, goodness, revoltingness, cuddliness, smiliness, sleepiness—sleeplessness—that that is *all* of baby.

Not so. There is no greater magic than to wake in the morning to see that your baby has changed during the night. There is no more extraordinary a process than watching the unfoldment of another human being. From the moment a woman arrives home with her first baby she often becomes completely enveloped by his presence. This is a phenomenon few mothers realise may dominate their lives after their first baby is born. During a discussion, Pauline, whose first child is now five, said:

> I was so obsessed with my children I did not have time for anybody else. I did not want to know anybody else. If the phone rang I did not answer it. If they came to the door they were a nuisance. I was so involved and so focussed, only now am I able to come to something like this [forum].

There is little warning in the literature that a formerly sane, upstanding, responsible member of the workforce will become the kind of woman who delights in blowing raspberries at her baby just for the pleasure of watching him try to copy her—and claps and dances with delight when he succeeds. Who could have told that this once-elegant human being will now 'broom-broom' the trolley around the shops, oblivious to amused or disdaining glances, in order to elicit a laugh from her four-month-old baby? How many of us suspected we could while away whole hours shaking rattles and talking to a baby who will not be able to respond in words for at least another eighteen months?

How can anyone transmit to another person, sometimes even to the father of the baby, the satisfying joy of becoming immersed in our baby's world of discovery, delight and emerging beingness? How can we explain that we were drawn like a magnet to the bassinette at nine in the morning and were still standing there appreciating this miracle of life half an hour later, an hour later, just watching baby sleep?

REALITY SETS IN

Because it seems difficult to justify this 'leisure' time some women 'pay their dues' by developing into overly responsible, self-driven work machines. Sally told one forum:

> I felt my husband was working his little bunions off for us and so I should always have dinner ready no matter what time he arrived home. He was away from home for up to fourteen hours every day and arrived home tired and stressed. It took five years before I understood that he would not die if he sat down to baked beans or tinned soup sometimes.

Because he was 'working' and Sally was not (read: 'because he was paid and she was not') she also felt it was her duty to always be the one who arose at all hours of the night to tend their baby, to clean their home—even when she felt she would die from exhaustion.

Once a new mother is at home with her baby she may find that things she previously ignored suddenly and inexplicably become urgent. Instead of resting while her baby sleeps she often finds herself trying desperately to clean, sweep, polish areas of the house she had never before thought of as needing attention. She may try to work from home only to be frustrated by interruptions. Somewhere in the doing of 'things', she reasons, she may regain her sense of herself as a worthwhile person.

This is called an immersion-mania continuum. It can manifest simply as an overwhelming desire to be with and enjoy the baby. It can be a need to do and achieve more than can be reasonably expected. Or it may progress until a woman's thinking processes are severely impaired, causing poor judgement and distorted perceptions. At the extreme end of the spectrum, although she appears to be working hard, little is accomplished other than further chaos. Her mood swings grow more pronounced and she is easily excited or irritated or depressed and her attention span is limited.[20] When this side effect of motherhood reaches unmanageable proportions a psychiatrist may prescribe lithium carbonate which, in 80% of cases, relieves mania rapidly.[21]

Whether the expression of mania is clinically diagnosed or merely another side effect of becoming a mother, the impact of this need to get things done can be extreme. Even those women who do not do these manic things often feel

---

20 A. Dunnewold & D.G. Sanford, *op.cit.*, p.29
21 Martin E.P. Seligman, *Learned Optimism*, Milsons Point, 1991, p.55

they *should* be doing them and so beat up on themselves both mentally and emotionally. They harbour a suspicion, a guilt, that they are wasting time, that they should be 'doing' something—'achieving', 'succeeding' at tangible goals. A day of play does not fill the bank account, it does not fit into a ledger, cannot be captured or held. It is seemingly valueless. If we have at any time felt this way then we have fallen victim to the intolerable ethic that all things of value must convert to dollars and cents. If experience does not convert to money then it is worthless. This is not so!

It is easy for a new mother to believe this immersion in the life of a baby is something which will go on forever and therefore must be resisted in case she becomes an intellectual blob. She does not yet understand that all phases in a child's life do pass, and ever so much more quickly than she can anticipate. The early months of a baby's life are over so fast. Baby changes daily and sometimes by the hour. The unfoldment of a human being is so precious that to miss it because one is busy trying to fit into the values of the doing paradigm is a tragedy. Your baby will only be completely dependent upon you for a very short period. By the time she is twelve to eighteen months old she will be running away and will act out 'no' long before she is able to say it.

We need to know that these days are to be cherished. Even if we do feel that our entire lives have been, and ever more shall be, consumed by babyhood—they will not. We need to keep in mind that nothing lasts forever, least of all the baby in our child. The first smile will never be repeated. The first baby talk. The first intentional reaching for mother. The first roll over, sit up, crawl, step, word. Enjoy and give yourself permission to be immersed in your baby's life. The time will never, ever come again and it is a shame to waste it feeling guilty and inadequate.

TRAPPED

- 59% of women surveyed did not expect this aspect of motherhood
- 59% reported an impact on coping; 43% severe to extreme
- 57% experienced intrapersonal conflict; 38% severe to extreme
- 55% engaged in interpersonal conflict; 40% severe to extreme

When a woman is in the paid workforce she knows that she has, to a certain extent, autonomy over her life. She knows if she changes her mind about going to work on any particular day she has the right to call in sick—or quit. If she does go to work she is taken seriously, at least by her peers if not by management. In this country there is no such thing as enforced labour—in the paid workforce. But we do have mothers who are not free to call in sick or resign or take holidays.

In subtle ways and in not so subtle ways, the collective social expectation conspires to have mothers conveniently disappear into their homes with their children where they are expected to make no demands for assistance. They are to raise their children alone and without complaint. For the most part, this is what the majority of mothers do. They put up with the isolation and abandonment and they adjust. A subculture springs up consisting entirely of women who complain to each other about the inequities of motherhood and the way they have become trapped in the role. Few speak out publicly because if there is anything lower than a complaining, nagging woman, it is one who admits she cannot cope with motherhood as it is defined by the society in which she lives.

Yet the way things are is not okay and many aspects of living in our society keep a woman feeling as though she is trapped in a role which is not recognised as being of value. The following are three common examples of this entrapment.

Public Facilities

To a new mother her baby can seem to be exquisitely vulnerable, fragile and infinitely valuable. So, when a woman is out in her local shopping centre she needs somewhere she can take her baby to change and feed her and which meets an acceptable standard of cleanliness and comfort. Certainly, there are some well-appointed baby changing and feeding rooms. However, some of the words women have used to describe those rooms in their areas are 'filthy', 'dark', 'hovel'. Other complaints were that they were tucked away in difficult to find corners and attached to public toilets. Even the least fastidious of us often find ourselves repelled and repulsed by these less than hygienic conditions which offer no warmth or comfort to the nursing mother. The country's parks and beaches offer no better facilities and often there are none at all.

This problem is magnified for rural women who may have to travel for an hour or more to the nearest urban centre and who, upon arriving, have immediate need of a baby friendly change room. Janelle, who lived in the Hunter Valley when her first baby was born, said:

I used to sit in the car to feed the baby and to change him. In summer that is awful and stressful.

Entertainment and Study

Women reported trying to continue their lives amongst mainstream society by taking their babies with them to theatres and restaurants. They found these places did not accommodate or acknowledge their babies and toddlers and, in many instances, made it clear that they were not welcome. Maureen was indignant when she said:

> We expect our women to have babies yet we do not allow our women to participate in mainstream activities.

Similarly, a woman who takes time out from her studies to have a baby soon finds that it is difficult to slot back into the system. Her baby is not welcome in the lecture hall but our institutions of learning do not provide adequate child care facilities either.

A Mother's Own Psyche

Sometimes a woman becomes trapped by her own instincts and obsession with her baby. She puts immense pressure on herself to meet her baby's every single need instantly, fearing he will grow up damaged emotionally or psychologically if she does not.

The older mother is more likely to fall prey to this belief than the very young, since she may be more aware of how a young life can go astray. Her child may also seem more precious to her since she knows her child bearing years, and thus the number of children she will have, are limited. On top of this lies the expectation that, because she was able to effectively direct her life before the birth of her baby in the complex world of paid work, she should be able to handle 'mere' motherhood easily. When she finds that motherhood is a far more difficult and demanding occupation, she feels trapped in a role in which she seems to be less competent than she has imagined her adult self to be. Charmaine, normally a devoted mother, admitted:

> Sometimes I feel like going out and never coming back. Always doing everything for others and getting no positive feedback like, 'you are doing a good job'. I feel trapped.

That is the thing with the early days of first-time motherhood. It is so in-your-face that a woman cannot see past the present moment of endlessly giving until she feels as though it will never end. She gradually begins to feel trapped forever in exhaustion, crabbiness and a mundane existence.

Most women surveyed and interviewed said that it was not until their second babies were born that they realised that their children would not be permanently damaged if they had to wait a moment for attention. And it is precisely this kind of psychological entrapment which can be and should be alleviated early by mothers sharing this common experience.

ACHIEVEMENT

- 75% of new mothers surveyed did not expect to experience a lack of ability to 'achieve'
- 71% reported an impact on coping; 43% severe to extreme
- 60% experienced intrapersonal conflict; 43% severe to extreme
- 51% engaged in interpersonal conflict; 32% severe to extreme

If a woman has been out there in the world working for several years before becoming a mother she has grown accustomed to achieving certain levels of accomplishment each day of her life. Especially if she has had a solid career for more than ten years she is likely to feel confident that, within reason, she is able to fulfil the expectations she has of herself and those which others have of her.

Many women, prior to motherhood, thrive on challenges and working out problems. They measure their self-worth against their ability to rise above complications and to turn chaos into order. If they enjoy predictable jobs they measure themselves by their ability to maintain that order. Even if their jobs are monotonous they know they are able to achieve a specified quantity 'doingness' in the course of an average day. Lisa wrote:

> I have five-year-old and six-month-old daughters. Before I gave birth to my first child I could run a household, work, party, anything. Now I find it a chore even to get dinner ready in the evenings. I find it takes all day just to do the laundry and clean one room. What happened to the superwoman that I once was?

Before bringing a baby into one's life it is difficult, if not impossible, to imagine how one tiny baby could take all of that away. But they do. To find one's self still in a dressing gown, hair unbrushed, beds unmade, the previous night's washing up still coagulating in the sink at midday is unthinkable to a self-determined, childless woman. Countless non-mothers and pregnant women believe, in their heart-of-hearts, that if and when they become mothers they will be more organised. They look down on the 'disorganised mother'. When I have tried to relate this slice of reality to a non-mother, although she nods in all the right places, I can tell that in her brain she is usually saying, 'Yes, but ... that will not happen to me.' The truth is that it happens to rather a lot of women and the reality is all the more awful because their expectations have been shattered. Anna confided:

> I thought they just eat and sleep and that's what babies do. That's what Mum said and I believed her. When David had colic it was just awful. I was in shock.

This mother's expectations were brought to an abrupt halt by a baby who rarely slept (and then only in short snatches), who had colic and who fed every three hours, day and night. This same mother said she felt she was a lesser person because her baby did not conform to the model, because she found it difficult to cope and because she did not live up to her mother's image of motherhood. Dianna found herself in similar circumstances. She said:

> I must be really hopeless. Other women go out to work and I haven't even folded the nappies yet.

Her remark, made during a group discussion, brought howls of protest from every other mother there. Each one felt compelled to assure her that she was not hopeless, that they had all had the same experience and that staying at home was far harder on a woman than going out to work. This feeling of being useless is undoubtedly one that most mothers have believed of themselves at some stage in their mothering days.

Denise's first baby often cried for three hours at a time, did not sleep and suffered severe reflux problems. Her entire life revolved around pacifying and feeding him leaving her an emotional mess at the end of every day. Denise described her situation:

I wanted to be a mother. I wanted to be at home, I wanted to do all that. But I didn't ever imagine that I would have a child who would be hard to manage.

How do you explain to someone who has never had a child that a mere baby can reduce the household to total chaos and the mother to feeling incompetent in even the most basic of menial duties? The problem arises out of two misguided notions: the expectation that life will not be severely disrupted by the introduction of a baby; and the fact that achievement is measured by the quantity of what we have done during a day rather than by the quality of our interactions with those people (especially our babies) whom we love.

I could not count the number of women who reported that their spouses arrived home at the end of the day with, 'What have you done all day?' on their lips or in their minds. There is an unspoken assumption by both the spouse and the new mother that now she is 'not working' she will be able to do more around the house. When a woman tries to justify her existence by explaining all she has achieved while he has been at work, the list is short and it sounds banal. This is only so because we measure achievement by how much we do.

Her appropriate reply would be to say, 'I have been a mother'—anything else she may achieve above and beyond that is a bonus.

RECOGNITION AND ACCLAIM

- 66% of the women surveyed did not expect to need recognition for their mothering
- 52% reported an impact on coping; 30% severe to extreme
- 54% experienced intrapersonal conflict; 37% severe to extreme
- 52% engaged in interpersonal conflict; 28% severe to extreme

Nikki was thirty-eight when she gave birth to her daughter. This child, although unplanned, was brought into the world with great rejoicing as she was much wanted. However, when her daughter was about three months old Nikki said these words to me:

> Wen, I love her so much. You know how much I wanted her. Some days I just sit and watch her be her and I feel like I need nothing else in this

world to make me happy. And yet ... I don't understand why I feel like this.

The answer is, by the time a woman has worked out there in the world for ten or twenty years she has grown accustomed to receiving rewards for the job that she does. Even if this only comes in the form of a pay packet each week, it is still acknowledgement that she has achieved at a standard recognised as valid by her employer and therefore by society. Kylie admitted:

My experience was that this [paid work] was what defined me as a person.

External recognition of who we are as individuals is essential to maintaining our sense of identity and when it is withdrawn it is both confusing and painful. If acknowledgement of the person we have come to know ourselves to be suddenly vanishes, as it often does with the onset of motherhood, then we may feel as though a significant aspect of ourselves has died. If the person who was once worthy of acclaim no longer exists then we find ourselves asking, 'Who was I back then, who am I now, and who am I becoming?'

One moment a woman is a successful banker, secretary, nurse, company director, editor, journalist, teacher ... and the next? A mother. Where is the acclaim? Where is the recognition? We women have grown accustomed to assessing ourselves against performance-based criteria only.

Mothering cannot conform to rigid standards since every woman and every child are different. A mother's performance cannot be measured or rated. She must be infinitely flexible if she is to meet her children's needs. How we bring up this generation of children will determine our future and that of the planet. Our children will need to be extremely strong and resourceful people if they are to be able to create anything like the degree of comfort we have always expected for ourselves. It is awesome to realise that an army of women are raising these children unpaid, unknown, unrecognised, with no applause or acclaim for doing what is also one of the most demanding, testing, tiring, wide ranging and potentially rewarding jobs open to humankind.

Pauline wrote to me:

To me, motherhood is a vocation, a career, especially up to at least seven years. It is a huge responsibility and sometimes a burden but doing it well is something to take pride and joy in.

REALITY SETS IN

Is there no room to acknowledge a woman for her labours of child bearing and rearing? Is there not some way we can honour our mothers with acclaim and recognition commensurate with the dedication, compassion and personal sacrifice they so endlessly pour into their children? Eileen said:

> I was in shock after my baby was born. I felt like an all-powerful goddess after giving birth and there was no-one who reflected that back to me.

Without recognition or acclaim for a job well done it becomes increasingly difficult to maintain a sense of worthiness and it becomes ever easier to believe that, as a mother, one is a person of little intrinsic value. Kristina first became a mother seventeen years ago and now has three teenage children. As I interviewed her, her husband came, sat beside her and joined our conversation. He reached out and held her hand, looked lovingly at her and said:

> You were beautiful with our babies. [turning to me] You should have seen her, Wendy, she was gorgeous. [and back to his wife] Do you remember how I would come home and the house would be all a mess and no dinner cooking and there you would be so contented in our big, old chair with the stuffing coming out of the arms, with our babies on your lap and at your breast. That was beautiful. God, that was beautiful.

His smile, his inward reminiscence and the look on his face told me that she was indeed beautiful. And that is all it takes, isn't it? Someone who matters telling a woman that she, as a mother, is wonderful.

TIME OUT

Once a woman becomes a mother she can no longer think only of her own needs or simply allow the day to unfold as it will. Sometimes it seems that life is flying past her simply because she is perpetually focussed on the future, making contingency plans so that her baby, her friends, her family will not be in any way inconvenienced. Often she does not realise she needs to take time out for herself. Glenda told me:

> Someone would have had to tell me it was safe to take time out, that I

needed it and that Sonya would be safe without me for short periods. I was too tired to rationalise.

When a woman does look after herself by taking time for herself she returns to the home feeling refreshed and rejuvenated. She has had enough time to miss her child and looks forward to seeing her again. Then she is able to lavish attention on her baby or toddler with a genuine desire to be close once more. Anna agreed:

It does not take long to recuperate—a few hours is all it takes. Then you enjoy the kids more when you come back to them.

If time out is not forthcoming a woman begins to feel trapped in her role as mother and may come to resent her child, her husband, her home and the role itself. Denise admitted:

I would kill for time out—much as I love my kids I would kill for more time out.

When every day is dominated by the needs of someone else, is it any wonder that women feel depleted of the ability to go on giving unconditionally? Women have their needs, too. The longer they are denied and left unfulfilled the harder it is to meet, or want to meet, another's needs. How much easier may it seem to escape back into the paid workforce where one's needs for space and recognition appear to be more easily met, than to eternally give with little or no prospect of ever getting in return. Although, as Mandy points out, time in paid work is still not time out simply to 'be':

Time to myself, time for me—it is such a big issue. It is OK to work. It is OK to look after others. I CRAVE time to myself, to be alone, on my own.

Eventually, when a woman does create time for herself she may find she becomes less than sympathetic towards any intrusion, demand or expectation that cuts into her precious private time and space. Adelle and Pam, respectively, said:

REALITY SETS IN

> I am resentful if people take up my own time out. I have to have quality time for myself.
>
> I resent others intruding on my time. I hate daylight saving because it cuts into my time for me because the kids go to bed later.

Almost universally the women interviewed for this book said they felt guilty for taking time for themselves and yet it is the one thing they each craved above all else. Amongst those who still had preschool children, not one had been shopping alone with the express purpose of buying something to please herself. Even the most closely bonded relationships cannot withstand such togetherness without it creating stresses.

Should a woman feel she cannot take time out for herself without her children, she cannot easily rejuvenate herself. She becomes absorbed by the role so completely she forgets she was a person and a woman long before she became a mother. Without distance she is unable to dispassionately evaluate her successes and failures. She finds it difficult to bring into balance her identity as a human being, a woman and an independent person—who happens to be a mother as well. Melanie summed it up:

> A mother needs time out when she feels as though she is going insane.

Many women reported to me that the only time out they ever got was when their spouses 'minded' their own children so their wives could go and do the shopping. Pam's story is typical:

> My day off is when Steve minds the children so I can do the grocery shopping in town. He does nothing else, mind you, like household chores or tidying up. When I come home and ask what he has been doing all the time I have been away he says, 'looking after the children'. He thinks he is doing me a favour looking after the kids.

No person can or should be expected to be a support person to another human being 100% of the time. It is recognised that people who look after the disabled and who care for the elderly need respite from their roles as carers. So too, our mothers need time to themselves on a regular basis in order to recreate themselves as people and as women of independent worth. It is not possible to instil a sense of worth into our children if we do not equally recognise our own worth. It is not possible to ensure that our children consider their needs to be valid if, equally, we will not recognise, validate and seek to fulfil our own needs. If we do not take reasonable time out for ourselves we may as well say we believe it is OK to use up women until they become ill, burn out or break down. More importantly, we will ensure the current status quo slides insidiously into yet another generation.

ASKING FOR HELP

Few women today feel it is acceptable to ask for help. Once she has become a mother there seems to be some unwritten rule which says she must be able to do everything herself and that to ask for help is to admit inadequacy. The logic is, that now that she is 'not working', a woman who is a mother has all the time in the world to accomplish anything and everything. Mandy's story brought forth gasps of envy around the room making it clear her experience was atypical:

> One woman saved me by coming in and immediately taking the baby, changing its nappy, making a cup of tea. At the same time she told me that I was doing a great job and was a good mother.

When I asked women why it was they were reluctant to ask for help they tended to reply in one of two ways. Dianna's answer was typical of one when she said:

> I know how hard it is with my own children, I don't want to burden another woman with my problems.

On the other hand, Marilyn's response was typical of the other:

> I resisted help because I felt that I had to do it all myself.

It was with disbelief that another group listened to Melanie tell how she had asked friends to take her baby so that she could have time out for herself. This same woman went on to say how she had a neighbour who would go down the shop for her to fetch a litre of milk or a loaf of bread to save her from having to go through the rigmarole of organising the baby for the trip. She also had an older woman friend who came in occasionally and did a load of washing for her, cared for the baby and made her, the mother, a cup of tea. The reactions of those women who did not receive, did not expect to receive and could not ask for help made it very clear that the majority of women, once they become mothers, expect to have to cope on their own. Many will not even ask their partners for assistance. Faye admitted:

> I feel really guilty asking William [her husband] to mind the children. He is not happy to baby-sit. He usually lets the children cry as I drive off.

Any help which is offered to a mother tends to be seen as charity or a one-off gift for which she ought to feel grateful rather than seeing help as her natural right. As Linda observed:

> We are encouraged to have a career. Most of us worked up until we had children. We should expect our husbands to be involved. We must look after ourselves, we must value ourselves.

Faye concluded our discussion on the need to ask for help as she realised:

> Maybe William doesn't make me feel guilty for asking for help—maybe it's just in me.

That puts the problem into a nutshell. So long as a woman does not perceive herself as worthy of help and does not honour her mothering role as a valid profession which requires support every bit as much as any other profession, she will not receive either help or support. We must learn to ask for help from that place of conviction inside ourselves which absolutely knows that we, and the job we are doing, are worthy.

THE CONSPIRACY OF SILENCE

- 60% of women surveyed did not expect to encounter a conspiracy of silence
- 71% reported an impact on coping; 31% severe to extreme
- 51% experienced intrapersonal conflict; 28% severe to extreme
- 47% engaged in interpersonal conflict; 19% severe to extreme

NAKED MOTHERHOOD

This is the essence of the matter. The ideology of motherhood and the reality are two entirely different concepts. Yet the myths live on and too many of us remain tight-lipped about our all too real experiences. Why do we do it? Several reasons come to mind (some of which have been discussed in the previous chapter in relation to pregnancy):

- If we give voice to our experiences we fear we will discover that we are the only mother in all of history who is abnormal and thus will be judged accordingly. Even if we do know others who have suffered similar defeats to ours, the mother, or prospective mother, to whom we speak may not encounter such an experience, leaving us looking foolish or less than adequate. So we only tell her the good bits (of which there are many, of course).

- We do not wish to be responsible for being the one to frighten a mother-to-be or turn a would-be-mother off the idea of having her own child—just in case she turns out to be the mythical 'perfect mother' with the equally mythical 'perfect child'.

- We divide women into mothers and non-mothers, and there is a feeling they are two distinct species. We believe the more of one, the less valid the role of the other, and that in order to increase the validity of motherhood, we therefore need more mothers. We don't tell the truth because it may scare the non-mothers permanently into the camp of independent, corporate achievers who highlight our lack of independence and freedom by their very existence.

- The mothers of non-mothers want grandchildren. They are highly unlikely to tell their daughters the truth of mothering for fear of reaching their deathbeds grandchild-less.

- Mothers forget. The majority of the women I interviewed had pre-highschool age first children. The drama of raising a teenager can make babyhood seem as though it was easy and there is a tendency to forget the rigours of babyhood.

- Mothers have selective memories. Motherhood is such a defining life role that to remember any part of it, especially the baby years, as painful, difficult, debilitating is to admit the loss of her *raison d'être*. Increasingly, after the children start school and the mother begins to return to a more balanced lifestyle she rationalises away the exhaustion, the uncertainties, the inner turmoil. To the extent that her self-worth was wrapped up in being a 'good mother' she will deny the hardships she suffered in those early years.

- A small percentage of women do thoroughly enjoy every aspect of motherhood and see no reason to speak about its darker side since they have not experienced it. I stress that amongst those who look after their own children entirely without family or paid help, this is indeed a rare woman. A larger percentage think they 'should' be able to be the perfect mother and so, rather than admit to their human failings, become judgemental of those who are not making it. It is hard, and somewhat pointless, for a woman to express the difficulties she is experiencing as a mother in the presence of those for whom the hardships do not exist or who will not admit they, themselves, are experiencing them.

- Mothers want revenge! How many times did you hear your own mother say to you, 'You'll know what it's like when you have your own children'? And after you have had your child and it behaves exactly the way you did, do you not see that tiny hint of an 'I told you so' on her face?

- Mothers need to be vindicated. When your child has thrown a monster tantrum, have you ever seen that judgemental look on your non-mothering friends' faces which said, 'If this were my child he would never behave that way'? Is it not secretly satisfying when your friend does have a child and it does behave that way—and worse? Do you not feel just a little vindicated and a tad smug? Be honest …

Throughout my research, over and over again women of all ages and of all walks of life admitted that there was a conspiracy of silence around motherhood. Nurses, midwives, child care workers, Nursing Mothers counsellors and mothers said, in aggrieved tones, they felt women actively partook of the conspiracy. Mothers everywhere said they felt cheated, conned, sucked in, manipulated. The most common single thing mothers said to me was, 'But they never tell you about that' or 'Why didn't anyone tell me?'

Women must talk about their realities. If another mother does not have the same experiences as you do this does not make you a failure or a fruitcake. What it does mean is that should your experience prove to be similar to hers in the future, she will know she is not crazy, that others have felt as she does and that there is light at the end of the proverbial tunnel.

A woman who is forewarned may not initially believe that any of the experiences in this book will affect her. But if they do, and women she knows who are already mothers have spoken honestly about them, she will know she can talk to them, ask how they handled it, how long it lasts and what steps to take to look after herself. She will be more inclined to reach out for help. Her expectations prior to birth may be more realistic and she may even take preventative steps before her baby arrives and so be less affected than when the consequences of motherhood strike unexpectedly.

Sometimes a woman feels that, for her, the negative aspects of motherhood outweigh the biological imperative to breed her own offspring. If this woman chooses to be a non-mother she is likely to lead a far happier life than that she would have led had she been compelled by social pressure to become a mother. We do her no favours by glorifying the institution of motherhood. If this potential candidate for the mother 'species' is turned off by hearing about its reality, you have probably done her a favour and, perhaps, the child as well. The following is one such example.

During my pre-mother days I had a business acquaintance who strongly felt she never wanted to have a child. However, she also felt she 'should' have a baby in case she regretted not doing so when she was older. (Another variation on this line of thinking is 'for the experience' or 'so I won't be lonely in my old age'.) Later, I ran into her and she admitted she was pregnant saying:

> It always was going to be a nuisance having a baby. I guess now is the time for the nuisance to arrive.

This woman might not have succumbed to the social pressure to bring a child into the world who was unlikely to be loved as unconditionally as children deserve if she had been informed of the difficulties of motherhood.

Having received letters and comments from women of all ages, I have discovered a deep and unacknowledged well of silent suffering amongst those whose experience of motherhood has been disappointing or debilitating. One such letter, which moved me more than a little, came from Beverley whom I have never met. Bev had been told she could never have a child, not even on the IVF program. Yet at the age of thirty-three she became pregnant and felt she had to grab the opportunity. Although she had been in a long-term relationship and her partner assured her he would be there for her, he was not. In fact, without consulting her, he moved interstate when their baby was one month old. The all too common story of exhaustion, isolation, crashing self-esteem and poverty drove her first to follow him and move in with him again and second, to return to paid work. Beverley's partner moved interstate again, and again she followed, only to find this time he took a job six hours from home. Her own job was so stressful, and she found juggling virtual single motherhood and paid work so debilitating that she finally suffered a breakdown. Not surprisingly her son bore the brunt of her disappointment, stress and anger until she finally left her partner. The conclusion to Beverley's letter speaks of the effect the conspiracy of silence had on her:

> Despite all this I love my son dearly, but if I had my time over again I would have had an abortion. Indeed, I found myself pregnant again ... and did not hesitate.
> Through all this my female friends and colleagues still insist that motherhood is the be all and end all of existence. They will not say anything against the state of motherhood and are extremely disturbed when I say that I am not coping or that I sometimes wished that I had opted for an abortion instead of motherhood.
> Their disapproval makes it extremely hard and I often feel ashamed and guilty—is it just me that thinks this way? 'There must be something wrong with me.'
> I feel that women should learn to be more open about motherhood—it is not the bestowing of sainthood on one, and there are incredible problems and obstacles to be overcome.
> Most importantly of all we have to learn to be honest with each other—especially with those women contemplating motherhood. What is needed is more support—emotional, physical and spiritual for mothers.

Unlike Beverley, if I had my time over again, knowing everything I now know about motherhood, I would unequivocally choose to be Daniel's mother once more. It is inconceivable that I could have lived this life without his presence—I simply would not be the person I have become without our relationship. Having said that, I also heartily wish that those who had gone before me into motherhood—friends, relatives, full-time mothers and those who rejoined the paid workforce, and representatives of the media too—had been more honest about the difficulties. This conspiracy of silence denies women the right to prepare for the daily reality of motherhood and generates more heartache than it saves.

HELP FOR HANGING IN THERE

Acknowledge and Own Your Natural Desire to Nurture

If you feel the need to nurture and protect your baby upwelling inside you, do not allow your instinct to be diminished by those who would dismiss it as merely another skill which anyone can learn as though it were nothing special. It is special and it is precious.

Rather than trying to suppress your instinct to nurture for fear of looking foolish—honour it, trust it, go with it. If you do not resist it, this instinct will adjust itself to appropriate levels as your baby grows older and becomes more independent. I am told by grandmothers, however, that it never quite goes away. Even when your children are middle aged it is quite likely you will still worry about them and wish you could protect them from the pains of life.

Don't Be Shocked By the Way Other Adults Treat You

Be prepared for the fact that many people will now treat you as though you no longer have a brain in your head, are incapable of directing your life and exist only to care for your baby—and them. Be assured that they are not actually out to get you personally—they would do this to any new mother. Rather than allowing yourself to feel defeated by their attitudes, let them know you are still alive, still have needs and still have a high and valid expectation that these needs will be met.

Before the Birth of Your Baby Create a Support Network

Before transforming into a mother many women, if they think about it at all, do not believe they need or want the support of other women. However, every woman would be well advised to ensure she has at least one like-minded and like-aged friend in her vicinity who is also beginning her career as a mother. This is not necessarily an easy process but one which will bring obvious rewards within the first six months of becoming a mother. Once one friendship is established it is likely to fan out as each of you brings new members to the group. Places to begin the search are in the antenatal classes, by asking other friends to introduce you to women who are at a similar stage of life, by going to the local baby health clinic or through Nursing Mothers.

If you find you are lacking in self-confidence or are too depressed to push yourself into new friendships do not hesitate to seek out a postnatal depression support group. I cannot stress how vital peer support is to most new mothers.

Nurture Your Sense of Humour

Too many of us get bogged down in exhaustion, low self-esteem and feelings of having been abandoned. Somewhere in the mire we lose our sense of humour—which is unfortunate since it is the one thing guaranteed to help you survive when all else fails. The real danger is that once your sense of humour is buried beneath the rubble of motherhood you may forget that you ever had it. Sometimes it takes years to dig through the debris of self to stumble upon it once more.

Watch at least one funny video every week without fail. Pull faces at yourself in the mirror. Blow raspberries with your baby until you are both laughing. Allow yourself to play with your baby. Give yourself permission to become immersed in his world, to rediscover the wonder of even the most insignificant object. Play racing cars with him in the trolley in the supermarket. So what if people think you are crazy—you probably are, so why not enjoy it?

Reclaim Your Freedom

Before you even become pregnant realise that having a baby will curb your freedom significantly. Like all things we take for granted we do not realise how precious this is until it is lost. The sooner you can reclaim some of it, the sooner you will feel good about yourself.

Organise with your partner, family, friends to care for your baby regularly while you take some time for yourself, preferably within the first three months of motherhood. If you find it difficult to separate from your baby, begin by removing yourself only as far as the other end of the house. Use the time to read a book or to take a nap. By the following week you may venture a walk around the block, and there find you can complete whole thoughts uninterrupted.

After several weeks, when no harm has befallen your baby, you may feel trusting enough to go to the shopping centre, see a doctor, have a haircut —alone. Even though you may feel anxious for your baby the whole time you are away from her, the day will come when you realise you have not thought of him in an entire hour (or two). This may make you feel guilty. Let that thought go and in its place acknowledge how good it feels to be at least a little free again.

Spontaneity Returns—In Time

To a certain extent spontaneity is curbed as soon as we enter any relationship with another human being, since their needs and concerns must be balanced with our own. To a baby, her needs are not negotiable and yours do not exist. While you are immersed in early motherhood it can seem as though your own life has ceased for all time.

However, every mother of older children will tell you that babyhood passes so quickly and in retrospect, that is true. All too soon they stop needing morning and afternoon sleeps, leaving you free to move around at any time of the day. They stop throwing up in the first year and grow out of nappies in the third so you no longer need to pack an overnight bag just to go next door.

Between toddlerhood and school, spontaneity begins to return as you find you can come and go more freely. After school begins, if you have not returned to paid work, you will have six hours a day to yourself.

Develop Flexibility

Nothing you do, short of shutting your baby, toddler or child in a sound-proof cupboard, will stop them from interrupting you—constantly. Certainly you can try ignoring them until they give up but a child's need for attention is so great they can be truly creative in developing less direct ways of getting it—most of them destructive of themselves, others and others' possessions. If you refuse to voluntarily accommodate persistent interruptions to your thought processes and activities, rest assured that your baby or toddler will wear you down until you do—or until one, or other, or both of you break.

When a baby or toddler feels secure in being able to get her needs met she does not have to continually prove to herself that she can. Learn to give the attention as and when it is needed when the baby is small. If you do, as the years go by, the demands on your time will diminish. Note: *years* is the operative word here, especially if you have a more demanding child.

The upside of learning to cope with hundreds of interruptions per day is that mothers become flexible and adaptable. They find they are capable of holding several dozen thoughts in their head at one time, eventually without muddling them. They are able to accomplish diverse tasks almost simultaneously. If, occasionally, a mother finds a sausage defrosting in the linen cupboard or baby's singlet in the fridge, it is but a small aberration.

Coping with Crying

Until your first baby is born the crying of another's baby may never have bothered you. Afterwards you may discover that the cry of your own is enough to tear your heart out and that other people's babies have almost as great an effect.

Do not be afraid to admit you have been unable to pacify your baby. This does not make you a failure as a mother. I can guarantee that the vast majority of mothers have suffered exactly the same agony at some time in their mothering careers. Before you reach your breaking point phone anybody you know who may be willing to support you until he stops crying—your partner, a neighbour, friend, relative. Take your baby outside if possible because there his crying will seem less loud, less all-consuming.

Many women reported that homoeopathic chamomile or rescue remedy, a Bach flower essence, worked miracles with colic or continuous crying. Other mothers said that a little acidophilus yoghurt diluted in expressed breast milk worked equally swiftly.

It is worth noting that the only woman who reported experiencing no sleepless nights, no exhaustion and little crying by her baby, carried him with her everywhere and had him sleep between her and her husband every night. All ape babies are in constant physical contact with their mothers during their first half year of life. They are what Ashley Montagu calls 'mother-huggers'.[22] So, too, are human babies. Notice how they cling to an adult, especially their hair, as soon as they are picked up.

If your baby is crying a great deal she may be crying out for something as simple as more physical contact. A sling in which to carry her while you go about your daily activities may be the single most worthwhile investment you can make. A baby who feels safe and secure in its earliest months of life is

---

22 A. Montagu, *op.cit.*, p.146

usually ready to begin separating from its mother within six months or so and does not need to spend the rest of its days trying to gain reassurance through the only avenue open to it—crying.

Recognise Mania

It is difficult to realise that one is being manic because the very reason one behaves that way is one believes it to be necessary and normal. A symptom of mania is refusing to relax when your baby sleeps even though you are exhausted. Another is regularly reaching the end of the day having tried to do so many tasks at once that none has been completed.

When mania is mild it can be a warning that your sense of self-worth has been depleted to a level of desperation for recognition. Take stock of what you are trying to achieve and why. Make a list of all the things you think need to be done and do only the single most urgent one each day. If that means all you do is to hang out the washing, so be it.

Note how you feel about doing so little. If this has been a long-term problem, its source may be rooted in a childhood where nothing you did was ever good enough to earn your parents' praise. You may need to do some work on that issue, perhaps with a counsellor or therapist. Meanwhile, look for people who will give you positive feedback about your role as a mother and ease up on yourself.

When mania is extreme, a woman's thought processes become incoherent, muddled and illogical. At this level, it is unlikely that you, yourself, will recognise there is anything wrong with your behaviour, so it will be up to your partner, family or friends to ensure you receive the treatment you need. Whether a doctor prescribes lithium or not, you will recover your sense of self-worth all the more quickly if you also see a therapist.

Speak Up and Speak Out

When you feel trapped in the role of mother, speak up, talk about it, share how you feel. When you feel as though there is a conspiracy to shove you back home, speak out about the inequities. Nothing will ever change if each individual mother bottles up her misgivings, her fears, her discontent inside her. As Gwenda said:

> Isn't it amazing that when you admit you are vulnerable you find that everyone else is vulnerable, too?

Be less concerned about what others think of you. Secretly, every one of us is vulnerable in some way—it is just that some of us are better at covering it up than others. One thing is for sure, though, if I am open and honest with you, you will be much more likely to feel comfortable being open and honest with me. And in that sharing we are likely to find that even if we are fruitcakes, we are not fruitcakes alone. This is comforting.

Raising a Child Well is a HUGE Achievement

The one thing that continues to astound me is how mothers themselves believe that raising a child well is not a particularly notable achievement. The difficulty for new mums is they do not know whether their brand of mothering, today, is going to produce a healthy, happy, well-adjusted adult in eighteen or twenty years. The delay between action and result is, literally, a lifetime. Parenthood is the one profession which requires no training, has no objective system of evaluation and offers virtually no way out. Yet we expect mothers (and fathers) to be expert parents from the moment they hold their first baby. This is not reasonable. Allow yourself at least the length of a university course to learn your trade before you judge yourself a non-achiever in the mothering stakes.

Look at your baby or toddler. Is she essentially happy, healthy, curious? Does she have a sparkle in the eye? Does he laugh and cry easily? Is he pleased to see you when you walk into the room? Is she eating, growing, learning at appropriate rates? If so, you are obviously achieving in your profession of motherhood.

If your child is not thriving do not leap to the conclusion that it is necessarily your fault. First check with a medical practitioner or clinic sister to see whether he is in good health. Second, look to your own unfulfilled needs to see whether they are affecting your child. Third, understand that babies do bring with them their own karma, their own personalities, their own lessons to learn and do not beat up on yourself just because you cannot control these.

Although it is impossible to see into your future, those mothers who have traversed some years of motherhood can assure you that, by the time your child goes to school, you will be looking back upon these early days with awe at what you are now achieving. Hold that thought.

Get the Recognition You Deserve

First, recognise in yourself your need to receive positive feedback about your abilities. Second, find people who will give it to you. Third, when they tell you that you are doing a great job, believe them. Do not brush away positive comments; say 'thank you' and let them sink in. Few people will say you are doing well if they think you are not.

The single most positive source of feedback a woman can receive is from her partner. He needs to know that when he spends time supporting you with his positive physical and emotional presence he is making a far greater contribution than if he spends his time trying to prove his worth through excessive amounts of paid work.

If you can convince your partner especially, or those closest to you, that their recognition of your worth and the value of your role as a mother are vital to your wellbeing, you will have taken a major step towards preventing many of the more difficult potential side effects of becoming a mother.

Take Time for Yourself

Every mother I interviewed, whether in paid work or not, said that time to themselves was their most precious commodity. If you establish a pattern in the very beginning of always putting yourself last on the list of priorities, it is likely you will still be doing so even when the family no longer needs you to be fussing over them. Then you really will feel worthless.

No human being can give of themselves all day every day. If you believe you must be there for your baby every second it is likely that, sooner or later, you will begin to feel resentment either towards the baby or towards others who are allowing you to take on more than you can cope with.

Negotiate with your partner or family or friends how you will get time out from mothering. If you want to spend your personal time in or around your home, it is better that they take the baby elsewhere so you will not be drawn back to mothering the moment she cries. Whatever you do, make sure you use this time to please yourself.

You Are Worth Helping—Ask

If you never ask for help you will never receive it. As a mother, you are one of our most precious resources and you deserve support. Do not think, even for a minute, that you are so insignificant as to be unworthy of help.

One creative solution a group of mothers told me about was that they developed a collective action plan for tackling the mundane daily tasks of keeping house. They jointly cleaned, washed and cooked at their alternating homes, all the while sharing the load of child care. Although this may feel strange in the beginning, provided you are reasonably compatible with your workmate, you will find the drudgery melts away.

Whether this is a viable solution for you or not, other people will not know you need help unless you ask. They may see you struggling, may want to help, but feel uncomfortable in offering for fear of offending you. Make it easy on them—drop the mask and ask.

Don't Buy Into the Conspiracy of Silence

If the only thing this book achieves is to stimulate discussion between mothers of how they really feel about the role, I will be pleased. Until we all become more honest about how the institution of motherhood affects us we will continue to feel isolated, insignificant and inept. Every one of us must begin to tell our own true story—perhaps quietly at first amongst trusted friends. Only when enough of us are willing to whisper our truth will the hushed silence of inadequacy and personal pain transform into the roaring wind of healing change so desperately needed today.

I have probably made it clear by now that I do not believe the way we, as a society, relate to and have structured motherhood (or indeed parenthood) is supportive of mothers, fathers or children. It is only a matter of eight or ten generations, at the very outside, since women mothered in a collective atmosphere sharing the chores, the responsibilities, the aches and the joys of mothering. Today we are expected to do it alone and vast numbers of us are finding it difficult. If you find it difficult to speak out, keep in mind the costs to yourself and your children of remaining silent. For you those costs may 'only' be continuing isolation or stress, for the children the consequences may be devastating. The symptoms of our collective failures are all too plain to see in their suffering.

There are 25,000 children who live on the streets in Australia[23] some of whom are less than ten years old. They are there, not necessarily because their parents do not care, but because the parents can no longer cope with their own lives, let alone their children's as well. The dictates of the doing paradigm have squeezed us into nuclear and single-parent families many of whom are time-stressed, unemployed, isolated, disconnected from the greater community, and/or living in poverty. Not surprisingly many have found it difficult, if not impossible, to adapt to these stressful conditions. Yet those who cannot cope

---

23 C. Sidoti, 'Giving Children a Voice', *NSW Child Protection Council State Conference*, February 17, 1997

individually bear the burden of blame as if they deliberately chose their family's demise. Add to this the appalling statistics on youth drug addiction and suicide and we have to acknowledge that something is terribly wrong. If we women are paying a high price in terms of depression and feeling marginalised, our children are paying with their potential and even their lives. Since the children are more powerless than their mothers, perhaps it is time we took responsibility for altering our circumstances.

If there is one thing most mothers want for their children it is 'the best'. Marginalised mothers cannot give their best to their children; instead they raise adults who feel marginalised themselves. Only when mothers feel strong can they raise strong children.

To hold inside all that is wrong with the current structure of motherhood is, at best, to condone it. At worst it is to condemn another generation of women to the shock of discovering that being a mother in today's world is a million miles away from their expectations. For the sake of the children, if not for yourself, please share your truth—today. Be honest with your family and friends about your sadnesses, fears and worries, just as you would share your joy. And similarly, when another mother reaches out to you for support, don't offer her a platitude or dismiss what she says because it makes you feel uncomfortable—let her speak. The unravelling of this conspiracy begins here—with conversation.

THREE
THE CHANGING SELF-IMAGE

In keeping with the conspiracy of silence, those women who have moved into motherhood do not discuss with those who are of pre-mother status how a woman's image of herself alters once she gives birth to her first baby. In part this is because mothers often do not realise that they have been, and still are, struggling to come to terms with a self-image which no longer fits the reality of their lives; that the person who stares back from the other side of the mirror is a stranger.

It is a rare person who is able to define herself in isolation. It is human nature to accept, to a certain extent, that the way other people treat us reflects the true worth and value of our abilities, appearance, feelings, intelligence, ideas, beliefs, fears, dreams. To the degree that we truly know and accept ourselves we will be more or less in need of this affirmation from others in order to define our identity and self-image.

If our need for acknowledgement prior to motherhood is great it is likely to mushroom afterwards—especially if we plummet into the downward spiral of exhaustion and feelings of failure. In many ways though, the more a woman believes she knows her deepest self and the more certain she is about who she is prior to motherhood, the more shocked she may be by the reality as she discovers aspects of herself hitherto hidden from her consciousness. No matter what we bring to the new role, all of us require feedback in order to ascertain whether or not we are acquitting ourselves adequately.

Until a woman becomes a mother she may feel she has accepted meaningful and difficult challenges and tackled them with commitment, guts and determination—and conquered them. She may have climbed the corporate ladder—or mountains; battled men in the boardroom, in the courts, universities; overcome the adversities of being a woman going places in a doing paradigm. If a baby never enters her life she may well go to her grave believing that she has tapped every strength, emoted every emotion, plumbed the very depths of her psyche and that she knows herself intimately. But if she never has a child she will never unleash the mother in herself and therefore cannot develop that dimension of her potential.

A woman who becomes a mother becomes multi-dimensional and discovers aspects of herself—both beautiful and terrifying—that she, as a non-mother, never suspected to be a part of her reality. The first hint that she might be someone other than the person she believed herself to be is the altered look and feel of her body.

PHYSICAL CHANGES

- 71% of women surveyed did not expect their body to be significantly altered by giving birth to their first baby
- 84% reported an impact on coping; 45% severe to extreme
- 63% experienced intrapersonal conflict; 39% severe to extreme
- 33% engaged in interpersonal conflict; 20% severe to extreme

Most women give birth to a child fully expecting their bodies to return to their pre-baby shape and size within a matter of months. There is little warning in the literature that her body, both internally and externally, may never be quite the same again. The magnitude of body changes can impact dramatically on first-time mothers.

External Body Changes
The Face
The changes to a woman's body throughout pregnancy are obvious. Essentially we expect to grow a fatter tummy and bigger breasts. What many women do not realise is that this additional roundness extends to her face, smoothing out many of the little lines. This is the 'glow' of pregnancy which affects the older mother more profoundly than the younger one. Because this bloom grows

THE CHANGING SELF-IMAGE

gradually it is quietly incorporated into her self-image and she does not realise it is a temporary phenomenon.

After pregnancy the lines which appear on some women's faces are truly astonishing. Fluid which has built up in the body during pregnancy rapidly returns to normal levels, withdrawing its plumping support from every cell—notably those in the face. Kate found this side effect of motherhood to be her hardest hurdle:

> I had days when I cried when I looked in the mirror and saw so many lines. I didn't want anyone to look at me ever again.

As the exhaustion and the drudgery begin to take their toll most of us age noticeably. This is especially distressing in contrast to the fullness of face we experienced during pregnancy. It is disappointing in the morning to look into the mirror and to see wrinkles that were definitely not there a month ago—or even yesterday.

Hair

During pregnancy a woman's hair grows more vigorously all over her body. As a result she often finds that the hair on her head has never been thicker or more shining as it grows rapidly and billows around her face. Some women develop waves or curls which have never been evident before. Again, this is a change which sneaks up on her in such a manner that it quietly becomes incorporated into her identity. Most of us, if we think about it at all, assume this unexpectedly pleasant change will remain with us forever.

Not so. Within weeks of baby's birth our flowing, curling locks may begin to wilt. The shine fades away. The once-prized hair may begin to fall out with every washing or brushing, producing drains and brushes filled with hunks of lank hair. Nikki was distraught over her hair loss:

> Every day handfuls of hair would come out. I didn't know how
> to stop it and I thought I'd go bald. Because I am a red-head
> my hair has always been an important part of my identity—and
> I was losing it!

In time the vast majority of us cut our hair shorter, usually under the pretext that it is easier to look after in our busy schedules. Few of us admit to ourselves that this is an attempt to lift our sagging faces and rid ourselves of hair which no longer looks particularly attractive.

Breasts

Breasts bulge, bestowing upon the most meagrely endowed of us the voluptuous proportions of the movie stars. It is a pity they ache, leak, tingle, twitch and burn with the milk's let-down response. Their nipples protrude, no longer the virginal, flat pink extensions of the breast, but patently obvious baby feeding instruments. They need to be encased in maternity bras so they can be held up and let out with speed on demand. They must at all times be encased in clothing which is loose enough to be lifted to free them whenever called upon to feed baby or they must be behind buttons which can be quickly undone. Many women told me they felt like a cow because their breasts were huge and/or they leaked all the time. Leonie wrote:

> The change in my breasts was a much bigger issue than I ever expected. I breastfed for 12 months and took another 18 months to feel 'sexy' about them again and feel comfortable with my husband's touch.

Nipples can change dramatically, too. Sally lamented:

> My nipples went from being flat and pale brown to protruding dark brown sagging appendages on my breasts. I mourned the loss of my pre-baby nipples. I still feel embarrassed about them.

By the time we have weaned our babies, returned to normal bras or none at all and are ready to show off our prized breasts—alas, they are no more. The brief display of big-breasted womanhood is now sagging and shrinking but we're left with the protruding nipples. For the women who shoot up to a size 40 and revert to a size 36 the shrinking phenomenon is not so distressing as the sagging. For the women whose breasts blossom forth into a size 34 or 36 for the first time in their lives the shrinking effect is sadder.

Tummy

The obvious change is to a mother's abdomen. There may be stretch marks, the skin may be softer, its shape may be rounder than before baby. Although weight has been lost in the form of baby, placenta and fluid, the tummy

THE CHANGING SELF-IMAGE

remains flaccid and floppy like a balloon that has been stretched to its limit and then had the air let out. Balloons never return to their pre-blown shape. Fortunately women are more resilient than balloons. But it takes time, as Sally soon discovered:

> When I left the hospital I had my husband bring in my favourite, pre-pregnancy pair of jeans. They used to be a little loose on me so I really thought they would fit now I was no longer carrying our baby. I was distressed and dismayed to find that their button did not meet by more than three inches.

With exercise we can lose the extra weight, trim down the waist and tone up the muscles again but it is unlikely we will push it all back into the exact same shape of our girlhood days—especially if the new mother is in her thirties or forties. For some women it takes only one child to irrevocably alter her shape. For months after childbirth many women are aghast when they see themselves in a full length mirror and, for the majority, a bikini never quite looks the same again. Maureen exclaimed:

> After the birth of my first child I threw away my bikini and bought my first one-piece—with a skirt!

and so did Sally:

> I spent all my twenties on the beaches topless. Since my baby was born [nine years ago] I have never been topless again—or even worn a bikini.

The Bottom, Hips, Thighs, Calves and Ankles

Hips which once looked like those of a boy may fill to matronly proportions and never return to their former slender shape. Thighs may thicken and show stretch marks, too. Bottoms become rounder and maybe they drop just a titch. Some ankles and calves grow larger. Varicose veins developed during pregnancy do not necessarily vanish after the birth and in some cases grow worse as the mother is on her feet most of the day carrying a growing baby's weight as well. As Faye experienced:

> I never wear a dress anymore because my legs are so ugly. I need so

many operations to fix all my veins that I do not think I will ever be able to get them done.

These are the externally obvious alterations. Inside there are others that are often completely unexpected.

Internal Changes
Bowels
Constipation after giving birth can be frightening. It seems that after pushing out the baby the muscles have used up all their push-power and will never return to normal. Just as the pelvic floor muscles require retoning, so too do the muscles of the bowel. The difference is time. It is critical that these muscles resume their normal functioning within a week of giving birth, yet it can take weeks. In the meantime the daunting prospect of continually using laxatives and enemas becomes an aid to survival. Kylie's case was extreme:

> Tell me about it! My bowel muscles were torn and it took over twelve months to regain control!!!

If nobody has warned a woman about this aspect of the post-birth experience she may become severely distressed by it, even frightened.

Haemorrhoids
These are a common result of the strain of the birthing process and are varicose veins of the rectum. Again, they generally recede of their own accord, sometimes helped with creams and ointments. The condition should be treated as soon as possible or there is a risk they will become prolapsed, meaning they will protrude through the anus, in which case surgery may be required to remove them. Untreated they may ultimately cause damage to, and bleeding from, either the haemorrhoids or the bowel. Elaine was frightened by this effect of birth on her body, and said:

> I was kind of scared—I had this bunch of grapes hanging out my bottom. That was the worst part. I ended up with the biggest pain in the arse.

Haemorrhoids will always be painful and certainly do not help a woman to feel good about herself, especially if she is already suffering from constipation.

Bladder

Damage done to the bladder during pregnancy and childbirth may be such that a new mother feels she needs to rush urgently to the toilet only to find she could hardly pee to fill a teaspoon. Worse still, she may find she cannot hold onto that teaspoonful and it leaks out before she can find a toilet. This problem alone can double the stress of a trip to the local supermarket.

In extreme cases a new mother may need surgery to bring her bladder back to normal functioning but for the majority, pelvic floor exercises will, in time, rectify the problem. Many women do, however, find that their control over their bladders, whilst not diminished enough to require surgery, is never quite as good again as it was before baby. Nikki was severely affected by this problem:

> I experienced great concern, irritation, anger, grief over difficulties with my bladder.

Vagina

Perhaps the vagina is the least talked about alteration to a woman's body after she has given birth to her first baby and it must be the one which worries many of us a great deal. After birth most women experience weakness in their vaginas. Some will have developed varicose veins therein which may be painful, some needing surgery (although this is not common). Still others will find as Elaine did:

> When I went to have a shower after the birth all my innards were outer—and nobody tells you that. That was really frightening because I didn't know that could happen.

With the birth of the baby the pelvic floor drops and for a small percentage of women it drops so far that the uterus becomes prolapsed. Once again, unexpected surgery may be required.

Surely though, one of the uppermost questions is whether her vagina will ever be the same again. Has it stretched noticeably and irretrievably? Jennifer confided:

> I went for a smear six weeks after and couldn't even feel the instrument. That was a shock.

and Madelaine:

> Every time I had a bath after the baby was born, when I stood up afterwards water came pouring out of my vagina—and it is still happening. Nobody talks about that.

The other major question about the post-birth vagina is; will I be able to control the muscles the way I used to when I make love and will it feel any different to him? Many women secretly, and in silence, worry there will be a difference but hope most fervently there will not. Nikki wrote:

> Sex was never the same again. I felt like a virgin and was very self-conscious of the size of my vagina as in before vs after.

Pelvic floor exercises will strengthen all the internal muscles but it is unlikely these will return a vagina to its pre-baby status within the first few months of birth; six months to a year later, perhaps.

GENERAL HEALTH AND FITNESS

- 52% of women surveyed did not expect their health or fitness to be affected by the birth of a baby
- 41% reported an impact on coping; 21% severe to extreme
- 34% experienced intrapersonal conflict; 24% severe to extreme
- 21% engaged in interpersonal conflict; 10% severe to extreme

Because giving birth to a baby is considered to be such a 'natural' event in a woman's life few expect it to create on-going health problems or to impact dramatically on their level of fitness. The advent of modern medicine has obviously taken much of the risk to a woman's life out of the process of birth and this seems to have lulled us into a false sense of security regarding its impact on the health of the new mother. Tracey wrote to me:

> Labour—eight hours, James would have been born earlier but he got

stuck. Delivery—forceps (mid) delivery, pain excruciating. Results—coccyx was bent back, pain excruciating for months.

Diabetes may also persist. When a woman is pregnant the volume of blood running through her body increases as does, therefore, the amount of blood sugar. Thus the risk of becoming diabetic rises if the kidneys are unable to deal with the additional sugar levels. Normally, diabetes contracted during pregnancy disappears very soon after birth but in a small number of cases it requires normal life-long treatment for this condition.

Other side effects which may continue to affect a woman's health after giving birth are tears and episiotomies. Sandra revealed her bitterness in saying:

Nobody told me episiotomies remain painful for six months and make sexual intercourse agony!

and Nikki told of her horror when her midwife recounted how another client had said that sometimes, when she was standing in a cold wind, her scar still ached—seven years later.

There is also a general assumption that if a woman is fit prior to the birth and if she has been exercising as instructed by her antenatal trainer she will do well during labour and automatically return to fitness immediately after the birth. Neither of these assumptions is necessarily so, and particularly if she had been anaemic throughout her pregnancy—that is suffering from low levels of iron in her blood. Since iron is vital to the production of red blood cells which carry oxygen around her own body and to the foetus, its deficiency can make it difficult for her body to manufacture new cells after the blood loss of birth. Any woman affected by anaemia is, therefore, even more likely to feel tired or exhausted than she would have otherwise. To counteract the loss she will need to ensure her diet includes leafy green vegetables, pulses, nuts, brewer's yeast, liver and vitamin B12. An iron supplement may also be necessary which, when taken with vitamin C, absorbs into the blood more easily.

Another major reason some women do not recover well from the birth process is the exhaustion factor itself. When a person never gets enough sleep to recuperate from the initial physical shock of birth, the immune system grows weak and cannot fend off even the minor ailments. Anna's health was chronically affected:

> People used to ask me, 'Why are you always so sick?' It seemed that I was sick continually for years. Even my sister didn't understand until she had her kids.

Because exhaustion is so endemic in most new mothers' lives, they find little time or energy to exercise and their diets may be inadequate. They are unable to quickly return to their pre-baby level of fitness.

The effects of reduced general health and fitness are many, as these comments show:

Adelle: I lost weight after the kids—too much. Other people were very judgemental.

Nikki: HORMONES! What a roller-coaster. That was quite unexpected.

Judy: I developed asthma after the birth which is now controlled, but sinus and hay fever cause me continuing trouble.

Jackie: I developed insulin-dependent diabetes as a result of pregnancy and childbirth.

Beverley: Within four weeks of my son's birth I was diagnosed with pregnancy-induced arthritis. I also suffered acute PMT which I had never previously experienced as well as irrational, uncontrollable rages. As soon as I went back on the contraceptive pill the PMT and rages went away.

Bianca: I had a low breast milk supply, an unwelcome slothfulness, low self-esteem and PND which led to overeating and huge weight gain.

For a woman who is used to being healthy and whose body image used to be one of being a particular size and shape, large weight fluctuations and inferior health feed into a cycle of low self-worth, stress, anxiety and even depression. Janine's letter to me expressed her underlying grief and helplessness:

> My health, from being perfect, has diminished to zero after several episodes of thrush (12 months continuously); bad fissures of the anus

due to corrective surgery (removal of skin tags left by piles); back and hip problems (slipped pelvic bone from 24 weeks of pregnancy and still causing problems two-and-a-half years later); and many unrelated illnesses because of low immunity.

I'm still suffering and I've suffered with 'systemic depression' because of it. Life by November 1993 (two years after the birth of my first child) was almost non-existent.

Most older mothers, especially, agree with Nikki's realisation that:

Physical energy and repair took much longer than I ever imagined!

Yet again, one of the greatest hurdles for women is that they are expected to cope with their sudden ill-health in isolation and with little or no preparation for the possibility. And if they are unprepared, their partners appear to be even less so. Women report that their partners are often unable to appreciate the difficulties they are experiencing and as a result become judgemental, treating them as though they are malingering hypochondriacs. This does little for the self-esteem of a woman who is exhausted, in pain or feeling unwell and who is already suffering an identity crisis. Janine's letter concluded:

I believe that better preparation and more support are essential.
Especially for the partner who cannot really relate to this sort of conflict.

If being fit and healthy was an integral part of a woman's self-image prior to motherhood she may find it most difficult to come to terms with being unwell or unfit. Exhaustion, ill-health and the daily rounds of tending to a baby may make it impossible for her to return to any fitness regime no matter how much she craves physical activity. The less fit she feels, the less energy she can muster to get fit. The pervading feeling of unwellness can become a self-perpetuating, downward spiral.

SELF-PERCEPTION

In the earliest months of motherhood we tend to assume these changes in our bodies and our health are immutable and will last forever. Just as exhaustion seems to stretch from horizon to horizon so, too, these alterations appear to be permanent. However, the human body is a remarkable thing and given good food, enough rest and the right kinds of exercise it does tighten up again, although perhaps not overnight as we may have hoped. Pauline expressed some of this sentiment in her letter to me, saying:

> I enjoyed the breastfeeding and nurturing and regained my physical state to my satisfaction—but I felt a lot older and uglier as a result of the constant demands and lack of sleep and time to tend to myself.

A new mother may find it a shock to catch sight of herself in a mirror or a shop window and realise that the person who stares back at her is not the image of the person she has always imagined herself to be. Glenda grieved enormously over the loss of her lithe body:

> I feel so ugly. I cannot even bear to look at myself in a mirror and I want to die when I catch sight of myself in a shop window.

Coming to terms with the new body a woman wears can be truly difficult and a trigger for depression. Believing that her good looks and beautiful body are gone for all time she may feel she has become, forever, an ugly duckling. If much of her sense of self-worth was derived from knowing she was pleasing to look at, her self-esteem may crash. Nikki told me:

> I used to have a wardrobe full of beautiful clothes, all size 8. Only just recently I realised that I am never going to be a size 8 ever again. At first I was angry at not fitting into them but now it is fine. I am not a girl anymore, but a woman with a woman's body and I am proud of it.

Nikki found this change to her self-image easier to cope with than some women might because her husband rather revelled in her new curves and rounder shape. She felt she had discarded the body of a girl and, at the age of thirty-eight, finally donned the body of a woman. Glenda's experience, on the other hand, was quite different. Her husband was insulting, pointing out to her regularly that 'it was all over now' her body was no longer that of a teenage girl but one of a thirty-three-year-old who was over the hill. She found it nigh on impossible to continually recreate a positive image of herself in the face of his cruel, carping criticism.

Natalie's reaction was different again. She wrote:

> I grieved over not being able to fit into any of my old clothes, over the enormous varicose veins such a big baby produced. I found so very little time to exercise. My body image and the reality were very different!

Whatever the changes to your body, know they are normal. Know that many of the alterations are temporary, although they may take a year or more to work their way through all the various stages of change—especially if you are an older mum. Be prepared that some will remain, to a certain extent, forever and that this, too, is normal.

The process of becoming a mother is also a process of developing the body of a woman and letting go the body of a girl. The two identities cannot reside in the one person comfortably and the faster a mother can accept her woman's body the sooner she will discover a whole new level of personal acceptance, sexuality, elegance and sense of being attractive to others. There definitely are sexuality and elegance after baby. It just takes a little longer than most of us hope.

THE HEALTH OF THE BABY

There is an expectation that modern medicine will ensure that the health of the baby will always be perfect as well. Michelle, whose first child was born with cerebral palsy, wrote to me putting the problem so clearly that I reproduce most of her letter here:

> When your first child is born with a disability all your preconceived ideas of motherhood are in total disarray. You feel:
> 1. A failure
> 2. Immensely different and isolated
> 3. Angry and resentful
> 4. A huge loss of self-esteem and feel unable to cope with anything
> 5. Embarrassed
> 6. Frightened of the added responsibility
> 7. Guilty
> 8. Scared to have another baby
> 9. Unprepared and unqualified

10. Intimidated by medical/paramedical staff
11. Cheated
and of course you go through all the stages of the grief cycle.

Friends don't know how to cope and I avoided them. Family refused to acknowledge it and I had to confront them. It's a position of confusion—you have to take the lead when all you want is someone to lead you. It's lonely although you're never alone. The constant repetition of history and progress (or lack of it) is profoundly damaging to your psyche and you constantly wonder what it's like to be a 'normal' mother.

In the end you get there but you always feel apart from other mothers—even mothers of other disabled children as no two are alike. To keep sane—keep busy. I feel going back to work early, however, compounds your guilt feelings. It's not all negative though as I believe it strengthens the mother/child bond.

Aside from congenital health problems babies come into the world with all manner of milder but nonetheless distressing problems such as birthmarks which parents may wish were paler or less obviously positioned. Babies can also suffer from colic and reflux. They get thrush, become constipated, have allergies, do not sleep. No amount of medical expertise can alter the fact that some children simply do not settle into 'normal' feeding or sleeping patterns, sometimes for years.

Babies are also born with their own peculiar temperaments. Some are placid and docile but some are born with a temper which defies explanation. Some babies bring with them a sensitivity to physical, visual, auditory or emotional input which causes them to feel pain when they are overstimulated. Others demand constant stimulation. The New York Longitudinal Study showed that 10% of children are difficult to handle in the extreme; 15% are a 'major challenge'; the ease or difficulty of handling 35% depends on the parent–child dynamics—and only 40% are described as 'easy'.[24] Until it is born, no woman can know for sure what challenges her particular baby will present her with in terms of its physical, mental and emotional health.

Probably the worst part, initially, of having a baby who does not fit the 'perfect' mould is that the mother tends to blame herself. She searches every nook and cranny of her memories of her pregnancy and birth trying to find

---

24 Christopher Green, *Toddler Taming: A parent's guide to (surviving) the first four years*, Lane Cove, 1984, pp.11–12

where she went wrong. Unfortunately, she will often encounter other people who believe that she is at fault. They judge that she did not sleep enough, eat well enough, did not prepare for the birth well enough, was emotionally unstable, worked too long or too hard ... These judgements, whether spoken or not, are the last thing she needs at this difficult time in her life.

IDENTITY

- 63% of women surveyed did not expect their identity to alter in any major sense
- 63% reported an impact on coping; 33% severe to extreme
- 57% experienced intrapersonal conflict; 30% severe to extreme
- 55% engaged in interpersonal conflict; 32% severe to extreme

A baby, when it is born, is recognised as having attained new status in the world, no longer a foetus but a person. A mother, when she is born, also becomes a new being but without any recognition that her new identity is quite foreign to the woman she once was—indeed, without any recognition that her identity has changed at all. Suddenly it is as if she has always been a mother and the independent woman never existed. Cathy did not find this adjustment easy:

> When I became a mother, that's when my identity began to suffer, because then I wasn't anybody.

If a woman holds a responsible job before the transformation of motherhood she is used to making decisions and acting upon them with every confidence she will achieve her desired outcomes. Unfortunately, most women enter motherhood expecting to be able to continue as though nothing has changed. Sandra wrote to me from New Zealand:

> I had unrealistic expectations of what I could achieve in addition to being a new mum. They are right when they say it's a 24-hour job.

When the expectations are unrealistic and a woman begins to realise that she can no longer maintain the identity she once had she finds herself in limbo, unsure of who she is anymore. Adelle was indignant about her identity change:

> Moving into a mother capacity was a bit of an insult to me. The extra baggage, unpredictability, the work, the discipline. I used to think, 'This is really futile, this is a waste of my intelligence.' Initially it shattered my confidence.

One moment a woman is an independent, self-determining, relatively integrated personality. At the moment of giving birth to her first child she becomes a mother. No longer is she independent but is driven by the needs of a small human being. In the first three months of motherhood 31–40% of mothers are uncomfortable with someone being so completely dependent upon them.[25] A new mother may feel as though her life is controlled, not by herself, but by a mere baby. Her personality may begin to fragment to the extent she is unable to predict her own reactions—they surprise her as much as everyone else.

Where once she spent her days in the company of other adult workers making a valued contribution to the world and was paid an income in acknowledgement for so doing, she is now 'just' a mother amongst mothers. She is unpaid. She is alone for whole days at a time with no opportunity for adult company and no-one who is able to reflect, support or help her mould her new identity. There is a great truth in what Margaret said:

> Identity must come from inside yourself. We must pat ourselves on the back for raising beautiful children and find value inside ourselves.

But this does not necessarily occur overnight. It takes time, and work—and acknowledgement that it is even necessary.

If a new mother is stunned at her inability to complete even the simplest of tasks she may begin to doubt her own competence. It is as if, when she becomes a mother, all her skills and identity vanish.[26] Although an older woman generally has a more firmly established identity than a younger woman, she may feel as though she is giving up a great deal to be a mother. She does have the advantage, though, of knowing she is more than 'just' a mother. She knows what she has achieved in the past and of what she is capable. Sarah said:

---

25 Joan F. Kuchner & Jane Porcino, 'Delayed Motherhood' in Beverley Birns & Dale F. Hay, eds, *The Different Faces of Motherhood*, New York, 1988, p.270

26 Arlie Hochschild, *The Second Shift*, London, 1989, p.7

THE CHANGING SELF-IMAGE

> When you are older you know who you used to be. You have to retain your identity. I am a woman, I am a person, not just a mother. I am a person first, a mother second.

For many women it takes years to rediscover the woman, the person, masked by the name of mother.

SELF-ESTEEM

- 64% of women surveyed did not expect their self-esteem to decline after the birth of their first babies
- 71% reported an impact on coping; 45% severe to extreme
- 63% experienced intrapersonal conflict; 43% severe to extreme
- 52% engaged in interpersonal conflict; 35% severe to extreme

One of the first qualities to suffer when a person's identity is called into question is that of self-esteem. Add exhaustion to the equation and a new mother's sense of self-worth can be totally shattered. Nancy recalled:

> I took on all the responsibility. It was huge for me. I felt stressed, felt I couldn't cope and my self-esteem went way down.

In today's world mothers are judged more publicly than they once were and the expectations put on them seem to grow by the day. No longer are a clean home and well-mannered children considered the only hallmarks of a successful mother. She is now also judged by the physical, psychological, emotional, intellectual and creative capacities of her children, as though she were solely responsible for their human potential. Even as the family unit becomes ever more estranged from the input and support of a community it is watched ever more closely by teachers, neighbours, doctors and welfare workers, all of whom are more highly attuned to detecting inadequate parenting or child abuse than at any time in the past. Unfortunately they often make judgements (both positive and negative) without the benefit of understanding the immediate circumstances in which the family lives or the effects of its past history. As Beverley wrote:

> I was not coping. I found that I would lash out at my son and would

shake and hit him when he annoyed me. But when I mentioned this to doctors and said that I felt it was hormonal and could, therefore, be fixed, they all (male and female alike) basically ignored me. It then got to the stage where I was too scared to tell anybody in case I was charged with child abuse. During this time I felt terribly guilty and extremely depressed.

Too often, even when a woman knows she needs help, she is quite unable to convince those whose role it is to offer such help that her concerns and needs are real and valid. Add to this the fact that nearly every woman surveyed or interviewed agreed that the pace of life, and so the demands on a mother's time, is increasing dramatically and it is clear that there is considerable pressure on women to look as though they are coping at all times. Janelle voiced the puzzle of modern day motherhood when she said:

My mother had six children, I've only got two. She coped, why can't I? I feel pressured by this past history even though life is really speeding now. Expectations have gone up and I feel I am always trying to keep up with others.

Isolation contributes to the drop in self-esteem which so many new mothers feel. When they realise they have little or no support system around them and few, if any, mothering friends with whom to compare notes on the processes of motherhood, they find themselves floundering in a foreign land. Christine, living over one hundred kilometres from the nearest city, found herself so stranded.

Tim, who is now ten, gave me no trouble at all but I did not feel good about myself. There was no-one else in the area with a baby then. I felt weak when the children were hanging around me all the time and just being normal children.

However, comparing one's self to other mothers and their children can do just as much damage as living in isolation, as can reading all the advice columns and books on how to raise babies and children. Every child and every mother is different and cannot be judged against some arbitrary 'norm'. Martha, who lives in the suburbs, felt this pressure:

THE CHANGING SELF-IMAGE

Some mothers do recover from the birth quickly and their children do sleep through the night and these give an unreal picture of how it should be.

Unfortunately, few seasoned mothers discuss the issue of self-esteem and so it is left to each individual woman alone to discover her own pathway back to a healthy sense of self-worth. For many this takes years. The following is an excerpt from a letter written to me by Clare:

> For years I survived under a mantle of motherhood which I chose to wear myself, though unconsciously, I like to think. This mantle stifled me. I was previously assertive about my rights, passionate, involved, active in society.
>
> Once I became a mother I smothered myself—I hadn't previously thought much about women who stayed home with their children. I didn't consider myself one of them. I was different. I was proud and pleased to be a mother of a beautiful boy but no-one reflected this back to me and my confidence, self-esteem, etc. crashed.
>
> I feel so sad that I didn't honour my role then and that still I have so much trouble giving value to myself and other women as mothers in our infinite variety.

The difficulty is that it is hard to maintain a clear sense of self-esteem when the role of mother is so undervalued. Not only does a woman face a complete re-evaluation of her identity, not only is she shocked by the isolation and exhaustion, but she must learn to recreate herself daily in the face of a wall of proof that she is worth less as a mother than she once was as a member of the paid workforce. Without solid support from her partner, family and friends her self-esteem is in danger of slipping lower day by day. Cathy wrote to me:

> I started being Cathy again when my second child went to day care one day per week when he was two. [This was eight years after the birth of her first child.]

Another of the many driving factors behind this decline in feelings of self-worth is the decline in a woman's sense of herself as a sexual being, and this will be discussed later in this chapter.

CONVERSATION

- 65% of women surveyed said they did not expect to be challenged by the inability to complete a conversation after their babies were born, nor for the content to be baby/husband centred
- 78% reported an impact on coping; 39% severe to extreme
- 45% experienced intrapersonal conflict; 28% severe to extreme
- 41% engaged in interpersonal conflict; 26% severe to extreme

Completing a Conversation

It is difficult to imagine how a being so small and helpless as a baby or a crawling, toddling child could wreak such havoc on the art of conversation. However, when a baby cries the sound is designed to motivate the mother to meet his needs. If she is in mid-conversation at the time she may persist in trying to listen to another person or to finish saying what she intended to say. If she does, it is likely she will find her attention so divided she is neither able to hear what is said nor put her words together coherently. Whether she runs to pacify her baby or steadfastly remains in the conversation, the thread of shared meaning is broken. If the baby is quickly quietened that thread may be reconnected. All too often, unfortunately, the baby does not settle instantaneously and by the time the mother has returned to the conversation it has been lost or others have completed what needed to be said and moved on. The disturbed mother may never catch up.

Since women with children tend to gather together for support, the likelihood of interruption is magnified by the number of babies and children accompanying each of them. The problem positively mushrooms when the babies become crawlers and toddlers. Then they can mobilise themselves into the mother's body space, or into potentially dangerous situations, until even the most steadfast converser can do nothing else but break her train of thought.

For a woman, especially if she is extroverted, the loss of the ability to converse freely is like cutting out the essence of her ability to know and accept herself. With little sustained mirroring of who she is by others, she becomes less sure of her self-image, less certain that she knows her true value and less able to understand her own inner processes.

THE CHANGING SELF-IMAGE

The Focus of Conversations

When a group of new mothers gather, whether at a playgroup, a shopping centre or in each other's homes, the conversation immediately turns to babies, toddlers and husbands. It is a woman's way to talk through her problems and major life changes.[27] It is entirely natural that a new mother will need such talk in order to work out what the changes mean for her as a woman and to make sense of the changes in her relationship to her partner. Sandra wrote:

> Gossiping is what the patriarchs would call it, as if that kind of gossip is not pure gold in a new mother's life.

A new mother may find she needs to compare her baby's development and responses to those of other women's in order to understand his behavioural normalities and abnormalities and to discover more and perhaps better ways of raising her baby. Unfortunately, these conversations often descend into a contest over whose baby is the more difficult to raise—which baby has the worst sleeping, feeding, burping, pooing, rashing, separation anxiety problems. New mums can be very creative about the ability of their child to cause them stress. In these circles any woman who is fortunate enough to have an 'easy' baby is labelled 'lucky' and is often dismissed as having no valid contribution to this conversation.

A similar scenario surrounds discussions about the birth of the babies. Certainly such an indescribable experience needs to be discussed until it finds a comfortable place in the woman's memory. Sandra wrote, after the birth of her second baby:

> I now know it is important for me to debrief (after birth). It's not true what the obstetricians said in med school, 'New mothers forget the bad things about the labour by the next day.' What a load of codswallop! Every time you handle the baby you are reminded of the birth. If it was a bad birth and you haven't got through the grief you just go through the horrors time after time.

All too often, however, this need to debrief also descends into a competition to see who had the worst experience. Rarely do those who found the process of

---

27 John Gray, *What Your Mother Couldn't Tell You & Your Father Didn't Know*, Rydalmere, 1994, p.42

birth difficult try to understand what made the process enjoyable for others. This often excludes those women who did not find birth to be traumatic. Instead their experiences tend to be written off, again as 'lucky'. This happened to Mandy:

> I joined a playgroup soon after my daughter was born but I hated it. All the other mothers wanted to talk about was their traumatic births. I had a great birth and they did not want to know about it. I couldn't stand it so I left. I didn't try again for another year.

In many ways this dismissal of a woman's good birth or baby is a protective mechanism against the inherent sense of failure which afflicts women when their experience was less perfect than they had expected. It also serves to protect against the fear that they may have caused damage to their child.

Husbands and partners go through their own postnatal reactions and readjustments. For many the advent of their first child is every bit as shocking as it is to their women. They, however, tend to cope in the entirely different manner of the man's realm, and that is to become more active.[28] Many will tend to extend their working hours to earn extra money while others will be out with the boys or begin reconstructing the house. To women this is bewildering. Her pleas for help are rewarded, not with attention and support, but more activity.

Therefore another prime topic of conversation amongst new mothers is 'The Partner'. These discussions have a nasty tendency to 'awfulise' the partner's behaviour as women out-bid each other with tales of woeful manhood. Women matronise his (in)ability to look after the baby adequately, to be supportive of her needs or to achieve anything at all when left in charge of the child. For a woman whose partner is supportive, for single mothers and for those women who detest being drawn into man-bashing cycles it is depressing to find this such a significant topic of conversation.

SEX APPEAL

- 51% of women surveyed did not expect to experience a decline in their sense of being sexually appealing
- 61% reported an impact on coping; 31% severe to extreme

28 J. Gray, *op.cit.*, pp.67–70

THE CHANGING SELF-IMAGE

- 43% experienced intrapersonal conflict; 33% severe to extreme
- 44% engaged in interpersonal conflict; 31% severe to extreme

Nowhere is self-esteem impacted more greatly than in the bedroom. Yet, underlying the issues of sexuality are the 'strong cultural forces which desexualise women as mother'.[29] Once a woman becomes a mother, whether she has been married for years or not at all, she is tacitly recognised as being somebody else's property—her baby's—and she is divested of her sexuality. If her sense of herself as a sexual woman pre-motherhood was centrally important to her positive self-image, the new mother may find this loss in her life difficult to bear. Sally wrote:

> All my life I have been used to men looking at me—and I enjoyed it! But after my baby was born I wore jeans and runners and nobody even noticed me anymore. I find that sad.

A woman with a baby on her hip becomes remarkably invisible and there is nothing guaranteed to kill an admiring glance more than the sight of an attached baby. It is as if a woman goes from being part of the greater world to the exclusive property of Baby—a sacrosanct relationship not to be molested even in thought. Neither do people anticipate speaking to a person with a brain in her head when they speak to a mother. It is difficult to feel sexy when one is being treated as though she were out of her depth shopping in a hardware store.

It is also difficult to maintain a self-image of sexiness and elegance when one is ignored by, or seldom comes into contact with the male half of the population. For just as the supermarkets are frequented by an almost homogeneous group of mothering women, so too are the streets and the parks of the suburbs between the hours of 9 a.m. and 4 p.m. The only place one is likely to encounter a male of the species is in the butcher shop or the greengrocer's. When these are a woman's major contact with males, her scope for feedback as a woman who is still attractive to the opposite sex is somewhat limited.

In the home the new mother may find that her partner is no longer as interested in her as he used to be. He too may be finding it difficult to come to terms with the changes to her body. He may find her flabby tummy or varicose veins or slack vagina less than appealing and he may not be able to relate to her

---

29 Adrienne Rich, *Of Woman Born*, New York, 1976, p.183

the way he used to and she may find she is even embarrassed to be seen naked by her own husband, as was Faye:

> To be spontaneous you need a good body. I used to walk through the house in my undies but not anymore. I do not feel confident enough.

Furthermore, a woman's partner generally does not understand her bone tiredness and may interpret her diminished interest in lovemaking as a specific rejection of him. If he fears that the onset of motherhood has robbed him forever of his sexual partner he may let her know, in no uncertain terms, that the physical, mental and emotional changes she has undergone are less than acceptable to him. This, of course, only serves to diminish her ability to believe in herself as a woman of sexual (and sensual) worth. As one man said to me:

> Face it. Once a woman has had a baby, it's all over. After that everything drops and flops and there's no fun in it anymore.

Whatever a woman may think of such a remark, it verbalises the unspoken reality that many men do find the post-birth woman's body to be less attractive than that of a twenty-year-old non-mother.

It has to be said, however, that some women have reported that their partners have found their more rounded shape and their fuller breasts to be a major turn-on. For these women their feelings of being sexually appealing have been enhanced by bearing a child, although this does not necessarily go hand in hand with wanting to participate in lovemaking.

STATUS

- 59% of women surveyed said their drop in social status as a mother was totally unexpected
- 51% reported an impact on coping; 22% severe to extreme
- 36% experienced intrapersonal conflict; 21% severe to extreme
- 34% engaged in interpersonal conflict; 26% severe to extreme

Status in this era is closely linked to occupation and earning power. Since mothering does not pay a wage (unless one is mothering another woman's children), the moment a woman ceases to do paid work her status drops significantly.[30] Sarah's is such a common cry:

> When you are a mother they assume you are doing nothing.

Being a mother is seen to be an occupation that is second rate and one to be fitted in the cracks between economics, politics, industry and commerce, relationships and social events. Whilst there is a pervasive belief that a woman should be responsible for her child's welfare, there is little latitude or sympathy if she allows that child to impinge on these more important areas of endeavour.[31] At best, the societal attitude towards motherhood in general, and mothers specifically, is ambivalent. The lack of regard in which women who are mothers are held is the cause of widespread outrage amongst many of this country's mothering population. Margaret expressed hers, saying:

> When you say you are a mother that is the end of the conversation—they do not want to inquire further—and that goes for anyone and everyone. It is a status thing, as though you are doing nothing.

Motherhood has been steadily devalued across this century and women themselves have grown to feel that the role is of lesser value than it once was. With this decline in value there has been a commensurate drop in the status and power of women who are mothers. Margaret continued:

> A lot of the relationship with self has to do with relationship with others. If that is all negative it is hard to value yourself.

Once women were encouraged and supported in bearing the children who were to be the future workers in the fields and their parents' guarantee of security in their old age. Today technology has replaced the need for physical labourers so children are no longer an indication of a couple's wealth. Social security, pension plans and superannuation have replaced older people's dependency on their children perhaps, in part, contributing to the breakdown in family

---

30 Diane Richardson, *Women, Motherhood & Childrearing*, London, 1993, pp.24–25

31 Anne Woollett & Ann Phoenix, 'Psychological Views of Mothering' in eds Ann Phoenix, Anne Woollett & Eva Lloyd, *Motherhood*, London, 1991, p.37

continuity. Children used to be a blessing. Today they are an expense for which a couple must plan and save alongside (or after) the car and the house.

Because her family is smaller and she is likely to give birth to her few children over a limited time frame, motherhood appears to be merely a short-term diversion instead of the life-long concern and commitment it once was.[32] Where once a woman was honoured for bringing new life into being now she is often seen to be adding to the population bomb and the subsequent economic and environmental problems.

JUDGEMENTALISM

Although this item was not included in the survey given to women it came up in every discussion group and clearly caused a great deal of anguish for the majority of mothers. Unfortunately, it was felt by most that women are far more judgemental of other women than are men of women. It is clear that the issue of mothering is so fundamental to a woman's sense of self that, whether she has children or not, many feel the need to justify their own choices by denigrating the different choices of others.

Division by Child Bearing Status

Childless women judge those with children. There was not a mother I interviewed who did not admit that she 'knew' her children would be better behaved than everybody else's—before she had them. All said they used to feel it was the mother's fault if her children were clingy, interrupted conversations, screamed, cried, threw tantrums, did not sleep, got sick, did not eat, had attention or hyperactivity or developmental or behavioural problems. As Melanie said (sarcastically):

> If there is a problem it is never the baby's problem, always the mother's.

All thought, before having their own children, that if a woman was stressed by motherhood it was her inability to manage, her disorganisation, her problem. After having their own, of course, they felt differently but that does not help the new mother who is struggling and is judged to be incompetent by her non-mothering peers.

---

32 A. Hochschild, *op.cit.*, p.3

Division by Birth Experience

There is a tendency to judge harshly a woman who has a long, difficult or exceptionally painful labour as if she has done something to cause her problems. This is especially noticeable amongst women who have experienced relatively easy labours. Rather than looking at a woman's body structure or her genetic history for explanations she is blamed for doing the most fundamental process of womanhood incorrectly. In the world of modern medicine it is easy to forget that childbirth once was considered a dangerous undertaking.

Division by Style of Child

Even women who do have children will be judgemental towards other women whose children are relatively less 'easy' to manage. Leslie told me she used to judge her friends for feeding their babies to sleep:

> I used to think they were wrong and were the ones who caused the sleeping problems. But now, that's the only way I can get Catherine to sleep.

Similarly, Susan, whose two children were sweet, quiet, well-behaved girls and whose third was a boisterous boy, wrote:

> I thought it was all the mothers of boys making them so difficult. Now I know better. James climbs on everything, pulls everything apart and loves noisy trucks. Nothing is safe when he is around—and the noise! Boys *are* different.

In an age when children's behavioural problems have been linked with allergies and an intolerance to the chemical overload of the late twentieth century, it makes no sense to judge a mother before investigating other possible causes. If her child is indeed more difficult than the average child what she needs is support—not judgements.

Division by Choice of Career

Nowhere is this more obvious than in the division between mothers who return to the paid workforce and those who choose the career of mothering and home care. It is generally felt by those who are in paid work that those who stay home are 'doing nothing'. One woman, mother of two children, who works full-time in an academic career asked me:

What do they do all day while they are home doing nothing?

This fundamental question is echoed a thousand times over by women who are mothers who work in paid jobs. Apparently they either do not realise or have forgotten all the things they no longer have time to do for themselves, their families and their communities. Perhaps, sadly, they have had to accept that it is 'normal' to have their weekends and evenings eaten up by household chores rather than being able to spend this time in leisure and pleasure with their children, partners, friends and community. Since two full-time jobs cannot be accomplished in the time allocated for one it is only a matter of logic to deduce that something has to be given up. It is this attitude that a full-time mother is idle which upsets, hurts and galls career mothers so very much. Pauline sums up their opinion:

> Far from being 'Just a Mother' I really thought I was doing great guns. As far as a job goes I felt I was far more valuable doing that than what I had done before.

Having to face people who are in the paid workforce can be daunting for a full-time mother. Cathy felt her intelligence was being questioned:

> I go to these wretched cocktail parties with my husband where he works and their first question is, 'What do you do?' and you say, 'I'm raising my children.' It doesn't go over well at all. They just walk away from you. They feel sorry for you. Women are absolutely worse than men. They go away because they've got all their little guilt complexes about where their kids are or who's got their kids or they haven't had them yet. They've got their own set of problems.
>
> You are not supposed to enjoy being a mother. You have to almost apologise for enjoying yourself. It is as though it is illegal to enjoy your children.

On the other hand, unpaid mothers tend to judge working mothers as selfish or neglectful of their children's needs. They assume that all children of paid working mothers are missing much of what they are entitled to in terms of being loved and nurtured. This can be crushing for the mother who has no

THE CHANGING SELF-IMAGE

choice but to work. As much as salaried, working women apparently do not want to hear about a career mother's experience, the career mothers equally do not seem to want to know about *their* jobs or achievements. This may be because the full-time mother already feels herself to be of lesser value and therefore will not, or cannot, hear of another woman's successes for fear of feeling and being seen to be even less adequate.

Women who make money are, on the whole, more independent than those who do not. They 'highlight the powerlessness of the dependent woman'[33] who, in turn, may feel antipathy towards them. So, instead of offering the paid working woman support and congratulations for her ability to juggle two jobs, there is a pervading tendency to believe that she is inadequate as a woman and is running away from her family responsibilities and involvement. Kate gave voice to this all too common belief:

> Why do women want to go back to work? Someone has to do the nurturing. I find it a fault in womanhood that everyone wants to get away from motherhood so much, because it is so natural for us to do it. I feel there is a lack of responsibility in trying to get away from it.

There are, of course, pluses and minuses in every choice whether that is to return to full-time paid work or to mother full-time, and every point in between. Some women find they cannot bear being at home with their children and say that they are far better mothers for having returned to paid work. Others have no desire to go back at all and still others have no alternative but to try to juggle motherhood and paid work because the family cannot survive without their incomes. Below are three contrasting opinions expressed in letters or during a discussion forum on the effects of motherhood on the women concerned. Margaret wrote:

> I enjoy blissful days with my absolutely 'perfect' new baby, and her father supports me as a person/mother/lover at all times. I am free to follow whatever hobbies/courses, etc. I wish—plus ... my days are spent with the world's most engaging child. I think everyone else ought to envy ME!!!!

---

[33] Jenny Phillips, *Mothers Matter Too!*, Melbourne, 1985, p.117

On the other hand, Natalie said in her letter:

> It was this business decision which saved my sanity, replenished my feminism and made me 'strong' against the odds of patriarchy. It was through this work in the first year of motherhood that I was able to connect my feelings, my ambitions and my fervent feminist consciousness. I was able to affirm to myself that, for me, it is a necessity to have independent work as well as motherliness.

Margaret said that she knew she could not be a mother and a paid worker. She felt that when she tried to do both she was a 'pretty rotten mother'. Yet for Natalie, work restored her sense of autonomy and of being a worthwhile person, whilst also empowering her as a mother.

Unfortunately the choice to work or mother full-time is not always so clear cut. Many women are trapped in jobs they do not enjoy, which they desperately wish they could leave, but simply cannot for financial reasons. Marge was passionate about her feelings towards work:

> I've waited a long time to be a mother and I want to be at home. But financially it's just not going to happen. My husband asks me how work is going and I go, 'I just hate it!' My priorities are so different. If I could be at home full-time, I'd do it tomorrow.

Marge works for a department of the public service where she is entitled to 12 months maternity leave and to work on a part-time basis for a further two years. Thereafter she must choose to either leave or work full-time. Her second child will be born almost three years after the first and she is already planning for a third to be born three years later.

Division by Age

Older mothers judge younger mothers. Mothers of the previous generation raised their children expecting they would grow into a world which would be ever more prosperous, more free. Instead the world has grown faster paced, expectations have boomed and, on every front imaginable, the world is looking more unstable and threatening. Children, via the medium of television, know and understand aspects of life at the ages of eight and nine that yesterday's teenagers did not know existed and, in fact, did not exist, for example AIDS.

By necessity children must be raised differently today than they were a generation ago. Yet, as Adelle said, the rift exists:

> There is a huge gap between the older generation and now. My own mother admits that it is much more stressful to be a mother today. There are more demands placed on women. Their lives were kept simple.

Recently my own mother realised how judgemental her generation was being of mine and wrote:

> My generation is so closed-minded. I suddenly realised how critical they are of the younger generation. I am going to spend the rest of my life trying to be a less critical person.

This is a hard won realisation on her part and comes after years of criticism, both direct and implied, of how I and my friends have been raising our children.

Division by Selective Memory

Because the early years of mothering are so stressful for so many women and because they often pass in a blur of exhaustion there appears to be a tendency to forget how difficult it is to make the adjustment to motherhood. It is for this reason that the majority of the women I interviewed had children who were still pre-teens. Yet it became clear that even once the children go to school women tend to forget how little time they used to have to themselves, how little was their ability to get things done and how very much they longed for a break and support. Adelle experienced this dynamic:

> It is a deceitful trick of memory. When we see our children at older ages we take the credit for their being successful—because they survived— and therefore assume that we must have been good mothers. But the truth is that they would have grown up anyway.

I could not more strongly urge women, whether mothers or not, to be more supportive and less judgemental of each other. We each must relate to motherhood in our own way. Sarah recalled:

> The best advice I had was from a nurse who said, 'No matter what anyone else says, follow your own instincts, you are the mother, you know best.'

No-one has the correct method and no-one can know what is right for another woman. What we can know is that if we do not support each other, no-one else will.

FAILURE

The mixed messages and inequities, the lowly status of mothers, the expectations and the lack of discussion about the reality of motherhood converge to convince many a new mother that she is a failure at her most fundamental level of being. The number of ways a mother can experience herself as a failure are legion.

Failure to Cope
When exhaustion deals continual body blows to a woman's self-esteem, when expectations are unrealistic and when few women talk honestly about their experiences of motherhood it is easy to believe that one is the only woman on earth who discovers that being a mother tests her to her limits—and beyond. It is easy to believe that she alone is failing to cope with the role which is still seen to be the most defining one of womanhood.

Failure to Meet Everyone's Needs
Some women have such high expectations of themselves as mothers they believe they ought to be able to meet their babies' every single need so that they never cry, fret, grizzle, whinge, whine, complain, say 'no', throw tantrums. Such women assume that anything less than perfect behaviour exhibited by their children automatically brands them as failures in the profession of motherhood, no matter how much they love them. Marilyn was one such mother.

> I used to say that I should have him adopted out because 'I'm no good as a mother.'

This comment brought howls of protest from Marilyn's friends who know that she is a most committed and caring mother. It is her expectations that are too high rather than her mothering skills being too low. Pauline wrote:

> My mental health ... was certainly dealt a huge blow. I never felt certain about my approach to problems I encountered in mothering. I doubted all my decisions when I finally made them. As I became more experienced I realised that all babies and mothers are so different and one just needs the confidence to make it up as one goes along. Looking back, a lot of the worry and concern was unwarranted. I am possibly in better shape now mentally and spiritually although it was touch and go for a while.

Pauline was fortunate to have a husband who believed in her. Other women are not so lucky and, try though they might, never seem to be able to fulfil the needs of their partners. If she is subjected to constant overt or implied criticism a new mother's sense of failure skyrockets.

Failure to Relate

One area of unstated expectation is that all mothers will automatically feel, and be, close to all their children. It is taboo to suggest that a mother may not like one of her children or that she may find her relationship with one to be irresolvably traumatic. Carol, aged sixty-five, wrote to me saying:

> I'd felt I was prepared for motherhood as I had been a successful children's nanny and governess and had a three-month-old baby to look after when 17–18 years. It gave me the confidence, as did being a Tawny Owl in the Brownie movement. But I was not prepared for the traumas of my first child.
>
> It changed my life as I searched for answers with all my might ... I have done a lot of work on myself to try to understand this child who is now forty years old. I am no closer to her now than I was then. But I keep trying. The failure is a source of bitter disappointment to me. I feel I have failed as a mother with this child.

In her letter Carol said that this daughter had had the umbilical cord wrapped around her neck three times in the last month of pregnancy and it was originally thought she might have been born mentally affected. She was not.

Yet her mother reports that she was a difficult baby right from the beginning of her life and that their relationship has always been one of distance.

The work of Arthur Janov[34] suggests that such an experience *in utero* can cause a person to mistrust and feel hostile towards her mother from the moment she is born. However, it is almost always the mother who is blamed for this failure to relate. Even if she does not take Carol's path of self-exploration in order to understand but, in self-defence, chooses to blame and reject the child, it is the mother who feels guilty. When the social taboos are so strongly against a woman admitting to an inability to like and/or relate to a child she has no alternative but to hold the pain of her presumed failure inside—sometimes for a lifetime.

Is it reasonable to assume that just because she gives birth to a baby a woman will be able to understand, like and relate to the personality which develops before her eyes? As Karen said to me:

My older daughter is my gift, my younger daughter is my karma.

As is so often the case this mother found that the character and personality of her first born fitted her own in almost every way whilst those of her second born were quite foreign to her, and she found this difficult to come to terms with. These differences do not necessarily have to mean that a relationship cannot develop—but it might happen that way. It does not mean that a mother may love her 'different' child any less than the ones whose personalities suit her style better—but it might.

Failure to Achieve

Women who are at home with small children or who are working in less than exciting jobs often compare themselves to those who are publicly achieving in politics, academia and business. Knowing they cannot do as these other women do they feel as though they are failing at life and must, at some fundamental level, be inadequate.

The pressure to succeed at those things valued by the doing paradigm makes successes in mothering seem insignificant. Even the desire to value them is somehow seen to be immature and certainly politically incorrect. Anyone aspiring to be 'just' a mother, therefore, aspires to failure in the 'real' world.

34 Arthur Janov, *The New Primal Scream*, London, 1993, pp.151–155

There seems to be a fear amongst some feminists, who have fought on the front line for a generation, that if we honour motherhood and accept it as a valid profession in its own right we will remove the choices which have opened up for women in the late twentieth century and create a trap for our young women from which they may never escape. Yet, could that trap be dug any deeper than the one we build for them with our walls of silence and our disavowment of the place and value of mothering our children fully and well and of the difficulties of so doing? How much further from the truth can we go than our modern myth that the choice to mother is a choice to underachieve?

SOCIETY

Again, this was not an issue covered by the survey but is one which raised its head at every discussion group, one which inevitably comes up in most classes I teach and often when I am simply in the street talking to women who are mothers. At issue is the marginalisation of the profession of motherhood. Many women feel this to be the fault of both the patriarchal nature of our society and the feminist movement. Margaret railed against the latter:

> The feminist movement has undermined women as mothers. You are supposed to have the kid, park it in day care and get back to work. Get your identity, your money, your self-esteem from paid work and power through the glass ceiling.
>
> They are not acknowledging that women do want to have children and not acknowledging the rights of the under-sixes. Why should mothers be negated and their children raised by strangers?

Although not a politically correct sentiment it is echoed throughout the mothering sorority. Women, themselves, have become accomplices in valuing only those pursuits which are considered worthwhile in a doing paradigm—and in devaluing the occupations which would be considered of paramount importance if our social structures were built upon a relating paradigm. There is real indignation amongst mothers in all walks of life about the way they, and their young children, are treated. Eileen says it all:

> Where is the honour and respect we need ... where do we recognise the cornerstones of society, the world? Where is the celebration of

children—not to mention women who want their children to be involved in their life pre-school and who aren't really into child care centres (without devaluing their use)?

Women, and men, who have not been privy to the phases of babyhood need to be taught that nothing lasts forever, that babies do not dominate our time endlessly, that there is a limited and finite time in which to enjoy our children and in which to discover the value of being a mother or a father. Annette wrote:

> With the breakdown of family support systems it is new mothers who feel the brunt of responsibility and the overwhelming emotions of motherhood with little or no sight of the balance to come, not to mention the joys, pains and gifts each child brings to us.
> Far too little emphasis is granted to mothers in this age and society. The 'art of mothering' is being lost in the clamour for more! I have learnt that formal studies, entertainment, careers, etc. offer a fraction of the lessons learnt in motherhood. What a pity we are unaware of and insensitive to this and/or are scared of losing a little to learn and share so much in those early days.

The tragedy is that 'in the clamour for more' many women are never able to discover the value and the joy of being a mother. It is all the more tragic for women who face the choice of returning to work or living in poverty. Ironically it is these women who so desperately need 'more' who find themselves with the most limited choices. As Megan, a single mother of a nine-year-old and a one-year-old, cried:

> It is too hard. I just want my life to be better than this.

For her, and others like her, the support systems we offer are inadequate. She is blamed for having two children out of wedlock—but the two men who ran away from a responsibility this mother thought they were ready to honour are not similarly condemned. It is she who pays the price in unhappiness and depression and it is her children who pay the highest price in guilt and referred unhappiness. Ultimately, the nation is likely to pay dearly as the children leave home and school feeling as though they themselves are unvalued; as, in reality, they are.

THE CHANGING SELF-IMAGE

After the birth of their babies many women feel they have accomplished the greatest creation they are ever likely to achieve in their lifetimes. They are proud beyond description of their beautiful babies and they want to hold them up for all the world to see and to honour. Women find a well of giving inside them they never suspected existed and a powerful desire to meet their babies' basic needs whenever they arise. Elaine continued:

> I used to feed my baby anywhere. I felt like an earth mother when I was feeding my baby but I felt defensive nevertheless because you see so few women doing it.

The messages coming through to women are mixed and confusing. On the one hand we expect our women to bear the babies and to raise the future generation on whose sense of responsibility and compassion we will have to rely in our old age. On the other, we treat mothers as if motherhood happens in isolation.

We design our shops in such a way that queues at the checkout ensure youngsters are held interminably in holding pens constructed solely of every sweet temptation imaginable and then frown upon the poor mother who, in saying 'no' to another chocolate bar, now has a pleading, crying, tantrum-throwing child on her hands. We blame her, not the store layout. And if she succumbs and buys the sweets, unable to withstand another round of discipline, we cluck our tongues and judge her to be weak and walk away knowing that she is spoiling another child.

We expect our mothers to raise children who are kind, compassionate, co-operative and who are able to resolve conflict in the most constructive manner. Yet we screen endlessly violent children's TV programs which epitomise the philosophy of 'if you do not like what the other person is doing, flatten him'. But we will blame her for not having taught her child proper ethics and for having been lazy or soft in her discipline.

We expect our women to care for the children but we also expect them to get back to work as soon as possible and treat them as indolent if they do not. Denise wrote:

> The other thing which still continues is society's attitude to 'at home mothers'. We are treated so badly and made to feel as if we are worthless just because we are not paid in dollars. The almighty dollar—it always causes trouble! If I was working as a paid nanny or housekeeper for

someone else people would ask me how was my day at work and how do I manage. But as an at-home mother people say, 'Oh, you don't work, do you?' The assumption that anything we do is only valuable if it is paid in dollars is a sad reflection of our community.

There is little entertainment that is geared towards mothers with small children. Women themselves organise playgroups and there are parks—but where do women go for adult entertainment when they have a baby? Cinemas and theatres do not provide space where a woman can take a crying baby and still participate in the entertainment without disturbing the entire audience. She must leave and miss the performance. Few stores provide toys and a play area where a child might be happily (and quietly) occupied while its mother shops. Is it any wonder that few women shop for themselves when their children are young? Natalie wrote strongly of her feelings post-motherhood.

> I was acutely aware of how unjust and unsupportive society was towards mothers and babies. Getting on and off trains, up and down stairs, in and out of buildings was a nightmare with a pram. There were days when I felt that society was telling me, 'stay home!' Wives and mothers were non-people. I felt society no longer valued me because I wasn't a professional or even 'interesting'. In having a baby I fell in love with a baby, with motherhood, with my partner and in some small measure with myself and my own strengths. The long haul of raising a child did not dampen my raised consciousness of the enraging inequities of a patriarchal society.

The whole milieu in which we raise our children must change so that the profession of motherhood is honoured as a foundation stone on which we build our ability to live together harmoniously. It is, after all, the foundation on which our children build their sense of worth, understand their place in the world and develop their potential.

It is admirable that we have begun to install lifts at the railway stations and access ramps in all new buildings. These innovations, however, were not created to help mothers and their children who make up 34% of the population. Their construction has been in response to a realisation that lack of access discriminates against the disabled and elderly. The fact that mothers have benefited from this growth in the collective enlightenment is but an accidental bonus.

THE CHANGING SELF-IMAGE

Natalie's letter to me continued:

Motherhood has been such a defining and clarifying process for me. In becoming a mother I have asked myself how I can be a mother and a feminist as well as a lover of my partner; a daughter; a daughter-in-law; and a sister to my siblings ... The interpersonal conflict has been enormous but not nearly as enormous as the conflict I felt when, after being pregnant, being visibly about to become a mother, society expected me to stay at home, invisible, once I was a mother.

Mothers' needs, *per se*, are met only if they are able to be conveniently piggy-backed onto changes which meet the needs of more vocal, more powerful, more politically visible sectors of the community. The degree of priority we allocate to meeting the needs of our mothers is a direct indicator of where, on the priority ladder, we value our children.

HELP FOR HANGING IN THERE

Accept That Physical Changes Will Happen

The younger you are when you have your first baby (within reason) the more likely your body is to bounce back into shape. The older you are the more likely it is your body will either not return to your 'old' self or will take longer to do so.

Obviously, the more fit a woman is prior to childbirth, the better are the odds she will pull through with little damage done to her body. So get fit; eat well, walk, swim, jog, go to the gym regularly before becoming pregnant. Keep up the exercise routine during pregnancy as much as possible—without jeopardising the baby, of course. Understand, however, that fitness does not necessarily guarantee an easy pregnancy or birth; nor does it mean that your body will not alter.

In our youth culture of the present time it is difficult to lose the body of a girl so suddenly and to have to adjust to that of a 'matron'. Be proud of your age and the new stage of life you have entered. Alter your wardrobe to suit your new body image.

Look After Your Health and Fitness First

The more exhausted you are the more difficult everything else becomes. Sleep when your baby sleeps. You are absolutely no good to anyone, much less your baby, if you get sick. Do not give so much of yourself that you begin to resent him or your partner. Your low moods, your tendency to become angry or tearful will only impact negatively on all of you.

As soon as possible, establish a routine for getting fit again. A daily, half hour walk with your baby in a stroller will help both your body and your psyche. Eat healthy foods. Don't forget to exercise your pelvic floor muscles to tone up the bladder, the vagina and the tummy.

If your health is impaired and you are unable to get back on your feet, do not hesitate to get medical help or to book yourself into an institution, such as Tresillian Family Care Centre, which will care for your baby while you recover. It is not a measure of failure to ask for this level of support if exhaustion and/or ill-health are dragging you down.

Get help with your baby early. If you have problems in feeding your baby, Nursing Mothers Association of Australia and their breastfeeding counsellors can provide invaluable help and support. Many women have also extolled the virtues of homoeopathy in curing their babies of a wide variety of ills from colic to constipation, sleeplessness to viruses. A difficult temperament, on the other hand, is something each parent must learn to accept and deal with over time, without blaming themselves.

Equally, the more serious abnormalities are not the parent's fault. They just are. To beat up on yourself for something you could not have prevented is only to waste energy which you might otherwise give to your baby. If you continue to blame yourself, your child will grow to feel guilty for having been less than perfect and for causing you such anguish. Acceptance is the first step, although never an easy one. Getting proper medical advice and treatment is the second. Third, once again, is to get help and support. Having a disabled child more than doubles the difficulty of becoming a mother—do not try to cope alone. If you do try to cope in isolation your health and ability to mother as well as you want to will suffer.

Your New Identity Will, Ultimately, Be Bigger

Many women admitted that, in their earliest days of mothering, they felt themselves to be 'better' than 'just' a mother and all the other 'just' mothers they'd met. Their identities were still rooted in an image of their pre-mother selves. They kept trying to re-enter their old identities only to find they no longer fitted or belonged. Even as each one resisted, she found her feelings for her baby grew, drawing her steadily deeper into the role of mother without even realising it was happening.

THE CHANGING SELF-IMAGE

In order to speed up the process of accepting your mother identity, begin to talk to other mothers honestly about your feelings and listen to their honest appraisals of theirs. Here you will discover the enormous well of strength and compassion we women harbour inside us; our ability to give of ourselves even as we feel ourselves drained of the last drop of giving; our ability to endure physically, mentally, emotionally—and still continue to love. You will soon discover you are not alone in this strange dimension, after all.

It is interesting that, when you begin to talk to others from the most real part of yourself, others begin to talk from the most real part of themselves. Then comes the sharing. Then the caring. Then the belonging. It takes time to get to know a new friend. Likewise, it takes time to get to know the new you. Be patient. Be kind to and tolerant with yourself. Give yourself time and you will find your identity grows bigger and stronger every day.

Conversation Does Improve

Interruptions to conversation are excellent training for lateral thinking, although it does not feel like it at the time. Get used to them because they will be with you for many years to come.

When you first realise that the focus of all conversations is on your baby and your partner, do not be dismayed. Women need to talk out these matters in order to adjust to their new life circumstances and you are probably no different. Just because the central topics of your conversations have changed from business to nappies, from spiritual enlightenment to teething does not mean you have become an intellectual moron. It simply means you have entered a new profession and need to discover the ground rules. Usually it is only during the first year or two of motherhood that this talk may be a bit obsessive.

Your Sex Appeal Will Return

Like everything else about motherhood, a diminished sense of being sexually attractive need only be a temporary phenomenon. Once sleep and a balance return to your life you will begin to look better and feel better about yourself. It helps, of course, to live with a partner who finds you attractive and who lets you know it.

If he does not or if he ignores you or actively puts you down, let this be an opportunity to grow strong inside yourself. Rather than allowing him to undermine or degrade you, learn to dress and groom to please yourself. Walk tall, throw your shoulders back and be proud to be you. Others will notice even if he does not. Let their compliments sustain you. Stop seeking his approval. Know that this is his problem, not yours.

In time you will learn that a woman's sense of sexuality matures whether she has children or not. With age she gradually gives up needing to be the teenage centre of attention and becomes a woman of discerning taste who appreciates compliments of quality rather than quantity. Having children just speeds up the process.

Don't Judge and Don't Allow Others to Judge You
It is unbelievable how judgemental we women can be of each other. Many women said they had thought, prior to motherhood, that women would stick together and support each other. However, there is a universal tendency amongst all peoples to distance themselves from the group to which they rightly belong if they perceive that group to be less powerful than another. Thus, when mothers criticise other mothers they imply they are better than those who belong to this low status group. In creating this illusion of distance they hope to be accepted in the dominant—and powerful—doing paradigm.

Until women recognise that the paradigm of nurturing, creating homes, building relationships is of equal importance to the paradigm of building an achievement oriented empire, they will always judge each other unkindly. In so doing we divide ourselves from our collective power. We rob ourselves of the opportunity to return balance to a society which has become severely lopsided. We cheat ourselves of our rightful place as equal directors of our own and our children's lives and our collective future.

Do not judge another woman until you have taken the time and the trouble to step into her shoes for a moment and to understand why she behaves in a manner you consider to be 'less than'. Do not accept the judgements other women impose upon you. Know that the more they judge you, the weaker they are feeling inside themselves. A secure person does not have any need to build their self-esteem upon the ruins of another's.

Above all, do not judge yourself.

The Only Failure is Not Learning From Mistakes
Mistakes are different from failure. Parenting is the only job which changes its criteria for success almost daily during the first few years of a child's life. Babies' and toddlers' needs and wants, fears and concerns change and multiply as they

teethe, grow and learn to relate to the world. What worked one day will not necessarily work the next. A baby is a very different being from a toddler, a preschooler is different from a child in junior school. And, as any parent will tell you, teenagers are in a class all of their own.

There is no manual to tell you how to do each age and stage the right way. There is no check list to be ticked off at the end of the day (or year) which will comfortingly tell you that you have succeeded as a parent. There is no chance that any parent is, or can be, perfect. If you were, your kids would probably hate you for it anyway.

But you can be a good parent and still make mistakes. When you travel uncharted waters every day you must occasionally run aground—sometimes on sand and sometimes upon the jagged reefs. It does you no good to beat up on yourself for failing to navigate the unknown as though you should know. Instead, ask yourself given what you knew, did you act in the best way you were able at the time? Had you known how to do it better, would you have done so? Many of us struggle eternally to do better but few of us deliberately set out to be the worst parents we can be.

When the ship hits a reef and looks as though it will sink, you have two alternatives. You can waste precious time beating up on yourself and/or blaming others for your mistake. This will prevent you, and others, from repairing the damage. Then you will all go down with the ship. Or you can learn from your mistake, apologise if you have hurt anyone in the process, learn the lesson the mistake was sent to teach you and change the way you do things in the future. That is not failure. That is what makes successful people, successful parents—and, coincidentally, successful children.

If you find you are unable to relate to your child because of behavioural problems, personality clashes or mismatched emotional temperaments, understand it is not your fault. Look inside yourself and see if the very characteristics you find difficult in your child are not ones which are secretly lurking in your own personality and which you find difficult to accept in yourself.

The interpersonal dynamics which result from a parent–child clash can herald a lifetime of personal growth or one of continual conflict and grief. Should you find yourself embroiled in a relationship with your child which is fraught with disagreement and misunderstandings, do not hesitate to seek the assistance of a counsellor or psychologist or family therapist. By taking the high road of growth and understanding you will reap rewards for all members of the family, even if the clashing personalities eventually agree to see little of each other. Taking the low road of resistance, recriminations and blame only ever creates pain for everyone.

Whatever you do, make sure you measure yourself against your own standards and not others'. Acknowledge your successes. Develop realistic expectations of what good enough parenting can achieve and do not give yourself a hard time over things you could not have controlled.

Society Needs You

The major thrust of the social support in the form of government assistance offered to mothers is the creation of more child care places and a meagre amount of money for those who choose to raise their children full-time. Admirable though this is, it is not enough. Nearly one-quarter of single mothers in Australia live in poverty.[35] Almost 11% of the total population in this country are mothers who care for a further 24% of the population—their under fifteen-year-old children.[36] Despite their significant numbers and the vital role they play in raising these children, the social devaluation of motherhood is pervasive and subtle. But passive resistance can create change.

Since women do the vast majority of the shopping it is not reasonable that the stores are not designed for their convenience. If they do not offer easy access for your pram do not be embarrassed when it knocks clothing from the racks or tins from the shelves. If the checkout queues in the supermarket are lined with children's books and sweets at a child's eye level, do not feel as though it is your responsibility to protect the supermarket's merchandise. It is their choice to locate these goods in so vulnerable a position. Let them accept the consequences.

If public transport makes it difficult for you to get the stroller onto the bus, do not be concerned that you may inconvenience the other passengers who must wait while you struggle. You have as much right as they to (convenient) transport.

Watch the children's TV shows with them. Make note of the advertisers who sponsor programs which teach the children how to nurture other people and the planet, and how to deal with conflict constructively. Support

---

35 C. Sidoti, *op.cit.*, 1997

36 The Australian Bureau of Statistics, 'Women in Australia', *ABS Catalogue No.4113.0*, 1994, p.19

their products whenever you can. Switch off the violent TV shows and video games.

If you can afford it, do not feel compelled to return to work before you are ready. And definitely, do not feel as though you must be all things to all people in order to justify your decision.

Speak up about the difficulties of mothering. Honour motherhood as a valid choice for a valuable career. Let us hope we all wake up to this simple fact before we suffer any further deterioration in the quality of our society.

FOUR

THE EMOTIONAL ROLLER-COASTER

When a woman becomes a mother she experiences a range and depth of emotions which may not only startle her but cause her to wonder whether her sanity is at stake. Few new mothers are able to live up to the mythologically glowing, calm, all-knowing, soft mother our media would have us believe represents the average experience. Taking into account the hormonal readjustments, the mental spaciness that breastfeeding may cause, the zombi-like state of exhaustion, the loneliness and generally ill-founded expectations, it is considerably more normal for a woman to feel as though she is in danger of going crazy.

CONTROL AND COPING

- 76% of women surveyed did not expect to feel out of control once they became mothers
- 82% reported an impact on coping; 52% severe to extreme
- 76% experienced intrapersonal conflict; 50% severe to extreme
- 64% engaged in interpersonal conflict; 49% severe to extreme

THE EMOTIONAL ROLLER-COASTER

Many years ago the wife of a colleague gave birth to her first child, temporarily suspending her career as an accountant. Within a matter of a few months of becoming a mother her husband told me she wanted to have another baby. With some horror in his voice he said:

> Quite frankly, Wendy, she is not coping with one. How does she think she is going to cope with another one?

In spite of the perfect mother myths the majority of women occasionally find themselves or others still in their gowns with their faces unwashed and hair unbrushed, and the house in total disarray mid-way through the afternoon. A great many of us find ourselves there more than just once or twice, too. For Marilyn, this was the living end.

> Losing my routine, my organisation was absolutely the worst thing. Finding myself in my dressing gown still at 10 a.m. The worst thing.

Any woman who once lived a life of regular routine and schedules and who needs that level of order in her life finds the disruptions brought about by living with a baby or toddler especially distressing. Marilyn continued:

> I need to be punctual. Having my schedule thrown out by the kids was my number one trauma.

Nikki echoed her feelings:

> My life was thrown into chaos with my first child. By the time I had fed her and changed her—and changed both of us again when she sicked up all over us—packed a bag full of her stuff, it was practically time for her to go to sleep again. She was only awake for two hours at a time and you can't get anything done in that time.

When a woman is used to making a decision and acting upon it immediately, the adjustment to the need to plan every movement in the finest detail is tedious and vexing. It is tiring for a mother to continually have to project herself into the future and imagine everything she and her baby might need in every situation. It is wearing having to be prepared for every contingency so that she does not wind up with an inconsolably screaming baby in the middle of the supermarket. And it is disturbing not knowing when, or if, disruptions will occur. Sally handled the experience thus:

> I took my baby with me when I went to get a haircut. I walked down the street until I found a hairdresser who could do the job right now, this second. All the while I was terrified that in the middle of the cut my baby would wake and begin to cry. Then what would I do?

During an interview Adelle encapsulated the extent of the impact of feeling out of control on today's mothers when she said:

> I was used to being in control, not at someone else's beck and call. I worked for twenty years, studied at university twice. I don't like relinquishing control. It's like bananarama land.

The trouble is, of course, that a baby cannot be controlled. This realisation either causes a woman to expend heroic amounts of energy trying to pull her routine back together or she re-evaluates that which is important to her and she learns to relax into the chaos. Caroline took the latter option.

> I did not look to find fulfilment through motherhood therefore I was not controlling. But whatever there was of routine before he was born just went out the window. I didn't realise that there even was a routine until it was interrupted. The world revolved around this little being.

When a woman feels out of control she also feels that she cannot cope. She feels as though other people are judging her competency by the standard of her housekeeping, her appearance, her baby's behaviour. Often, they are. Madelaine told me:

> As soon as others know you're not coping they either avoid or patronise or offer more advice. They don't offer help, though. When you are not coping you wind up leading a double life—OK on the exterior, dying inside.

Women seem to expect that because they are good at their paid jobs they should also be good in all areas of life—especially at being a mother. This is an unrealistic expectation and one which often causes a new mother to try to put on a brave, but false, front. The result is much guilt and grief—often labelled postnatal depression.

Being in control of one's life is fundamental to a person's wellbeing.[37] Most of us can bear being out of control for short periods of time but when a baby arrives it can feel as though it has been lost forever. If a woman is unable to establish a sense of control over her life she may give up trying. There is a fine line between helplessness, hopelessness and depression.[38]

Depression is often the result of desiring one style of life, feeling trapped in another and believing one is quite unable to alter the circumstances. The trap for a woman with a young baby is that she feels compelled to keep on being a good mother regardless of the cost to herself. As John Gray says, a mother gives her all to mothering her child/ren whether she has one child or one dozen[39] and, in giving her all, she often feels as Nancy did when she said:

Hey, it's not like a dog. I can't put it outside. I have had enough!

That baby will be in your home for the better part of two decades. The good news is that some semblance of control does begin to return. Sometimes this will happen within the first year but perhaps not until the baby begins to sleep through the night, which may take from four weeks to four years or even until the child goes to school. Once a woman feels she has regained control of her life she begins to feel she can cope again. The bad news is that if you thought babyhood was bad, watch out for the teens!

These problems could be considerably alleviated if every mother followed Charmaine's advice:

If everyone spoke up and was honest you would realise you are not alone, not the worst off. Women do hold a lot in and do not talk because they feel that they alone are not coping.

---

[37] William Glasser, *Control Theory*, New York, 1985
[38] M.E.P. Seligman, *op.cit.*, pp.29–30
[39] J. Gray, *op.cit.*, p.37

When people are not able to be honest about what is really happening in their lives and can see no escape they have little choice but to try to hide their reality. This must eventually result in either ill-health or rage as the internal pressure builds up.

EMOTIONALISM

- 72% of women surveyed said they had not anticipated increased emotionality
- 88% reported an impact on coping; 62% severe to extreme
- 78% experienced intrapersonal conflict; 52% severe to extreme
- 78% engaged in interpersonal conflict; 58% severe to extreme

It is acknowledged that a pregnant woman can become emotional at times. It is also acknowledged that in the two or three weeks after the birth of her baby a woman may also be emotional. What nobody warns her about is that the change may be permanent.

Emotionalism is naturally heightened by exhaustion which no doubt plays an important role in this startling effect of motherhood. However, exhaustion usually wears off in a matter of years—often emotionalism does not. Sarah said:

> I became more emotional. I cry at the drop of a hat. I cannot watch violent things now or anything about brute mentality.

and Jennifer laughed when she admitted:

> No. I didn't expect to cry at the television commercials.

In the giving of birth a woman's life focus changes. Suddenly she is no longer the centre of her world, her baby is. Much of what she sees and hears is filtered through the baby's needs rather than her own. Seen through the eyes of a vulnerable baby the world looks more sad, more unpredictable, more threatening—more surprising, more beautiful, more joyous.

The range of emotions a mother experiences often changes rapidly, leaving her feeling elated or drained according to the moment. If her self-image once was that of a woman who could be in control of her emotions, she may see these swings in mood as proof she is less than the person she once thought she was.

In fact she is in the process of becoming a fuller and deeper personality, often capable of a level of compassion and love far beyond anything she ever believed herself capable of feeling before she became a mother. She may also experience a range of emotions which once played no part in her life and which feel frightening, foreign or wonderfully uplifting.

JOY

There seems to be a pervasive attitude that a woman must not, or indeed could not, enjoy staying home and raising her children. Yet Camille said:

> It was the first time I shed tears for joy. I had never done
> that before.

When a baby enters a woman's life she is drawn to its world where even the most insignificant of objects are capable of generating a baby's smile, a toddler's laughter. Insects and sticks, dirt and clouds become wondrous and magical things. Blowing raspberries, playing peek-a-boo and swinging on a swing in a park are sheer joy when they cause your baby to laugh, causing you, the mother, to laugh out loud—and to repeat the performance endlessly. As Sarah told me:

> Your whole life takes on a completely different perspective. Before kids I
> got pleasure from activities, etc., now I get the greatest pleasure from
> the smallest thing my child does. I enjoy that more than any party.

The joy that a baby brings to a woman's life is like no other. It is untainted by the trials of everyday living. It is fresh and it refreshes the world-weary older soul with a feeling for what is truly important in life—and that is the process of life itself. I knew no greater joy, when I allowed myself to do it, than to stand by my sleeping baby and watch him grow. Sometimes I felt (and still do feel) I could burst with pleasure just knowing he is mine.

FRUSTRATION

- 65% of women surveyed did not expect to be frustrated by being unable to meet their baby's needs
- 84% reported an impact on coping; 47% severe to extreme

- 72% experienced intrapersonal conflict; 45% severe to extreme
- 50% engaged in interpersonal conflict; 26% severe to extreme

As wonderful as the joy of having a baby can be it certainly does not fill every corner of every day for most women. Almost three-quarters of those surveyed reported they did not expect to encounter the raft of emotions involved in being unable to meet their baby's every need. Adelle is still bewildered:

> What do you do with a baby all day? I used to leave him on the floor and he'd basically cry all day.

Until a child begins to talk, all a mother's caring actions, especially with the first baby, are guesswork. If her guesses bring positive results a new mother tends to feel positive about her ability to mother. If they do not, at the very least, she will feel frustration. This may spill over into self-doubt, feelings of incompetence, or anger.

While feelings of frustration with a baby are normal they are exacerbated by women having to mother alone. With no-one to turn to for help and with no respite from the baby, a woman can grow certain that either she is a hopeless mother or the baby is deliberately frustrating her efforts to please and appease. In either case frustration can soon turn to anger or depression if the mother cannot rely on some time out from her baby.

ANGER AND RAGE

- Only 10% of the women surveyed were able to say that they had never lost their temper at their babies or toddlers
- 90% admitted to having, at least once, smacked their baby harder, shaken him more vigorously, dumped him into the crib or onto the bed more forcefully than they would have liked

Alongside the pleasant discovery of the joy of living with a baby, is the unpleasant discovery that on the other side of the coin may be rage and, as Maureen admitted:

> ... frightening emotions—anger, hate, despising a child. It was scary.

THE EMOTIONAL ROLLER-COASTER

When any person feels as though they have lost control over their lives and as though they are trapped interminably in this frustration, it is natural to feel anger or resentment against that which holds a person captive. If there is no other way of expressing those emotions the baby often bears the brunt of the rage. Nikki has been shocked by her anger at her children.

> I am only just emerging as a decent human being. The last 12 months have been as much hell for her [her three-year-old daughter] as they have been for me.

Pam handles her anger through her imagination:

> I visualise being violent first. That's what stops me from really doing it.

Sally, however, found herself pushed beyond her limit.

> He had been crying for five hours and I had been crying for four and a half. I knew if I stayed near him one minute longer I would kill him. I took him into his bedroom and threw him into the bassinette. I slammed the door, went into the lounge room and cried and cried.

When this mother regained her ability to cope she immediately hurried to her small son and, seeing him lying helplessly howling, dissolved into new floods of tears of regret and guilt.

> How could I get so angry? At a baby! There must be something wrong with me.

Whilst the majority of women do become short-tempered with their babies and toddlers, most realise before serious damage is done that the child is simply being a child and not deliberately designing its every waking moment with the intent of driving its mother insane. Some women do, however, become convinced that their baby's cries are judgements upon them and blindly go to the most extreme lengths to make their internal pain cease—even to the point of murder.

Everybody publicly condemns a woman who physically harms or kills her own child. It is the ultimate 'unnatural' act. Yet every woman I interviewed understood how this could happen—not the premeditated torture a very small number of women inflict on their children, but the blind rage that kills.

The less supportive a woman's partner is and the fewer the choices she has, either because of his control over her or because of poverty, the more likely she is to not only feel rage but to act it out with her baby as the target. During this period in our history when women are expected to mother in such isolation, it is a testimony to the strength of a mother's love for her children that more children are not seriously hurt in their earliest years.

GUILT

- 56% of women surveyed did not expect to feel guilty about the quality of their mothering
- 64% reported an impact on coping; 36% severe to extreme
- 67% experienced intrapersonal conflict; 43% severe to extreme
- 47% engaged in interpersonal conflict; 24% severe to extreme

In the mythology of motherhood there are two kinds of mothers—good ones and bad ones. The good ones never, ever harm their children and are patient with them at all times. They are always nurturing and able to meet the child's every need instantly, no matter what their own life circumstances are. The bad ones are the witches and wicked step-mothers who beat their children, work them to the bone and then push them into an oven.

One or two angry or unsupportive incidents do not make of a woman a 'bad' mother. Yet most new mothers feel guilty even when they are unable to meet their baby's every need and all feel guilty if they in any way treat their baby less than gently. Adelle's feelings about her mothering of her first child are not unusual.

> I feel guilty about my first one. I'd like to have that one back because I would do things differently.

Even if a baby or toddler is hurt through no fault of the mother's she is still apt to feel guilty. She tells herself she 'should have' foreseen and prevented the unpreventable.

Guilt often extends to a woman's perceived inability to run the perfect household, serve the perfect meals, be the perfect wife, daughter, sister, friend—and her inability to remain emotionally stable at all times, never needing or asking for any form of support from anyone. Again there is this strange expectation that because a woman trades paid work for the unpaid career of motherhood, she has nothing better to do than to look after everyone else. Since she will 'obviously' have time later to take care of herself, nobody seems to feel compelled to look after her.

For the woman who does return to the paid workforce her guilt load often soars. Not only is she trying to fulfil the requirements of a part-time or full-time paid job, she is also trying to fulfil the expectations of her unpaid one. There simply are not enough hours in the day to do both. Some things have to be given up and for each one of these she tends to load herself with ever more guilt.

RESPONSIBILITY

- 54% of women surveyed did not expect to be affected adversely by the responsibility of caring for a baby
- 54% reported an impact on coping; 32% severe to extreme
- 48% experienced intrapersonal conflict; 33% severe to extreme
- 40% engaged in interpersonal conflict; 20% severe to extreme

In the past a woman was seen to be a successful mother if she raised her children such that they survived physically into adulthood. Today the expectations are that she will raise a child who is intelligent, well educated, socially conscious, acceptable and adept, physically well coordinated, emotionally secure, psychologically stable and, in some cases, spiritually aware.

We are bombarded with advice from the experts in each of these fields telling us how to nurture and educate our children better, faster, earlier. Many women believe that if they do not begin teaching their toddlers to read, appreciate music, draw, make all manner of crafty things they will deprive them of the head start they need for tomorrow's competitive world.

There is a fundamental flaw in the thinking of many new mothers and that is that a particular phase in a baby's life will automatically extend into adulthood. Thus, feeding difficulties in early life can equate, in the mother's mind, to a fear this will lead to eating disorders during the teens. Two-year-old tantrums may cause her to feel her child will be socially unacceptable forever. Refusal to learn how to read at an early age may be seen as inevitable failure in school and beyond. But these phases in a child's life do not go on forever—unless the parents become so obsessed with them that they may actually cause the problems to continue.

Everywhere I found women who were afraid that their own less than perfect behaviour may have psychologically and emotionally injured their children for life. Adelle's comments are typical of how many new mothers feel when confronted with this sense of responsibility:

> That overwhelming responsibility was there all the time. That was depressing. It reduces you to the very basics of life—how frail it is. You seem very powerful when you work. I thought kids would be just like that.

It is said that it takes a whole village to raise a single child. Today a single mother can be expected to raise several children on her own. She is essentially expected to give up anything that is dear to her if it will interfere in her mothering—except paid work. After hours, however, she must return to the role of nurturing, need-fulfilling mother; regardless of her own needs. This is not reasonable. It is time we realised that the responsibility for the children rests with all of us. All of us, after all, will pay dearly if our children do not feel they are important and as though they belong when they come to take their places beside us in adulthood.

FEAR

With the onset of motherhood a woman may find herself experiencing fear which could well be an emotion she has never felt before and one which was totally unexpected. It can manifest itself in several ways.

Fear for the Baby
- 74% of women surveyed did not expect to fear for their baby's life
- 70% reported an impact on coping; 36% severe to extreme
- 61% reported intrapersonal conflict; 46% severe to extreme
- 27% engaged in interpersonal conflict; 16% severe to extreme

If you did not know you could love a baby so much it hurt, then you probably did not know you could become desperately afraid of losing her or him. Fear for the baby's physical wellbeing begins in simple ways with simple questions. Will I be able to bath him without drowning him? Will I know what she wants when she cries? Will I be able to carry him without dropping him? Will my baby be one who succumbs to cot death? Nikki's walk with fear began the day she took her baby home.

> I left the hospital after a very difficult birth—blood transfusions, etc. but still a very proud mother. I had been through, what I thought, was a totally shattering experience but delighted to have this gorgeous 8lb bub. Then the matron said, 'You thought that was hard work—the hard work is just beginning.' I felt afraid.

Within a few days of first holding her baby a new mother may begin to see a yawning gap between all that was known and certain before, all the beliefs of which she was so sure, and the ocean of unknowing which now stretches before her. Such uncertainty combined with such responsibility cannot help but engender a little fear.

Many women reported seeing in their mind's eye clear visions of their children dying in gruesome circumstances. They told of 'seeing' them being burned, falling from great heights, suffocating, being kidnapped, tortured and murdered, being harmed in a car crash, dying in their sleep, suffering from terminal illnesses. Charmaine reluctantly admitted:

> I picture it in my mind like a torture. I see them floating in a river, face down. I see it in every detail. It's like I am preparing myself. I must be crazy.

Some women cannot stop themselves from imagining every conceivable accident the environment could devise happening to their children. Once the inner scene begins to unfold she seems powerless to halt its inevitable progress even as she suffers spasms of guilt and fear simultaneously. Suzanne told me:

> I sit here and I can see the light fitting falling off the wall and the wires coming loose, falling onto his head and electrocuting him. I see every bit of it happening and I can't stop it. It's crazy; I hate it; but I can't help it.

Each woman felt afraid that by visualising these terrors she was in some way willing them to happen. The fear that she may be responsible for creating the imagined disaster enables some to push their visions aside. Those who are unable to quash their imaginations, however, experience guilt in addition to their fear and tend to secretly doubt their sanity.

Perhaps instead of being an energy for creating catastrophe these imaginings are a way of putting a face to, and understanding the underlying fear of losing a child. It is also a powerful way of foreseeing potential danger and therefore motivates a mother to take preventative measures before circumstances have a chance to wreak havoc. In an electronic world which bombards us with scenes of tragedy daily, a new mother often becomes hypersensitive to how vulnerable her baby really is.

Women who have lost children often report that the worst thing for them is the way other mothers ignore them or will not acknowledge their child's death. The first time I met a woman whose nine-year-old son had died in a bike accident I realised that simply knowing someone to whom this had happened made my vague fears for my own son all too real a possibility. I believe for many parents that acknowledging the loss of another family's child is to open that Pandora's box in one's own life.

Fear of Damaging the Baby

- 60% of women surveyed did not expect to feel afraid of damaging their baby through being less than perfect mothers
- 58% reported an impact on coping; 36% severe to extreme
- 59% experienced intrapersonal conflict; 36% severe to extreme
- 36% engaged in interpersonal conflict; 22% severe to extreme

A new mother may find she becomes afraid of damaging her baby physically, mentally, emotionally and, sometimes, spiritually. In today's world there has been considerable emphasis placed on the nurture side of the nature versus nurture argument. There are a plethora of child raising books which tell parents how to raise their child's IQ and how to teach them self-discipline. There are books about mothers who love too much and toxic mothers who poison their children with their own problems and hang-ups, and the consequences of having one. All subtly insinuate it is the mother's responsibility to raise an optimum adult from the baby she has given birth to. She is left in no doubt as to whose responsibility it is if her child deviates from the socially acceptable norms.

Thus a new mother may find herself obsessed with meeting her baby's every need for fear of damaging the future adult's potential, emotional wellbeing or mental stability. It is not until the second child is born that many women realise children are certainly stamped with their own genetic make-up and that this contributes significantly to the development of the evolving adult. Even then her fear of being judged a 'bad mother' may cause her to remain fearful of outcomes over which she could not possibly have any control.

Personal Mortality
- 74% of women surveyed did not expect to fear their own mortality
- 58% reported an impact on coping; 28% severe to extreme
- 43% experienced intrapersonal conflict; 26% severe to extreme

Fear can manifest as the new mother realises that she is mortal. Even though adults know about death at an intellectual level, it is a concept some women do not personalise until they become mothers. Sarah's experience is not at all uncommon.

> Death took on a totally different significance to me. Before I did not care if I lived or died. Now I have got to survive until they become individuals themselves—so I gave up smoking and I never would have done that before.

This sudden awareness of her mortality can make a woman feel extremely vulnerable and afraid for her own wellbeing, causing her to notice body pain more often and wonder or worry about its meaning. Sally's experience sometimes bordered on panic.

> When my son was ten months old I became obsessed with the possibility that I may have contracted AIDS before I met my husband. It played on my mind so badly I finally went and convinced a doctor I needed to be tested. I was panic-stricken that I might die before he got to be an adult.

Sometimes, as a mother, a woman will give up activities which have been a core part of her being since childhood. Anna, who had been riding horses since she was in primary school and had designed her living space and lifestyle around her passion for them, said:

> I used to get on any horse. After I had David I had a young horse that had just been broken in. I was like a leaf shaking, worrying about my kid. It took three months to get confident again. Nothing had changed. I was still a good rider. It was just because I had a child.

In some cases a new mother may become unduly fearful for her partner's wellbeing believing that if he were to die she would not cope. As Pauline wrote:

> The whole responsibility was felt so keenly—any sickness or pain resulted in extreme anxiety. Fear of the baby's death was sometimes experienced but I was far more anxious about the possibility of my husband's death. I felt if I died (which I sometimes prayed for) my husband would be able to meet all their needs because he is so close to them.

Every woman I interviewed felt a heightened sense of her own mortality yet all said that if anybody was to die or be harmed she hoped it would be she, not her children.

EMPATHY

Empathy is the ability to understand how particular circumstances or events are likely to affect another person in the present moment and their likely impact on their future. When we look in on another person's world with empathy there is a sense that we, too, participate in joys and heartaches that might never have been part of our life experience. In its most powerful form, it is a gateway to feeling 'at one' with another human being or with all of creation—it is the beginning of the end of separation and loneliness. It is also the starting point for understanding that we cannot always control our environment, that unfortunate events do not befall others because they 'deserve' them and that to judge others because their lives are less blessed than ours makes no sense.

When we break through into empathy the emotions we feel may be so strong that we will do anything to assist or defend another person in need. If, however, we are unable to relieve their suffering we may equally experience distressing inner conflict ourselves as we try to deal with the painful realisation that we are powerless to help. With the birth of their first baby many women experience a marked increase in empathy on many levels as they fully understand, perhaps for the first time in their lives, that they are no island and that they and their children are truly as vulnerable as any other mother and child. In the comparative safety of a Western society this knowledge does not always sit comfortably with a new mother.

Empathy for Her Baby

- 65% of women surveyed did not expect to feel emotional pain whenever their baby was in pain
- 73% reported an impact on coping; 35% severe to extreme
- 59% experienced intrapersonal conflict; 28% severe to extreme
- 42% engaged in interpersonal conflict; 18% severe to extreme

Sally's reaction is very common.

> When he cried, if I could not figure out what was wrong and he continued, then I cried. It hurt me like a physical pain to know my baby was unhappy when I could not fix it.

There is a special symbiosis which occurs between mothers and babies. Suddenly the new mother does not just experience her own feelings but those of her baby as well. She knows by her baby's cry whether he is feeling hunger, pain, frustration, rage, helplessness and she often feels these as well. It is this symbiosis which drives her to cure her baby's problems and to bring him back to laughter so that she, herself, can feel pleasure and happiness. As much as a contented, happy mother can positively affect the mood of her baby equally a contented, happy baby will positively affect her mother.

Empathy for Other Mothers

- Only 20% of women surveyed expected to be affected by other mothers' traumas with their children
- 60% reported an impact on coping; 30% in the severe to extreme range
- 37% experienced intrapersonal conflict; 20% severe to extreme
- 20% engaged in interpersonal conflict; 16% severe to extreme

One of the common things said to me during the research for this book was that women who were not yet mothers would not understand what I was writing about. This assumption was derived from their own experience of having looked down on mothers before they became one themselves. Sarah spoke for many of us when she said:

> I was dogmatic, critical, thought others should do it my way. Now I am more empathic. I don't judge until I have been in that situation. Prior to having kids I couldn't understand how women could leave children, hit them. I was judgemental. But after my own I understood. I used to think there was something wrong with other mothers.

Not all women make this transition to empathy for other mothers, however. It is so easy to see a child who misbehaves and blame the parent for not exercising enough control without considering the child's temperament, the mother's circumstances and without knowing their history together. Advice and judgementalism flow, if not verbally, then in the privacy of our own minds. Yet how many of us have experienced behaviour in our children for which we can find no explanation and no answers, no matter how hard we search our inner selves to discover where we went wrong?

The majority of women, however, once they have had a child of their own find they more closely identify with other mothers and other mothers' children. They take on board the trials and tribulations of others as though they were their own, sometimes to a degree which is quite unexpected. Camille said:

> When I hear of deaths of other people's children it really eats inside me.

Empathy for Those Caught Up in World Events
- 78% of women surveyed did not expect this to affect them
- 58% reported an impact on coping; 34% severe to extreme
- 46% experienced intrapersonal conflict; 22% severe to extreme
- 22% engaged in interpersonal conflict; 11% severe to extreme

World events can take on an unexpected significance when a woman becomes a mother. Penny told me:

> Before I became a mother I could watch the news and not cry for all

those starving children out there in the world. Now I have to leave the room.

Watching the evening news on television can become a draining, emotional experience if a mother identifies with harm done to completely unrelated children and the consequences this has for their mothers. Adelle's reaction was unequivocal:

> I shouldn't have had them—boys—I should have had girls if there is going to be a war. I don't know what I would do. I'd die. I'd die. I've given them life—I could have chosen not to. I don't know—I think I would take them away, hide them.

To know great love is also to know great fear and pain. Women all over the third world sit and watch as their children die from starvation or wounds or diseases, helpless to save them. Women all over the developed world stand mute as their children die or are injured in accidents, succumb to cancers or are harmed by others. As television brings these tragedies into our homes we are all affected in some small measure. Only a parent who has lived through these dreadful experiences can know what this is like, yet a mother often experiences an empathy for them which causes her to feel spontaneous heartache and shed unbidden tears. As each new loss touches her life she may find that her core fear for her own children rises and subsequently, so too does her need to protect them.

In my own life, each time I see or hear of a mother suffering a loss of or damage to one of her children I feel as though she suffers so that I may be spared so incomprehensible a pain. For I know in my heart that that mother could be me but for the grace of God. I do not suppose many days go by during which I do not thank God for my good fortune and pray that She keeps on protecting my son forever.

CHILDHOOD ISSUES REVISITED

- The upwelling of childhood issues was the second least expected aspect of motherhood with only 19% of women surveyed expecting to be affected
- 65% reported an impact on coping; 52% severe to extreme

- 59% experienced intrapersonal conflict; 43% severe to extreme
- 53% engaged in interpersonal conflict; 40% severe to extreme

Becoming a parent may shock and surprise a new mother (or father, for that matter) when this dramatic change in her life role brings back difficult feelings from her own childhood. If those unresolved issues have been repressed or suppressed for all of her adult life so far, their eruption into consciousness can be disturbing.

When we know a person's name but cannot quite remember it, the misplaced memory nags at our brains, sometimes for days, just out of reach. When we leave home with a sinking feeling that we have forgotten to bring a significant item with us, or have misplaced it, our minds churn and sift through lists and possibilities until we recall what it was we have left behind or where it is to be found. Incomplete issues are like this except they do their nagging, not on a conscious, mental level but on a subconscious, emotional level. When a person's inner self is being emotionally nagged with unresolved and uncompleted angers, hurts, regrets from the past she cannot get on with the business of living fully in the present. To a greater or lesser extent, depending on the depth and scope of her unconscious memories, she will be condemned to acting in the present as though the past were perpetually replaying itself. Madelaine told me:

> We were abused every day as children. My mother can't remember any of that. We used to get hit with the jug cord leaving welts up and down our legs. The scary thing is that when my little boy does something I could just throttle him and it is such a rage!

The further in her past these key, unresolved issues were buried, the less conscious a mother will be of their influence on her present day behaviour. When things do not go well for her, she will tend to interpret her problems as being caused by others and feel as though they are 'doing it to her'. Her negative feelings from the past will then be projected onto those who are most closely around her at the time—her partner and her baby—as if they were the perpetrators of her original pain. Incomplete issues, whether from the earliest days of existence or yesterday, will always adversely affect relationships, usually with those closest to us.

The hurts of childhood are imprinted on us from the moment we first draw breath, and earlier. Often they are manageable until we have children of our own when the lost memories are stirred into life once more. As a woman watches her child develop and grow she is reminded, at the deepest emotional level, of her own early days and what they meant for her. Emma wrote:

> I had always assumed that there was something innately disgusting and unacceptable about me due to the way my father distanced himself from me and seemed to disapprove of my every word and action. Also I was incredibly ashamed of my sexuality—a shame communicated by my parents as they insisted that I cover myself up and stressed the dirtiness of those lower, unmentionable, untouchable bits of the body.
>
> When I first saw my daughter—naked as they all come—I thought she was the most beautiful and perfect thing I'd ever seen—every bit of her. Through my love for her I have gradually been able to accept, at last, the possibility that I was lovable and beautiful as a child but that my parents hadn't been able to communicate that. And as I have watched her grow and chatter and play I have been able to see that silliness is quite normal—not just restricted to me.

Experiments have shown that baby monkeys when removed from their natural mothers will choose to be in contact with a mother substitute which does not feed them but is soft, warm and nurturing, for up to eighteen hours per day. Conversely, they will choose to be in contact with a mother substitute which feeds them but is hard, cold and non-responsive for approximately one hour per day. To a newborn primate the need for affection completely overshadows its need for nourishment.[40] Similarly, other experiments show that if a newborn female ape does not have the opportunity to develop a normal mother–infant relationship she grows into an adult who does not know how to mother her own offspring. If her mother figure feeds her but is cold and distant, the daughter will develop into an indifferent mother herself—or an abusive one.[41]

Human beings are not so biologically different from apes that we can afford to distance ourselves from these findings. Genetically there is only a 1% difference between a chimpanzee and a human being. The way both species are treated as infants imprints everlasting impressions upon the

---

40 A. Montagu, *op.cit.*, pp.38–40

41 A. Montagu, *ibid*, p.42

chemistry of their bodies and brains, their hormonal flows and their immune system.

> A traumatic event remains deeply imprinted as organic memory, but the accompanying shock creates a neurochemical barrier of repression between the unconscious and conscious mind ... Imprints influence perceptions and personality development; they do not fade with the passage of time.[42]

In later years these imprints spring up to haunt and direct the behaviour of the adult, seemingly from nowhere. They cause people to behave in ways which they would otherwise rationally reject. Bianca told:

> My mother used to force me to eat all my vegetables no matter how cold they were or how much I hated them. I was determined not to force feed my son so I give in to him all the time. Now he eats only junk and I cannot find a balance.

For Bianca, any discipline regarding food automatically feels as though she is exerting unacceptable force because her own childhood issues are confused with today's reality.

As we grow up our role models are our own mothers. We absorb their mannerisms, their beliefs and taboos, their prejudices and limitations, their expectations and their ways of doing things without even realising it is happening. In adulthood we may mentally reject much of what our mothers said and did, avowing never to inflict such conditioning upon our own children. But often we do. Pretty well any woman who has ever had a child in her care will attest to having heard her mother's words pour out of her own mouth even though she had sworn never to repeat them. Our behaviour patterns spill forth in a similar fashion and often we do not even recognise that we are repeating past history. Linda wrote:

> One of the most thought provoking (not always positive) issues for me in mothering Emily, travelling long distances and working, has been that my own mother experienced enormous stress in balancing all these

---

42 Elizabeth Noble, *Primal Connections*, New York, 1993, p.56

> commitments and without the support of a husband. As the eldest child I often felt that I had to grow up quickly and frequently felt under pressure to 'help set an example'. I feel that I am subjecting Emily to similar pressures.
>
> Of course, all this results in a feeling of guilt and frustration that no matter how well I try to organise myself and the household ... I never seem to achieve what I consider to be a satisfactory result for all concerned! Doesn't it seem a little like history repeating itself??!!

Until a woman becomes a mother she may have coping mechanisms which enable her to deal with incidents and influences from her childhood which she experienced as negative. She may have stayed busy with work, friends, parties, hobbies, sports; she may have developed a professional persona thereby proving she was a worthwhile person in spite of parenting which often demonstrated otherwise when she was a child. In these ways she blocked out the old hurts so they could not make their way into her consciousness. I have listened to many a woman deny anything was amiss in her childhood even though the most superficial examination of those days revealed emotional, psychological or physical abuse.

For a woman who believes she achieved a significant degree of personal growth before she became a mother it is a shock to find she was playing children's games in comparison with the level of growth thrust upon one at the onset of motherhood. It is a shock to find that issues one thought were resolved were but the tip of the good-old iceberg. Nikki admitted:

> I used to think that being a mature person would aid me as a mother but it was like snakes and ladders. All the neuroses and hang-ups that I thought I had dealt with came back to haunt me times ten! It was like going back to the beginning and starting again.

Left alone with their newborn babies, many women encounter their real selves for the first time in their lives. There is nowhere to hide. The baby keeps them at a level of exhaustion in which no defence mechanism works reliably and often they all fail at once leaving the new mother face to face with a total stranger—herself. Even if by an act of supreme willpower she manages to rebuild the barriers and defences, sooner or later they will be breached again. And again she will have to face the stranger in the mirror.

GRIEF

- 74% of women surveyed did not expect to experience grief at losing their pre-mother selves
- 50% reported an impact on coping; 30% severe to extreme
- 57% experienced intrapersonal conflict; 33% severe to extreme
- 33% engaged in interpersonal conflict; 20% severe to extreme

Some women welcome motherhood as the fulfilment of their destiny. Some embrace it as a way of escaping from the world of boring or pressurised work. Others, even though they may have looked forward to including a baby in their lives for years, experience an unexpected sense of deep grief. Margaret said:

> I actually grieved when I had my son, that I could no longer be the person that I was. I used to contemplate leaving him in a basket on the steps of a convent.

While motherhood brings many joys and benefits to a woman's life, it also heralds many losses. These are all the more profound because they are generally not publicly acknowledged and because a good mother is supposed to be able to instantly and totally embrace her new role in life. New mothers grieve for their loss of freedom, control, sense of achievement, youthful body, quick mind, the ability to decide and do, financial independence ... the list is long and the losses are not trivial. A woman's career or studies go on hold sometimes for years. Her friendships change. Her support systems changes. Her relationship with her husband may have changed dramatically—perhaps for the worse.

When a person is going through an identity crisis, when she is trying to adjust to irrevocable and new life conditions which have not turned out to be quite as rosy as expected, when the new mother feels suddenly undervalued, she may look upon her past life as having been more ideal than her current circumstances seem to be. It is not uncommon that she wonders why she ever did this to herself. It is not uncommon that she grieves for the non-mother person she used to be.

More 'natural' societies than those of Western civilisation help their women make the transition to motherhood by means of rituals which honour the person she once was and which appropriately lay to rest that identity. Even in our own society, becoming a mother was once seen to be the attainment of the pinnacle of a woman's destiny and the ultimate contribution she could make to her community. Today she is expected to pretend, along with everyone else, that nothing much has changed and that she is delighted, totally, with her new circumstances. Above all, the new mother is not given the opportunity to grieve for her losses. Perhaps this explains, in part at least, why she gets the blues and why so many go on to develop depression.

BLUES, STRESS AND DEPRESSION

It is well documented that some 80–90% of women experience a let-down period a few days to a week after the birth of their babies. This is a period of hormonal readjustment which may leave the new mother feeling as though she has lost control of her emotions. One moment she is elated with her achievement and in love with her baby. The next she is weeping inconsolably feeling as though her life has come to an end.

And in a very important sense, it has. Never again will she be a non-mother; never again will she be without responsibility to another human being; never again will she be the carefree person she was only nine months ago. Or so it seems a mere week into motherhood. It is often during this time she realises that carrying and giving birth to her baby was not the end of the process but only the beginning.

These realisations may come as a genuine shock and subsequently it may take years for her to come to terms with them. Under normal circumstances, however, the hormonal upheaval will subside within a few days and cease to contribute its weight to this otherwise surprising awakening.

More serious is postnatal depression about which a great deal has been written. It is now recognised that up to 88% of new mothers suffer, at the very least, from what is termed postnatal stress disorder (PNSD).[43] I do not agree that this is a 'disorder' since such terminology assumes deviation from the norm when in fact it is the norm. I will, therefore, refer to the condition as postnatal stress/depression or PNS/D. Whilst researchers almost universally agree they do not know what causes either, they are clear on the symptoms. If one or more of the following affect a mother for more than two weeks, depending upon the severity of her symptoms, she may be suffering from either PNS or PND:

---

43 NSW Women's Consultative Committee, *op.cit.*, p.19

- Loss of control when usually competent
- Inability to do household tasks
- Poor self-image, low self-worth
- Fear of social contact
- Fear of being alone
- Poor appetite or overeating
- Tearfulness for no apparent reason
- Exhaustion and over-concern about lack of sleep
- Inability to concentrate or think clearly and coherently
- Inability to sleep
- Overwhelming feelings of anxiety or depressed mood
- Feeling helpless in caring for her baby/child
- Irritability and/or apathy and/or despondency
- Inability to bond with her baby
- Inability to separate from her baby
- Acute feelings of grief
- Feelings of guilt
- Feeling worthless
- Avoiding going out
- Lack of confidence
- Becoming obsessed, eg: with the baby, cleanliness
- Exaggerated fears about health of self, baby or partner
- Palpitations
- Constant headaches or non-specific body pains
- Feeling upset with her baby for no apparent reason
- Thoughts of harming her baby
- Suicidal thoughts, plans or actions[44]

PNS/D can attack the new mother within days of giving birth or it may not manifest until a year or even two later, or until she weans her baby. It may not even affect her until after her second or third child is born. Certainly the inability to escape the role of mother contributes significantly to stress and depression but sometimes this sense of entrapment does not surface until further pressure is brought to bear on her life. Sally and Sarah woke up to this one and two years later, saying, respectively:

44 NSW Women's Consultative Committee, *op.cit.*, pp. 18 & 58

THE EMOTIONAL ROLLER-COASTER

> When my son turned one year old it hit me that this, motherhood, was FOREVER. I panicked. I felt trapped. In retrospect I realise I became depressed around that time and stayed at a low grade depression for years.
>
> PND does not necessarily happen until the child is two. That's when I realised this could go on forever.

Postnatal depression does not normally strike suddenly on any particular day but takes hold insidiously in such a way that its presence may never be recognised or acknowledged by the mother, her spouse, the clinic sister or even her medical practitioner. Instead her sense of wellbeing is steadily eaten away day by day until it seems to the mother, and everyone around her, that this is her normal self. The longer the depression goes undiagnosed, the harder it becomes for a woman to admit that all is not well in her world. Madelaine said:

> Everyone else says they are fine or great so I used to think, 'What's wrong with me?'

Pam's realisation that she had suffered PND did not come until after it had passed.

> Looking back I think I must have had PND but didn't know it at the time, thinking this is how it is. I didn't know I needed help. I didn't know how to ask or how to articulate what I was feeling.

Postnatal stress/depression may last for several weeks to months and even years. Studies show that 30–50% of women who have experienced the depression end of the spectrum are still depressed after twelve months. Recovery has the sense of being two steps forward, one step backwards. Every time there is a step backwards a woman feels fear that the downward spiral of depression may be about to suck her into the terrifying whirlpool of blackness once more. Nikki, who did battle with serious PND after the birth of her second child, wrote the following to me when he was eighteen months old:

> I can feel the spectre of depression pulling at me again and it scares me to death. I couldn't stand it again.

The fear of slipping into depression once she has escaped its tentacles may powerfully motivate a woman to take whatever measures are necessary to prevent its recurrence. It is often this fear which motivates and steels a woman to leave an unsupportive or destructive relationship, to actively seek counselling or new friendships or return to the paid workforce. Margaret experienced these depths before she finally left her partner.

> I've gone so low that I'll never allow myself to get so low again. It was scary. Curlers and dressing gown syndrome at 5 p.m.—to think I got so low.

When 88% of a particular section of a population are experiencing difficulties adjusting to what is, biologically speaking, the most fundamental experience of life, perhaps we ought to be asking whether the way we expect women to be mothers is what is disordered. Could it be that the 'disorder' of postnatal stress and depression is, in truth, symptoms and indications of the disordered health of the society rather than an abnormality in our mothers?

Think about it. Once women used to mother collectively. They gathered their food together, they talked as they worked and shared their inner worlds. Even as the human race began to live in villages their children of all ages washed through the community. Their needs were tended by whichever adult was closest to hand. If a biological mother was unwell, tired, busy, disinterested or disinclined to attend to her child's demands the child simply moved on to the next mother figure in the community. When a child was ill or smitten by accident the pain felt by the parents was the pain of all and the work of caring for the child was shared. If the baby or child died a whole community experienced the loss and mourned together with the parents.

Today we expect our mothers to take their children into the four walls of their homes within a week of giving birth, there to undertake every single responsibility of raising that baby alone. A mother is expected to be nurturer, gatherer of food, cook, nutritional expert, educator, psychological expert, emotional support person, cleaner, washer woman, expert problem solver, medical diagnostician and practitioner, eternal giver of unconditional love ... Most women arrive on the threshold of motherhood with not a single day's training in any of these skills and without a word of warning that she may find them difficult, tedious, boring or soul-destroying. And she is considered 'lucky' if her partner, family or friends help her. She is expected to perform these duties in isolation with little or no support from the community. Indeed, she will often feel as though she has been actively shut out of the community whether she resides in the remotest corners of the country or in the middle of the largest city.

However, if she feels depleted by the endless giving, if she weeps for the trapped and lonely and exhausted person she has become, she will be labelled 'disordered'. It is she who will be judged to be in need of 'treatment' to help her 'adjust'.

In terms of evolution this raising of our children in isolation from the flow of community has come upon us in the blink of an eye. Only since the Industrial Revolution have we begun to withdraw into our separate houses and to exclude our wider communities from collective parenting. In the space of 200 years we have devolved from communal life to the nuclear family to single parenthood. Genetically we could not have even begun to mutate to the degree necessary such that we could possibly find this style of mothering 'natural' or acceptable. Thus, women are being asked to raise their children in a manner diametrically opposed to their genetic programming.[45] Is it any wonder 88% of us find it difficult to adjust!

One of the recommendations made by the Women's Consultative Committee was that all antenatal classes include a component on 'adjustment to parenthood'[46] since it has been shown that just two 40 minute sessions significantly reduce the likelihood of PNS/D.[47] This recommendation lends weight to my contention that it is not just the antenatal teachers who must be more honest about the reality of motherhood. Mothers themselves must freely share their personal experiences—both the positive and the negative. If our young women are ever to have the opportunity to base their choices on knowledge rather than myth they must be told the whole truth, not just the half we think they want to hear.

When she knows what changes she may encounter as a new mother a woman is less likely to be shocked and left floundering for solutions if they do eventuate. When she is educated as to the possible effects of these changes on herself, her partner and her relationship she will know that others have experienced the same stresses; that she is neither odd nor crazy. She will have

---

45 Daniel Goleman, *Emotional Intelligence: Why It Can Matter More Than IQ*, New York, 1995, p.5
46 NSW Women's Consultative Committee, *op.cit.*
47 Women's Consultative Committee, *op.cit.*, p.6

heard of strategies for dealing with the changes and will not need to reinvent the wheel whilst in the pit of depression—surely the most difficult time imaginable to be called upon to think creatively.

The debate over whether PNS/D is a medical phenomenon or a social one will go on for some time yet. Certainly there are some factors which predispose a woman to either one or the other. They are:

- Stressful life events during pregnancy or the postnatal period, eg: moving house, financial problems, death of someone close, caring for three or more children
- Lack of a confiding relationship—particularly with partner or own mother
- Unresolved past grief, eg: miscarriage, abortion, adoption, stillbirth or the loss of a parent as a child (especially mother)
- High levels of intervention during childbirth with low levels of explanation
- Low levels of social support after childbirth
- Lack of information about the possibility of stress and anxiety after the birth
- A difficult or handicapped baby
- Medically there is a link between women who experience severe PMT and then suffer PNS/D in that they appear to be more susceptible to hormonal changes[48]

Whatever the accurate figures are on PNS/D and by whatever pathway a mother arrives at its door—be it physiological, psychological or social—it is unacceptable that so significant a proportion of a particular population does suffer this excruciating and debilitating handicap. Certainly mothers need to learn to adjust to our current definition of motherhood (for the time being) for their own self-survival. But they do not have to accept that motherhood must forever remain an isolating experience. Nor do they have to accept that motherhood be forever relegated to one of the least recognised, most undervalued roles a woman can play. Nor do they have to remain silent.

---

48 Women's Consultative Committee, *op.cit.*, pp.20–21

POST TRAUMATIC STRESS

In rare instances a woman may find she is subject to post traumatic stress disorder after a particularly distressing birth process. The condition is recognised amongst those who are victims of violence, accident and natural disasters but perhaps not amongst women whose birth processes were equally terrifying.

A person is considered to be suffering from post traumatic stress when the following symptoms repeatedly impact on her life more than a month after the traumatic incident:

- Flashbacks to, or nightmares of, the trigger incident which have the intensity of reliving it and which cannot be halted by mere conscious willpower
- Inability to get to sleep or constant waking with an inability to return to sleep due to repetitive replaying and analysing of the incident
- Panic attacks which are set off by an unrelated event which reminds her of the original incident or occur when she re-enters the environment where the trauma occurred
- The traumatic memories are so intrusive as to significantly diminish a person's ability to enjoy life
- Sudden and dramatic mood changes which cannot be explained
- Heightened state of arousal, hyper-vigilance and an inability to inhibit the startle response, which is the tendency to jump when faced with a sudden and unexpected occurrence or loud noise

Although little research has been done in this area, Kym Kilpatrick who is a psychologist at the University of New England says that a woman who experienced a traumatic childhood may be predisposed to suffer from post traumatic stress disorder if she subsequently lives through a traumatic birth experience. Certainly, of all the women I interviewed, the only one whose postnatal depression was recognised as having encompassed an element of post traumatic stress disorder had also grown up in a family where anger, overcontrol and sexual abuse had festered. Sandra wrote:

> It took a while to make the connection between my panicky, bad feelings and the flashbacks of post traumatic stress disorder. Books on

PTSD never mention childbirth as a source of trauma intense
enough to cause this reaction, but I am not alone in the universe.
I heard of one woman who had been a political prisoner and a torture
victim who then had a baby and felt 'abandoned and overwhelmed'
and developed PTSD with flashbacks both to birth and to torture—
there are similarities. I am glad she exists, otherwise I would feel a
complete freak.

However, having listened to the stories of others with similar tales of horror births and subsequent attacks of panic and anxiety, I cannot help but feel the condition may be more prevalent than the current lack of diagnoses would indicate. There is some indication that it may even precede postnatal psychosis, a condition that causes a mother to lose her grip on reality to the extent that she can no longer be relied upon to care for either herself or her baby. Clearly more research is required.

LOVE

A small but significant minority of women (12%) found their profound sense of love for their babies difficult to deal with in the extreme. Most, however, simply expressed surprise at the depth of their feelings and genuine delight in discovering they were capable of loving another human being so much. Even the mothers who had not bonded with their babies for years still expressed this depth of love once they had bonded. Elaine's words give hope to all mothers who have had difficulty bonding.

> I did not think it was possible to love my little boy so much after
> having such despair. They say you have to have that special bond in
> the beginning—with him it was 12 or 13 months.

The majority of women expressed feelings of profound love for their babies and, although we all expect to love our children, it is true that nothing can prepare a woman for the depth and passion of that love until she holds her own child. After my son was born I realised how naive had been my assumption that the feelings I had for my beloved German shepherd would in any way compare with those I instantly had for Daniel. Leigh confessed:

THE EMOTIONAL ROLLER-COASTER

> I have never cared for anybody as much. I've never loved anybody before, but I do Teresa.

When a baby responds to being fed and cuddled and raspberried with smiles and laughter it is difficult not to feel good about yourself. Their acceptance of you as a person is complete. They are non-judgemental no matter what your social status or IQ or looks or organisational ability or levels of achievement. Their forgiveness of your foibles, in the early days at least, is total. Babies do not harbour grudges nor seek revenge. Practically nowhere else in the world can a woman feel so totally accepted for who she is, as she is, as when her baby responds positively to her. Maureen said:

> Kids just know you are Mum. They do not care what you look like.

This astounding blossoming of the ability to love is by no means confined to a mother. As my brother recently gazed adoringly at his six-year-old daughter his eyes filled with tears and he said:

> I didn't know I could love like this. I never knew love could be so big it hurt.

I began a diary for Daniel when he was ten months old which I hope will give him some insight into his early life when he is older, should he be interested. The second entry reads:

> I love you. I have just spent the last half hour kneeling by your bed and gazing into your sleeping face. So perfect. So peaceful, serene. I love you more deeply than I ever thought I could possibly love anyone and I shall be grateful to you to the end of my days for unlocking that vault in my heart.
>
> What fills me with wonder is that for the first time in my life I truly know how it feels to love another human being unconditionally. I love you totally and I cannot tell you what a miracle that is.

Notwithstanding everything else in this book, *this* is what makes mothering, indeed parenting, worth all the pain and exhaustion and heartache. There is no other love to compare with the love for a child. It is a testimony to the power of this love that women find a million creative ways to overcome the devaluation of motherhood and continue to experience deep pleasure and meaning in being a mother.

HELP FOR HANGING IN THERE

Learn to Let Go

Accept that there is a distinct possibility your household will be thrown into chaos occasionally (or often). Becoming a mother is an opportunity to re-evaluate what is urgent and what is important or merely trivial. When you hear yourself giving yourself a hard time because some household chore has not been done, yet again, ask yourself whether it will matter in two years time.

Learn to relax and let go. The need to control and direct every moment of your life is tiring and unnecessary. As surely as the sun will rise tomorrow, if the washing is not done today it will wait for you to do it the next day—or the next. Will the world really fall apart if you run late for an appointment? For whom do you need to keep up appearances? Do you do it for yourself or is it to make others think you are capable and worthwhile? If they need you to kill yourself to prove your value, they are not the kind of people you need in your life at this time.

All things pass. Trust that this chaos and lack of control will too.

IQ vs EIQ

IQ is a poor predictor of success and contributes to, at best, only 20% of the qualities which contribute to an individual's success. Goleman writes, 'People with high IQs can be stunningly poor pilots of their private lives.'[49] A person's emotional intelligence quotient (EIQ) contributes more predictably to their ability to succeed in life. Unfortunately, emotions are considered illogical. According to the doing paradigm, therefore, a person displaying them openly must be less intelligent than one who is able to hide or deny them.

Reconnecting with the inner well of emotions is possibly one of the most rewarding side effects of motherhood. In here you will find the core of your intelligence which you may have lost in the business or academic world. Emotions are the foundation on which we build our evaluation and

---

49 D. Goleman, *op.cit.*, p.34

understanding of people and events. Without them to guide us, we are dumb to possible danger and we are numb to joy, love and our creative potential.

Our psyche goes numb in the same way our legs do when we sit for too long and cut off the blood supply. When the blood begins to flow again we experience the unpleasant sensation of pins and needles. Similarly, when emotions begin to flow after a period of suppression, the sensation is one of being on an emotional roller-coaster. Just as with pins and needles, rest assured that the roller-coaster effect settles down when all the new emotions have found their rightful place. After that, the life-blood of your emotions will flow through your psyche as naturally, as painlessly, as your blood flows through your veins. It is the restriction which creates the pain, not the release.

So, do not allow others to put down your increased emotional output. You cannot expect to experience deep love and joy without also experiencing a heightened awareness of many other emotions. Motherhood is a magnificent opportunity to reclaim your emotional intelligence.

Frustration is Normal—Rage Needs Help

Know that no baby deliberately sets out to thwart a parent's good intentions or to ruin her day with disruptions. A baby does not intend to pass judgement on his parents when they are unable to figure out what it is he wants. He cannot consider your needs because he does not know you have them. He only does what must be done in order to get his needs met.

Some babies have simple needs, others more complex ones. If your baby is difficult to please and you cannot cope with the disruptions to your life, get help before frustration turns to rage. Find anger releases which work for you. Beat the bed, scream into a pillow. If you are as fortunate as I am and live in the middle of nowhere, stand out in the field and holler even until the cows move paddocks.

Be aware of taking out anger on your baby which has been caused by your partner, your own parents, social structures or poverty. If you see yourself becoming unreasonable with your child stand back for a moment and try to ascertain what lies behind the emotion. Learn to deal with the appropriate source of your anger even if that means seeking out a counsellor.

If you feel violent towards your child, visualise your violent actions vividly— and their consequences. Notice how helpless your baby is, how unable she is to defend herself. If you cannot control your anger get help. Get help. Get help. Children are taken away from their parents these days only as a last resort—in fact, often not soon enough. Child welfare authorities try to help long before they resort to separating a child from its mother. The embarrassment of admitting to feelings of violence is nothing compared with the life-long physical, emotional and psychological damage you may inflict on your child and the life-long sentence of guilt you may inflict on yourself.

Guilt Has Meaning—Pay Attention

Guilt has only three purposes; to let us know we have done something wrong; to alert us to the fact that we need to repair the damage we have caused by our wrong actions or words; to signal that we need to change our behaviour.

If we have done something of which we are not proud, which we know has hurt another, then we must apologise and make amends to that person. This is especially so if the person to whom we have done wrong is our baby or child. Children respond exceptionally well when a parent admits her behaviour was less than caring. They forgive readily because they want to be able to trust their parents and, in that trust, to feel safe and secure. Children have an innate sense of basic right and wrong[50] so when a parent habitually cannot or will not admit to her mistakes or imperfect behaviour, her child will feel she cannot trust her.

Guilt is not meant to drive us to unrealistic heights of perfectionism. It is not meant to make us feel bad every time something outside our control goes less than well. We are not given this emotion so we can worry eternally about what might go wrong and whether it will be our fault. It is given to us only as a signpost towards becoming better people.

True maturity, it is said, lies in knowing what one can and cannot fix, having the courage to act on the former and the wisdom to leave the latter alone. Feeling guilty for what was not one's fault and for that which one cannot rectify, is a monumental waste of emotional energy. Be wise enough to know that there is no chance of ever being a perfect parent. Have the courage to admit your shortcomings, make amends and learn how to do it better next time.

Responsibility in Moderation

Being overly responsible is detrimental to your health. It keeps you on guard and in a state of tension when you could otherwise be nurturing your own need

---

50 Frans de Waal, 'Good Natured: The Origins of Right and Wrong in Humans' as quoted in the *Sydney Morning Herald*, Sydney, 24.2.96

to let down. Women become exhausted because they try to be responsible for everyone else's wellbeing without equally looking after their own.

Do not try to mother in isolation; do share it around. Your child will be all the healthier psychologically if he learns, early on in life, that other people have different ways of coping with the world and that these ways are as valid as his parents'. His exposure to other caring adults and their different routines and expectations will expand both his world and yours.

Feeling one has to be responsible for every nook and cranny of a family's existence robs the other members of the family of their ability, and their right, to take responsibility for themselves. Even very small children feel empowered when their all-powerful parents entrust them with responsibility for clearly defined areas of their lives. And if children are capable of taking their share of this load, so too is your fully grown partner. Let him. If you can make yourself stand aside, he will often alter his behaviour surprisingly quickly.

The longer a woman goes on taking responsibility for all members of her family, the longer it will take to wean them all off it. In the long run you do nobody any favours by doing for them what they could and should be doing for themselves.

Fear Fades

Unless a new mother has been accustomed to being around babies, she is unlikely to be prepared for the absolute vulnerability of a newborn baby—especially her own. Be prepared for your fears to change as your baby becomes a toddler, goes to school, becomes a teenager. The early fear of sudden death gives way to fear of accidents, cars, drugs, as your child moves further and further out of your control. Perhaps you will become less obsessed with the fear, but it will, most likely, never completely go away.

Fear of your own mortality or that of your partner will pass as you see your child growing more independent of you. The older she gets, the less likely it is you will be concerned about her being left motherless or fatherless.

If you fear you will damage your baby or child by being less than perfect yourself, know that babies bring with them their own agendas, their own lessons to learn and their own way of relating to external circumstances. Not everything you do will suit your child—an absolutely normal fact of life. Nor can you protect your child from every hurt in life, no matter how much you would like to. What counts above and beyond anything you could engineer for her is your love for her.

Again, should your fear of hurting your baby begin to feel as though it may become a reality, seek professional help before it does. There is no shame in admitting to the fear that can compare with the shame of actually hurting a baby.

Empathy is Such a Bonus

Notice how your empathy for others blossoms once you become a mother. Actively develop it. It has been shown that a child brought up in an empathic household will go on to develop empathic relationships. The reverse also holds true.[51]

As a mother, a woman's first task is to get to know what her baby wants by the way it behaves. The more empathic she is, the sooner she will understand him; the less empathic she is, the more likely it is she will blame the baby for being dissatisfied. Your baby comes into this world with an in-built ability to empathise at a crude level. He soon learns to gauge your state of mind and how to modify his behaviour in order to get what he wants from you. If crying works, he cries. If rage works, he rages. If laughter works, he laughs. If all his best efforts to get his needs met are rewarded only with let-down or exasperation, he soon learns to give up—or rebel.

Empathy begins as a survival mechanism and, given the right conditions, evolves into an ability to understand the world in which another person lives. When in empathy, a person cannot judge, blame or harm others for they know intimately what impact those actions will have. They feel another's pain. Conversely, when one is capable of being in empathy with someone who has succeeded or who is overjoyed by a life event, one gets to experience the other's feelings of success and joy as though they were one's own. There is no need to feel jealous or belittled by another person's success since one is able to experience what their success means for them. If every person in this world was capable of bringing themselves into empathy with other people, there could be no crime, no war.

So when you find yourself crying over the television ads, angering over the state of the world, hurting over someone else's hurt, know that this is part of the pins and needles of re-emerging emotional intelligence in its highest form. Know that you will automatically pass this talent on to your children and, in so doing, make a valuable contribution to the betterment of the world.

51 D. Goleman, *op.cit.*, p.192

Personal Growth

It is not easy to know when your actions and reactions are irrational or being driven by internal, unresolved pain. One way is to try to objectively look and see whether others are treating you in a less than supportive manner. A single incident or a single person undermining you may not indicate personal issues are on the rise, but a pattern of others doing so may. If you begin to believe that your baby is deliberately trying to thwart your best efforts at motherhood it is almost certain your own issues are getting in the way of seeing the picture clearly. A rigid need to control and achieve unrealistic goals can also be an indicator of unresolved issues nudging to be noticed.

One of the best ways to begin to resolve these aches and pains of your past life is to begin to talk at a real level with other mothers. Find out if they are experiencing similar concerns. If they are you are probably within the 'normal' spectrum. If they are not, listen to their suggestions as to how you may deal with the situation and give it a go. A surefire symptom of old issues arising is when you hear all the suggestions as to how to better deal with a particular experience and you refuse to give up your old ways of doing things.

Should you continue to feel uncomfortable or angry or upset even though you have tried every strategy offered it is probably time to consult a counsellor. Becoming a mother is one of the fastest pathways to personal growth and although this can be painful in the beginning the rewards of reclaiming lost pieces of yourself are immeasurable in the long term.

Grief is Part of Motherhood

Allow yourself to grieve for the loss of your old self. The grieving will go on with or without your conscious consent anyway, but to hold it inside is to create a stress you do not need at this time. Because you grieve for your old self does not mean you love your baby any the less. It is simply acknowledging a very real loss.

Ceremonially say goodbye to your old self in order to welcome the new you. There is no shame in articulating regrets or talking about the things you miss about the person you used to be. Write a list of all the things you feel you have lost in becoming a mother—and then write all you have gained—your emotions, empathy, strength, endurance and, not least of all, your baby. Honour the strengths of the pre-mother woman you used to be and which you now bring to motherhood. Rest assured that many of the losses of motherhood which appear to be so permanent are only temporary and that grief will pass as the losses are gradually replaced by the gifts of motherhood.

Stress and Depression are More Common Than You Think

If, a few days or so after giving birth to your baby, you find yourself howling huge tears which plop onto her head as you feed her, it could be an upwelling of the grief I have just spoken about. The medical profession calls it the 'baby blues'. It is considered 'normal', it does pass very quickly and it is not an indication that you are likely to reject your baby or fail as a mother. The blues will only last a few days.

Stress and depression affect up to 88% of women at some time after giving birth to a baby—not necessarily immediately, nor after their first baby. So if you are feeling depressed or severely stressed, far from being a freak, you are in the majority.

There are three major steps to curing depression and the first one is the hardest:

- Acknowledge to yourself that you are stressed or depressed and take it seriously. Do not try to brush it aside, explain it away, feel guilty or put yourself down for it.
- Talk about it. If your partner is a sympathetic listener explain to him that you just need to talk and that you do not expect him to solve your depression for you. If he is unable to help you, talk to friends and other mothers.
- Get help. Join a PND support group where you will find you are not alone. Ask your doctor for advice. See a counsellor or a psychologist or a family therapist.

The single biggest mistake depressed mothers make is to try to ride it out alone without telling anyone how they feel. They tend to think there is something wrong with them, that they will be judged inadequate if they admit to this 'weakness' of character; that tomorrow will be different. If all the tomorrows for two weeks have not been any different, then you need help.

If you will not seek help for yourself, do it for your baby. Babies need unconditional love. A depressed person cannot give unconditional anything because they are so overloaded with simple, day-to-day coping. Babies also absorb the emotions of those around them as though they were their own. There is more than a little evidence that children who grow up with a depressed mother have a much higher risk of succumbing to depression in their teens and adulthood.[52] This is not to make any woman feel guilty about her depression—it is to encourage her to seek help for both her own sake and that of her baby. Few women would knowingly feed poisoned food to their babies. Similarly, if they knew that their unacknowledged and untreated depression was an emotional pollutant they might develop the courage to seek its cure before serious damage is done.

It is interesting to note that anthropologist Buck Schieffelin tried to find evidence of depression among the Kaluli, Stone Age tribesmen who live in Papua New Guinea. He found none. It seems the community so strongly nurtures its individuals there is no possibility of one person feeling isolated or helpless and, therefore, depressed.[53] It is equally interesting to note that in a country where this level of community support is considerably diminished, it is the sufferer of depression who is considered to be out of step and in need of 'treatment'. Perhaps women who express the symptoms of postnatal depression are expressing the symptoms of an ill society rather than those of an ill individual.

Unfortunately, society is not likely to admit to its own illness, so each woman who suffers from depression will need to find her own cure. Fortunately it is curable. In most cases it tends to go away of its own accord when some semblance of control returns to a woman's life or when she faces, and deals with, the issues causing it. If depression is debilitating, drugs may be prescribed to break the negative mental cycle. Most often what is needed is support, encouragement, sleep and a few new coping mechanisms.

To not acknowledge or speak about your depression is to compound the problem. It also adds to the lie that only bad women and bad mothers find mothering hard. You are not weak because you have grown depressed. In fact, you are in the process of becoming stronger than you have ever been in your life. Do not waste precious months or years of motherhood lost in this awful and insidious suffering. Get help fast.

Post Traumatic Stress Needs Treatment

Although many of the symptoms of stress, depression and post traumatic stress are similar, PTSD, in this context, is characterised by flashbacks, either to the

---

[52] M.E.P. Seligman, *op.cit.*, p.128
[53] M.E.P. Seligman, *op.cit.*, p.286

birth experience itself or to a previous violent episode, which may cause a woman to enter an unreal and terrifying world. If this happens to you, do not try to cope alone. You need to talk out the circumstances of your trauma, so find a therapist who specialises in it as soon as you can. There is no way a woman can adequately care for her baby if she is being terrorised by her inner demons—no matter how she acquired them.

Nothing Compares with the Love

Whatever you do, if you find your love for your baby is wonderful beyond your wildest imaginings, spread it around. Never feel embarrassed about your feelings and never, ever feel you should hide them. There is too little love in the world as it is. Mothers have a gaping window of opportunity to redress this imbalance. Imagine if all the world loved as deeply as a mother is capable of loving her baby.

A word of warning. Realise that most other mothers feel just as strongly about their children as you do about yours. Do not fall into the trap of believing yours to be the quintessentially fabulous child. Give other mothers the space to tell you how great their children are and do not try to one-up them with stories of how much better yours are. All children, in their own mother's world, are the most wonderful.

FIVE
A MOTHER'S RELATIONSHIP WITH HER PARTNER

- Approximately half the women surveyed expected their relationship with their partner to alter after the birth of their first child yet not one person said it was easy or not a problem
- 85% reported an impact on coping; 52% severe to extreme
- 69% experienced intrapersonal conflict; 48% severe to extreme
- 73% engaged in interpersonal conflict; 44% severe to extreme
- 17% stated that becoming parents had been a direct cause of their relationships coming to an end

Simplistically speaking, the majority of women are not only genetically but hormonally programmed before birth to detect and understand emotions, to value and develop relationships and to be able to see the big picture without losing sight of what this means in terms of day-to-day living. A man's prenatal programming, on the other hand, causes him to compete for status via his ability to control and manipulate objects and the environment.[54] Clearly both talents are essential for the survival of the species, yet in our society males' strengths are honoured whilst females' are deemed to be inferior.

---

[54] A. Moir & D. Jessel, *op.cit.*, pp.144–145

When a woman becomes a mother, therefore, she may be shocked to her core to find she has entered a valueless vacuum wherein everything she does, says, thinks, feels and believes suddenly carries less weight than it did when she was living by and accepting the value system of the doing paradigm. The first and most obvious relationship to feel the impact of this abrupt shift from honouring the doing paradigm to living in and needing to understand and honour the one of relating, is that with her partner.

It is almost taboo to suggest that the arrival of the first child in a family may cause the relationship to be put under the extremes of stress that the figures from this study would suggest. Thus women (and men) enter parenthood completely unprepared for this likelihood, with few, if any, contingency plans in place to help them cope. The enormity of the anguish this causes cannot be understated. Glenda wrote:

> The immense joy and fulfilment I felt as a mother in Sonya's first year of life by far outweighed the heartache I was enduring in my marriage. She remains the only warmth around my soul.

This letter was written to me when Glenda's daughter was almost five years old. She had finally separated from her husband when their child was three and her feelings are by no means unusual, as the following finding shows:

> Four out of five marriages go through a severe crisis at the birth of the first child. All the literature suggests that once the novelty factor of the new child has worn off, the father tends, to a greater or lesser extent, to resent the newcomer.[55]

During each of the discussion forums this problem of relationship to one's partner arose continually and it would be fair to say that husbands and partners took something of a beating. The following is by no means a complete list of problems which can arise between parents during their first few years of parenthood but they are the most commonly cited areas of difficulty.

---

55 A. Moir & D. Jessel, *op.cit.*, 1989, p.143

WOMEN CHANGE

I spent my twenties in a relationship with a man who had had a family and did not want to go through it again. When I raised the subject of children his response was always to say that having a baby changed a woman so completely he was not prepared to go through the experience again. At the time I, a non-mother, did not understand. Now I do.

Women today believe that having a baby is just another experience to be had. They do not appreciate that it will irrevocably and forever alter their lives, their priorities, their identities. They do not comprehend that the woman to whom their partner originally committed himself will become a new being after the birth of her first child. Her partner will have to learn to adjust to this new creature in his life. Most women agreed with Anna that:

> Men also need help with the changes. They lose their wives, get dumped with the extra responsibility without the benefit of having grown the baby inside them.

Prior to baby a man may have come home to a woman whom he could expect to be rational, together, a person with whom he could have a civilised conversation and dinner. After the baby's arrival he may instead find he comes home to a gibbering wreck who shoves a screaming baby into his arms, who yells at him for having forgotten to pick up the milk and then throws herself sobbing onto the bed for no apparent reason. Marilyn admits to having been horribly unpredictable.

> My husband never knew who he was going to come home to—the lunatic or the lover.

Because women bear the brunt of the life changes brought about by the birth of their children, they may slip into survival mode where little else matters to them other than getting through the day. They can become self-absorbed even whilst expending heroic amounts of energy in tending to the needs of everyone else, and ploughing through mundane household chores that are no sooner complete than they need doing yet again. Many find it difficult to understand that their partners are just as likely as they to be in shock or that a man deals with these life changes very differently.

SECURITY

- The unfulfilled need for security contributed to 15% of women surveyed and interviewed leaving the fathers of their children
- 30% said that, in spite of living in a relationship which was of a significantly lesser quality than the one they would choose if they had their time over, they felt their need for security outweighed the need for a more intimate relationship and stayed with the father of their child for this reason

The need for security comes as a surprise to many women, particularly those who have wandered the globe, who have never considered owning a home to be important or who have been content to live day to day without concern for their future—financial or otherwise. As their pregnancy draws closer to the date of birth they sometimes find themselves needing to put down roots, to create a beautiful, safe nursery for their baby, to ensure they are able to provide for their baby's needs and comforts. Linda was one who did not expect this reaction to motherhood.

> I did not anticipate I would want the sort of security I would want once I had a child. Prior to Emily's birth it had not been a huge issue. This was a big change. The level of my security needs surprised me and I became obsessive about it. Security meant having a house of my own, an income in keeping with having a child. It was bizarre and overwhelming. We had a lot of conflict over it in the first twelve months.

Living in a home which is too cold, too hot, too inconvenient, too hard to keep clean, too far from social activity, too expensive to be maintained on a diminished income can all impact upon a woman's feelings of insecurity. At the very time she most wants to build her 'nest' a woman may decide that the circumstances in which she lives are not adequate for her baby. She decides to move house quite unprepared for the distress this upheaval will cause her. Sandra, who had lived in several foreign countries and thought nothing of changing cultures, let alone houses, found it deeply distressing when she had to move again after her daughter was born. She said:

I recognised my need for stability and my aversion to moving only after Bettina was born.

This desire to put down roots and establish financial security, at least in the early years of motherhood, can cause real difficulty for women who find themselves unable to create these circumstances. If she is unable to articulate her fears clearly or if her partner is less than understanding and sympathetic to her needs, the new mother may find herself becoming tetchy and prickly towards him. He, believing he is doing the best he can to provide security, may view her as having become neurotic as a result of motherhood. If he continues to deny or refuses to take her need seriously their conflict can grow to such proportions as to cause them to separate, perhaps permanently.

Many women stay in relationships which become ever more destructive because they believe they could not provide the same level of security for their children as their partners can. It has to be said, however, that in surviving the early years of parenting, provided they do not destroy the relationship in the process, many couples do ultimately grow closer together for having lived through and overcome those obstacles.

DEPENDENCY

- 63% of women surveyed did not expect dependency to affect them
- 70% reported an impact on coping; 47% severe to extreme
- 61% experienced intrapersonal conflict; 40% severe to extreme
- 57% engaged in interpersonal conflict; 40% severe to extreme

Most women expect to become dependent upon their partners, or others, to a certain extent when they have their first baby. The surprise comes when the new mother realises that her world has shrunk to husband, home and baby and that her dependency is far more profound than she had imagined. We all tend to take for granted the emotional, mental and spiritual support we derive from interaction with our friends and workmates. Like most things we take for granted, we do not know that we value them until they are gone. Only then do we find that life can be very difficult without them.

Financial Dependency

The loss of an independent income was felt keenly by almost every woman who participated in this book. Although it is obvious that a couple's combined income will drop significantly when a woman gives up work to become a mother, it is less obvious that she will feel dependent and experience this as limiting, demeaning and claustrophobic. As Mandy found, it can be a huge issue:

> This is really big and I am still working on it five years later. I tend to blame my husband, asking why he can't earn money like I could. My attitude is you earn it, you enjoy it, you spend it. He is more conservative and more stressed by money. It's a big issue.

When a woman ceases to contribute to the income of the household it is common for her partner to assume a significantly greater proportion of the responsibility for the distribution of (his) income. The more a man earns, the more family power he wields. When money is available the woman often feels that she must get permission to spend anything on herself and may go without in order to buy for her child. There is a tendency for both the wage earner and the mother, either overtly stated or covertly implied, to believe that she must earn the right to utilise money for her sole benefit and that he who earns has the right to dictate those terms.[56] Catrina confirmed this dynamic:

> When I need a new anything I have to make do for years because we cannot afford it but let him need something expensive for the boat and we can afford it immediately.

With only a few exceptions, most women felt uncomfortable spending money on themselves if they were not earning. Yet nearly all noted that their husbands did not seem to suffer from this restriction. Anna, whose oldest child is fourteen, revealed:

> I bought stuff without his approval a week ago for the first time. Yet my husband went out and bought a $1,000 TV for Christmas when I thought he was buying a cheap second TV.

56 D. Richardson, *op.cit.*, p.25

A MOTHER'S RELATIONSHIP WITH HER PARTNER

Of all the women interviewed and surveyed for this book, a significant minority—13%—had neither a joint account with their spouse nor access to his bank accounts nor an account of their own. This is in spite of the fact that all had owned their own properties and cars prior to marrying and had contributed these assets to the combined assets of the marriage. Sally's experience is repeated all too often.

> I owned a car and a house with almost no mortgage on it when I married. I earned a huge salary. Now I find myself constantly having to justify why I spend $X on a birthday present for a member of my family and fighting for the right to do so.

Whether or not a woman is able to access her own or joint accounts, many women must ask for or justify their need for money even to do the weekly shopping. Financial dependency contributes to a woman's sense of being trapped in the role of mother and devalued as a person. Charmaine said:

> I feel very dependent. I hate holding out my hand for money.

Physical Dependency

The majority of women understand that they will require help with the physical aspects of running a house such as cleaning, cooking, shopping, etcetera during the weeks after the baby is born. Few realise that exhaustion may force her to need this support for, perhaps, years. When once this woman was able to do for herself she now finds herself pleading with her partner to help with the most mundane of tasks. If he does help she may be grateful but she may also feel inadequate in his presence, believing that she 'should' be able to cope on her own. If he does not help or does the job half-heartedly she may develop feelings of ill-will towards him.

Mental Dependency

Prior to the birth of the first baby a woman may read a book a week or the newspaper cover to cover every Saturday. She may have enjoyed the cut and thrust of deep and meaningful conversations. Her work may have offered mental challenges and stimulation. She may have been studying.

Post-baby she reads two paragraphs of the *Women's Weekly*'s Christopher Green column on the toilet once a week. She peers momentarily over her partner's shoulder at the paper and tries to get him to tell her the world's affairs in one minute or less. Conversations disappear. Paid work and study may have ceased. Because of a new mother's isolation neither her peers in the workplace nor her friends are available to provide mental stimulation. No matter how much we love our babies, their ability to stretch our mental capacities in the directions we would otherwise choose will not be in place for years. Thus a new mother becomes dependent upon her partner for affirmation of her mental capacities. It is asking a lot of a partner that he fill the gap left by study, work, colleagues and friends.

Emotional Dependency
Hormonal readjustment, exhaustion, stress, loneliness, isolation, relentless and tedious work, not to mention the enormous redefinition of her identity, combine to throw the emotions of a new mother into chaos until she can begin to feel as though she is going crazy. Under these circumstances it is imperative that she receive emotional support from her partner. To the extent that he is able to do so in an empathic and non-judgemental manner, the sooner the new mother will be able to begin to rebalance her emotions. To the extent that he cannot, but rather is critical of her, she is likely to feel as though her emotions are out of control for a more prolonged period of time. Sometimes this can go on for years.

When a woman spends her every day with a child she gives of herself emotionally almost constantly. Without a community to turn to she can draw this support from her only source of replenishment—her partner. If he values her and her role as a mother then he will fulfil her emotional well. If he does not she will soon find herself emotionally depleted, feeling worthless and struggling to retain her sense of identity.

Spiritual Dependency
It is easy, if a woman is so inclined, to be spiritual when she has time to read, discuss, meditate or pray, participate in courses which will encourage her personal growth or regularly attend church, free of interruptions. During these times she is able to feel as though she is growing as a person and integrating, accepting the pluses and minuses of who she is. However, when the new mother has not an uninterrupted minute to herself she can come to feel as though she has not only ceased to grow as a human being, but slipped further back into a spiritual void than at any time in her memory.

A MOTHER'S RELATIONSHIP WITH HER PARTNER

Then she turns, again, to her partner for support. Women who receive unconditional support from their partners report feeling neither diminished nor depressed by motherhood and tend to be astonished to find any mother feels thus. The quality of her partner's ability to value her appears to be of paramount importance to how a woman feels about herself when she becomes a mother.

Pauline did not find the transition to parenthood an easy one, but how much harder might it have been if her husband had been unable to support her? She wrote:

> Parenthood has been an enormous strain for both of us in every way but I could not have managed without my husband who was exceptionally supportive in every way—he held the whole family together, gave endless love and understanding to me and the boys.

MEN CHANGE

The father of a newborn baby may discover that his socialisation has primed him to be overly responsible in an almost panic reaction to the realisation that the wellbeing of this mother and this child—his child—rests solely upon his shoulders. Many are frightened by the prospect of not being able to adequately care and provide for these new beings. Never before has he seen his woman so vulnerable. Never before has she been dependent and it seems the baby's entire future rests upon his shoulders. It is not unusual for a father to extend his existing work hours, change to a more demanding, better paid job or take on a second job in the first year of his first child's life. In so doing he feels that he is contributing, at great cost to himself, to his family's wellbeing. Therefore, when his wife criticises him for not doing enough for the baby and around the house he is both mystified and hurt.[57] This was Margaret's experience of early parenthood:

> I had all these expectations of having a lovely baby and family but it separated us. He thought he had to go off and work harder.

At the very time a new mother craves his physical and emotional support and his company the father often moves further away for longer periods of time

---

[57] J. Belsky & J. Kelly, *The Transition to Parenthood*, New York, 1994, p.135

arriving home tired, full of his own day, certain of his importance and the importance of his work. He cannot comprehend that 'just' looking after a baby all day could possibly be so hard. The fact is, that for all the talk about fatherhood having altered, evidence says that the father in the late twentieth century is technically present but functionally absent; the actual man hours spent in the care of his children have not changed.[58]

In researching this book, however, it has become abundantly clear that men also suffer from postnatal stress and depression in significant numbers. Nobody tells them, either, what fatherhood will mean for them as people. Most recently written books on motherhood and parenting mention the possibility that a man may feel threatened by suddenly having to be the provider for a growing family. Some even note that men have a tendency to withdraw from their partners and new babies. Few acknowledge postnatal depression in men. Although a great deal more research needs to be undertaken, the following list of symptoms are indicators that a new father may be suffering PNS/D:

- Feeling trapped
- Agitation, irritability
- Excessive worrying
- Constant tiredness
- Inability to bond with the baby
- Feelings of rejection by his partner
- A sense of deep loss and grief
- Withdrawal into work, hobbies, external interests
- Overworking
- Panicky feelings
- Feeling useless or superfluous around the baby and his partner
- Resenting the baby
- Feelings of guilt
- Aggression towards his partner and/or the baby
- Obsessions
- Feeling inadequate
- Overwhelmed by responsibility

---

58 K.M. Baber & K.R. Allen, *Women and Families*, New York, pp.170–171

A MOTHER'S RELATIONSHIP WITH HER PARTNER

Put together a woman who is in shock over the unexpected changes a first baby brings to her life and a man who is equally in shock over the unexpected changes to his and there is a recipe for disaster. The deeper a person is immersed in shock, postnatal stress or postnatal depression the less their ability is to empathise with another's predicament and the greater is their need for support. With neither side able to give this support and both so desperately in need of it (and with little or no outside help available) it is no surprise so many relationships become strained and even tear apart during the early years of parenthood.

SELFISHNESS

Many women felt that their partners became more selfish once the baby was born. Since men are as oblivious to the changes brought about by having a baby as are women, they apparently are quite unprepared for the fact that their women folk will become baby-centred rather than man-centred for some considerable time. Charmaine showed her bitterness when she told me:

> The hardest thing to overcome for me is the husband problem. He is selfish. It is the hardest thing to cope with a husband who still expects to come first. His attitude seems to be that he is bringing in the dollars so he deserves to be number one.

When her partner returns to the home at the end of a day's paid work, often the new mother's overriding need is for him to take the baby so she can disengage from the role of mother for a moment.[59] The second thing she wants her partner to do is to validate her as a woman, reconnect her with the 'world out there', reassure her that she is still a part of it. If he is empathic and supportive he will meet her needs. If he is not or if his day has also been stressful he is as likely to want to withdraw. She may feel that his lack of appreciation of her work devalues her and so judges that her discomfort is caused by her partner's self-focus and preoccupation with his own wants and needs.[60]

It was a common complaint that many husbands seem to think new mothers have all the time in the world to organise the household simply because they

---

[59] A. Rich, *op.cit.*, p.23
[60] J. Belsky & J. Kelly, *op.cit.*, p.40

are no longer in paid work. Thus, rather than pitching in with additional help, many men withdraw support and the male/female roles become more polarised. She finds herself gradually picking up more of the household duties as well as caring for the baby's needs, her partner's needs, and her own. Meanwhile, he actually contributes less and less in these areas until he is taking responsibility for his personal concerns only. Christine recognised this scenario, saying:

> It took me years—like until the kids went to school—to get around to realising that I had to get my husband organised. Now I just tell him what he has to do.

Because women tend to assume that their men are able to see what needs to be done and to feel they ought to volunteer assistance without having to be asked, they will often say nothing about these imbalances until their load grows too heavy to bear. When they do finally speak up and object their men are often surprised—and the women are just as often astonished that the men simply did not notice the lopsided division of labour.

LACK OF EMPATHY

Underlying a great many complaints about partners was the lack of empathy they displayed for the new mother's situation and feelings. Sandra wrote:

> At my last therapy session I'd been trying to describe how I felt after the birth: alone, vulnerable, abandoned, devastated, lost, suicidal—you know, about as bad as a human being can feel—and that my husband just didn't seem to be there for me. And my therapist said simply, 'Yes, lots of women complain that their male partners lack empathy.' Something in my brain went 'click' and I thought, so he's not totally blind and he doesn't deliberately misunderstand just to make me feel bad! And I felt much better about him because empathy is something he can be encouraged to learn

Some men, not all by any means, seem to think that having a baby has little to do with them and that they have no vital role to play. Rather, they expect their lives to go on unaltered while their women take responsibility for all the parenting, meeting the baby's needs and running the household, even if they

A MOTHER'S RELATIONSHIP WITH HER PARTNER

have returned to paid work. Often women interpret these actions as uncaring and feel rejected by their partners. Christine did.

> My husband doesn't realise what it is like. He went on a cattle buying trip the day I arrived home with our first baby. I felt rejected and that the baby had been rejected.

Linda was having her first child at the age of thirty-three and lived over 100 kilometres from the hospital into which she was booked to give birth. She said:

> It was a major inconvenience having Emily because it was March and they wanted to buy bulls. I was anxious—how was I going to get to the hospital? The attitude was, what was wrong with me? Why was I so upset about this?

It seems to a person who is not vitally involved in the nitty-gritty of caring for a baby that the job ought not to be difficult. A woman's partner who goes out to work does not see the constant demands placed on her all day long and throughout the night. Even if he does participate during the evenings and weekends, he always knows that he will escape back to work the following day or week. Without making a conscious effort to do so he may never understand what the new mother is going through. Martha said:

> Men can't imagine or understand that bone tiredness or what it is like to have your body pulled out of shape.

Perhaps a partner can only understand the unrelenting drag on a woman's psyche when he becomes a divorced father, thus having sole custody of his children on the weekends, holidays or as is increasingly happening, full-time. As one satellite father said to me of his five-year-old daughter, and with heartfelt conviction:

> I could not look after her every day. That would have to be the hardest job. I don't know how women do it.

This particular man said he would be a very different husband today if he remarried and had another child. Primarily, he would come home, assess the situation and be prepared to take the baby, allowing the mother some real time out regardless of how hard he felt his day had been.

COMMUNICATION

- 54% of women surveyed did expect communication with their partners to alter
- 74% reported an impact on coping; 39% severe to extreme
- 55% experienced intrapersonal conflict; 36% severe to extreme
- 56% engaged in interpersonal conflict; 32% severe to extreme

It has been shown that conversation between husbands and wives declines by as much as 50% after the baby arrives.[61] Significantly it has also been shown that 50% of marriages decline in quality after a baby's arrival and yet the most common of expectations is exactly the opposite, that is, that the birth of their child will draw the parents closer together, bond them as a family with a common interest and a common future.[62] Mandy acknowledged:

> You need time alone with your partner, time to sit down and talk about what each is feeling and what they are going through. We have no communication. Usually it is me who feels it and says something, not him.

A woman's way of interacting is to talk and to listen. When that is taken away she feels depleted and finds it difficult to work out the validity of her needs and concerns. Pam finds it difficult to rise above the interruptions.

> I try to talk to my husband but the kids always interrupt and I always wind up screaming at them. Then I give up and won't try anymore.

An American study by Hite discovered that 98% of women want their men to talk to them more but 84% say their men do not seem to hear them, or want to hear them.[63] Not surprisingly she writes:

---

[61] S. Kitzinger, *Ourselves as Mothers*, Toronto, 1992, p.193
[62] J. Belsky & J. Kelly, *op.cit.*, p.6
[63] Shere Hite, *Women and Love ... The New Hite Report*, London, 1988 pp.5 and 13

A MOTHER'S RELATIONSHIP WITH HER PARTNER

> Eighty-three per cent of women say they initiate most deep talks—and try very hard to draw their men out ... Sixty-three per cent of women meet with great resistance when they try to push their husband or lover to talk about feelings [and] only 17% ... say the communication in their relationship is good, makes them happy, adds to their life.[64]

Some women find they are too tired to want to talk even if their partner does, especially if their baby or toddler has been particularly noisy or demanding all day long. Come the end of the day when the baby is asleep a mother may want nothing more than to sit and relax into blissful silence alone in her own head to complete whole thoughts. This situation Marilyn recognises all too well.

> I don't want to talk at the end of the day, even to my husband. I have been answering questions all day. I have given of myself all day and now someone else wants a piece of me.

If the relationship was already shaky or has been seriously shaken by the introduction of a baby to the household, a woman may find that she has little to say to her husband that is positive. He may be so shocked at the changes to his life and wife that he says nothing, believing he will only make matters worse. So neither of them talks and, as Sandra found, this is sad. She wrote:

> I am haunted by the spectre of the nagging or complaining wife—it was definitely not OK for women to say anything negative in my family. But still, in those early months, I would try as hard as I was able at the time, to tell him how I felt ... and that it was very important to me to talk ... he just didn't seem to understand. It puzzled and saddened me that I couldn't get support from the only source available at the time.

In almost any situation the lower the level of communication between people the lower will be their ability to understand and empathise with each other's different life focus and to support each other in those circumstances. Communication between new parents is vital to the wellbeing of their relationship. Time for uninterrupted conversation needs to hold a high level priority or intimacy soon fades.

[64] S. Hite, *op.cit.*, pp.6–10

INTIMACY

- 49% of women surveyed expected intimacy between partners to be affected
- 76% reported an impact on coping; 42% severe to extreme
- 63% experienced intrapersonal conflict; 39% severe to extreme
- 63% engaged in interpersonal conflict; 43% severe to extreme

A reversion to traditional roles can drive a wedge between a couple surprisingly quickly. The resultant loss of intimacy in their relationships is most distressing to women and most unexpected. As Nancy said:

> When the baby comes along the honeymoon period is definitely over!

It takes a conscious effort to maintain intimacy after the arrival of children in the household, which is impossible if neither parent realises it is in jeopardy. Like exhaustion, the death of intimacy does not happen on any one day so a couple can look back and pin-point the exact moment they became isolated within their marriage. It wears away over the weeks and months of limited emotional contact. By the time they realise that something valuable has gone from their relationship neither can recall what it is they have lost and they begin to wonder what they ever saw in each other.

Sarah realised early in her mothering career:

> You can get so tied down, so wrapped up in the children that there is no spontaneous love between husband and wife. There needs to be a consciousness of that. We need to give each other treats and rewards.

Those who had maintained intimacy in their relationships said they had had to work hard to do so. Some had made a conscious decision to separate children's and adults' meal times. Others regularly set aside time to be together without the children.

However, only two women reported having taken a weekend away without their children in the first four or five years of parenthood. It could be that Charmaine's reaction to the opportunity for time with her husband may be more common than is generally thought.

> If we had a weekend away he would think it was just for sex so it would be no holiday for me. I would like a weekend away to hold hands ONLY! Just to lie there without the kids jumping all over us.

How a couple are going to maintain intimacy needs to be discussed before the birth of their first child so that coping mechanisms are in place before the stress of parenthood is allowed to damage the relationship. Once the downward spiral of emotional distance has set in, each partner's feeling of alienation grows. Unless a conscious effort is made to rebuild intimacy in this new world of parenthood the point of no return is reached and the relationship grinds to a halt.

SEX

- 65% of women surveyed did not expect their sex lives to alter after having their first baby
- 69% reported an impact on coping; 41% severe to extreme
- 53% experienced intrapersonal conflict; 30% severe to extreme
- 63% engaged in interpersonal conflict; 37% severe to extreme

One area in which a new mother's partner may find it difficult to be empathic is that of lovemaking. Often she experiences a marked decrease in her image of herself as a sexually attractive woman.

On average the sex life of new parents drops between 30% and 40% in the first year of their baby's life.[65] For the new mother exhaustion is a major contributing factor as it saps her energy for anything other than sheer survival. It is difficult to feel sexy when breasts are sore and leaking milk, when the stomach has wilfully refused to return to its pre-baby tautness, when she knows full well that every moment spent in pleasuring her partner is a moment during which she cannot sleep before being woken, yet again.

Often the new mother's total absorption in the baby supplants all thoughts of sex. Having cradled, rocked, cuddled baby all day and perhaps half the night as well, breastfeeding on demand every two hours, the last thing she wants is to share her body with anyone. She finds she is in desperate need of reclaiming

---

[65] J. Belsky & J. Kelly, *op.cit.*, p.40

her own body space at a time when her partner may feel that he must compete with the baby for her attention.[66]

Many women approach their first lovemaking after the birth of their babies with trepidation. What if lovemaking has been changed forever? During the discussions with each focus group, sex was a much seized upon subject bringing forth both acrimony and hilarity. Probably the best way to describe the reactions of women to sex after birth is to quote them.

Nikki: I have always had men in my life and sex has always been important to me, but forget it. It's too much like hard work.

Martha: ... you've got to be kidding.

Nancy: It is just one more chore to be faced at the end of the day. I expected my sex life to change but the degree was surprising. I thought, 'I am supposed to be a sex symbol, and look at me!' I thought I would spring back but it takes a while.

Melanie: My husband doing the dishes is the best foreplay I could have.

Jennifer: I would rather have 20 minutes more sleep.

Maureen: I would rather have another bar of chocolate—at least you won't get pregnant again.

Sarah: I thought things would be back on track after six weeks.

Madelaine: The first time I had sex afterwards, I felt like a virgin.

Eileen: I definitely did not feel like a virgin. I was scared he would not want to sleep with me again—especially after watching the birth.

Pauline: I felt holy—like I had a birth canal, and I did not want him to violate that.

---

66 M. Rivka Polatnik, 'Why Men Don't Rear Children' in ed. Joyce Treblicot, *Mothering*, Totowa, 1983, p.35

A MOTHER'S RELATIONSHIP WITH HER PARTNER

Pam: It is something you must do because you are a wife as well as a mother and it is expected. I think, 'Well come on and we will get it over and done with—and then it might be right for another couple of days,' but then it is back again. This will pass as the years go on. I just cannot be spontaneous anymore because they [the children] are there and if we are home alone it is hard to be spontaneous, to really get back into it again. It takes a while to relax.

Christine: I can remember lying stiff in bed right over at the edge of the bed and thinking, 'Oh, don't touch me. I have had kids hanging off me all day. Don't touch me. Can't you just lie still over on your edge of the bed.'

Anna: I think I should just do it and get it over and done with. You want to be good at everything you are doing and then your husband becomes part of that—the sex becomes part of that.

Catrina: I was out to prove that I could do it all. I felt I must not inconvenience him. Life has not changed for my husband except for his sense of responsibility because I took it all on—including the extra sex.

Glenda: I said no—and then I left.

Anna: I wish I had said 'no', because all that time I suffered because I did not want to. I am still really resentful of it.

When a woman is dependent upon her partner she often feels 'morally obliged'[67] to make love on demand regardless of how she feels.

Across the board there was a consensus that what these women most wanted was to be held and cuddled by their men in full trust that no demands would be made on them for sex until they felt ready. It was almost universally felt that if they could be close to their partners, safe in the knowledge that sex would not be the natural progression of physical contact, they would relax more easily, feel warmer towards their partners and perhaps return to more 'normal' sexual relations sooner.

---

67 J. Phillips, *op.cit.*, p.119

Although these discussions brought much hilarity there was also a sense that it was a relief to be able to admit that all was not glorious in the lovemaking department. Unfortunately, because it is such a personal subject it is rare that prospective parents are told this truth.

EQUALITY

Women who reached adulthood in the seventies, eighties and nineties have grown up believing in the equality of women. Although the glass ceiling has been raised considerably during that period, once a woman becomes a mother it may seem to bear down upon her like a ton of bricks. She finds herself thrown quite unexpectedly back to the 1950s, cast in the watertight role of 'mother'. For Terri this was a shock:

> I came into marriage expecting to be an equal partner—and I was.
> Nobody told me though, that once I had a baby I would suddenly
> have only 49% of the vote.

There are women who would consider themselves blessed if they held so high a proportion of the say in controlling their lives once a baby is born to them. Where a woman's expectations are that mother and father are in this together, equally committed to the raising of their child, she finds that he expects her to do 90–95% of the child caring, the extraordinarily increased organisational work, the on-call duty around the clock, all year long, and all the household duties that once her partner may have shared. In short, she finds herself demoted from equal partner to gofer overnight.[68] Judy stated emphatically:

> A man does not take responsibility for the child. The woman does
> whether she goes back to work or studies. She is the one who organises
> the care and takes the child to the carer.

Countless women have regaled me with the story of how their men folk look after the children while they go to shop or to work, only to return to the house to find that it looks as though a bomb has hit it. She casts her eye around realising that every chore that needed doing before she left still needs to be

---

68 J. Belsky & J. Kelly, *op.cit.*, p.135

done—and then some. When she asks in hurt tones what he has been doing all day he, in equally hurt tones, replies, 'I have been looking after the children for you.' Many women feel it is pointless having a day off because all it does is increase their work load when they return home.

Recognition for the job of caring for children is not equally distributed either. There is a persistent tendency to praise a man for helping in the house or for taking care of children whereas a woman is simply expected to do these things with little or no thanks and certainly without complaining. Madelaine observed:

> He gets the praise she should be getting all the time when he says, 'I'll look after the kids for you.' He thinks he is doing me a favour instead of seeing that they are OUR kids and equally his responsibility.

In 1994 there were, according to the Australian Bureau of Statistics, 507,908 single mothers[69] in Australia. Many of them are working; the majority in low-paid jobs. Yet attitudes towards the 111,492 single fathers are, as Maureen pointed out, that:

> If he is a single father AND works he is the greatest thing since sliced bread.

It is considered heroic if a man takes care of his family in any way other than financially, whereas a woman who does it all is not seen to be doing anything special. It is unthinkable that a father should have to juggle his schedule or give up his work to look after his children in the same way a woman is expected to.

POWER

The onset of motherhood can signal an immediate loss of power in a woman's life. Across the spectrum most mothers are so stretched to the limit with their family's demands, school support and/or paid work, that they are unable to stand up for themselves. They are not a united group. They do not have a union or a political party to represent their interests. Their diversity of cultural, social, educational and economic backgrounds, which could be of such strength

---

[69] Chris Masters, 'Other People's Children' in *Four Corners*, ABC Television, 1.4.1996

to them, in fact divides them. Thus it is that each, alone, becomes powerless in a culture which is dominated and evaluated by the dollar. Nikki's outrage was evident when she said:

> Powerlessness equals no money. No matter how much we try to cover it up, money equals power.

The demotion of status within her relationship, extended family and community after a woman becomes a mother can be shocking. It is all the more shocking if, before the birth of her first baby, she was independently in control of a career, had owned her own home and car and was used to making the decisions which affected her life. No woman expects to lose these powers just because she becomes a mother.

Yet, from the moment of birth a new mother seems to become the responsibility of someone else—her partner or, if she is single, her own family or social security. It is as if they believe she can no longer think about and decide for herself what is best for her and her baby. Advice flows in from all sides, most of it less than honestly representing the widespread difficulties of motherhood, leaving her feeling as though she is inadequate. The media presents soft-focus pictures of idealised motherhood which do not often match the reality. All these undermine a woman's belief in her own power and ability to direct her life and to care for her child.

Because many men do not understand the changes a baby will bring to their lives either they can find themselves feeling as though they, also, have been demoted in the family structure and may compete with the baby for their partner's attention. If a power struggle ensues between husband and baby, the woman becomes the meat in the sandwich, powerless to meet both their needs adequately. For example, my own father admitted to me when I was well into my twenties that he had been jealous of me when I was born and that he had found it difficult to forgive me for taking away his wife.

So many women joke about having two babies to care for, not just one, after their first child is born. Many agree that their partner is the more difficult of the two since he is capable of being more demanding and is able to (and does) question her every decision. Some men will punish their wives for giving them less attention after their children are born by withholding affection, support, money and by staying out late. Others do it with verbal, emotional or physical

A MOTHER'S RELATIONSHIP WITH HER PARTNER

abuse. New mothers can become so worn out with over-coping that they do not have the energy to assert their own rights. Charmaine sighed:

> I get so sick of arguing and justifying why I do what I do and want what I want, that I give in.

The birth of a baby has the potential to unleash a power battle between the new parents which neither suspected was on their life agendas. If a balance is not found each will tend to dominate in their own spheres of influence—he in the domain of earnings and expenditure, she in the running of the household and the upbringing of the children. Such traditional polarisation does not necessarily bring about a balance and, as the years go by, can cause deep divisions within the family for which the children ultimately pay the highest price.

ROLES

- 46% of women surveyed did expect to revert to traditional female/male roles
- 77% reported an impact on coping; 52% severe to extreme
- 57% experienced intrapersonal conflict; 43% severe to extreme
- 60% engaged in interpersonal conflict; 44% severe to extreme

Many women realise after the onset of motherhood that equality of the sexes only holds true for women who work and who do not have children. Because the socialisation of men and women today is more subtle than it may have been in the past each gender perceives their roles as parents very differently from the other and yet the myth is that we are equal. The expectations that develop around the idea of parenthood are often subconscious or unclear until the moment a baby is brought home. Only then do they begin to bubble to the surface and crystallise. A couple who thought they knew themselves and each other well can be surprised (and devastated) by their own and their partner's reactions to becoming parents and their expectations of each other in those roles. Margaret described her first marriage:

> There was a lot of blame on either side. He put me into the traditional mother role and I put him in the 'you should be able to feed us' role. It

was a total disaster right from the start. We did not know that until we had this screaming kid and that just really blew things apart. Otherwise we might still be together now.

The arrival of a baby can cause both men and women to suddenly polarise their roles along traditional lines. Women become the caregivers, the nurturers, housekeepers, accepting responsibility for the health of everyone's emotions and relationships. Men become the breadwinners who stoically bear up in the face of nagging wives and screaming kids. In a world where women are increasingly being raised to expect equality with their partners this situation is quite unacceptable. As Charmaine said:

> You have to train men. We make excuses for them. But I get sick of being told that I am whingeing because I want the kitchen to be left clean.

Anna's response to that was:

> Your home is your office so you are entitled to have it as you want.

This puts into perspective a woman's right to ask for what she considers to be the minimum of acceptable working conditions.

ENVY

- 71% of women surveyed did not expect to experience feelings of envy towards their partners
- 67% reported an impact on coping; 41% severe to extreme
- 56% experienced intrapersonal conflict; 42% severe to extreme
- 57% engaged in interpersonal conflict; 29% severe to extreme

The never ending cycle of housework and child care, lack of recognition for a job well done, exhaustion and a sense that one day melts into another with no definitive landmarks can combine to make a woman feel as though life is happening for everyone else but is beginning to pass her by. As a result, for those women who do not take maternity leave but become full-time mothers, it may come as a surprise to find that they grow envious, or even jealous, of

A MOTHER'S RELATIONSHIP WITH HER PARTNER

their partner's continued participation in 'the world out there'. Catrina was one who found this adjustment difficult.

> You have to put your life on hold but your partner never does. My husband has not had to make any major change to his mental and physical lifestyle. He has not had to change his friends or his career whereas I had to stop, have the baby and cope with all of that; plus all the pressure to start a new career; plus society telling us that the mothering years are not valid as a job; plus it is the mother's fault if the children turn out to be neurotic.

When a woman becomes a mother, particularly if she has had a career prior to motherhood, she gives up an enormous slice of her life. Her working peer group ceases to be available to support her and she may find herself feeling envious of their continued freedom, recognition and success. She no longer receives a wage in acknowledgement of a job well done and which guarantees her independence. Her daily routine and expectations are shattered; her body will never be the same again; and in fulfilling the needs of others, she has no time to herself yet may find herself perpetually lonely. Achievement may seem to be a thing of the past; exhaustion scrambles her thinking processes until she wonders if there ever was a time when she was sharp of mind. Every day reduces itself to a battle with the most mundane and boring of household tasks.

More than a few new mothers soon begin to ask themselves, 'What have I done to my life?' They look to their partners' apparently unaltered circumstances, blossoming careers and prospects for a successful future with enviously green eyes and fear for their own futures. The intensity of these feelings may drive a woman to being overly critical of her partner, to under-acknowledge or even denigrate his successes, or to demand more validation of her own worth than might otherwise be reasonably expected. She may experience even mild criticism as proof she is failing in her role of mother and react with either anger or depression, or a redoubling of her efforts to be seen to be coping with and enjoying the role of 'mother'. Unless she is able to admit these feelings, talk them through and work towards a more balanced lifestyle in the future, it is highly likely that she and her partner will increasingly find fault with each other and even engage in destructive conflict.

RAISING THE CHILDREN

Most couples do not discuss how they want to raise their children before they are born, nor their beliefs about what each should contribute as a parent. This can be a significant source of conflict. A representative comment was made by Christine when she said:

> In our family I am overly protective but my husband will let the kids do anything. There is a constant tension between us over it.

Other issues which tend not to be settled before the birth of the first child are: who will do how much; how the parents feel about discipline; baby-sitters; how quickly they will agree to respond to their baby's cries; and how protective they will be. When these have not been discussed and when the parents' expectations are widely differing they are likely to find themselves embroiled in conflict with each other. Nikki gave voice to her fury over the conflicting issues she and her husband have over raising their children.

> He is always criticising the way I raise our kids. He even thinks that I deliberately hurt them when they fall over by themselves. He doesn't trust me and I really resent that.

Parents may discover that their ideas differ widely as to how much respect will be afforded this new person in the household, how much support it will be given, what is expected of the baby itself. Sally was also cross when she said:

> I can't stand the way he always blames our children first and doesn't see that other people's children might be to blame, too. I am afraid for what that is doing to our children's heads for the future.

While childless, it is difficult to comprehend that these matters can become vital once one has experienced the powerful, emotional attachment to and love for a baby. For some new parents, anything which they believe threatens the mental, emotional, spiritual health of their child is completely unacceptable and non-negotiable.

The real difficulty in making agreements on how to raise children before they are born is that none of us really know how parenthood is going to affect us and nobody knows exactly what a particular child will need and demand. This is not to say that there is no value in the parents-to-be discussing these issues. Indeed it is vital if for no other reason than to bring them to the surface and to acknowledge and clarify ideas which may not be apparent or clear, either to themselves or to each other.

THE BRADY BUNCH

When I asked women how long it took for them to feel as though they were a family the answers surprised me. Not one said they felt like a family in the first year of their first child's life. Most decried the fact that there is an unstated expectation that simply because two people produce a child its parents will automatically and immediately feel as though they have created a 'family'. In fact, what often happens is that their relationship is thrown into chaos as both parents struggle to renegotiate their roles and to rebuild their identities. This struggle can be so intense and so traumatic as to destroy the feeling of being a family before it even gets started. Catrina laughed at her pre-mother naivety.

> What I imagined would happen was 'Brady Bunch Quality Time' but that took about ten years.

Some women said they were simply too busy or too exhausted with small children to consider themselves a family. Others had partners who had undertaken additional work as soon as the baby was born. Far from feeling as though they had created a family they felt as though they had been deserted and had lost their relationship altogether.

Because so many relationships deteriorate rather than improve after the birth of the first child, new mothers often find themselves passing through the various stages of grieving for the family which seems to take forever to evolve—or which never eventuates. First, she denies the problems that are pulling her family apart and makes excuses. Second, she grows angry with her partner for not being able to fulfil her expectations and, perhaps, also with the divisive impact the current economic and social structures have on their relationship. Third, she accepts that her family is not going to live up to the 'Brady Bunch' image and she experiences grief, regret or bitterness.

Estimates of how long it had taken to feel like a melded family ranged from two years, to when the second child was born, to five years, to ten years. Some said 'never'. Yet all had expected that the birth of the first child heralded the birth of the family. This expectation often led to disappointment, feelings of failure and additional stress on the relationship.

BREAKDOWN OF COPING MECHANISMS

Once a baby arrives many of the coping mechanisms a couple have developed over the course of their relationship begin to break down. Where differences have been avoided, skirted, managed, denied, ignored, these defences no longer seem to work. Under the stress of declining communication and sexual interaction, emotionalism, reduced social activity and anxieties over money and responsibility they find it difficult to raise the energy or will to resolve this plethora of unexpected conflicts of needs, values and expectations.[70] Margaret's marriage unravelled during early parenthood.

> I felt like Cinderella in the kitchen. My husband was a SNAG on the surface. But he grew up with a single mum who did everything for him so he put me into that role instantly which was a real shock to me because I thought we were going to have this partnership of parenthood. His great statement when I was tearing my hair out was, 'other women cope'.

When the normal coping mechanisms begin to break down all the unsaid accusations, all the unstated and failed expectations and all the unexpressed hurts of the relationship can no longer be contained and held in check. Emma's relationship with her husband broke down, finally, after the birth of their second child. She wrote:

> I guess having children magnified all the flaws in our relationship. I certainly did not expect the jealousy and over-demanding behaviour that came with the stress of a first baby with whom my husband had to compete.

These issues bubble (or explode) to the surface sometimes with the force of a pent up volcano. If the couple are unable to face and deal with them they may be reburied causing additional stress or depression and destructive conflicts.

[70] J. Belsky & J. Kelly, *op.cit.*, p.13

A MOTHER'S RELATIONSHIP WITH HER PARTNER

The ultimate result, if they are not resolved, is the eventual breakdown of the relationship itself.

These conflicts generated by bringing a baby into the home are almost universally unexpected, they are painful in the extreme and because of the dramatic decline in interpersonal contact between the new parents (physically, mentally, emotionally, sexually, spiritually) they are exceedingly difficult to resolve. Nikki admitted:

> I am still trying to figure out how it all works together. I wanted this marriage so badly, but the reality ... I am seeing him in such a different light. Now I could quite happily live in a women's commune and not have anything to do with a man ever again.

When Nikki married her husband after the birth of their first child they had known each other for 18 years and been lovers for six. There was nothing she wanted more than to be this man's wife and to have his children. Until a child is born we tend to believe we know ourselves and each other but often we only know the surface person. As Maureen found:

> I wound up discovering new depths to the person I thought I was and who that person, my partner, really is. I moved him out.

All couples considering having their first child would do well to understand that the 'first year with the first baby is considered the most hazardous for any marriage today'.[71] Martha acknowledged this reality when she said:

> I thought it would bring you closer to have a baby together—but it doesn't. Before, I didn't understand, but now I know why we get divorced.

Parenthood brings with it challenges that are so unexpected and sometimes so huge that some parents feel as though they are tested to the limit of their ability to endure. Under no other circumstances would they tolerate the degree of conflict with their partners in which they find themselves ensnared, other than that of raising their children.

---

71 Silvia Feldman, *Making Up Your Mind About Motherhood*, New York, 1985, p.57

Women have told me that their levels of rage and frustration against their partners have been so extreme that they have punched holes in the walls of their home, have wanted to murder their partners, have willed them to die. A few admitted that their pent up anger was so ferocious they had hit their heads against hard objects until the physical pain became greater than the pain of the rage inside them, giving them something tangible to cope with and control.

Belsky and Kelly, working on the Penn State Child and Family Development Project of the early 1980s, found over the three years of their study that 12–13% of marriages suffered dramatic negative alterations after the birth of the first child. A further 38% grew more polarised, 30% neither declined nor grew closer and a mere 19% found their relationships improved.[72] These are not the statistics of the average expectation. The common belief that having a baby will bring a couple closer together could not be further from the truth. In fact it is difficult to think of any other single event which more glaringly defines and highlights the differences between women and men. The trouble arises when:

> ... men and women fail to acknowledge, or begin to resent, each other's complementary differences.[73]

In general, the feminist movement appears to be appalled that we should accept there are these innate differences between the sexes. There seems to be a fear that if we publicly accept that they exist and, therefore, acknowledge the existence of the paradigm of relationships, we will automatically doom women to a life of subservience, sacrifice and servitude in a paradigm that is inferior to that of material achievement.

> But deemed inferior by whom? By men, of course ... It is only when women judge their own worth at men's valuation that the problem arises ... why should any woman consciously adopt a male value system which devalues her own female values?[74]

---

72 J. Belsky & J. Kelly, *op.cit.*, pp.14–15
73 A. Moir & D. Jessel, *op.cit.*, p.140
74 A. Moir & D. Jessel, *ibid*, p.131

In most areas of endeavour people who express a talent for detecting fine emotional nuances, nurturing, understanding human behaviour and motives and who are able to develop deeply meaningful relationships are seen to be weaker, less intelligent and less worthy of recognition than their tougher, goal oriented counterparts. Both men and women buy into and accept these judgements as much as the fish accepts that the polluted water in which it swims is the only water available to it. If the fish would only believe that its quality of life could improve it might be motivated to swim towards the original source of the water where it will find clarity, cleanness and a place where the environment nurtures it rather than depletes and kills it.

Since the people who display the nurturing, relationship building qualities are overwhelmingly women, and since these talents are honed and often enhanced by motherhood, it follows that mothers tend to be relegated to the polluted realms of the weak, feeble-minded non-contributors. Nothing, of course, could be further from the truth. But the reality is that until women begin to honour and publicly value their qualities and the priceless contributions they make to our collective wellbeing, the doing paradigm cannot and will not change. The relating paradigm will remain forever polluted with ridicule and worthlessness. When a baby enters their relationship the parents are offered an opportunity to re-evaluate the way in which they deal with their inevitable differences. If they insist on trying to mould each other in their own likeness, they will continue to come into conflict with each other. Equally, if they insist on employing their old coping mechanisms of denial or avoidance or blame these will only escalate—perhaps even into abuse or violence.

VIOLENCE AGAINST WOMEN

Nowhere is the inequality which still exists between men and women more evident than when violence enters the home. As statistics on violence against women are gathered, the magnitude of the problem is becoming increasingly apparent. In the United Kingdom in 1989, 32% of all violence against women was classified as domestic and in 1990, 43% of all female murder victims were killed by their husbands or lovers.[75] A study in 1985 by Finklehor and Yllo in the United States found that 10% of wives are sexually assaulted by their

---

75 Naomi Wolf, *Fire With Fire*, London, 1993, p.154

husbands at least once during their marriage.[76] In Australia in 1995, 50% of all homicides were domestic.[77]

Worse still, it has been found in the United States that 60% of battered women were pregnant at the time of their partner's attack. The sickening prospect that the onset of physical abuse may occur when a woman becomes pregnant with her first child is borne out in a study by Webster, Sweett and Stolz at The Royal Women's Hospital in Brisbane. They state that:

> Pregnancy may be a stimulus for the first episode of domestic violence or may prompt an escalation in an already abusive relationship.[78]

This study of 1,014 women revealed that 18% experienced their first abuse by their husbands after they had become pregnant for the first time, and 24% said previously established abuse escalated during their pregnancy. Punching, kicking, choking and assault with knives and other weapons was not uncommon and the abdomen and reproductive organs regularly became the targets of abuse.

> Characteristically, the abusive man controls his partner in multiple ways ... Pregnancy may threaten his dominance over the woman; he may also see the foetus as a rival. Blows to the abdomen may be a direct attempt to terminate the pregnancy.[79]

This problem affects women of all ages, socioeconomic backgrounds, cultures and educational status. It is distinctly not an exclusively lower class phenomenon, although lack of money and education may cause a woman to feel less able to escape her partner's clutches once violence sets in. Similarly, women who are more affluent are often embarrassed by their predicament, afraid they will compromise their children's education and lifestyle if they leave their partners and, therefore, can be reluctant to admit to the violence they suffer.

Just as motherhood has lost its value over the last two hundred years, so too

---

76 K.M. Baber & K.R. Allen, *op.cit.*, p.83

77 Kym Kilpatrick, *Breaking Free: Empowerment Program for Women & Children Escaping Domestic Violence*, Armidale & District Women's Centre, Armidale, 1996

78 Joan Webster, Sheila Sweett & Theresa A. Stolz, 'Domestic Violence in Pregnancy; A prevalence study' in *The Medical Journal of Australia*, Vol.161, 17 October 1994, p.466

79 J. Webster, S. Sweett & T.A. Stolz, *ibid*, p.470

A MOTHER'S RELATIONSHIP WITH HER PARTNER

has masculinity during the past thirty years. Men may not yet have relinquished their power but they have lost the absolute authority they once had, as women have infiltrated most previously male-held domains. Lacking any alternative and positive image of masculinity a man may feel a sense of despair for his own self-worth and rage against women who he believes have undermined the old world order.[80] If he feels inadequate or threatened out in the workplace and rejected in favour of a baby in his own home he may use violence as a way to regain control and reinstate his sense of dominance.[81]

Violence usually begins slowly and so it, too, sneaks up on a woman. At first it is a push, a shove, an abusive remark. She tries to explain it away—shocked. Once a woman has children the trap closes tightly around her as she tries to provide them with shelter, food and security. If she has nowhere to run or no money or little prospect of getting a job or feels ashamed for having chosen so inadequate a father for her children, she stays, hoping against hope he will change. He usually does not. Instead the violence escalates. Her ability to see that what he is doing is his problem, not hers, fades daily. Her will is broken in the same way a terrorist breaks the will of his hostages.

Physical and sexual abuse are the overt end of the spectrum of violence perpetrated against women. Less obvious are the more subtle forms of mental and emotional abuse that occur when a woman first becomes a mother and the balance of power tips into the hands of the father. The dripping tap effect of constant criticism, interrogation, put-downs, insults, humiliation, fault finding, lack of cooperation, half-done jobs and the belittling of her role, not only as a mother but as a woman, gradually eat away her confidence. Because she is not hit she is often made to feel like a whiner when she expresses objection and her feelings of inadequacy rise as she begins to believe there is something wrong with her.

As we know, it's not unusual for women to find themselves looking and feeling exhausted, haggard, incompetent, find their thinking processes are fuzzy, their memory unreliable, their sex drive non-existent and their emotions out of control when they make the transition to motherhood. Too many men find these initial alterations to their partners both incomprehensible and intolerable. Combined with his own problems of adjustment to parenthood, his inability to cure his partner's problems and the consequent sense of inadequacy,

---

80 N. Wolf, *op.cit.*, pp.20–25
81 K.M. Baber & K.R. Allen, *op.cit.*, p.52

he may blame her for being less than the idealised mother and wife he had anticipated she would be. At a time when she is too tired to counter his attacks, too unsure of her new identity to rise above them, too vulnerable to fight back and too powerless to leave, the new mother slowly crumples under a daily barrage of accusations and put-downs or physical abuse. Try though she might she can neither counter his attack nor disprove his criticism. Remarkably quickly she becomes conditioned to helplessness. She gives up, gives in and, all too often, becomes chronically depressed.

Any form of consistent abuse can have a devastating impact on a woman's desire and ability to care for her children well. There has been shown to be a direct correlation between the extent to which a man is able and willing to support his partner once their child is born and her ability to derive meaning, purpose and enjoyment from caring for their child. When the man is understanding, 75% of women enjoy child care and 85% find strong meaning and purpose in doing so. When the man is intolerant, 80% of mothers are irritated by the duties of child care and 87% derive little meaning or purpose from their role as mother.[82]

As abuse and violence increase, a woman's ability to give to her children must decrease proportionally. Her energy, rather than being directed towards them, has to be diverted towards anticipating her partner's next move and taking steps to protect herself, and perhaps her children as well, from his onslaughts. In effect she becomes hostage to his whims and his power. Her life revolves around his needs, not hers or her children's. To survive, she buries her emotions and becomes dead inside, her internal resources depleting towards zero.

Amongst the handful of women in this study who said they had had little difficulty in transforming their identities from non-mother to mother, the common denominator was that each was adamant her partner had been involved, supportive, caring and loving. In turn, they had found it easy to love and care for their babies.

Whilst women must take some responsibility for allowing their men to define their satisfaction levels with mothering, it has to be acknowledged that the institution of motherhood as it is socially defined and constructed, reinforces her downward spiral in value. All too often, the parameters of motherhood appear to justify not only her partner's complaints, but his right to

---

[82] M.G. Boulton, *On Being a Mother*, London, 1983, p.177

make them. Once a woman is financially dependent upon a man she may have no control over the way he treats her and there is little help forthcoming from the community until the family reaches crisis—or worse.[83]

As I have listened to women who have been seriously abused I have been dumbfounded at their ability to endure—and so appalled at this social disgrace. Perhaps the greatest injustice of all is that many people still blame these women, assuming it is they who have provoked the violence and that in some way they deserve what they are getting. I have yet to meet a single woman who 'deserves' to be abused. People who have not been in such a relationship find it difficult to understand what a fine line there is between becoming trapped in violence and being able to gather the mountain of strength needed to leave in the face of such a shattering of self-esteem and self-worth. There is little difference between what some of our women and children endure at the hands of their partners and fathers and that abuse which Amnesty International rails against in countries whose human rights laws are far less 'adequate' than ours.

Many women who become victims of domestic abuse have never before in their lives experienced such ugliness. They cannot understand its dynamics, nor its likely course of escalation. On the other hand, it is easy to see how children who are brought up with nothing but abuse as their role model for life go on to live with it in adulthood. They do not know there is another way and thus the cycle of violence perpetuates itself.

VIOLENCE AGAINST MEN

Women tend not to commit physical violence against their men. They do it in much more subtle ways; so subtle, in fact, few of them recognise their behaviour is abusive.

Until a woman becomes a mother it is unlikely she will have ever, as an adult, felt so vulnerable. If her relationship is far less than perfect after the birth of her first baby, she will often experience such a serious loss of control over her own life that the vulnerability feels unbearable. In her insecurity she will grasp any straw which appears to redress this glaring imbalance of power in her home. Unknowingly, mothers sometimes use their children as weapons in an attempt to control their partners, feeling it may generate more security for themselves and their babies.

83 Terri Apter, *Why Women Don't Have Wives*, London, 1985, pp.79–80

In our society the law does not always stand behind women financially, although that has improved somewhat. Its failures to protect them physically are glaringly obvious. But it does support them almost unconditionally when it comes to custody of their children.

We have asked our men to become sensitive new-age guys. We have drawn them into attending birthing classes and the births of their babies so they will support us and bond with their children more deeply. We have demanded they participate in all aspects of family life to a degree our forefathers would find astounding. As a result many men now find they bond with and love their children every bit as much as the mothers.

When a couple begin to realise their relationship is less than ideal it is the mother who is able to make decisions about her future without having, for a moment, to consider the possibility of losing the day-to-day intimacy with her children. Most fathers do not have that freedom of choice. Most know that should the relationship break up it is they who will lose this sense of intimacy.

For many men this outcome is so abhorrent they will endure almost anything. Some women allow their unhappiness to spill forth in verbal degradation of their men even in front of family and friends no matter how much he has, or believes he has, done for the family. Many men will allow their partners to dictate, even against his wishes or financial means, how the children are brought up, how much money will be spent on them, where they will be educated, what religion they will follow, rather than run the risk of losing their kids.

When a relationship does split up, men often—and increasingly—go through a grieving process which is every bit as profound as if they had suffered a death in their immediate family. More so, in fact, since the wound never has the opportunity to close. It remains always open—until the children grow up. These men regularly fall into the deepest of depressions which often last for years. They feel completely at the mercy of the law and helpless to alter their circumstances. They lose touch with the daily development of their children. They have little or no say over their schooling, health care, or even the way the mother chooses to care, or not care, for them. Sometimes the only way a man can cope with the pain of losing his children is to turn it into a hatred of the woman whom he sees as having taken them away from him. One man I know, who is normally the quintessential pacifist, said to me years after his marriage dissolved:

> I just wish she would die so I could have my kids back again.

I have watched several men go through this process of losing their children. Apart from standing by a person who has had a child die, I have never stood by people who have suffered so much. Their lives lose all meaning. Their hearts break. They wait all week to see their children on the weekends—and their hearts break again and again, every week, as they hand them back to the mothers.

In time satellite fathers do adjust. I am told by those who have been through it that it takes between three and four years, though. Then the pain just becomes an ongoing, ever-present ache. In keeping with the doing paradigm where control and achievement are hallmarks of success and emotions are indications of weakness, men do not readily seek out help when they are suffering.

In this sense women hold immense power over their men. It would do every one of us well to understand, fully, the consequences of wielding it—not only for ourselves, but for our children and their fathers. Just as men must take responsibility for the power they hold over their mothering women, women must take responsibility for the power they hold over the fathers of their children. It is not one to be used lightly.

HELP FOR HANGING IN THERE

Security is a Basic Human Need

Most psychologists rate security as the second most important human need after survival. There is nothing as vulnerable as your first baby so it stands to reason that you will want to make his environment and future as secure as you possibly can.

Women have greatly differing security needs. For some, it is a home of their own, for others, an involved father of the baby or a network of support. Others will find they need an income of their own in order to feel secure, no matter how much their partner makes. The more you can ensure your needs for security are met prior to motherhood, the less likely you are to be upset or unbalanced by their absence at a time in your life when you will probably feel at your most vulnerable.

Try not to make big life changes, like moving to a new area, for at least a year after the baby is born or until your life feels as though it has settled down.

It is a big enough life change becoming a mother and ceasing paid work without loading more changes onto yourself.

Do not stay in a seriously destructive relationship solely for reasons of security. Ultimately everyone in the family will feel even less secure and safe than if you took advantage of a women's refuge, public housing or prevailed upon family or friends until you can look after yourself and your baby on your own.

Choose Interdependence Over Dependency

Before having your baby, you are likely to have been a relatively independent person. So was your partner. After the birth of your baby you can either choose to become dependent upon your partner or you both grow towards interdependence.

If you see yourself as dependent you will be placing all your power into the hands of your partner and trusting he will treat you fairly. In many cases of course, he will. But in at least as many, he will not. Instead, he may grow to despise your dependency. In time, he may misuse the power with which he has been entrusted.

In an interdependent relationship both people must respect each other's contribution, must trust and be trustworthy, must love and be loved. Interdependence is to understand that to mistreat the other is to damage the relationship and so to mistreat one's self. Be sure to discuss the following areas of potential dependency and develop strategies for interdependence before the baby is born.

Financial Interdependence

A woman is not, just because she becomes a mother, suddenly an employee of her husband who must meet certain standards before she is paid. She is not a slave who must beg funds to purchase the very food the whole family will eat. Rather, you are the half of the relationship which will emotionally support and nurture the family. You will contribute the bulk of the work to run the house, keep the supply lines open. Whether you are in paid work or not and whether you run joint or separate accounts, there must be some agreement as to how you will always have fair and equitable access to the money which is rightfully your income as much as it is your partner's. You are not only raising your children; you are raising his as well. Above all, expect to be treated as an equal partner in all decisions relating to money.

A MOTHER'S RELATIONSHIP WITH HER PARTNER

Keep in mind that you both have only 168 hours per week to invest in your life. Nothing makes the ones you have left on this planet more or less precious than anyone else's whether you are earning money or not. So if you find your partner makes continual snide remarks about how hard he has to work to make the money you spend, hand him the shopping list and tell him to go and buy it all until he gets a feel for how much things cost—and how long it takes to do it. Make sure you send him with the baby. Point out the food items, drinks or alcohol you buy exclusively to cater for his tastes. Go through the next credit card bill with him, making a clear list of his and your purchases and those which are for your baby. Ask him to point out all the items you have bought over the past month which he considers to have been excessive or extravagant. Can he find any and, if he can, is there a chance he might be right? If so, perhaps you could consider putting these purchases on hold until you are in a more comfortable financial position. If not, ask him what he thinks you should have done or bought in place of the items you still consider to have been necessary.

Money and power are closely interrelated. It seems women are just as susceptible as men to making the mistake of believing that the right to power is automatically bestowed upon the one who earns the money. Kylie, a woman who fervently believes in the equality of the sexes, said:

> For a while I worked while my husband stayed home and looked after our baby. I came home every day to a clean house, dinner cooking and a clean baby. It was wonderful. I basically cuddled this baby until it was time for him to go to bed. But I started to think that the money was mine and I started to resent him spending it. It was scary.

Physical Interdependence

You both need to know that, during the first six months at least, you will need more physical support than you have ever needed in your life. If your partner escapes into the workforce every day, he must know that he will be needed to physically relieve you of the baby for a period every day after he returns to the home and for substantial periods of time during the weekends. You will also need his help to keep the house in running order. If you are both in paid work, then both of you will need to share, equally, the back up work at home—unless you employ someone to do it for you.

Mental, Emotional, Spiritual Interdependence

It is a funny position we have placed ourselves in. Since the dawn of the human era there has been recognition that men and women are different. We have different strengths and weaknesses, different values, hopes and fears and different ways of relating. Generally speaking, a woman needs to talk, a man needs to do. Once men gathered together to do men's stuff and women gathered together to do women's stuff. At the end of the day when the two sexes reconvened they needed little from each other because the men's masculine needs had been fulfilled by men and the women's feminine needs had been fulfilled by women.

Today, as the pace of life hurtles into the next century, this sense of community has all but vanished. Men spend their days frantically keeping pace with the workforce and have little time to stop and simply be with other men. Women who are full-time mothers are shut in the isolating boxes of their homes and have difficulty finding other women with whom they can relate. Women who are back in the paid workforce are doubly affected as they, also, frantically try to keep abreast of the changes and pressures in the working world *and* look after their families; they have no time whatsoever to stop and relate.

Now when the two sexes reconvene at the end of the day, neither having had their needs met, they turn to each other for fulfilment. Women everywhere decry their man's inability to talk at a meaningful level, his inability to share his emotions, his refusal to listen to her problems and concerns without telling her how to run her life. Men begrudge the lack of appreciation when their efforts to support the family are not glowingly acknowledged and they are mystified as to why a woman's problems do not go away when he seems to be working harder and harder to try to solve them.

Because we are unable to give to each other everything the other needs to feel fulfilled, we believe our sense of lack to be the other's fault. If you are dependent solely upon your partner for your mental, emotional or spiritual fulfilment you are probably asking more of him than he is able to supply. Rather than blaming him and judging him to be inadequate, learn to accept your differences. Get out into your community and find women who are able to talk at your level, who understand your emotions and who can support you spiritually.

Interdependence Benefits All of You

Both of you made the baby. Both are financially, physically, emotionally, psychologically—and legally—responsible for this new life. When a baby enters the household the two people who created it must necessarily lose a certain amount of their independence. The choice is to either fall into a dependent relationship where antipathy and blame bubble just below the surface, or to grow towards true interdependence where you acknowledge that both of you:

- Have given up much to build this family
- Are coming to terms with what these changes mean for you and your futures
- Are responsible for someone who will need your unconditional support for two decades, and more
- Will find the road ahead infinitely easier to negotiate if you cooperate and pull together
- Need each other to make it work

If you can make the transition from independent people to interdependent people without becoming stuck in dependency, not only will your relationship grow as the years go by, not only will you both evolve and become more whole as individuals, but your child will bloom in the security and harmony you create around her.

When All Else Fails—Communicate

Every book emphasises communication as one of the most important foundation stones on which healthy relationships are built. Similarly, one of the fastest ways to destroy a relationship is to cease to communicate.

Communication, especially after a baby enters the family, takes effort, commitment and planning. When your differing schedules conspire to keep you apart, it is all the more important you let each other know what is happening for you. Otherwise assumptions are made which may not be accurate and offence is taken which may never have been intended. A hurt feeling expressed today, before it has time to fester, may prevent The War of the Roses in six months time. Make sure you make time to talk with each other even if it is only for a few minutes before falling asleep every night.

The following are essential areas of discussion which new parents often neglect, ignore or are afraid to approach. Yet to let them sit in limbo is like leaving the leftovers in the fridge for too long. When you finally acknowledge their existence, usually because they are stinking, you find they have turned to a mouldy, irredeemable mush. Do not let your relationship slide into something which is only fit for the compost heap for want of a commitment to talk and to listen to each other.

Express how motherhood has changed you as a person
Your partner cannot know how you feel or what you need unless you tell him. He cannot help appropriately unless you tell him where, when and how. When you do tell your partner what is going on for you, he needs to be told in a manner which is non-blaming. Be sure you do not imply it is his responsibility to fix you or to turn you back into the woman you were before you became a mother.

Understand how fatherhood has changed him as a person
You may need to help him identify his feelings. If you think your partner is suffering from depression, bring the subject out into the open. Do not let him hide it behind a wall of overworking or aggression or withdrawal. Men generally do not talk enough amongst themselves to know that their individual experiences are repeated across the spectrum of fatherhood. They, also, think they are alone in their world, are afraid they will not cope and cannot see any end to babyhood and responsibility. Often first-time fathers are anxious about their changed roles and about how fatherhood is affecting their relationship with the mother of their child. You may be more than a little surprised at how fatherhood is affecting your man if he's encouraged to express his feelings.

Role Changes
It is possible you will begin to envy each other after a period of time as parents. He may envy you your relationship with your baby and, because you are not going out to paid work, he may think you have more free time than he does. You may envy him because he does escape back into the workforce daily and because he seems to have more free time than you.

The problem is compounded by the 'politically correct' assumption that equality means there is no difference between the sexes other than that men grow penises and women grow breasts. Men are not supposed to feel a deep need to protect and provide for their families and women are not supposed to want to nurture their babies and gather those items of comfort which will please her family. Neither, therefore, expects to polarise into traditional gender roles and both may feel guilty for doing so or confused as to what their roles ought to be.

A MOTHER'S RELATIONSHIP WITH HER PARTNER

Trust your instincts. They have a longer evolutionary history than political correctness.

Changed Priorities

The first thing that happens when a new mother brings home her first baby is that most men lose their place at the centre of her attention, usurped by the baby. This is a shock from which some never recover.

Should your partner be one who tries every which way to get back the attention he did not know he was receiving until he lost it, he needs to be reassured that his demotion is not meant personally. Rather, it is part of the process of balancing and meeting the needs, equally, of every member of the household. You may need to point it out to him when he does get the attention he wants and let him know when you do not get the attention you want. It is possible he has not noticed either.

While you may love your partner every bit as much as you did the day you agreed to live together, he may not understand that you are exhausted and consumed with love and concern for your baby. Unless you tell him that you simply do not have the physical and emotional resources left over at the end of the day to give as much to him as you used to, he may assume you have lost all interest in him as a man, as a person, as a partner. You both need to keep in mind that this is not a forever situation. It is one which will pass as your baby's demands begin to ease. But you also need to know that it could be well over a year, or more, before you regain enough energy to give to your partner anything like the level of attention he feels he needs.

Your Sex Life Will Change

One of the key ways a man knows he is still important to his woman is by her willingness to engage in lovemaking. After the birth of her baby, even the most willing of sexual partners is less interested. All the books which assure a couple that things will return to normal after six to twelve weeks do both men and women a serious disservice. The women tend to feel there must be something wrong with them when they find their libido has vanished—and the men tend to think so, too.

The majority of women have said that, at the end of a day of giving and nurturing, what they want more than anything else is simply to be held; to hug, to cuddle, to hold hands. Some women need to be reassured of their sexual appeal for some time before they are able to return to the intimacy of sexual relations, especially if they feel their body was significantly altered by the birth process. If this is you, you have a right to take your time about returning to lovemaking, but you also have a responsibility to tell your partner how and why you are feeling as you are, and to let him know what it is you need from him.

Sex is a subject so laced with social and personal expectations that when it does not live up to those ideals, both men's and women's identities are cut to their core. The damage can be minimised if you communicate, with empathy, your individual perspectives.

Put Intimacy High Up On Your Schedule

I know intimacy is supposed to be spontaneous, a mutual twinkle in the eye which culminates in warm, fuzzy time together. In the early days of parenthood you may find the time lag between the twinkle and the warm fuzzy is so long, you forget one preceded the other. It is too easy to lose all intimacy and once it is gone it can be surprisingly difficult to rekindle.

Make time for you and your partner to be together without interruptions from your baby or other family members. Placing a high priority on maintaining and regenerating intimacy in your relationship will ensure you both have a time to look forward to and it will give you a regular space to discuss matters which are important to you but which may get lost in the day-to-day scrabble to cope. When your baby sleeps, drop everything and talk, hold hands, be together. As soon as you are able, find a baby-sitter and take an evening off—go out together and eat pizza. Take a walk, if only once around the block. Do it regularly whether that is once every week, or once a month.

Most importantly, understand that if you have not made the effort to place central importance on intimacy, when your children reach an age when they no longer need you, you will find yourselves staring at a stranger across the breakfast table. Do not leave intimacy out of the equation. To do so takes an enormous toll, not only on your relationship, but ultimately on your children as well. You are, after all, the primary template on which they build their understanding of intimate relationships. If you and your partner are able to model companionship, friendship and solidarity—including constructive conflict (that is conflict that is resolved to everyone's mutual satisfaction)—your children are far more likely to emerge as adults who feel comfortable in a close, adult relationship and who know they have the right to have their relational needs met. Distant relationships do not meet the fundamental human needs to feel loved, valued and as though one belongs and they are not the optimum model for children. Just as your children will copy your speech patterns, so too they will look to you to learn how to manage their relationships.

Equality is Your Right

Equality ought to mean you have a right to express yourself in a manner appropriate to your situation. If your situation is that of being a mother, and you choose to play the role to the best of your ability, you are as worthy of support and recognition as any person who chooses to play the role of paid worker to the best of his or her ability. Some partners cannot, or will not, understand that you, who care for his children, are doing a job which is at least as demanding and worthwhile as his. Ask him if he, who is president of whatever, is really more important than you, the woman who may be raising the future Prime Minister.

A woman needs to be strong to insist on equality in the face of a man, or a society, who does not believe she deserves it. A new mother does not usually have the energy to fight this battle by herself. Collectively, if we women who are mothers feel we have a right to be treated as equals, we have a responsibility to acknowledge the inequities, to work towards changing them and to support each other when we are vulnerable. To the extent we are unwilling to face up to this, we forfeit our rights.

Once you have regained your physical and psychological strength, if your partner deems himself to be more equal than you because he earns the dollars, you have a responsibility to put him straight and to gather support around yourself if he will not hear what you say. If you let him think and behave as though he were more important than you, you support him in his delusion.

Should your partner refuse to understand your inherent right to equality, try withdrawing all your support services in the house other than those necessary to keep you and your baby in comfort. Come and go according to your own rhythm, pursue your own interests exclusively. In a relationship where only chauvinism (as opposed to violence) is operating, he will soon realise how valuable your contribution is to the smooth functioning of his life and may, at the end of a week, be ready to reconsider. These are drastic measures but sometimes the only way to gain equality is to demonstrate the consequences of not getting it.

Don't Be Afraid to Exercise Your Power
Once the downward spiral of powerlessness is established it is extremely difficult to break—and downright impossible while you are exhausted. Preferably before you become pregnant, and definitely before your baby is born, work out a power agreement with your partner. Afterwards, you may want to renegotiate some of the details but if there is no initial agreement there is no starting point and you may well be too tired to think straight or to stand up for yourself by then.

You need to be able to agree on exercising cooperative power rather than trying to take power over each other. He needs to know that, for a while, you will not be able to give him the same level of attention to which he has become accustomed and that this does not mean you care any the less for him. You need to establish that it is going to be OK to ask for support, help, time out and that you can expect to be given them without having to justify your need.

Support for your personal power at home will assist you to stand strong in the face of your diminished power in the outside world, too. Notice that amongst those women who reported no sense of power loss after becoming a mother, all experienced cooperative equality of power in the home.

Raising a Child Does Not Just 'Happen'
Long before anybody has a child they ought to have thought about how they want to raise it. As a couple you owe it to your children to discuss your beliefs about babies and children, your notions of what parenting is supposed to be and what each of you expects of the other as a parent.

No matter how much you discuss this issue before your baby is born, be aware that new ones will arise after your baby's character and personality begin to emerge. As she grows into a person in her own right and begins to have ideas, values and beliefs which may or may not match yours you will, no doubt, have to readjust your ideas of parenting again and again. However, if you have no foundation on which you both agree, the years ahead may be fraught with disagreements or arguments or, worse still, the two of you playing tug of war with your child.

Brady Bunch Quality Time
Like intimacy, the feeling of having become a family does not happen by itself. The united family which spends quality time with all members equally involved, respected, loved and supported is the exception rather than the rule.

A MOTHER'S RELATIONSHIP WITH HER PARTNER

It happens in TV sitcoms where children never cry or argue, where parents are never tired or stressed and where money and time are never a problem. The rest of us have to work at it.

Quality family time does not have to mean going anywhere or doing anything in particular. It can be sitting in the backyard playing with blades of grass, watching the clouds go by; a simple walk with the baby in a backpack or a stroller; building sandcastles in the sandpit with a toddler.

It is difficult to feel like a family when every member spends whatever time they get together frantically trying to gain the love or attention they feel they are lacking. This is the essence of dependence. Interdependence, however, is when you and your partner are willing to state your own needs and concerns, are prepared to listen to, understand and validate each other's, and are able to work together towards meeting those needs and alleviating those concerns. This interplay of assertiveness and empathy is the starting point for building a quality family.

Conflict Resolution

Today 40% of fathers do not live with their children and the majority of the single mothers who do have custody are exhausted, stressed and financially deprived. Marital conflict is taking an extremely high toll on the next generation when partners in parenthood are unable to work out their differences. In many cases adjusting to these role changes is so stressful that it prevents both men and women from being able to see and acknowledge the contribution each is making to the partnership. When you find yourself dwelling upon what he is *not* doing, make yourself search out three things he *is* doing which assist and benefit you and your baby. Are you willing to do these yourself? Could you? Ask yourself if you have the energy to raise this child and provide for all its needs on your own.

In a world which presents soap operas in which all dramas are fixed within an hour it is difficult to come to terms with the fact that human relationships are far more complex and may require years of work before they function smoothly. Whilst in the midst of marital/parental conflict it is also hard to appreciate that both partners are likely to be contributing to the situation. Next to raising a child, living in a relationship has to be the fastest avenue for personal growth if the participants will only look for and integrate the lessons their partner has been sent to teach them.

Conflict can be a gift if you know how to look for the positives in it. It does not always have to spell the end of the relationship and may, over time, bring a couple closer together. If you have chosen to bring a child into the world you owe it to that child to do everything possible to resolve your conflicts and to maintain the relationship. Sometimes this will require outside help in the form of a mediator, marriage guidance counsellor or relationship counsellor. Do not be embarrassed about seeking one out. The consequences of temporary discomfort are far kinder than those of single parenthood for both you and your children. The only reasons for not continuing to work at the resolution of conflict are when your partner has an addiction (such as alcohol, drugs or gambling) that he refuses to acknowledge or address, or when he is abusive or violent.

Violence is Always Totally Unacceptable

It is recognised that physical abuse is so not OK it is illegal. We provide refuges, financial support and counselling services for women and children who have been victims of physical and sexual violence. In theory, at least, we also have laws which should protect them from ongoing abuse by a particular perpetrator. In practice protection is reactive rather than preventative.

A man who has committed violence against his partner or children will usually do it again, and again—usually more severely each time. If you find yourself in a relationship which is physically violent towards you or your child, get out. Do not make excuses for your partner no matter how sympathetic you are towards his past or present circumstances. Do not waste time blaming yourself.

Do not, for a minute, believe his protestations of remorse or his promises he will not do it again. It is highly unlikely he will look for help, or even admit he has a problem, if you stay. Basically this is because you are sending him the message that his behaviour is acceptable to you. If he loves you as much as he says he does, he will seek help and cure his problems. Only then is it safe to consider returning to the relationship.

Abuse takes many forms, some of them not so obvious. It can be difficult to pin-point when it is 'only' dealt out verbally, emotionally or psychologically. It may seem as though you are perpetually complaining if you object to insidious abuse. Yet it is deeply damaging to a person's psyche to be controlled by another person. Controlling behaviour can include some, or all, of the following:

A MOTHER'S RELATIONSHIP WITH HER PARTNER

- Put-downs, dealt out both privately and publicly
- Withdrawal as punishment—physically, mentally, emotionally
- Having to beg for money
- Inquisitions every time you spend or want to spend a dollar
- Having no say in the distribution of available money
- Restrictions on your movements or who you are allowed to see
- Enforced physical or psychological isolation
- Deliberate destruction of your possessions or ruination of your work around the home
- Being yelled at for minor infractions of his rules
- Withholding of relevant or vital information
- Threats of abandonment or violence for non-compliance
- Insistence that you hold the same world view as his
- Occasional kindnesses which seem to offer hope of improvement but which make you feel guilty for having had negative thoughts about the abuser

After years of suffering this sort of treatment a woman feels battered internally, but the bruises do not show. A man who so degrades his partner will often be the sweetest, most witty, most helpful person everywhere else in the community. This leaves a woman who complains about him looking and feeling ridiculous. Everybody understands and supports a woman who leaves a physically abusive relationship. It is very much more difficult to justify leaving an emotionally abusive one.

If you feel trapped in an abusive relationship do not, under any circumstances, use your children to try to control your partner. Do not ask them to take sides. Do not threaten to stop him from seeing them unless he is violent towards them, and do not accuse him of harming them if he has not. In the long run you only drag yourself and your children down to his level. Nothing is gained and the children will not thank you for it in years to come.

Whatever you do, do not try to handle an abusive relationship alone. Seek out friends with whom you can share your disappointments and fears. See a counsellor. Suggest to your partner that you both take a course on parenting, relationships, communication or that you see a family therapist together. The Department of Community Health and the Anglican Counselling Service both offer free counselling. If he refuses, point out to him the impact your relationship dynamic is having on your children and in what ways they are suffering.

Get strong on the inside so the barbs do not hurt. Once you have gained that strength, tell your partner how his behaviour hurts you and how you would prefer to be treated. If he still cannot see that his behaviour is unacceptable or he is unable or unwilling to change, it may be time for you to seriously consider other options. Should you desperately not want to split up the family and if the abuse is mild enough to be tolerable, it could be you will simply look to building a separate life outside your relationship and learn to ignore his behaviour.

If this fails to work for you, you may need to go through another strengthening process in order to finally draw a line in the sand. Before you say anything you will need to have thoroughly thought through what the immediate and long-term consequences are likely to be for you and your children if he still refuses to change. Put in place contingency plans which you are able to act upon and with which you are able to live. When you do deliver your ultimatum, let him know clearly what crossing that line will mean for him and his life. Be sure you mean what you say. Only then will your words carry enough impact to make him realise he is about to lose his family. If you are not strong enough to back up your words with action your partner will know you are making hollow threats and he will know you remain in his power. Do not let that happen or your position is likely to deteriorate further.

To treat any other person as less than equal is abusive. To what degree we each tolerate such abuse is a personal decision. No-one else can draw your line for you. Only you can exercise your right to do so and you can only do that when you are willing, and able, to take responsibility for the consequences.

SIX
MOTHERS WITHOUT PARTNERS

The pathway to becoming a single mother varies enormously from woman to woman yet their experiences can be remarkably similar. The women who contributed to this chapter came from across the spectrum of the single motherhood continuum. Some had ex-partners who were supportive, others who were destructive in the extreme. Some of the biological fathers were never involved with their children, others were very involved. Many of the women are still single while others have teamed up with new partners.

There are basically five ways women become single mothers:

- Those who consciously choose to become pregnant without a permanent partner in their lives. It would appear they are in a minority.
- Those who become pregnant accidentally to a casual partner who does not want to share the responsibility. They then have the choice of abortion or lone motherhood. Because they discover they cannot philosophically or emotionally face up to a termination and/or find they are pleased with the pregnancy, they choose the latter.
- Those whose pregnancy is unplanned but who believe they are in stable relationships—until their partners leave before, or shortly after, the baby is born.

- Those who are in a stable relationship, but discover, once the baby is born or shortly thereafter, that their partners are not people with whom they can continue to live.
- Those whose partners' lives come to an untimely end.

Women who belong to all but the first group tend to become single mothers reluctantly. They do so because they cannot bring themselves to terminate their baby's life, because they want to be mothers, because they are widowed, because they feel that choosing between leaving or staying in the relationship is a choice between psychological, emotional and/or physical life and death—or because their men abandon them.

There are both pluses and minuses to single motherhood. Obviously many of the experiences of single mothers are similar to those of women who are in relationships, many of which are intensified a hundredfold. Some issues, naturally, are very different and those mentioned in this chapter are by no means definitive. The issues surrounding single motherhood deserve a book of their own.

CELEBRATING BIRTH

If those of us who were married when we gave birth to our babies found it difficult to get anyone to acknowledge what an incredible achievement it was, imagine how hard this is for the woman who gives birth to her baby without a man in her life. Jackie still feels hurt and incensed about this.

> Having a child is supposed to be this wonderful euphoria and here I am going through, 'This doesn't exist—we didn't do this and she [the baby] is not here.'

When a woman goes to a hospital to give birth to her baby she is already unsure, uneasy and in need of support from the staff. She is about to undergo a life-transforming experience about which she has little knowledge of what to expect. The last thing she needs to encounter is judgementalism because she is there without a partner. Suzanne told me:

> The hardest thing was the emotional trauma of being in hospital without the father being there. I felt there was a very unsympathetic air in the hospital.

> The lady who came in to register James's birth gave me the papers. I filled in the name of the father. She looked at it and said, 'Oh, you're not married,' and just scratched a line through the whole section as though James had had no father or as though, because we weren't married, I, of course, didn't know who the father was. Really cruelly, I thought. The implication was that I was sleeping around with so many men—I really resented that. It was a very emotional issue for me. If you are not married it is 'father unknown'. That was terrible, shocking actually. It was like being slapped in the face.

In the ensuing days Suzanne's friends came to see her, which she enjoyed, but:

> I felt different because I did not have someone coming in and sharing it with me. It was just really traumatic because they weren't who I wanted to be there.

Nikki's daughter was created in one wild fling with an old flame. At thirty-eight she had all but resigned herself to living a life without children—an ongoing source of deep disappointment for her. When she found she was pregnant the father decided he wanted to have nothing to do with the baby. She was delighted and made the choice to go it alone. She wrote:

> I stopped teaching at seven months and slowed down to allow for baby time. My anticipation was very high, having looked forward to motherhood for so long. My connections with the child were very strong. Mum stayed for the first eight days after Laura was born. I was in love with my baby, blissed out, enjoying the breastfeeding, feeling proud of my womanhood. But I howled like my daughter when I was left alone. I was shattered.

If a woman is already strong in herself, the judgements, the blatant injustices and the loneliness of being a single mother can serve to strengthen her determination to prove she can care for her child. As Suzanne said:

> I felt I had a lot to prove. I had to struggle to prove I could do it because everyone assumed I would have an abortion because I was pregnant and not married.

On the other hand, to a woman whose self-esteem is already low and whose confidence in her abilities is shaky, these attitudes of blame only serve to confirm her self-image of being worth little and may cause her to relate to her child as though he is worth little as well. Megan, whose life since the birth of her son has been one of poverty and restriction, often shows her frustration in front of her son referring to him as a 'pest', a 'nuisance', a 'waste of time'. Stephen, now in late childhood, was once an average little boy. He now thinks of himself as a 'pest' and often acts it out.

Of course, single mothers are not the only ones to project negatively onto their children. However, their chronic lack of support does put them under greater pressure which can make it harder for them to see their children as separate from themselves.

BLAME

There is an attitude afoot which blames single mothers for their circumstances. It is incredible that thirty years after the liberation of women this tone of judgementalism should still exist. Every sole mother I interviewed expressed anger that she was treated as if she were the only one who had had anything to do with her pregnancy. At no stage are the men, who are also responsible, called upon to account for their actions in the same way she is.

Suzanne was twenty-six and living with her partner when she discovered she was pregnant. She was pleased, not only with the prospect of becoming a mother, but that this particular man was to be the father of their child. She told me:

> He packed his bags and went to the laundromat and just didn't come back. It was like B-grade movie stuff. Unbelievable. I thought, 'This just doesn't happen to people I know.'

Yet it was she who bore the brunt of accountability for their combined actions. Suzanne continued:

> I think that was always the thing I resented the most. Because I chose NOT to terminate the pregnancy therefore it was totally my responsibility. I still don't really understand that thinking. In fact, I chose not to do something I could not do.

Jackie, also in what she thought was a stable relationship, discovered her partner's inability to deal with their joint actions when she was seven months pregnant and he denied paternity. She told me:

> That was one of the hardest issues I had to deal with. I had blood tests come back with a 96% positive result which is the highest they give. He didn't manage to prove he wasn't the father, but I wasn't able to prove he was. So my daughter's birth certificate does not have a father's name on it.

Almost universally, sole mothers agreed that the general attitude to women who become pregnant 'out of wedlock' is, as Gillian said:

> Well, you chose to fall pregnant by yourself.

Phillipa discovered it is equally unacceptable to leave a marriage. When she told her father she was leaving her husband he asked:

> He doesn't hit you, does he?

When she replied, 'no', he told her that she 'had no right' to leave. Yet she said:

> Even though people knew about his drinking and accepted that he wasn't great husband material, I don't think they would ever understand the degree of fear I had because I kept my end up all the way.

It seems, even at the very end of the twentieth century, women are still expected to put up with diabolical treatment at the hands of their men unless their physical life is in danger. If he does not shoulder his 50% of the responsibility for the children he has created, it is not he who is blamed but she for either tricking him, trapping him, driving him away or leaving him.

NO RELIEF IN SIGHT

The stress of being a single mother is relentless and every lone mother I talked to referred to her lack of relief from mothering as an almost unbearable burden. Glenda wrote:

Many single mothers never get a break from their kids and often suffer a real loss of identity and self-esteem. They never get a chance to be anything else other than somebody's mother. From my own experience and that of other single mothers I know, stress-related illness is one of the typical by-products of our lifestyle, particularly depression, high blood pressure, insomnia, just to name a few.

On the other hand, some mothers remain incredibly healthy until they have time to be ill. Gillian said:

I don't get sick. It is amazing. Single mothers have to be really healthy because they don't have time to be sick.

However, Jackie finds:

Whenever I have a holiday from work I get sick—nothing major—just a cold or I put my back out or something. I think it's because I have the time.

The risk is that women who are coping with so much and with so little support or relief simply push the stresses underground, sometimes for years. When the children are grown, when they finally have time, that is when they become ill. My own mother, who had been impossibly healthy throughout her fifteen years of single motherhood, study and work, crashed when the last of us left home. Essentially she collapsed for a full year under the weight of accumulated exhaustion until her body and mind had recovered.

The lack of time out for single mothers, particularly those whose partner in pregnancy refuses to be a partner in child rearing, is chronic. Bianca's desperation was evident when she said:

I used to think, 'Wouldn't it be wonderful if his family accepted him with open arms and they wanted him to come and stay for a weekend.' I would love a weekend off—I really, really would. I envy women who are divorced and their kids go off to the father for a weekend or school holidays.

It has been over five years since Bianca has had a whole day to herself.

Jackie, whose daughter is now eight, reiterated this desperate need to have some time away from the children.

I went to a work-related conference eighteen months ago for three days and left her with her day care mother and it was sheer bliss. I was at the point where I was going to put my hands around her throat and press very hard.

This is the point. It is so totally unreasonable to expect that one person, alone and unaided, can be eternally giving and patient with a child, year in, year out, with no relief in sight. If the mother pays the price with her health, the children pay, too. Julie admitted:

Basically I didn't cope. I was overemotional. I tended to take my own anger at the broken relationship out on the kids. I was just so stressed out. Being stuck in my situation stressed me most. I was poverty-stricken, a lot of bills to pay, didn't have a lot of friends.

I was very lonely—incredibly lonely at night. There are only so many TV shows to watch and books to read. I just couldn't cope. I craved human, adult company. I had no money to pay a baby-sitter and go out to meet people. I didn't have the self-confidence to join groups. I had always been in a relationship and I was scared I would never get into one again.

I was just really loving and caring before my marriage broke up so the kids must have sensed it was a different mum afterwards. We broke up because of his drinking. And I drank more after, which only made it worse but that was the only answer I had at the time. They would go to bed and I would get drunk most nights. It didn't help at all.

When they went to school things just generally lightened up a lot, more time to myself. I made friends and got a support circle around me.

Where was the support for this mother when she and her children were at their most vulnerable? Her ex-husband paid her no money, ceased all contact with his children and continued his life as though his three-year-old and eighteen-month-old had never happened. In desperation, Julie remarried five years later. Her evaluation was that:

It was disastrous. My second marriage was not so much an escape from single motherhood as an escape from loneliness. He was a control freak and wanted to run everything. He tried to change the kids into these darling little angels. He really rode them.

Again, the children paid the price.

Sole mothers who lack another adult with whom to share the stresses of parenthood regularly feel as though they will break under the strain. The really remarkable thing is that, usually, they do not harm their children in the process. Bianca told me:

> In the middle of the night I would get up with a crying baby—I would be walking around with this baby over my arm thinking, 'Please don't cry any more. I'm going to kill you. I can't stand this. I'm going mad!' I would turn the radio on just so I had someone else to focus on.
>
> When Joe was little and he was a fair little bastard and people asked how I was coping and I'd say, 'Well, actually I'm that close [holding her thumb and forefinger a millimetre apart] to grabbing him by the ankle and swinging him around and smashing his head against a wall,' and they would go, 'Shock, horror.'
>
> I used to think about all those married women with husbands in bed—even if they did not get up, at least they had someone to hand their baby to if they felt they were going to kill it.
>
> I used to be intensely jealous and I am sure it coloured my relationships with other women. Every time I saw them, I saw them as somebody who had back up.

Relief only comes five or six years later when the children go to school and the mother has a whole six hours a day to herself. Once she has that respite she may find it very difficult to re-accept the constancy of parenting when the holidays arrive. Bianca continued:

> I never thought I would say it, but when Joe went to school it was so nice. The one and two week holidays through the year were nice but the six weeks at Christmas were Hell! Where can we go? What can we do? What am I going to do for six weeks? I didn't think this would happen.

With the perpetual demands being made on her, a single mother has no time to herself, especially if she also works or studies. There is little or no input from outside the closed circle of her relationship with her child from which she can draw sustenance and strength. Suzanne, whose son is now twelve, told me:

> I was desperately lonely. I can remember crying in the night when
> James was asleep, 'Help me, help me, help me.' I was always exhausted.
> ALWAYS. Just chronically exhausted.

When I asked her how long it took her to get over the exhaustion she laughed and said she was still waiting.

Hard though it is for any new mother to cope with the incessant demands of a baby or toddler, a woman who has a partner knows that at some time in the day another adult will enter and share her living space. Single mothers never get that break in the stream of mothering. I do not know whether anyone who has not lived through it can begin to comprehend the sheer loneliness of a mother who is trapped, in isolation, with only her children for company and support.

POVERTY AND HUMILIATION

Added to her interminable work load and aloneness, single mothers are amongst the most poverty-stricken people in our country. Their children grow up acutely aware of how much they do not have compared with the rest of the population. Worse still, they spend their formative years living with a mother who is perpetually stressed, depressed or just plain unhappy. Phillipa told me:

> Financially it was bloody awful in the first years. Beans and rice; cold
> water; not enough money to pay for the gas; having to go to other
> people to eat because we actually didn't have any food left in the house.
>   My big problem was pride because I had to cope and taking charity
> was not something I had been brought up with as an acceptable thing.
> I had lived in a world before where I just charged everything. Money
> was not a problem. I remember feeling really, really embarrassed at the
> checkout of the supermarket going through the basket and thinking,
> 'what can I go without', putting stuff back in front of everybody.

The adjustment from having had money to having none is a process fraught with, not only difficulty, but perhaps rancour and hostility as well. It is widely acknowledged that when a marriage breaks up it is the woman and her children who suffer financial deprivation and a significant downgrading of their lifestyle and expectations. Robyn said:

> One of the hard things for me is knowing that my kids are growing up with poverty consciousness. I really hate that! I get really peeved—he [the father] went to private school and my kids don't have that opportunity from him.

Almost invariably single mothers are forced, at least initially, to live in conditions which in themselves are stressful. While she is trying to adjust to motherhood she is also trying to adjust to a dramatic decline in her standards. The double load is often too much to bear. Suzanne recalled:

> After a couple of months of living in a very dingy little flat I found myself sitting day after day really going out of my brain. James got sick. It was just a really oppressive existence. Even doing the grocery shopping was really difficult. I had to take a bus and train to get there, with baby and stroller and coming back with groceries. I thought, 'I just can't do this.'

Bianca, too, lived in conditions which stressed her beyond her limits.

> I was living in a shoe box with a three-year-old. My son had to bath in the laundry tub and by then he was too big for it. There was nowhere to get away from each other. I was going mad.

It is simply not possible to live in such stressful conditions and remain the eternal, beatific Madonna.

Many mothers reported feeling totally humiliated at having to seek financial support from the government. Suzanne told me:

> It was a shock to me to find myself on social security. Pregnant. On my own. Here was I, the girl most likely ... That was a fairly humbling experience—more like humiliation!

Nikki kept up her private teaching practise after her daughter was born but found, after five months of struggling to juggle baby and clients, that the interruptions were too frequent. The source of income on which she had thought she could survive dried up. She wrote:

> I hated having to get financial assistance, having to stand in line with my hand out. In a nutshell, my relationship with single motherhood was ambivalent—half proud and half filled with fear and loathing of the handouts and vulnerability.

There is a general feeling that if a sole mother needs to ask for financial help she automatically brands herself as being worth less than anyone who has an independent income. She is treated as if she were stupid, lazy, loose. Yet because so many mothers would do anything rather than see their children deprived even further than they already are, they do not rock the boat. They simply feel degraded. Bianca said:

> If you are really doing it tough you have to humble yourself—you have to act as though you are in the bowels of the earth to get help. If you look clean and well dressed they think you are OK and just complaining. If you look lousy you get the help but you are judged as incompetent. You have to grovel and beg to get help. You can't have any pride left. I always wanted to cry out, 'The fact that I walked in here to ask for help was hard enough in the first place!'

Even for single mothers who go back to paid work the pull towards poverty is ever present. Because she is truly trying to fit two full-time jobs into a one-time life she will often choose part-time paid work which offers her, almost always, a lower hourly rate than a full-time worker and often none of the benefits. Jackie works at two part-time jobs in a university, one academic and one administrative. She is not entitled to pro rata study or research leave as are her full-time colleagues. She told me:

> I earn $600 per week. By the time I pay day care fees, medical expenses, travel costs, the costs of having to have a car to get there, my HECS repayments, tax on two part-time jobs, not to mention the loss of rate,

telephone and electricity subsidies, I am $50 better off than if I was on the pension.

And Jackie is well off financially by comparison with many of her sisters. In Australia 80% of women earn less that $18,000 per year.[84] On that amount and less they are expected to pay rent as well as provide food, clothing, education and entertainment for themselves and their children. Under these conditions even the need to purchase a single pair of shoes is a source of major anxiety and stress. Gillian stormed:

> It costs the taxpayers around $50,000 per year to keep a prisoner in gaol but look at what we pay our single mothers! Where is the logic in that?

It has been shown over and over again that when a family is forced to live in poverty and isolation the parents, especially when single, are placed under such pressure that they are more likely to neglect or abuse their children. There is, also, a clear (although not inevitable) pathway from an abusive childhood to teen and adult delinquency, aggression and violent crime (especially if the family lives in an area where criminal activity is an established feature).[85] These are factors that are known to create the circumstances which predispose children to becoming inmates of the adult gaol system. Yet because there is little or no immediate political or economic gratification in increasing support for single mothers and their children the resources allocated to alleviating their problems are woefully inadequate. This is the logic of the doing paradigm.

The indignation which poured out of these women over the degrading conditions in which they were expected to mother their children was enormous. They were infuriated at the men who had dumped them and with the society for expecting so much of them while giving so little help and support. In every case their anger was not so much for the hardships they, themselves, were suffering but because the hardships limited the lives of and opportunities for their children.

---

[84] Women's Advisory Council, *op.cit.*, p.7

[85] Adam Graycar, 'Poverty, Parenting, Peers and Crime-Prone Neighbourhoods', in *Trends & issues in crime and criminal justice*, Australian Institute of Criminology, April 1998, pp.1–6

DECISIONS AND RESPONSIBILITY

When a mother does not have a partner every decision is hers and the consequences are her responsibility alone. She often has no-one to whom she can turn for confirmation that she is doing a good job as a mother and making the right choices for her baby and children. Bianca said:

> That's the biggest thing I miss—somebody else who shares the load, somebody else who has an equal stake in this child. My sister used to be so critical of my parenting. But because I am the only parent in the house I can't be too extreme. I can't be too lenient or too hard. There is no-one to balance me out.
>
> My ideal fantasy is someone who will come up and say, 'there, there' and talk about how we will handle the problems. Instead it is like somebody has put a mixmaster in my brain and I can't think what to do next. So I just go and sit and cry because I've got this child and everybody thinks I am a bad mother.

There is a tendency to blame single mothers for any small quirk her children may display. All to whom I spoke said they felt this glare of public responsibility acutely. Glenda wrote:

> One of the tough things about being a single mum is the constant awareness that, whatever decision you take, whether it is how to respond to misbehaviour, how to deal with kids' problems or how your stress attacks are affecting the children, at the end of the day, if things go wrong, it is always going to be your fault. You have no-one else to blame, no-one to comfort you and tell you that you have handled things the right way. You judge yourself mercilessly every step of the way.

Even fathers who remain in contact with their children blame the mothers when things go wrong. They do not seem to be at all inclined to look to their own behaviour as having had the remotest possible influence on their children. There is an unspoken (or outspoken) suggestion that, 'with a mother like you …'

For some women the enormous responsibility of raising a child on her own becomes the catalyst which causes her to become extremely focussed and determined to rise above the hardships. Suzanne told me:

> I sometimes felt the responsibility was hard, but I got really organised. I went to see The Women's Investment Network and took out mortgage and income insurance and a savings investment insurance plan to cover James if anything happened to me. I made a will. But it did often get me down.

It is not only the responsibility for her children and their future wellbeing which falls solely to the single mother. No matter how organised she is every decision relating to the running of the household, repairs to the home and equipment, financial management, time management must be made by her alone. Phillipa remembered:

> There have been times when it has been intensely lonely and there have consistently been times when I have been overwhelmed by the responsibility. Not necessarily to do with the children but it was the times when I had to get another car; or when the lawn mower needed fixing and I couldn't lift it into the back of the car; when I had to decide whether I repaired a car that was already costing me more than I could afford.
>
> There are times when I think 'somebody just do it! Give me the answers!' I don't even want to talk about it. There is a build up of all these things over time and I have to decide. How am I supposed to know which is the right decision?

While the weight of the world may feel as though it rests upon these mothers' shoulders much of the time, it was interesting to hear how many of them valued their ability to control their own money and their right to raise their children without outside interference. When Julie spoke the rest of the women at the discussion forum nodded with heartfelt understanding.

> That is one of the big bonuses for me now. I really enjoy having my own control over my money. Making my own decisions even if I have to rob Peter to pay Paul. It is a big difference.

This feeling of having reclaimed control over her life was all the more clearly accentuated for those women who had lived in, then left, relationships which were controlling or violent. Phillipa's appreciation of her release was evident as she said:

> The sense of freedom, the liberation from the marriage. It was such a relief that living in poverty seemed minor by comparison. The constant negotiation in a traditional family can be horrendous. How nice it is to just make decisions and follow them through without having to play the games.

GUILT

All mothers feel guilt. It seems to be one of the most pervasive side effects of motherhood at this time in history. The ones who feel it most acutely and most constantly, however, are the sole mothers. Colleen wrote:

> My initial feelings after separation were of pure panic and loneliness, unworthiness and unloveliness. I believed the marriage breakdown was all my fault, that I was a terrible, ugly person. My married friends, I felt, were patronising. One even went so far as to tell me that she believed one 'has to work at a marriage'.

The fact that Colleen had, over a period of years, suffered broken bones and black eyes at the hands of a husband who became violent when he drank too much was apparently of little interest to her friends. Rather than help and support her they judged her to be inadequate and at fault at the very time she was already suffocating under her own sense of failure and guilt.

At the bottom of this well of guilt is the blame a mother heaps upon herself for having chosen a man to be the father of her child who turned out to be less than ideal. In an effort to make up for this yawning gap in her child's life she will often expend heroic amounts of energy trying to fulfil the roles of both mother and father, feeling as though she succeeds at neither. Suzanne, twelve years after her partner left her, said:

> I really feel that I have deprived James of his father. Sometimes I feel I should not have said anything when he would go to a party without me

and come home at six o'clock in the morning with his pants on backwards. But then I have to tell myself, 'Hang on, I couldn't have lived like that.'

Because a sole mother is the only adult in the home all discipline must flow from her. There is no other adult who daily says 'no' to the children. Glenda wrote:

> You wonder sometimes why it is that your kids can even stand the sight of you. After all, you're the 'Monday-to-Friday' parent; the one that is forever hassling them to eat their breakfast, brush their teeth, clean up the mess; the one who dishes out the punishment, who is forever tired and has not got time to play.

Being forced into the role of sole disciplinarian creates a dynamic of guilt and remorse for always being the one to say 'no' and never having enough space to be the kind, loving, nurturing mother she originally wanted to be.

Single mothers feel guilty because they often unwittingly accept the generalised attitude that they alone are responsible for bringing their children up in the poverty cycle. They feel guilty that their children are growing up without the same advantages they had themselves or the benefits they see accumulating in dual parent families. They feel guilty when their decisions do not work out as well as they had hoped and they feel guilty whenever their children do not respond to them, their schools, their community in ways which are socially acceptable. When they realise they cannot bear to be closeted in isolation and in deprived circumstances with their baby or toddler and they seek child care so they can study or work, their guilt load soars. Suzanne cried:

> I did not want to put James in day care. I felt guilty about it. I always felt guilty. Guilt was the biggest thing.

Gillian confirmed the wrench it is to leave a young child with a stranger.

> I stayed at home and did everything for my husband and children. After he left I put them in preschool one day a week. They would stand at the fence and cry, 'Mummy, Mummy, don't leave me,' and I would walk away all shaking. Then, when I go to pick them up they don't want to

come home! I feel guilty when I leave them and guilty when I pick them up.

Gillian felt as though she was being judged a bad mother by the preschool because her children did not want to go home with her. She had no-one to tell her that this is very common behaviour in young children and in no way reflected on the quality of her mothering.

More than a few single mothers told me hair-raising stories about the treatment their babies and toddlers had received from their day carers. There is more than a little suspicion amongst them that, in part, the mistreatment was due to the carers' negative judgements about the mothers' abilities to parent their children. If the carer treats her child with judgemental callousness the single mother often accepts the guilt for having put her child so at risk. Jackie related her not so unusual story:

> I am a no-hit parent and suddenly I had this uncontrollable child on my hands. I blamed myself. I thought, 'I am a single, working parent. She is not coping with it. She must need more time out.'
>
> Just before my daughter turned three, I found out the day care mother was hitting her. I had taught my daughter to kneel up to the table to eat because she was too little to sit. The carer hit her for that. My daughter spat her food out at her so I was told she had 'behavioural problems' and I was asked to remove her. I was also told I was a rotten parent. I felt blamed because there was no father there and because I was working.

As if these avenues to guilt are not enough, the single mother sometimes has to contend with the physical and psychological damage her ex-partner has inflicted or continues to inflict on her children.

THE EX-PARTNER — THE FATHER

Few women consciously enter a deep relationship with a man expecting it to crash after they have children. But it happens every day of the week. During the period from 1986 to 1992 the number of single mothers in Australia rose by 30%, primarily due to the increase in broken marriages. Today, nearly 50% end in divorce and the odds of two people remaining married until death do them part is still declining. For those marriages which begin in the 1990s, statistics say that 67% will be terminated by divorce.[86]

When a marriage ends, if there are no children involved, the ex-partners are able to go their own ways, resume their single lives and choose never to have anything to do with each other ever again. Unfortunately, when the relationship has produced children the parents remain parents forever. The divorce papers may signify the death of the marriage but they can never cut the cords which tie the parents to each other for all time—truly until death do them part. These are not contingencies for which a woman plans when she enters motherhood.

Some men are able to separate from their families with minimal recriminations. They continue to love and support their children. They pay the mothers regularly and see the children whenever they can. Even when the split is as friendly and cooperative as is humanly possible under such distressing circumstances, the mother will often suffer every week as she hands her child over to the father for weekend access. Glenda wrote:

> Then Dad's at the door, and you're all but forgotten as Daughter goes flying past into his arms, all starry eyed and ready for a good time. You wave goodbye and go back inside feeling strangely empty—your child has left to live her other life—a life that you'll only ever hear about but never share. It hits you every time.

When children leave their mothers to go with their fathers they do enter a totally different world. One thing which becomes abundantly clear when relationships end is that the two people involved have, and probably always did have, distinctly different values and different agendas for their children.

Parenting is very much about instilling one's values in one's children, a fact which is often not noticed when two parents have to negotiate with each other daily. After they have parted company, however, they tend to parent according to their own agendas which may be in diametric opposition. For the children the switching from one reality to another every week or fortnight is more stressful than anyone who has not been through it could imagine. During the week they do things mummy's way. On the weekend they change personality so they can do it daddy's way. Then they switch back again.

---

86 D. Goleman, *op.cit.*, p.127

MOTHERS WITHOUT PARTNERS

One of the most common complaints of the single mother is that when her child comes back from his visit with his father he is wild and uncontrollable. This stems, in part, from the father's desire to give his children a good time for the short period he has them each week. Or it may be his unconscious (or conscious) desire to take revenge on her by actively undermining her authority and her values.

Added to this is the almost universal phenomenon that men who have separated from their families are financially very much better off than the mothers who are raising their children alone. Separated fathers can, therefore, afford to be the 'good guys' and buy their children treats and toys and holidays their mothers only ever dream about being able to provide. He does not say 'no'. He does not waste his precious time with them getting them off-side by exerting discipline. He knows he will be handing them back in a day or two and that any discipline problems will become the mother's. He grows to look like the knight in shining armour; she grows to look like a nag—or worse—a thwarter of the child's dreams.

Not all men are committed to their children, however. Some become erratic in their payments and their visits. They promise their children the earth down the telephone line and then fail to deliver, leaving the mothers to pick up the emotional pieces of crestfallen children. It is not at all unusual for him to expect to be able to drift in and out of their lives as and when the fancy takes him. After three years of absence from their lives Suzanne's ex-partner rang her and said he wanted to see his son. She, hoping against hope that this would herald the beginning of a relationship between father and son, prepared him for the visit.

> James sat around and waited all day and he didn't show up. I was devastated all over again. I always felt he could hurt me all he liked but start hurting James and it is just not on. Even then I still really wanted it to work.

Even though James's father has never contributed to his son financially, physically or emotionally, and even though Suzanne has since married, still he remains an unspoken, unresolved part of her life. Her son is his son and, because she loves James ferociously, she can never quite disconnect herself from his father.

In far too many cases the fathers of the children continue to exhibit seriously destructive behaviour for years after the family has split up, sometimes taking out their feelings on the children themselves. The courts seem to be reluctant to address this unacceptable level of victimisation leaving the single mother with the sole responsibility for protecting her children. Even when the court rules that a man can only have access to his children under supervision, it is the mother who must arrange it through a volunteer organisation—usually a church or charity. In Australia there is no structured, government monitored system of supervised access. Gillian's distress was evident as she spoke.

> My husband was quite violent and threatened to kill us. I did the right thing and gave him supervised access for about four months twice per month. The church was doing the supervision and they told me he was a role model father, brilliant with the kids, wonderful. He played their game.

Because supervision became increasingly difficult to organise and because the father of her children seemed to be treating them well, Gillian conceded to unsupervised access. When her not quite five-year-old daughter came back from one visit with an unexplained split from her vagina to her anus, Gillian, understandably outraged and sick with guilt for having given in, took the matter to court. There, far from finding the support she needed and expected, she found the court judged her harshly for releasing the father from supervision.

This is not a one-off story. It is incredible the degree of terror with which some women live for years after they leave abusive marriages. Lynne told me that she lives in constant fear for her life and the lives of her two children—and it is eight years since she left her husband. He continues to live within her community and to phone and call at her home even though she has a court order which is supposed to prevent him from doing so. He has beaten her so badly in the past that she has no cause to doubt his potential ability to kill. Still, the law as it stands cannot assure Lynne of her or her children's safety.

In cases where the father of the children is not technically violent it is impossible for the mother to deny him access no matter how much she is afraid of him. Phillipa told me that one of the first things she realised after leaving her husband was that, although they had severed the marriage, they could never sever their relationship. She recalled those times when they had to meet to exchange the children.

Access was horrendous. His incredible anger. After I got away I was never with him alone again. But I had threatening, violent phone calls at 2 a.m., sometimes weekly, sometimes fortnightly. They went on for years. Probably ten years. Drunk usually. They were frightening—like he'd take a contract out on my life, reporting me to the local police for dealing in drugs, threatening to take my daughter away from me, accusing me of being a prostitute.

Basically I behaved passively for ten years after I left him and all the years I was with him. It took me many years after I left to recognise that I had actually been in fear of him while I was married to him. I had been very careful not to upset him. Constantly. And I kept doing it. I was frightened of him for a long time and I did not doubt his capacity to take Angie from me or to have me done in.

His bitterness against me for leaving him was such that, in those years, he would have done anything. So I played very carefully and in a sense my children paid the price for my lack of assertiveness at that time.

No woman enters motherhood expecting that just because she becomes the mother of a particular man's child she will be held psychologically, emotionally or physically hostage by him for decades to come. And, as Phillipa said, the children always pay the price since no mother can ever be relaxed when she is permanently in fear of her own and her children's lives.

In time the pain of separation or being dumped even before the baby was born does pass but the scars remain on the inside, and sometimes on the outside as well. They leave a woman feeling wary of committing herself again to another relationship, and wary of men. Phillipa concluded:

I no longer hate this man but there are times when I think over it I can feel very bitter and resentful still. I am certainly not prepared to forgive him or forget but it doesn't hurt anything like it used to. I'm not frightened of him anymore.

It is sixteen years since she left her husband.

THE FANTASY AND THE REALITY

Because the reality of single motherhood is anything but easy and because it is an experience so far outside the expectation of most women, many who find themselves in it tend to fantasise about how it might have been, how it could be one day. With the fantasy of a better, easier life ever present in their minds many of these women are vulnerable to believing professions of love from men who cannot, and will not, back up their promises.

Megan has made the same mistake twice, ten years apart. When she was twenty she thought she had found the man of her dreams, the one who was going to rescue her from her own impoverished upbringing. He dumped her when she became pregnant. Ten years later, in spite of her inherent wariness of men, she thought she had found a genuine one who would rescue her from the stresses and poverty of single motherhood. She was more than a little influenced by his firm relationship with her son who was already becoming more of a handful than she could cope with on her own. Again she became pregnant. Again he left her, now with two children. She cried:

> How can you tell if they are genuine? I thought this one was for real.
> He was so good with Stephen. I don't know how you tell.

Her misery, her emptiness and her helplessness were profound. It is difficult to imagine, if one has never been a single mother, the sense that love and kindness have passed, and always will totally pass them by. On a good day these feelings of loss fade into the background, on a bad day they can be all-consuming, rattle her judgement and cause her to regret her life's choices. Robyn said wistfully:

> When I am having a hard time with my kids, I sometimes wish my
> ex-husband was around to help me with a problem. But then, I have to
> remind myself, he never did help anyway. It is sort of a fantasy thing
> —how it could have been ... but it never was.

Other women wait, eternally living a fantasy that their absent partners will see the light and return to the family, offering love and support to both the mother and her children. Suzanne admitted:

> I used to wait to be rescued, I'll be honest about that. I used to think

that I could be rescued. It needed to be James's father. It had to be him. I used to think about him all the time. It's woeful, isn't it? I wrote to him and said, 'I really miss you.' He got in touch with me saying, 'I feel like I should settle down.' I thought, 'This is it, this is what I have been waiting for.' My heart was racing, I was so excited. But it just didn't happen.

When a woman is alone with her children she easily falls prey to any man who appears to offer her a way out. Her mind and heart will grasp at straws of hope only to be dashed time and time again. Colleen wrote:

I felt incredibly sad for my children and desperately wanted to find a fine man who would take care of me, be a kind and loving father to them, and who would enable me to be at home, to be there for them at all times. As a result I was terribly vulnerable, wondering if each man I met was 'the one'.

It is not until she realises that rescue can only come from within that the single mother begins to grow strong enough in herself to sieve the fantasies from the realities. Unless she is fortunate enough to find a loving partner, a woman has only two choices. She either spends her life regretting and feeling 'less than' because she does not have a man attached, or she rises up and claims her own power. Although it took her many years to do it, I am fortunate to have had a mother who was able to do just this. She wrote to me saying:

Now in my retirement, I look back and wonder why I wanted so badly to be a twosome. Security, yes; companionship, yes; but what a price I have seen a lot of women pay for them.
    Were I able to turn the clock back, knowing what I do now, I would have stopped yearning for a partner far sooner than I did and, therefore, would have given my children a far happier mother to live with.

It probably took her twenty years to begin to let go of the fantasy and to appreciate the reality of her own inner strength and talents. Today there are half a million single mothers in Australia who come from across the educational and economic spectrum. They are no longer an aberration but an integral part of the social structure. They are able to come together in numbers large enough to create support networks which can help each woman rise above the fantasy and reclaim her power. Today it is possible for the healing process to happen very much faster than it was only a generation ago.

THE SCHEDULE

Few people work as hard as a single mother. Should any of them ever doubt their inner strength they need only look at the schedules they run to in their daily lives. It is little wonder they fantasise about a way out. The stories which follow are not the exception, but remarkably common. What is exceptional is that so many women are out there living this reality.

Suzanne, realising she could not live in the isolation and poverty of single motherhood and the pension, found a job when her son was four months old.

> James was still breastfeeding. I handled that with enormous difficulty. I would leave home at 6.30 a.m. and catch a bus and then two trains. Then I had quite a long walk with the stroller and all his paraphernalia. I was also trying to be nicely dressed for work so I had the nappy over my shoulder so that when he threw up he did it on the nappy and not on my coat.
>
> I would walk from the second train, down the hill to the family day care place, then walk up the hill to work. In my lunch hour I walked down the hill again to feed him and back up the hill to work. At night I did it all in reverse. If I missed the 6 p.m. train I didn't get home till after nine, which happened often enough.
>
> It was tough, actually, and it cost a lot of money to have him in day care, too. I got into a routine though. I used to wash the nappies in the bath tub at night because I couldn't afford to use the laundromat.

When I asked Suzanne how on earth she managed to get out the door with herself intact and groomed, her baby clothed and fed and his bag of clothes and nappies at the ready by 6.30 every morning, she replied:

> That was easy. James woke at 4 a.m. every day. His day started then, so mine did, too. It amazes me now that I managed to get through those first few years, but by the time James was two I bought my first house.

> I saved really hard and worked really hard. It was a funny little run-down house with an outside bathroom, but it was mine.

Phillipa, after she left her husband, managed to borrow enough money to buy a small piece of land in a small country town. She put a shed on it and she and her three-year-old daughter moved in. She found a job teaching at TAFE. Her daily routine was incredible.

> I used to get up and make fifty mud bricks before breakfast. Then we'd get ready, I would take Angie to preschool and go on to TAFE and teach all day. After work I would make another fifty mud bricks before I got dinner. Then I'd go to bed.

Two years later they moved into the two bedroom mud brick house Phillipa had built 'in her spare time' almost totally on her own.

Jackie works at two part-time jobs and studies whilst parenting her now eight-year-old daughter. She told me:

> I work a sixty-hour week but at least my career is flowing. I will be in a better situation by the time my daughter leaves home, but it is exhausting. When you are a single parent you can't stop.
>
> Saturdays are all for her, her gymnastics and her riding and ten weekends a year are for those as well. But when Sunday comes and it is my day, I still have to look after her. That is why I like going to work, because that is my time away from parenting.
>
> I am doing my masters degree as well. I study every night from ten till midnight after I have put her to bed. There is no time for housework. The ironing gets done five minutes before we leave the house. There's no organisation at home whatsoever. There is no time to cook.
>
> I don't know how I do it but I know if I don't I won't be happier—I might be a bit less exhausted but not happier. My study is Me. It is the only part of me that is really left. Everything else is my daughter and my job.

Not every mother is able to run her life to these unbelievable schedules when her children are very young and it is not always because she is unwilling to meet the challenges. Bianca's son could not adapt to day care.

> I tried to work when Joe was four months old. I would take him to the carer at nine and breastfeed him trying to get him to take as much milk as possible. Then I would go to work and come back again at one to feed him again. He would always be crying when I turned up and he would not take a bottle. I'd go back to work and then pick him up at six. The day carer was just at the end of her tether. I kept it up for four months but finally she asked me to find someone else to look after him.
> I decided, 'Forget it. I quit.'

Today Bianca's son is in school and she is studying full-time at university. In spite of her efforts to improve her ability to care for herself and her son, Bianca still finds her parents are judgemental of the way she is running her life.

> My parents say, 'When are you going to have an income, when are you going to be off the pension? Joe is in school now, why haven't you got a job?' But even if I could get a job, what would it be? $300 per week? And no prospects of ever doing any better? I know I couldn't study and work and be a good parent. I made a commitment when Joe went to school that those thirty hours a week are sacrosanct—it is my time for studying.

Julie said she found it very, very difficult to be a parent and to work part-time and study.

> I wanted to study so I could be more employable. Something had to give. It wasn't going to be the kids and it couldn't be the work because the pension wasn't enough to support us. So it had to be the study, so I was stuck. It was virtually impossible. I needed a wife.

Eighteen years later Julie is finally studying at university.

These women are the ones who are judged to be irresponsible, immoral and sponges on our social security system. They are the ones who are judged to be incompetent as mothers merely because they are single. They are the ones who are blamed should their children display behavioural or developmental difficulties which are every bit as normal as those exhibited by children from intact marriages. These women are the least likely to be given physical, financial or moral support. These women are truly remarkable.

SOCIAL LIFE

'What social life?!' they cry.

'You ask a single mother about her social life?'

'It's going to see *The Fox and the Hound*.'

As I researched this chapter I was appalled to find that the social structure of a single mother's life has not altered one jot since my mother divorced my father in 1966. Of her experience she wrote:

> I was determined to show everyone that I was still a person in my own right and I repeatedly had married groups in for dinner parties, Sunday lunches, Christmas drinks. I felt that if I did this, surely they would invite me back when they had other guests to lunch or dinner. They didn't.

Because my mother was so very mystified and hurt by these people's behaviour, some of them friends from the early days of her eighteen-year marriage, I coped with her pain throughout my teen years by believing there must have been something wrong with her. Today I know, most assuredly, that there is nothing wrong with her and everything wrong with our social structures.

Nothing has changed. Every woman whom I interviewed reiterated her exclusion from the social life of couples. Bianca said:

> I never get invited to couple things because I don't have a man to take with me. If I do get invited to a married's house I feel like a sore thumb.

Phillipa told me:

> When I have made connections with people, male or female, through my work or study or whatever, I am very, very rarely invited home. As a single person we can have really strong relationships and meet for coffee but not be involved in the family.

Jeannette was astonished by her realisation that:

> Do you know, I have been single for three years and last weekend was the first time I have been asked to a couple's house. And I was the only one there.

The women who attended discussion forums went on to discuss why they think they are excluded from couple society. Almost universally they concluded that women with partners are afraid single mothers want to wrest their men away from them. Equally universally they expressed Phillipa's frustration with this archaic attitude:

> I sometimes feel like sending a note home to the wives saying, 'I don't want your husband. I wouldn't have your husband even if I could have him. I am not interested. I am not even looking for a man.'

What is probably a relatively new development is that men, too, are feeling the need to shun single mothers. Jackie admitted that she feels most lonely when she knows she is being excluded from a couple based activity. She said:

> I have come to the conclusion that men feel threatened by sole mothers who are coping. I think they are afraid that we might teach their wives they can live without them; that there is another way other than having to put up with their inadequacies.

Unfortunately, for whatever single mothers might think about men in general or their ex-partners in particular, many of them still enjoy male company. When they find they are cut off from it by those who live in couples they mourn that loss of balance in their lives. Phillipa lamented:

> My circle of friends tends to be other single women and I do find that difficult because I like male energy. I enjoy it. My closest friends are women and I am sure my closest friends will always be women. But I miss male company. You don't want them to look after you—just let's be friends, let's be companions. The air charges when you have got male and female company around and it is different. I like it and I need it. That is a real problem.

A single mother's social antenna becomes acutely attuned to the moods of other people as she tries not to be a burden on anyone. If she is she fears she will not be asked to join their company again—something to be avoided at all costs. Bianca said:

> When Joe was little I used to get invited to afternoon tea. We would be having a really good rave but about 4.30 I would see the eyes flicking to the clock and I realised I had better go now, I was not welcome anymore. There would not be an offer of another cup of tea. The cake would be put away. It was husband time.
>
> I was intensely jealous because they had a grown-up coming home to talk to. I was going home to emptiness and somebody who would probably scream for three hours. I used to sob inside, 'Don't make me go home. I don't want to be at home by myself with this little baby who cries all the time.'

Women who have partners do not understand this terrifying aloneness. Colleen wrote to me about her experiences with her old, married friends after she and her husband divorced.

> I was asked to dine with friends only when they were having a quiet night on their own—'We'll just have some spaghetti bolognaise on our laps.' Always I felt there was a strict curfew on these nights. When I noticed the husband surreptitiously roll his wrist in order to look at his watch, I knew it was time for me to leave.
>
> Many times, while dining 'a trios' I would be regaled with details of the dinner party the couple had held the previous Saturday. On one occasion the wife hastily added, 'Oh, we didn't include you of course, dear. You wouldn't have enjoyed it because the guests were all married couples.' Did she think that I had suddenly ceased to enjoy adult conversation?

Even when a woman's former friends are ready and willing to maintain the old relationships it is not always easy for the single mother to keep up her end of the bargain. Her life is consumed by her baby and their survival. Her interests change and the focus of her life alters radically. Suzanne found this the greatest difficulty.

> It was hard to keep up a social life. Even though the bubble burst on my career, my good friends were fantastic. But it is like visiting people from another planet in a way—they live such different lives and I could not maintain the closeness of those friendships. I could not do the same things, I could not afford to. I no longer had the same things in common with them.

This, in part, explains why single mothers find themselves excluded from the social world of couples. If having a baby alters the way most women relate to their world, having a baby alone alters it all the more dramatically. If, in becoming a mother it is patently obvious that there is no equality between the doing and the relating paradigms, then becoming a single mother sets off alarm bells of injustice. Therefore, single mothers tend to be, amongst their family and friends, more vocal about the inadequacies of our society and they make others uncomfortable, simply by their very existence. It is easier to blame her and to exclude her so the general community is not forced to see her living the injustices, do not have to feel guilty for their own good fortune and do not have to disrupt their tidy lives in any way by taking any responsibility for her and her children. Yet this is not a problem when the single person is male. He is often seen to be an asset. She a liability.

OTHER MEN

When a woman is excluded from social life because she does not have a man attached, when she lives in poverty because she is unable to earn as much as a man, when she runs a schedule which would kill a buffalo, is it any wonder she wishes she could find a man to help out? For many reasons achieving that goal is not as easy as it sounds. Yet, once again, the socially accepted truth is that there is 'something wrong' with a woman who does not have a male partner. Funnily enough, in spite of this patronising attitude, most single mothers I interviewed told me, as Julie did, that:

> People assume you must have a man somewhere, in the closet or under your bed because you couldn't be doing it all on your own.

Many of the women who contributed to this section of the book were very clear that they did not even want a man in their life, and not because they were lesbians. This is something of which the majority had been accused at one time or another. Because of the current social structure a single mother must mix almost exclusively with other single mothers which apparently causes others to suspect she has changed her spots. For most women this is not so; she has simply begun to turn to people who understand her, care for her and accept her for who she is. Robyn said:

> A lot of men want to come in and start running your family for you. I have done it for six or seven years now on my own and I don't need someone to tell me how to do it. I deal with men outside my parenting hours now.

Amongst these women there was a fairly universal agreement that men are more trouble than they are worth, that they do try to take over, that they do expect every bit as much attention as a child no matter how exhausted a woman may be. Phillipa fell into a new relationship shortly after she left her husband but soon decided that these were excellent reasons for remaining single.

> I found another man interfered with me getting on with my life. I felt as if, in my marriage, I had been standing still personally for such a long, long time. Here was this other man in my life who was again trying to fix me up. I wanted to look after my babies and I didn't want to look after any more grown-ups, thank you very much.

Until a woman comes to terms with being a single mother she is open to the manipulation of any man who professes concern for her, her children and her situation. Colleen wrote:

> In the course of my working life I discovered that there were plenty of married men who pretended they were unhappy at home and that I was the one they had been waiting for all along. It took me a while to wake up to them and I was badly hurt a couple of times before I did.

In spite of all the talk of female equality, too many men still believe a woman cannot exist, let alone happily, without one of them in her life. They approach mothers who are newly single with an attitude of 'you need me' and 'I am doing you a favour' because 'I know your life is a misery—especially because you are deprived of sex'. It is a cruel joke these men play on women who are in the early stages of trying to re-order their shattered lives. They offer the carrot of love and companionship and support until they get what they want and then they move on to the next unsuspecting victim. They leave behind them a trail of hurt, bitter and wary women. Not meaning to do so, however, they also play a large role in her growing inner strength, self-sufficiency and courage.

Single mothers find they have to assess men today, not only on how well they treat her, but on how safe it is to have them near, or alone with, her children. Everyone to whom I spoke was extremely aware of the violence step-fathers often inflict upon their step-children. Bianca asked:

> All this stuff about abuse and men—who do you trust? You just can't. There is all this anti-male sentiment out there in the community warning you not to leave your children with them. They could be perfectly wonderful but ...

the statistics are not good and many women feel they would rather remain on their own than to put their children at risk.

For women who have never lived with a man but who are now mothers, a live-in relationship is something of a mystery. Before having children women take for granted their romances and do not question their worth or their validity. After becoming a mother a relationship with a man takes on a whole new light. Leigh asked the married women present at the discussion forum she attended:

> Do you all love your husbands the same way you love your children? Is it the same? I don't know what it would be like to love a man.

Bianca continued with the same theme of unknowns.

> I think it would be scary to have to share with someone else. What if I got pregnant again and decided to stay home for the first two years (because I really like the idea of that) and I had to give up my income? I would have to rely on his. No way! Never mind the fact that I sit there with the budget now and think, 'Oh, God, it just won't work,' but at least I can decide. I have never had to negotiate like that, not since I was in high school.

MOTHERS WITHOUT PARTNERS

Often a woman will find a relationship which works for her and then she becomes acutely aware that it is not only her needs which have to be considered but those of her children as well. Suzanne discussed this issue with me.

> I found other relationships with men pretty tricky at first. You have an enormous amount of baggage when you are a single parent, and not just because you have a child (which many men consider to be baggage) but you've got a lot of emotional baggage, too.
>
> Also, you go into a relationship and you are not looking for a father for your child but that is the first assumption. But then you are. You first go into it looking for a relationship but that relationship can go no further unless it is going to include your child. There is a degree of contradiction. In the end you have to evaluate that man as a potential father.

The quality of the potential father is something many women do not consider before they choose a man to be their partner. It is of paramount importance to a single mother. Thus a man must qualify not only as her partner, a test he may pass easily, but as a father—a test not so easily passed. Many a potentially good relationship dies at this final hurdle.

When the relationship does culminate in marriage it is often a carbon copy of the first. If a woman does not look into her own reasons for requiring a partner in her life she will choose one who fulfils deep, unconscious needs but who may be less than ideal as a partner or father. Julie admitted of her second husband:

> He was a bit wild, a bit exciting which attracted me. But he wasn't a wild man at all, it was a cover-up. He was really very conservative and straight and he wanted us to knuckle under. He was a very strict parent. I am not. He overcompensated. Because he wanted to be seen to be a good father he wanted the children to be a good reflection of his parenting.

Without consciously meaning to do it Julie married a man who put her under exactly the same pressures her first husband had. As a result the marriage lasted only five years and she and her children suffered. She has vowed never again to enter a relationship until she has cleared all the debris of unfulfilled need from her subconscious.

Once a woman has tasted the true independence of single motherhood it can be very difficult for her to give it up. This is independence of child rearing as well as independence of choice, distribution of the finances, life-focus and style. Learning, or relearning, the art of negotiation can be tedious and vexing—to put it mildly. Nikki re-met and married a former lover two years after her daughter was born. She wrote:

> My sense of independence lessened and I was disappointed at not getting the support I had expected and hoped for. Compromise was something I negotiated on my own terms hitherto—now (in retrospect of course) it tasted more like acquiescence. Why did I lose that core of self-certainty so easily? I wonder if it would have been different if Laura had been Ian's—although he adores her—it is just a constant unknown.
>
> Essentially I loathe financial dependence. It is a difficult adjustment having to negotiate all financial transactions.

Whatever a woman's choices, once she has become a single mother everything is more complicated and more complex. She cannot spontaneously bring another man into her life with little thought about the consequences and ramifications. These have to be considered from every angle. Although Nikki has now been married for three years and has had a second child with her husband, her letter concluded:

> It has been a rocky road. I have great respect for women (or dads) who do it alone. I know that it takes a lot of endurance, dogged strength and resourcefulness. Swings and roundabouts. Not harder or softer, winner or loser, less or more. It is just another way. In this case my choice was partnership. It is still a struggle.

INTENSITY OF MOTHER–CHILD RELATIONSHIPS

When one adult is solely responsible for her children and there is little or no break in their contact with each other, their relationships are bound to become more intense than if another adult is involved. This intensity factor escalates if a single mother has only one child since there are not even other children to diffuse their relationship. Jackie said:

> I find having a single child is probably not best for her. I am not sure about a one-on-one relationship. It is very intense. Work is a pleasure—I can't wait because that is my only time away from her. I don't have anyone who takes her so I can go out on a Saturday night. I don't have people she can go to for a weekend and it has been over eight years now.

Like most other factors in mothering, this is a two-way street. When a child has only one parent she often feels vulnerable about being left with no-one to look after her. It is a stick the sole mother may use when all else fails. Jackie admitted to doing just this.

> When my daughter was two she was still not asleep at 2.30 a.m. I had to go to work the next day. By then I was screaming. I got the car keys and said, 'I'm going, I have had enough!' If there had been a bloke asleep in the bed I could have gone. There would have been no guilt in walking out. I got as far as the front gate and she was chasing after me saying, 'No, no. I'll go to sleep now,' and she did. That's the one thing single parent kids fear, you going. Because if you go, there is nothing. I use it; it just happens when I'm about to go over the edge. Rather than hitting her, that's what I use.

Jackie is not advocating using this sort of emotional blackmail as an ideal way to raise a child and she realises it is not good for her daughter to be made so afraid. She also knows there is a limit to how much one person can take and rationalises that this is better than physically harming her. When there is no-one else to step in to take the load, even occasionally, a woman must resort to whatever means are available to her to get through another day—or night. This problem is exacerbated if the child has a very different temperament from the mother's and if they both enjoy differing lifestyles. Jackie continued:

> She wants everything in life that I don't. I think that is why the relationship is so intense—because she wins all the time. I do not get lonely as a sole parent. I like to stay at home but she is the social butterfly. She can't do that unless I take her.

How different it would be for Jackie and her daughter if they were both stay-at-home people or both social butterflies. With this disparity in their personalities the problem is growing as the daughter grows up. As a result, far from the relationship improving with age, Jackie is finding mothering more tiring the older her daughter gets.

Like it or not, the single mother finds her child's needs come ahead of hers every day of the week. There is no second parent to give her time to herself, there is usually no money in the budget for baby-sitters or outings and so her world closes in on her. Bianca pondered her relationship with her son.

> I wonder, am I co-dependent on my child because he comes first? Sometimes I hate it. Sometimes I can just live with it. It is like this child is not my life—but he is. It is a decision I have made to have this child in my life therefore there are certain things I have to do but ... I have a life, too.

This is a perennial dilemma for many mothers but it is one which is intensified for those who are parenting alone. They often find themselves struggling with the pull to mother well and the pull to create a life for herself, neither of which fits together easily.

When a woman is supposed to be all things to her children at all times, it is inevitable she will fail sometimes. For the single mother these failures are felt acutely since there is no-one around to point out to her all the good things she has done over time. Again the responsibility comes back to haunt her. Nikki wrote:

> Had I been a married woman, or in a de facto partnership, my relationship with Laura would have been a bit less intense, for her as well as me.

YOU AND ME AGAINST THE WORLD

This is the bottom line for many single mothers. There is little help offered—and much judgement. Her man often goes free while she remains trapped in parenthood. She finds it difficult to obtain meaningful, well-paid, part-time work and when she does find it she is often denied access to the benefits a full-time job offers. If she works full-time she is perpetually exhausted and stressed and cannot look after her child as well as she might like. If she does not work she and her children live in poverty with all its stresses and injustices. The law cannot protect her from a violent, abusive ex-partner if he continues to threaten and harass her. She is socially ostracised. Indeed, all too often, her own family desert her, blaming her and disapproving of her decisions. Often her children are treated less kindly in the school system and she is not taken seriously when she tries to address the injustices. The list of isolating experiences just goes on and on. Colleen wrote:

> I envied women with family support. My mother disappeared to the Blue Mountains as soon as I was divorced. I derived no help from her. My brother and sister-in-law could have helped me enormously by inviting the children to spend school holidays with their children. They never did and took no interest in whether we were surviving or not. My children grew up without the benefit of a relationship with family and cousins. We were entirely on our own.

Of course, the children suffer these isolations every bit as much as does the mother, although they probably do not realise it at the time. As they grow up, however, their limited family circle becomes all too apparent and they are left to deal with the stresses of their mothers on their own.

Over and over again single mothers told me how financially well off their parents were and how little support they gave them. Being able to blame their daughter for her actions and choices is apparently a reasonable excuse for withholding love and assistance. Many of them felt their fathers were more judgemental than their mothers.

When a woman can glean no support from her family, she turns to the social security system for help where she is made to feel as though she is a burden. If she is going to need help it will usually be during the earliest days of her single motherhood. This is the very time she is most disoriented, most vulnerable and least able to assert her rights. Robyn told me:

> There is a lot of help out there for single parent families but the ones in need never seem to hear about it. The government says, 'See what we are doing,' but you have got to know the right questions to ask because they will not tell you. Single mothers are only worth the minimum. They make you feel even more degraded than you already feel anyway.
>
> I am pushy though. I knew my rights and my education is possibly a

lot better than many other people's so I got what I needed for my kids. Unless you are able to be really assertive, government departments walk all over you.

Even if there are no hurdles within her family to be overcome and even if she does not have to tackle the systems of government, the single mother will, undoubtedly, encounter blocks to her fulfilment out in the workplace. Glenda wrote:

Life as a single mother can be like starting out on a treacherous journey and never knowing whether you're ever going to get there. Being a working single mother is one of the hardest struggles of all. Whichever way you turn, you can't win! You are always feeling guilty—either about leaving work early and hearing the full-timers say, 'leaving already?' or by getting home late and having your child tell you what a rotten day she had and how she 'wished you could pick me up from school like the other mothers'. It's the old vicious circle—you've either got the money and not the time, or the time and not the money! Hell, what do you do?

The strain of trying to raise her living standard above the poverty line and still be a 'good enough' mother takes its toll. For all the rhetoric about equal opportunities for women the structure of the working world still does not do enough to accommodate their needs. Equality does not include the right to balance the doing and relating paradigms. The paid working world is still built around the belief that only a full-time worker who is spontaneously available to work overtime whenever necessary has value. The logical extension of this belief is that anyone wishing to work fewer hours cannot offer a worthwhile contribution to the company, cannot be serious about a career and, therefore, cannot expect to be treated as an equal. Glenda continued:

If you dare to want to work part-time, you might as well be walking around the office wearing a sign that says, 'I'm a bludger'. Suddenly it is assumed that you're not serious about your job, that you are constantly going to ask for time off and that, basically, you've become a risk factor to the business.

I think many employers are terrified that, by making a compromise to a single working mother, they might be setting a precedent or, even worse, risking a loss in business. They fail to see that single working mothers, in particular, are often the most reliable, most dedicated and hard-working employees. They value their jobs more than anything simply because that's the only income coming in and without it, well, there's no-one else there to keep the ball rolling.

Implicitly there is a covert social blame of the single mother for being single. Suzanne bemoaned these attitudes.

I knew that society was very hypocritical about it. They didn't mind me having sex before marriage, in fact that is what the Pill is for. They didn't mind me getting pregnant—that is what abortions are for. But because I had chosen not to have an abortion, that made it my sole responsibility and so it was my responsibility to suffer the consequences.

It is almost as if in becoming a single mother a woman deserves to be viewed as a lower class of citizen and ought, without complaint, to accept how she and her children are treated—no matter how unacceptable that may be. Yet just because a woman is a sole parent does not mean she loves her child any less than a woman who is living with the child's father. Suzanne said:

James was very important to me even when I was pregnant. I used to be very fearful that something would happen to him. After he was born he was the centre of my world. I just adored him savagely. A lot of the time I felt it was me and him against the rest of the world.

Even the school system contrives to make a single mother feel as though she, and her children, are worth less than women and children from two parent families. Julie related her experience:

There was an agreement between four or five sole mothers whose kids went to my kids' high school that the teachers really didn't care as much about what happened to ours as happened to those from together families. It was subtle. It wasn't overt so everyone in the community could see it. It was just the general impression that our kids weren't going to get anywhere anyway, so they weren't going to bother about them.

Suzanne agreed.

> I had to make quite a stance about being single and being proud of it when James went to school. Just because I am single doesn't mean that I am loose and dishonest.

When a woman is the sole defender of her child and his rights she becomes acutely aware of the social injustices and of her powerlessness to effect change. As Suzanne continued I could not help but think how many times, as I researched this book, I had listened to both single and partnered women saying essentially the same words.

> The thing I noticed the most was the lack of resources for children. It was almost as if children don't exist—babies in particular. They don't actually exist in our society. It is as though we go from being born to being teenagers.
>
> Going shopping, doing anything, with a small child in our society is just extremely difficult, physically. You notice that more when you are on your own because you haven't got someone you can physically hand the child to.
>
> There is this absolute lack of tolerance for small children. There seem to be so many people, in professional circles especially, who don't come up against children in any form and to whom they are simply a gross inconvenience.

When I have heard this same cry from well over one hundred mothers, I wonder what on earth it is going to take to revalue our children and give them back their rightful place—that of the future generation. Nikki captures the essence of this problem in her letter.

> When is this cock-eyed society, that measures power in monetary and material terms and treats children—tomorrow's people—as units of dependency, going to see parenting as the most difficult and challenging task of all?! I don't want money, I want support, a social web within which I can be respected as a mother and parent.
>
> I don't want to stand in a queue, waiting helplessly for a mite. I want a safe neighbourhood where my kids can play with other kids and I can

negotiate support with other parents. I don't want the government to be monitoring our lives with endless paperwork and probing, personal questions. I want to choose with whom I share my secrets and sorrows, and with whom, in turn, I offer my support. Do not make me a legal unit, a number of dependency, a beggar of taxes, impoverished and marginalised.

Let me make my decisions on the basis of my children's welfare—let me work if I choose either at a paid full- or part-time job or as a full-time parent. And if I choose the latter, let me be seen to be making a most valued contribution.

There is something dreadfully ill about a society which causes a woman to feel as though she must continually and vigilantly defend herself and her children against that society in order to survive.

NO REGRETS

Almost without exception these single mothers felt that, for all the deprivations, they would not change their choices if they had their time over again. Whether their choice was to go ahead with a pregnancy in which their partners wanted no part or it was to leave their partners after the child/ren were born made no difference to their conclusions. As Phillipa said:

> There have been some really lovely things. The independence, the freedom, the not having to raise adult men! I would not have missed it for the world. It has been a full-time job. It's the best job, the hardest job and the most rewarding job I have ever had. You are, after all, in the people making business.

Single mothers are, above all else, survivors. Whether they realise this in their earliest days is another matter. Those who are too newly single to appreciate what strength they harbour inside them need to listen to those who have gone ahead into sole parenthood. Suzanne said:

> People used to say, 'You're marvellous or brave.' But I wasn't any of those things. I just did what I had to do. In the end you just do what you have to do.

Women who are new to sole parenthood need to know that these exceptional women are mere mortal, normal mothers pushed by circumstances into becoming shining examples of just how resourceful and talented we women can be when our kids have no-one else to turn to. Suzanne admitted:

> For a long time I had a huge chip on my shoulder. Feeling like the victim. Fortunately, though, I classified myself as someone who could go through it all and survive and I think it helps to see yourself that way.
>
> I have no regrets at all—even about any of the circumstances. Because you can't change any of it without changing all of it. You can't afford to regret or it turns into blame. I don't regret leaving my career for James at all so I don't have an ounce of resentment towards him. Even when I was really down to rock bottom financially and emotionally I never regretted making the decision I did.
>
> Motherhood, for me, was the birth of compassion and empathy. I finally understood so much more. I cared a lot more about humanity. I can remember not having that compassion before.

Consistently women have said that one of the great things about being a single mother is having the right to raise their children the way they wanted to. Nikki wrote:

> I felt I had no power except that, as Mother, my word on Laura's needs was final.

and Phillipa said:

> You get a chance to raise a child the way you want to raise her with your values, your attitudes. So I have a daughter of whom I thoroughly approve because she's got a social conscience, she is an honest, reliable young lady —all the things that were really important in my life are also important in her life. That's a real bonus and I don't think many people get to do that in two parent families. I thought that was a really good little luxury.

Although it can be difficult to see the pluses of being a single mother while one is stuck in the enormous load of work and responsibility, those who have passed through it and come out the other side stand testimony to the strength and endurance of a mother—and her ability to rise above just about anything life can throw at her. My mother wrote to me as I was concluding this section of the book:

> On the plus side, I must say that if I were given the chance, I would still choose to have divorced when I did. Although it was difficult and very lonely, I did find I could achieve things I never would have achieved had I stayed married.
>
> I have grown in every direction and found a strength I would never have found as long as I was married. I carved out a career for myself and gradually gained confidence in myself. I am now superbly capable of managing my own affairs, have a very realistic approach to all problems and have no stress in my life. I have the time to do everything I want and to do absolutely nothing if the mood takes me. No-one is making demands on me.
>
> Over the years I have gradually become more understanding of other people and their troubles and, I hope, a lot more tolerant and less judgemental. I have become a whole person in my own right, instead of a half—a quite inferior half. I know I can survive on my own.
>
> None of this may ever have happened if I had stayed with the man I married. In fact, had I stayed with him I would probably be in a psychiatric ward by now, if not dead from some stress-related illness. The fact that I am alive and sane is the biggest plus of all!

If any other minority group was as dismissed, blamed, used and abused as are single mothers, they would generate a social and media-driven outcry loud enough to exert political pressure for change. The silence is deafening. Unfortunately, most single mothers are flat out surviving, caring and providing for their children. They have no energy left over to organise themselves into a coherent group, nor time to direct protest rallies, nor money to pay for publicity—and nobody else does it for them. Yet notice how vocal the gun lobby is over the comparatively minor deprivation of losing the right to bear automatic weapons. Notice how much attention the media and politicians pay them. In any sane society one would imagine, surely, that the issue of providing safe, non-deprived environments in which to raise our children warrants more attention than the issue of boys losing their deadly toys. Obviously not so—in the doing paradigm.

HELP FOR HANGING IN THERE

Give Yourself Permission to Celebrate

Regardless of how judgemental others are of your situation you are still breathing life into a newborn baby. That baby deserves to be welcomed into this world every bit as enthusiastically and lovingly as any child and you deserve to be able to revel in the marvel of your creation. Just because there is no man attached does not make your achievement any less a miracle. Before you give birth to your baby think about how you would like to celebrate his or her entry into the world and with whom you wish to share the experience. Ask others to support you and help you create your own rites of passage and celebration. Suzanne's advice was:

> Above all, be proud to be a mother.

Do not waste your energy feeling guilty. If you love your baby that is all that matters to her—let it be all that matters to you.

Blame is Not Part of the Equation

Women get pregnant for many reasons but money is rarely one of them. Sue told me:

> I have been a single mum for a long, long time and I have worked with lots of other single mothers. I have yet to meet one who deliberately got pregnant just to get the pension.

If you find yourself having a baby on your own, for whatever reason, do not accept the all too common belief that you are to 'blame'. Yes, you are responsible for making love unprotected. Yes, you are responsible for choosing not to have an abortion. Yes, you are responsible for choosing to leave a destructive relationship. These are not 'blame' issues. They are choices. Remember, always, that he also chose unprotected lovemaking, was at least half the problem in the relationship and that you have a right to not terminate your baby's life if you cannot or do not want to.

Network Fast

If you know you are going to be single when you enter the institution of motherhood, spend your pregnancy seeking out other single mothers who may be able to guide and support you while you make the transition. If single motherhood comes upon you at a later date, find women who are already in your position who can help you with the adjustment, warn you of the pitfalls and help you find you feet.

Being in contact with single mothers means you will have adult input into your decision-making processes and reassurance that the decisions you have taken were the best available at the time. It means having the company of adults who understand and share the stresses of your situation and who do not feel compelled to judge you. Ultimately, it means you have someone with whom to share at least a little of the responsibility of raising your child/ren and who can look after them when you need some time out from mothering. Jackie said:

> My life changed when I found someone else in my situation. Now I have someone to talk to, share the load with—even my social life has improved.

Be Humble, Not Humiliated

When you realise that single motherhood means either poverty or overwork (or both) do not be too proud to ask for help. Women with partners often do not realise how intense an experience it is to raise a baby on your own and, when asked, may be willing to mind yours for a few hours every week. Other single mothers will understand your need for some time out for yourself.

Your own parents may not realise how hard a job this is, either. If they are able, ask them to help you financially in the early days, even if only a little. It may make it easier to accept their generosity if you view it as a loan to be repaid when you are on your feet again or even as a down payment on your inheritance. Perhaps your parents could be encouraged to look at their contribution as one which is giving their grandchildren a less stressed start to life. After all, a mother who is constantly worried about money cannot give her children the best of herself.

If you find yourself on the doorstep of social security, understand that the system has been set up to help you, not to humiliate you, no matter how it may seem when you walk in the door. Before entering the world of the single mother's pension find out from other single mothers what your rights are and what you are entitled to receive. If the person you first see at Centrelink tells you they cannot help you, ask for someone who can. Unfortunately, all too often a woman who has freshly joined the ranks of single motherhood is at her most vulnerable and least assertive when she first confronts the social security system. Many find out years later that they were entitled to more income than they have been receiving and trying to have benefits back-dated is a nightmare, if not impossible. If you feel too vulnerable to be truly assertive take a friend who can support you.

Even if for yourself you would prefer never to have anything to do with your child's biological father again, your baby will benefit from his financial contribution. While the battle for acceptable maintenance is far from over, the law decrees that he should pay something towards the survival of his child and, to a certain extent, holds him responsible. Do not allow pride to stop you from accepting this source of income.

Some mothers have found their Local Exchange Trading System (LETS) scheme a financial blessing. This is a system of bartering goods and services in which no money changes hands. They have taken in ironing and washing or cared for other people's children in return for reciprocal baby-sitting services or physical labour which they would otherwise not have been able to afford. As Bianca said:

> Everybody has something to offer in return for the help they need.

Contact your local council to find out if a LETS scheme or similar system operates in your area.

Detach Emotionally from Your Ex-Partner
Whether the father of your child was a mad fling in the night or a husband to whom you were married for a decade, the loss of the potential 'family' can be devastating. It may be that you will feel angry towards him for not fulfilling his role as partner and father, for remarrying, for apparently continuing his life unfettered by the responsibilities which weigh you down and limit your life. You may find yourself grieving for your lost 'ideal' future. And you may feel guilty for having provided your child with less than perfect circumstances in which to grow up.

The sooner you can come to terms with these emotions, the sooner you can begin to focus on recreating your own life, leaving him to his. Although not an easy thing to do, there are counsellors and therapists who can help you work through the issues. Some women said they worked out their emotions in their journals. Others said they wrote (many) letters to their ex-partners which they never sent but ceremoniously burnt or tore up and flushed down the toilet along with their negative emotions.

Stand Tall

Many single mothers said their sense that they were less respectable than partnered mothers drove them, in the early days, to fantasise about bringing another man into their lives. However, all conceded, even if they have re-partnered, that there are some real blessings about bringing up a child without having to negotiate daily life with another adult. Although the exclusion from couple society and the on-going social stigma attached to being a single mother would seem to suggest that you are a less respectable member of the community without a partner, it is entirely up to you whether you accept so limiting a definition of yourself or whether you reject it as the nonsense it truly is. Noni's advice was:

> Believe in yourself no matter what others try to tell you.

Whether you have a man in your life or not says nothing about your respectability, or lack thereof, nor does it say anything about your personality or character.

Be aware that in your early, more vulnerable days of being single there may be men who see you as someone who will meet their needs and be grateful for their attention, without demanding much in return. Do not sell yourself short in the blind hope that one of them will rescue you from poverty, loneliness, overwork or social ostracism. Often you are very much better off taking care of yourself and your baby on your own and looking to your female friends for support.

Set Realistic Goals

Although experienced single mothers admitted it was difficult to know what 'realistic' goals were in the early days, they cautioned women in this situation to lower their expectations from the outset and not to set themselves up with a schedule which will eventually cause them to burn out. Noni said:

> At first I felt I was such a failure as a partner and as a woman and as a mother because I was single that I thought, 'I can't tell them I'm not coping as well!'

It is this sense of profound failure that often drives a single mother to try to prove to the world she can do it all on her own while still being all things to all people. This is certainly an unrealistic expectation.

It is also unrealistic to expect you can be a perpetually patient and loving parent. It is common for single mothers to feel as though they cannot cope with their children's less than perfect behaviour and to be afraid of completely losing the plot with them. Gillian's advice to anyone who feels pushed to the edge is to:

Stay calm and breathe deeply ten times before you say, or do, anything.

The one expectation single mothers, particularly, need to raise rather than lower is that she and her children are worthy of help and support.

Take Time to be You

Because the relationship between a single mother and her child can become intense, it is even more important that you begin to develop your own interests as soon as possible. The only way to do this is to find others who will look after your baby for a regular period every week. Whether that assistance is given by a relative, a neighbour, a friend or whether you find a day care mother who suits your baby's temperament, all the single mothers interviewed for this book stressed the importance of sharing the mothering load. To try to do it all alone is to sacrifice your own needs and dreams and to place the burden of your emotional and psychological wellbeing onto your baby or child. No matter how close your relationship, one day your child will become a teenager and not want to look after you and will, of course, eventually leave home. If you have made your child the centre of your life it is likely you will feel lost when this happens.

When asking long-term single mothers what advice they would offer those who were newly single, almost every woman's first response was:

Take time out to be yourself.

SEVEN
A MOTHER'S RELATIONSHIPS WITH THE GREATER WORLD

All relationships are affected when a child is born. A couple become parents, no longer a twosome. Grandparents are born. Brothers and sisters become uncles and aunts. Friends must move aside. The mother's relationship to her community undergoes a major transformation. Some of these associations adjust easily. Others do not.

When a woman becomes a mother she gives up a great deal, not only in terms of recognised achievement, personal freedom and spontaneity, but in terms of the stability, continuity and structure of her relationships. Given that the quality of her relationships is fundamental to how a woman defines herself, when they change suddenly, radically and across the board, whether those changes are for the better or worse, she finds herself negotiating a new and foreign landscape.

From the moment a first baby is born other people begin to relate to a woman differently. It is as though she ceases to be a person in her own right who has needs, wants and concerns of her own, and contributions to make outside her mother role. Her relationship with herself transforms, colouring her interpretation and understanding of every interpersonal interaction. Sometimes this colouring brings joy and clarity, sometimes pain and confusion. No matter which way the pendulum swings, until her new relational status begins to crystallise a first-time mother may feel that she has been thrown into a sea of uncertainty. She may not feel comfortable until she has regained a sense of being surrounded by supportive and stable relationships once more.

Women tend to derive their level of self-esteem from the degree of esteem afforded them by those whom they love and respect.[87] If that support is withdrawn by people who are important to her, her own ability to rebuild her sense of worth and identity can be impaired. If she is surrounded by supportive relationships she may experience an almost painless transition to motherhood; if her relationships are unsupportive and undermining it may take her until her children leave home to discover that she has any worth. Sadly, some women still go to their graves feeling worthless.

THE RELATIONSHIP WITH ONE'S OWN MOTHER

Giving birth to one's own child immediately highlights the relationship a woman has with her own mother and her mother-in-law. Caroline, like many of us, found her relationship with her mother deteriorated.

> For a while my relationship with my mother was really bad. It was really difficult because I was resentful and I felt that she was too interfering, always trying to tell me what to do and what not to do.

Sometimes the mother–daughter relationship grows closer when a woman becomes pregnant or gives birth. Or it may take time for the two women to adjust to their altered relationship. As a woman begins to realise the true difficulties of motherhood her appreciation of her mother may grow. This serves to bring the two women closer together in a mutual respect for the hardships and wonders of being a mother. Caroline continued:

> Now she lives around the corner and it is really good and we get on well with each other. We have emerged in a way that we can be close with each other.

---

[87] A. Moir & D. Jessel, *op.cit.*, p.159

On the other hand, many women complained bitterly about the lack of support and active undermining they experienced from the older generation of mothers. Natalie wrote:

> My mother went all 'strange' for quite some time. I can see now that it was difficult for her to think of herself as becoming a grandmother but also my being pregnant served as a major catalyst for her to examine her own years of being pregnant and her own abilities as a mother.

There appears to be a gulf of understanding between the older generation of mothers and those of today. It may be that their lives were less independent, more restricted with fewer choices and less mobility, but their lives were also less complicated. This is a factor which many older mothers do not seem to appreciate. Adelle told me:

> I think there is a suspicious gap between the two generations. My mother is still suspicious of my mothering and I am of hers. She will never respect my parenting—NEVER.

In the past, children were raised to be 'seen and not heard'—today they are taught to assertively speak their minds. Children were smacked for the slightest infraction—today that is almost illegal. Children by the age of eight or nine know about AIDS and safe sex, drugs, wars, sexual and physical abuse, the law, their rights. They know about the sorry state of the workforce, environmental disasters, the dishonesty and ineptitude of our leaders. Even the parents of bygone generations were ignorant in many of these areas and certainly did not openly discuss them—let alone with their children.

Children in primary schools have lost their innocence in ways that even the teenagers of yesterday never did and they are materially enriched in ways yesterday's parents could never have imagined. They have hurdles to cross which none of us can yet conceive so they must be raised to be aware, assertive, strong and able to believe in themselves—no matter what the world serves up for them to surmount. Many mothers from the previous generation do not appreciate that today's world demands a very different parenting style than the one that served in the world in which our parents raised us.

A mother is asked to do more today than at any time in the past, not least that she returns to the workforce or 'does something' with her life as soon as possible after having her children. Even doing the shopping is now a minefield of artificial colours and flavours, chemicals to be avoided, thousands of choices to be made, allergies to be considered, prices to be compared while trying to ascertain whether the product is made in Australia. Yet many of the older generation remain critical and judgemental of this generation's ability to parent.

In rural Australia there are members of the grandmother generation who, far from thinking a woman ought to be earning an independent income, frown upon it as an act of self-indulgence and selfishness. Linda, thirty-eight when she had her daughter, is receiving this message:

> My mother-in-law tells me how easy motherhood was for her but she had help from her mother. I will never have that. She says it is not OK for me to work. She says, 'how are the men to get their work done?' I did not realise this would upset me so much. Even though I thought I was strong it has been a slow wearing down process.

In the past, the wisdom of parenting was handed down from mother to daughter. Those women who reared their children according to the advice of their mothers in the twenty years or so after WWII undoubtedly expected that their daughters and daughters-in-law would listen to and accept their wisdom. Many an older woman has echoed the sentiments written by Colleen:

> As you had no prior knowledge of caring for babies you automatically turned to your mother for advice and believed everything she told you, as she had done it all before. Her methods had worked for her and we found they worked for us. We thought they would work for our daughters.
>
> Imagine, therefore, the bewilderment and even hurt suffered by today's grandmothers when they tried to pass on their experience, only to find that most of it was rejected as being old fashioned and no longer relevant. There has had to be a huge adjustment made by today's grandmothers; some have had difficulty accepting that their advice is outmoded; some have finally accepted the vast changes; some never will.

When the current generation of mothers do not accept the advice of the previous generation, the grandmothers tend to feel devalued, dismissed and displaced, unable to complete the cycle as their mothers had done. They then become even more judgemental as they try to carve out some value in being an elder whose wisdom is not only unwanted, but considered to be irrelevant in today's so very different world. Camille's mother-in-law has caused her much grief during her years of motherhood.

> My mother-in-law is undermining, unsupportive. Always telling me how I am doing it wrong and not coping. I feel anger and resentment towards her.

Older mothers may feel that if their advice is not accepted unquestioningly the younger mother is criticising the very essence of her life's work and therefore dismissing her as having no valid place left in the world.

Women do forget what mothering small children is really like and grandmothers seem to have a tendency to glorify those early years. Over and over again today's mothers reported to me that their mothers and mothers-in-law regaled them with stories of how wonderful they and their husbands had been as children—how they had slept through the night from day one, never thrown tantrums, always ate everything that was put in front of them and never answered back. Here are a few apparent glitches in their memory:

> *Eileen*: My own mother says, 'I have had five children, what is wrong with you?' She can remember exactly when everything happened to us like we were toilet trained at three months and so on.

> *Mandy*: If I do anything differently from the way my mother-in-law did it she criticises me. She remembers everything in a rosy light—how her children slept through, ate everything. Grandmothers forget what it is like to have small children, therefore they give endless advice, know everything and are constantly telling you how to do things.

> *Sally*: My mother insists I was toilet trained six months before I could walk!

> *Madelaine*: My mother does not think she ever got angry at us but she used to beat us nearly every day with the wooden spoon. But she has forgotten that.

Perhaps because mothers of the previous generation were judged only on their ability to raise well-mannered, healthy children and on the cleanliness of their homes, they find it difficult to admit that they were less than perfect in the role of mother. The heartfelt words of Sarah say a lot:

> The cruelty of my mother-in-law! She always gives advice rather than saying, 'It's OK, that happened to me.' Her kids were perfect. My kids were never at the right stage and age. You would think she would have been more supportive. She should have realised and been more sensitive. Instead she undermined me as a mother.

Some grandmothers rationalise that simply because their own children have reached adulthood they must have done everything correctly. When their daughters begin their own families they are reminded of their early mistakes and perceived failings and may dislike being forced to remember. Natalie's mother was one of those grandmothers.

> My mother was absolutely no support whatsoever throughout my pregnancy and very little after the baby was born. I think, if anything, she was extremely jealous of my ability to cope, to work, to be financially independent and to be *happy* ... all things I don't think she experienced in her own very unhappy life. I felt guilty about being happy ... and felt such conflict about this that I ended up staying away from my parents' home. I longed for some deeper, more meaningful relationship with my mother but she was not able to provide or partake in one.

It is said that every new mother needs a mother herself and not a single woman I interviewed denied this. Catrina, whose mother died when she was a teenager, felt the loss of hers acutely after she became a mother.

> I was jealous of women with mothers. I imagined them to be being helpful all the time.

Often it is not until a woman has her first child that she realises her own parents did not enjoy parenthood. Simply because a person becomes a parent does not necessarily mean that she or he will automatically like small children. Many parents are, therefore, quite unable to be the grandparents a new mother would like to have provided for her child. Leigh commented:

> When my parents came out from the United Kingdom I realised that my mother did not even like little children very much.

Upon reflection Leigh realised that her mother had not enjoyed her as a child either.

When their daughters have children many grandmothers are reminded of their own sense of inadequacy because they, of course, were completely enveloped in this conspiracy of silence. Most have never had the opportunity to talk about their real feelings towards motherhood in general and their own mothering experience specifically. In being confronted with their long-buried histories many find it easier to hide behind indifference towards, or irritation with, their grandchildren and criticism of their daughters' ways of mothering.

THE REST OF THE FIRST FAMILY

- 57% of women surveyed did not expect to see much change in their relationships with their greater family
- 47% reported an impact on coping; 29% severe to extreme
- 51% experienced intrapersonal conflict; 28% severe to extreme
- 47% engaged in interpersonal conflict; 19% severe to extreme

Somehow we expect that a baby will simply be an addition to our extended family and that it will make little difference to the relationships which have been established for decades. One of the most unexpected consequences of giving birth to my own son was that I lost my father. I did not expect his reaction and can only surmise, since he will not discuss the matter, that when my son entered my life he felt that he lost his daughter, just as he had lost his wife to me when I was born. Only once, when Daniel was eight years old, did I raise the subject saying, 'You are not even interested in my son.' His reply was, 'Only vaguely.'

Coming to terms with his judgements and criticism of, not only the way I raise my son, but the very fact of having had him, has been one of the more painful lessons of my life. It has resulted in my seeing less and less of my father as the years have progressed and has meant that I have always had to make arrangements so that my son did not have to be in his presence for any undue length of time. However, I know that in this I am not alone. Women have related stories to me of how sisters, mothers, brothers, fathers have found their progression into motherhood cause for withdrawing from or attacking them. Natalie poured out her pain in a letter.

> My relationship with my sisters was shattering. My younger sister ... has since confided that my being pregnant challenged her enormously and she ended up asking herself lots of questions about what sort of partner she wanted to have children with. My elder sister posed a bigger problem to me. She was very depressed. I took her out to dinner to tell her my good news [about being pregnant]. What a disaster. She burst into tears, made a huge scene in the restaurant and basically dumped me for getting on with my life. She would not see me even after the baby was born.
>
> In the first three months of being pregnant I felt as though I could not do a thing right by my family. Those relationships which were disintegrating prior to my pregnancy disintegrated completely when I, for the first time, made demands on people who had only ever made demands on me. Some of those relationships have been rebuilt on newer, stronger ground. Some were not worth rebuilding. At times the interpersonal conflict has been enormous.

Other women have noted that their non-parenting siblings expected them to continue as though nothing had changed in their lives and did not understand their exhaustion. Anna said:

> My sister was always asking why I was sick as if it was somehow my fault. She did not understand for years that I was exhausted until she became a mother herself.

Catrina added:

> They arrived and expected me to serve them like before. They never thought that I might like to be served.

Not all the changes are negative, of course. Some are quite unexpectedly the opposite. Caroline recalled:

> My father was a workaholic when I was a child. So I missed a lot. Now he is an involved grandfather, giving and receiving what he missed back then. I enjoy that.

The crux of the matter is that most women are used to giving to and supporting other members of their families. When they become mothers they find that they do not have the time or the energy to continue giving at the same level and they want to put what energy they do have into their own families. If the first family understands this natural progression of life and steps in to support the new mother in a non-interfering manner, the relationships will grow closer. If, however, the first family members still demand the same degree of support from the new mother she will find she has to distance herself from them in order to survive. Often this displeases others.

FRIENDS

- 52% of women surveyed did not expect any alteration in their friendships
- 56% reported an impact on coping; 18% severe to extreme
- 48% experienced intrapersonal conflict; 15% severe to extreme
- 35% engaged in interpersonal conflict; 13% severe to extreme

Although not a major source of readjustment, the change in their relationships with friends did have an impact on new mothers. Before a baby arrives a woman is able to either spontaneously choose to see her friends or plan ahead for a meeting. Once one of them has a baby neither course of action can be relied upon. Spontaneity gives way to the baby's sleeping and feeding patterns and planned activities are as likely to go awry because the baby does not cooperate.

Friends without children tend to find it difficult to be sympathetic towards the new mother if they think she is either unorganised or obsessed with her baby. Many 'know' that when they become mothers they will not allow a mere baby to dictate the terms of their life. They do not comprehend that exhaustion controls a new mother's brain, sometimes for years. Her focus changes and she finds that things her non-mothering friends believe to be important, things she used to think were important, now hold very little meaning for her. Instead she becomes child-centred which, to her friends, is all right so long as it is kept within the bounds of moderation.

To a new mother the often unspoken criticisms of disapproving looks, exasperated sighs or distancing are not experienced as being supportive, especially at a time when she may crave adult company above all else. Friends are less inclined to be tolerant of her baby's interruptions and may find them to be extremely irritating, especially when the baby becomes a toddler.

These days, when a friend announces that she is going to have her first baby, I know that we will not experience quality time together for several years at least.

OTHER MOTHERS

Often, as a non-mother, a woman will feel as if she is different from women who are mothers. When she becomes a mother herself, she realises she is the same. She begins to understand that we are all mothers, in this together. Once I accepted that I had stepped through the one-way door into motherland, I looked around and saw that I had entered a world where women of all kinds were routinely handling exhaustion, loneliness, confusion, guilt, enormous responsibility, great love, huge fear. They were largely lacking any meaningful support and generally were doing battle with low self-esteem and a yawning need for acknowledgement. Nobody was talking about not coping, not really. Whilst we will readily admit that mothering is difficult, few of us let on that we suspect we may not be cut out for this lifestyle; that maybe it was all a mistake. Few of us feel all right about asking for and accepting help. Our mothers did this. Other mothers are doing it all over the world. And so we feel that we should be able to do it, too.

Competitive Mothering

Perhaps this pressure we place on ourselves is what leads to the competitive nature of mothering about which many women have complained. Conversation develops a wilful mind of its own, returning time and again to some standard topics:

- Whose baby sleeps least, behaves worst
- Whose baby does what first

- Whose husband is the least considerate
- Whose husband has done or said the dumbest thing
- Whose husband is the least supportive
- Whose greater family has the most outrageous expectations
- Whose in-laws make the most unbelievable demands

It is almost as if women need these additional hurdles so they can define their value by their ability to rise above insurmountable odds. Being 'just a mother' is not enough to empower her with self-esteem so she must also struggle against unreasonable obstacles and, in surviving them and overcoming them, she proves her real worth.

Elaine wryly gave substance to what most of us unconsciously believed before becoming mothers.

> I thought mothers would be supportive but I found there was this big competition between them—how smart their child was, whose husband was the worst, whose child wore the best brand names.

Some women play down their feelings for their children, while others gush over how incredible theirs are. It can be galling to stand listening to a mother effuse over how bright, intelligent, creative, musical, witty, spiritually developed her child is while other women's children and their achievements are ignored. At first other women may try to compete with such a mother, eventually most go silent in her presence. A new mother would do well to note that while she may feel her baby to be the greatest creation on earth, most other mothers feel exactly the same about theirs.

Although most women go into motherhood with the expectation that they will need to make new friends amongst other mothers, 35% found it difficult to connect with like-minded women when the time came. This was especially true for the older first-time mothers who often found they were surrounded by much younger women with whom they had little in common. Mary told of her experience which was commonly repeated throughout all forums.

> The older you get the harder it is, I think. I joined the Baby Health Centre and met up with some new mothers, all of whom were much younger than me. These younger women just snapped into it. They hadn't had a career, they hadn't travelled, they hadn't done anything.

They'd grown up in this town, they'd always lived here, and they had family here. Motherhood was a breeze.

The Baby Health Centre had a psychologist come along to talk to us. At that time I was finding it *very* hard and they were stunned. They couldn't understand it. So I just shut up because I thought, 'It's a completely different experience for me.'

There is a glaring need for those who deal with new mothers on a professional level to take a more active role in helping them develop a workable support network.

Discovering Other Mothers

In the first year of my motherhood I developed an admiration for women that I had never before suspected possible. Our ability to handle all the crises of motherhood, the interminable demands of children, the exhaustion, the eternal thinking ahead and organisation amazes me. Other mothers have expressed similar feelings for their mothering sisters. Nikki said:

Motherhood introduced me to a whole new society—mothers. I am in awe of what we do, we are so strong.

Many women do not find the conversion from living in a male-dominated world to living in an all-female world easy. They often feel as though they have lost a significant and cherished slice of themselves, particularly on a mental level. This can generate a certain amount of discontent at being trapped in this strange land from which she can find no way back—indeed knows that there is no way back.

In time most of us accept that we belong to this exceptional 'species' called 'mother', for we are mothers ourselves. For me, this is now a comfortable belonging which probably took the better part of five years to develop. In this belonging I have found a powerful thread of commonality with all mothers in all lands on this planet. There is almost no woman on earth, who is also a mother, who has not experienced the same love and fear, anguish and joy that I have lived in relation to my son. Indeed, on the day we give birth to our first child we all enter a very special sisterhood which extends into every corner of the globe.

Other Mothers' Children

One of the facts of becoming a mother is that a woman inevitably and unavoidably comes into contact with other women's children. If a woman was already child-tolerant or child-oriented by the time she became a mother this is not such a problem. If, on the other hand, she had little contact with them or actively disliked them this adjustment to motherhood can be quite a challenge. How some women feel prior to having a child of their own is captured in the following comments by women who attended discussion groups.

Mandy: I didn't like other people's children. I couldn't even look at them.

Glenda: I really hated kids before my daughter, but then I developed a liking for them after she was born.

Charmaine: I had no interest in children before I had mine.

After the advent of motherhood it can come as quite a shock to realise that one's world is populated by other women's children. If one is going to survive in this world one had better find a way of relating to those children quickly. Fortunately there are strong motivating factors. Being able to compare your own baby or child to others and thereby gauge whether you are doing more or less the right thing as a parent is very comforting; as is knowing that your own baby is developing at a 'normal' pace. It is interesting to see how older babies and children develop and thus to gain insight into how your own may evolve. Most importantly, when you are hanging out for adult interaction it makes no sense to frighten another mother's kids with daggered looks when that will only result in more crying, more interruption and less conversation.

Ultimately there is the realisation that you must find a way to get along with your friends' children so that your toddler has the opportunity to develop friendships—and you to find baby-sitters so you can have some time out from mothering. The social benefits of deciding to like other children soon become apparent.

However, a small percentage of women choose to isolate themselves from other people's children as much as possible, finding no interest in them at all. Usually these women are either completely absorbed in their own offspring, are finding the bonding process difficult or are seriously depressed. Pauline has only just begun to accept other children, five years after becoming a mother.

> I am not a particularly sociable person ... I was totally focussed on and absorbed in my children—I could not concentrate on anything or anybody else. Child care is more valuable than anything I have ever done before.

Sometimes a woman will choose to isolate herself from other mothers and their children because she cannot bear the level of noise a group of babies and toddlers invariably generate. Playgroup can be a nightmare for the woman who discovers she is noise sensitive and who is jarred mentally, emotionally and even physically by the yelling, screaming and crying of twenty or more children. This problem is exacerbated when the playgroup is held in a hall that echoes. The louder the noise the louder she must shout to be heard and the more intensely she must concentrate in order to hear. If she is already struggling with any other stressful side effects of motherhood, playgroup may be intolerable.

THE LOST TRIBES

As I have said before, until very recently women mothered collectively, not in an echoing hall but in their own village environment. Only since the Industrial Revolution, and the advent of the suburb during the twentieth century, has it been expected that women should mother alone in their separate homes. In our tribal and village days we shared the responsibilities and the work with other mothers, grandmothers, young women and girls. In evolutionary terms this change has come about in a millisecond. Women need other women to develop those close relationships that today they so wish they could create with their men, but are finding it difficult to do. Because our lifestyles are filled with 'doing' we often do not appreciate how much we need each other until we become mothers.

Almost to a woman, those who contributed to this research believed that the social move towards isolation has cost families too much. At every discussion group women decried the loss of the extended family, not only for the support it once offered them as mothers, but for the support it offered them in their partnerships with the fathers of their children, the sense of belonging, history and variety of input it afforded their children, and the connectedness and sense of worth it afforded the grandparental generation. Indeed, there was a degree of anger amongst women that the economic climate and/or the pressures of city life had divided them from their families and that, therefore, they were expected to mother their children in an environment of such paucity of familial relationships. Also evident amongst women who did not have an effective extended family was a profound degree of helplessness at their inability to alter their situation.

One of the first impacts of raising a baby and child without the support of other women who have been through the experience and who have produced functional adults is a sense that the new mother is doing something wrong, is incapable, is 'not normal' in the way she feels. Heather's questioning of her normality is far too common:

> Am I normal with these feelings? Am I just some weird person who's not able to cope with motherhood? What's happening to me?

Those whose children were older than hers assured her that indeed she was normal and that they had all felt similar feelings to hers.

It cannot be emphasised enough how profoundly all women experienced this loss of not only the extended family, but the extended community as well. Even those few who did have a functional, supportive network were clear that they could not survive without it. As Betty said:

> I'm very blessed to have a wonderful mother-in-law who lives nearby and just loves kids. She has the kids twice a week and complains it's not enough—even on weekends she rings and asks if she can have them. In the first few months she takes the baby so I can get some sleep. That's how I cope. I wouldn't survive motherhood without her.

Those who did not have this level of support discussed the issues with a great deal of passion. In so doing there was a sense that they were attempting to understand, not only what was wrong with the structures in which they were trying to mother their children, but how those wrongs could be righted. Kylie expressed what has proved to be a very common opinion.

> How it's meant to be is tribal—we all go down to the river and wash

the clothes and watch the kids. But usually you are isolated from the extended family.

Essentially in agreement, Nancy lamented the difficulties she had experienced that were brought about by a lack of contact with other mothering women and which she felt had been compounded by the sheer 'busyness' of modern day life.

> My tribe's scattered all around Australia and I'm here on my own. People are so busy and there is so much going on. One of the things that sometimes let me down when I wanted to speak to another mother was that they were all so burnt out and so busy that we didn't create time to get together properly. When you're a career person, in between looking after your child, you charge off and you're out there doing it and you're not sitting there sharing a cup of tea and some ideas with your supports.

The lack of extended help networks resulted in some women having to 'outsource' the support they needed in terms of employing home help. Nikki told of her distress in having to hire a stranger to look after her children.

> My mother lived with us for two months when our second was born because I was so ill and he was ill. But after she left there were days when I had to ring up nanny services because I couldn't even get out of bed. It was *awful* having to have a stranger in my house to look after my two precious babies.

Although the majority of women had not experienced such extended illness, they had certainly experienced the lack of support. Many were angry about the structure of a society that cannot provide the assistance mothering women almost universally feel they need. Helen expressed her feelings on this subject.

> I'm very angry because I feel I'm at the absolute end of it. I use some child care now but the first time I did it all on on my own. This time there's been no way I could because my partner's not been around that much and it [child care] is very intense.
> What makes me angry is that it could be different. We could actually have a different structure. We could be not living in these isolated little

units of heterosexual, marital coupling which doesn't provide, for me, a hell of a lot of support. There could be much more extended family—or extended community involvement where there were little halls everywhere. Neighbours could be more strengthening.

When her words are compared to those of Kylie, who lived in a commune during her early days of mothering, it is clear that even the most difficult of mother–child relationships can be ameliorated when the support of an extended community includes women who are mothers of older children, who understand the difficulties a new mother faces and who have the willingness, resources and time to offer their expertise.

> The thing that truly saved me when Alex was little (and screaming 15 times in a night and I never got any sleep and he was always sick) was not my relationship with my partner—because he felt overwhelmed by this too. It was that at that time I was living in a well-established community. What would happen was that these other women would just come and put our son in a backpack and take him away and let me sleep. That's what saved me.
>
> I can remember going at three o'clock in the morning to a midwife who was a member of the community when he had a temperature. She just took over and showed me what to do. It was wonderful.

Rosemary's experience of having a child with similar health problems was quite different given that she lived in a regional town, in her own home with her partner, with no family nearby, and no social support structure. It is worth noting that those who may have helped her considered themselves to be 'visitors' and therefore a hindrance, rather than supporters or active helpers.

> When I was going through all the problems with Zac, probably the hardest thing was that I was on my own all the time. Everybody stayed away because they thought I was having such a hard time the last thing I needed was visitors. So I just spent all day on my own with a screaming child.
>
> When my husband came home I would go to bed because that was the only sleep I got all day. So I saw him for five minutes because then I was asleep. Then, when he had to go to bed he'd wake me up and I'd do

the night shift. I used to sit there at three or four o'clock in the morning sometimes on my own and I'd think, 'This is weird. I don't see anyone. I'm awake when everybody else is asleep.'

There was a clear and pervasive tendency amongst the majority of women to believe that they ought not to need help with mothering their own children and that to ask for it was to admit incompetence. Nancy pointed out that if a woman is older when she has her first baby, those with whom she has previously had a relationship do not always adjust well to the fact that a new mother may become needy for a period of time which adds to her sense of inadequacy.

> The thing is that when you are really down you don't have the energy to contact people because you're so wiped out. Or you are embarrassed if you are used to being in control and a capable person. I've noticed that when people are used to you being a certain style of person they tell you that this is not you, to pull yourself together if you are collapsing. I used to think, 'Don't you want to know this part of me? This is another facet of me.' You also find that if you've developed a relationship with someone they don't want you to be a needer because you've always been giving.

Nancy also found that her husband did not enjoy her going outside their immediate family unit for support.

> My partner was angry when I talked to my girlfriend because I'd hung out my dirty washing. But I felt a lot better. I need to talk about it and I do. There was this attitude that, 'We don't have problems and we don't talk about them to anyone else.' It's this isolation that women get, particularly if you are tired and you've got no income coming in and you're stuck at home and your partner feels that you shouldn't need other people to talk to because he should be enough. If I said I needed someone he took affront at that. It was like he felt he wasn't doing enough and he'd say, 'I'm doing everything I can.'

These mothers also regretted the fracturing of extended family relationships because of what their children missed. Jan had moved to a regional town because her husband's career demanded the move. She explained what her young life had been like in comparison with that of her children.

> I always had extended family around me as a child and it was really special. I remembered those times at birthdays when the people who were at the party were all my cousins, and at Christmas time there was this huge event with our uncles and aunts and cousins.
>
> When we had our kids I was really sad that there were no cousins, no uncles and aunts and thought we had to do something about it. But there was nothing we *could* do and there still isn't. We do stay in touch but a visit is a lot different from week-to-week contact. That is an issue and it is another kind of pressure.

It was widely felt that the broken continuity of intergenerational family relationships was almost as detrimental for the grandparents as it was for their grandchildren. Mary, who lives 600 kilometres from Sydney, said:

> It's bad for the grandparents as well. My parents live in Sydney and they just adore my kids. It's really sad. I'd love it for myself to have them nearby, but I really wish for them that they were closer because I know they are missing out.

There was, however, a widespread sense of conflict between these women and the grandparents of their children, whether they were on the maternal or paternal side, which was either generated or exacerbated by the physical distance between them. Marge's experience was that her child, at the age of 14 months, was treated differently from other grandchildren in the family.

> My mother-in-law is here at the moment. She lives in Sydney near my husband's brother and his two kids. One of them is the same age as Nadine who she's seen three times. All I'm getting is 'Lorraine doesn't do that.' I'm thinking, 'Well this isn't Lorraine, this is Nadine.' That's all it is—comparison, and my child isn't meeting the expectations, isn't up to scratch. I have to keep walking out of the room because if I don't I'm going to go off my head.

In a similar vein Mary found it difficult having to have a relationship with her parents because their only contact was during short but intense periods of having to live together under the one roof. She said:

> When my parents come to stay now it's such a pressure. I find it's OK for a couple of days but after three or four I've had enough of being in the same house with my father. I wish they were just around the corner in the next suburb when I could see them for two hours and then go home, instead of three days of them in my hair.

The difficulty of maintaining relationships between the generations was keenly felt by those women who found they were the ones who had to do the majority of the travelling. They found that having to pack up the multitude of clothes and toys required to keep their children occupied whilst on long car treks and extended visits to their family's home, combined with trying to give everybody a fair and equal share of their time when they got there, was stressful. Heather said:

> Not to mention visiting the rellies and the accusations of not giving them enough access to their grandson. All the guilt that you get thrown on you from the grandparents. And at Christmas! Trying to fit everybody in. 'Oh, you're not going to spend Christmas with us this year.' That *really* is a big problem for us.

Regardless of their personal difficulties with their parents and regardless of the difficulties of maintaining relationships with grandparents when they live at a distance, the majority of women very much wanted for their children the style of interaction that Kerry portrayed her sister's children as having with their grandparents.

> My youngest sister lives next door to my parents. Her kids have the *best* relationship with them. They'll get up and go next door and have breakfast and my sister will still be in bed. It's been like that forever.
>
> It was a wonderful thing for Dad after Mum died. Even though he gets exasperated, he wouldn't be without it. I'm sure they'll always remember Mum because they were there all the time. It is such a day-to-day thing, not a big thing, not like, 'Let's go visit grandparents.' They are just there, they are just part of their life.

THE GREATER WORLD

> After Mum died I was really jealous of the relationship my sister's children had with Mum—that Becky didn't have. I don't think Mum and Dad thought they were the 'special' grandchildren but just by the proximity, just because they were there, they were always buying them this, or taking them there. It is really interesting that you've got to be close by for that to happen. It can't happen a long way away.

Kerry believes her father's close contact with his children and grandchildren helped him weather the death of his wife after almost fifty years of marriage and that his resilience to such a major life change was enhanced by the depth of these intergenerational relationships.

There was clear agreement amongst these mothers that relationships require time and proximity if there is to be any chance of them being meaningful and intimate. Many women believed that being older when they had their first children combined with living at a distance from their families had contributed to their sense of isolation which, in turn, had exacerbated the difficulties they experienced in becoming mothers and coping with the rigours of motherhood. Although most had tried to integrate with other mothers the majority had not found it easy to replace their family with new friends. With the exception of those women who had supportive families living close by, every woman missed the opportunity to have intergenerational interaction on a regular basis without the pressure of having relatives visit them or being the ones to do the visiting. They missed the contact for the support they did not get for themselves, for the relationships their children did not develop with their grandparents, aunts, uncles and cousins, and for the relationships the grandparents did not develop with their grandchildren. Gillian wondered how this breakdown in the family would affect the next generation when she asked:

> Isn't it terrible that our lives have changed so radically? That our relations and our aunts and uncles and cousins, instead of living all together, are now scattered everywhere? That we don't like going to see them because it's such a hassle to get there? What's going to happen to our kids when they grow up? How much more is it going to be?

No woman had the answer to these questions other than to know that the breakdown in the ties between people is not, and if it continues will not be, conducive to creating a healthy society for anyone who lives in it. Nancy did not have the answer either when she said:

> Somehow the community needs to provide the extended family instead of the blood lines.

Because women now feel (and are) so disconnected from their extended families and communities the issues of child care have also become intense.

CHILD CARE

The first and most obvious relational change of motherhood is that a woman's primary relationship, in the sense that it will occupy the greatest proportion of her mind space and time, is the one she will have with her baby. Since the breakdown of communal parenting the responsibility for child care falls almost exclusively on the new mother. Dianna's experience is very common. She emphasised:

> My children are NEVER away from me.

Dianna is, if you like, a 'natural born' mother. Patient, kind, supportive, loving —the kind of mother who should have a large family. Yet even she said these words with a hint of despair.

In spite of their intense desire for more time for themselves, over and over again women told me that they did not allow their children to be minded by anyone in the first years of their lives. The reasons they gave are both personal and societal.

Trust

Trust is a valid issue in today's world. Where once a woman would readily leave her child with friends and neighbours, today she must question whether these are people fit to care for her baby. In some cases her memories of her own childhood are so negative that she will not trust even her own mother. Thus she never leaves her baby with anyone other than her spouse. Even then she is often anxious for the entire time they are separated causing her enjoyment of her free time to be impaired. Pauline told me:

> I never felt at ease until I was back home again and I could tend their

needs in what I regarded as a satisfactory way. I was quite obsessed ...
but I could do it no other way.

Especially with her first child a mother may feel she is the only person who will be able to meet her child's needs and does not trust that anyone else could attend to her baby as immediately or as completely as she can. Underlying this lack of trust is a feeling that her baby will be psychologically and emotionally damaged for life if its needs are not fully met. This is not the case. A child will certainly be damaged if its needs are regularly violated throughout its early years. It will not harm a baby or a child to go wanting for short periods of time. Logically this may be so but many women cannot get past their overwhelming need to be with their babies at all times. Pauline concluded:

> I find it very difficult to understand how people can leave their babies or toddlers with others.

Being a Burden

At a time when a woman is expected to be the sole caregiver to her children she understands the demands this places on every other mother. Few of us want to make the job harder for anyone else and so many women will not ask even trusted friends to take their babies or toddlers and give them a break. If she does reach the end of her rope and asks for help she will often spend all the time she is away from her child feeling guilty and anxious that she is imposing upon another over-burdened mother. As Dianna said:

> I don't feel I can ask my friends to look after my child. I know how it is. They are already struggling. How can I ask them to do more?

However, it is well to note that if we reach out for help we give permission to those who support us to reach out to us when they, too, are in need. Most mothers benefit from a break in routine, responsibility and from a short period of freedom from the continual physical and emotional demands placed upon them by full-time child care. Given a few hours to herself she may return to her job of mother refreshed, renewed and ready to be fully committed to the raising of her child. On the other hand, the reverse can be true, as was pointed out to me by Ellen, who said:

If I got away from the kids for a day when they were small it took me
days to adjust back again. I hated coming back.

It should be noted that Ellen is a committed, full-time mother of three who
adores her children. What her comment reveals is that even for those of us who
are fully committed to being mothers, the sacrifices are not easily made.

Child Abuse

If the myth were correct that the biological mother is the only proper person to
look after her very young children then the growing statistics on child abuse
would show that this is an all-male phenomenon. In fact it is not. In the first
year of a child's life it is as likely (and in some instances more likely) to be
abused by its mother as its father. Studies conducted in the United States show
that women are responsible for:

- 56.8% of major physical abuse
- 48.5% of minor physical abuse
- 7.6% of sexual abuse or exploitation
- 69.7% of abuse by neglect
- 52.2% of emotional maltreatment
- 65.5% of other maltreatment[88]

In light of the way we perceive, relate to and structure motherhood this should
come as no surprise. A woman may feel surges of anger towards her child
simply because there is nowhere else to discharge her frustrations which are
both unacceptable and undeniably real.[89] Sandra wrote:

> Most first-time mums think they can take care of the baby without
> help 24 hours a day or go straight back to full-time work,
> travelling, etc. and that is not the case. Apart from time off to
> catch up on sleep, we also need time to ourselves to do non-baby
> things, or we burn out.

The maternal instinct is not necessarily coupled with a desire to mother 24 hours

---

[88] N. Wolf, *op.cit.*, p.235
[89] A. Rich, *op.cit.*, p.24

per day in isolation from the rest of the community. Studies conducted in 1983 by Boulton revealed that only half the women interviewed actually enjoyed child care while slightly more than half found it to be irritating to their individuality. Over half found motherhood gave them a sense of purpose but a significant minority did not.[90]

Margaret Mead has stated that the mental and emotional health of both mother and child is enhanced by the interaction with other supportive adults. She concluded that the quality of care given to a child is of far greater concern and value than the quantity.[91] Similarly, Alice Miller believes that:

> Children need the respect and protection of adults who take them seriously, love them, and honestly help them to become oriented to the world.[92]

It is difficult to take the demands of a very young child seriously every minute of every day of every week with no relief in sight. There is considerable evidence to suggest that children actually benefit from the variety of interaction that occurs when they are left in the care of other *concerned* and *supportive* adults.

Sharing the Caring

As I have already pointed out, very few women who contributed to this book found it easy to separate from their babies and very young children and the majority discovered that leaving them with day care mothers, day care institutions or baby-sitters was very much harder and more painful than they had anticipated. Marge asked her discussion group:

> Did you have an emotional problem putting them into care? I just can't do it. Because I don't have family close I've never left her, she's never been left overnight.

Those who had put their children into care, particularly at an early age, said that they had suffered anxiety and guilt over the separation, over the quality of the care being given and over the fact that someone else was responsible for

---

90 M. G. Boulton, *op.cit.*, pp.58–61
91 Betsy Wearing, *The Ideology of Motherhood*, North Sydney, 1984, p.63
92 Alice Miller as quoted by Peter Knudtson & David Suzuki in *Wisdom of the Elders*, North Sydney, 1992, p.170

teaching their children values that were not necessarily theirs. Nevertheless, every mother said she wanted, more than anything else, to have more time to herself. Jan explained:

> I'd like to look after my kids full-time but I find it very difficult to be their full-time carer every day of the week. That just drives me crazy. There comes a time when I've really had enough!

This conflict of ideals and needs was one few mothers had resolved to their satisfaction no matter what their choices had been and it highlights the extent to which the loss of the extended family and community has affected them—as the following stories show.

Kylie returned to a job she loved when her son was 14 months old and experienced deeply the dichotomy of being both a career oriented person *and* a mother of a young child.

> I found that really traumatic. I chose child care centres as opposed to day care because of my fear of child molesters. The first centre was awful—another mother told me she had sat and held him while he screamed because no-one else would. I sent him to another centre. That early morning rush of getting your kid ready and then he'd be clinging and hanging onto me and I'd leave him sometimes in tears. There was a sense that I was abandoning him. There is no way that wasn't enormously heartwrenching.

Rosemary had had to go back to studying at a PhD level soon after her baby was born not because she particularly wanted to fulfil the requirements of her scholarship, but because she and her husband needed the income it afforded them. She said:

> I think that the guilt is always there when they are in care. I know that someone else is raising him and that's pretty obvious when he starts talking words that I know I haven't taught him, rhymes I haven't told him. And that means he's getting them from somebody else, which means he'll also be getting their values which are not necessarily mine. I found that hard.

Those women who had found carers whom they trusted implicitly or had access to quality child care in their places of work did not suffer from these feelings of guilt, anxiety, or emotional dislocation. Three such examples are Taylor who employed a child carer, Shirley who sent her daughter to a day care mother, and Geraldine whose daughter attended a workplace child care centre five days per week. Taylor's carer regularly took her two pre-school age children to visit her own grandparents and over time these people had become surrogate grandparents to her children filling the gap in their lives brought about by the physical distance between members of their own family. Shirley's day care mother had become her own mentor. She said:

> That's why it is so easy for me, her day care mum is the most brilliant lady. She is round and fat and jolly and she laughs the whole time. She's been doing child care for the past 25 years and her house is like a preschool. She's got so much equipment and she just loves kids. I use her as my mentor because I don't have grandparents close, so I often sound off things that we're going through because she's so experienced. So for me, day care was a really easy decision to make so I could have time to myself.

Taylor had not returned to paid work and at no stage felt guilty for putting her child into care or for taking that time for herself. Geraldine, on the other hand, did return to full-time paid work but had the option of placing her daughter into care within five minutes walk of her office. Although she was initially distraught at having to separate from her, six months later she said:

> It's so easy. I drop her off in the morning, I see her at lunch time and then I take her home with me. I know her carers, they know me, and they are the best. She loves it. I love it.

The majority of mothers, however, were not able to access the quality of care found by these three women and experienced putting their children into the care of strangers as 'difficult', even 'heartwrenching' and 'traumatic'. Their experiences highlight the need for affordable, quality child care that is close to the places in which women live and work and in which mothers, themselves, can participate. Paid child care has the potential to fill the gap left by the fracturing of the extended family and community and to provide the additional resources that single parents, in particular, so desperately need. Although it is an industry created by the rise in dominance of the doing paradigm, this same paradigm is now compromising the ideals of universal accessibility, affordability and quality of care as the industry is increasingly subjected to the pervasive objectives of 'economic rationalism'.

It is clear that very few women who are mothering in isolation find full-time child care either easy or eternally fulfilling. It is also clear that extended families and communities have fractured to the degree that mothering in isolation is commonplace; that dual parent families are increasingly in need of two incomes in order to survive; that single mothers and their children commonly live in poverty, and are therefore under additional stress; that most women feel desperately stressed by the lack of time they have for themselves either because they are the full-time carers of their children or because they have also returned to the paid workforce. Given that there is an acknowledged link between isolation and/or poverty and/or stress and child abuse, and that child abuse across the society is rising rapidly, it makes no sense not to increase the quality, accessibility and affordability of paid child care. If, in addition, the institutions which share in the care of our children (including infant and preschool care as well as infant, primary and high schools) were also supported in creating environments which encouraged parents to attend meetings, educational sessions and social events, either after hours or on weekends, there is every possibility that they could collectively become an important re-integrative force across the entire community. This, in turn, holds the potential to alleviate some of the more negative effects of the doing paradigm.

RELAXATION AND HOLIDAYS

- 47% of new mothers surveyed did not expect to have to alter their manner of relaxation or holidays
- 63% reported an impact on coping; 31% severe to extreme
- 47% experienced intrapersonal conflict; 30% severe to extreme
- 41% engaged in interpersonal conflict; 28% severe to extreme

After the birth of a baby all relaxation activities must take into account this small person and thus they tend to become baby-centred. Holidays and weekends need to be structured around the care of the baby, but this is not always anticipated. As one man vehemently stated when being advised of this by parenting friends:

> Our life will not change after he is born. The baby will just have to learn to fit in with us.

His wife agreed. Shortly thereafter they sold their home, which they had vowed never to leave, because it was not designed to accommodate children.

Women whose husbands travelled in the course of their jobs said their spouses did not want to take holidays and so did not realise they might need a break from routine occasionally as well. Others felt that holidaying with very young children was no break for them since they still had to do the lion's share of the caring. With only one exception no mother had had a holiday away from her children with her spouse in the first four years of motherhood.

It would seem to be fairly obvious that the addition of a child to a family would alter the way that a family holidays, yet it is not something people take into account until after the baby has arrived. Suddenly, people who used to think nothing of hopping into the car and travelling hundreds of kilometres for a weekend away find their baby does not settle well in a baby capsule and that the crying they must endure to get from A to B is more stressful than staying home. Or their children develop car sickness. Or the continual begging for the journey to end from the back seat is too aggravating to bear. Or, once there is more than one child, the fighting drives the parents crazy. No longer are weekends away viable so they never drive outside their city limits. Long plane flights are a similar nightmare and so overseas travel tends to go on hold even for the most seasoned and committed of travellers, sometimes for years.

Food becomes more of an issue once a child becomes part of the family. Expensive restaurants do not cater for a toddler's simpler tastes, nor its needs to move about, so the parents find themselves dining more often at the fast-food outlets whether they themselves like the food or not.

Accommodation alters its focus. No longer will it be evaluated by its ability to meet the needs of the adults but by how much entertainment it will be able to provide for the junior members of the household and at what cost. Above all, holidays cease to be a time when the adults are able to do as they please, when they please, together. Instead they find themselves doing exactly what they do at home—entertaining and meeting the needs of their children. The only difference is that they are doing it in a strange place without all the familiar toys, routines and foods being available and at great expense. Pam feels:

> Holidays are no holiday for me. I still cook, wash, pick up, chase after the kids all day long, get up to them all night. I would rather be at home where it is not costing me anything extra and where I know where everything is.

FEELING LEFT BEHIND

- 59% of women surveyed did not expect this aspect of motherhood to affect them
- 55% reported an impact on coping; 31% severe to extreme
- 47% experienced intrapersonal conflict; 31% severe to extreme
- 41% engaged in interpersonal conflict; 30% severe to extreme

Whether a woman is eighteen or thirty-eight when she first gives birth to her children, the world keeps on moving at its ever increasing rate of change. No matter what her age, when she leaves the workforce to become a mother she steps outside the daily flow of those changes and the longer she leaves her reentry to paid work the greater the gap in her knowledge. In the course of a single year cash registers can and do change, as do computers, phones and switchboards, libraries, teaching methods and curriculums, technical expertise and all knowledge, work practices and opportunities. As the years pass, her need for retraining grows and so does the daunting feeling of being left behind.

Particularly when a woman leaves a career in which she had been reasonably successful, she may feel that paid work will speed rapidly out of her reach if she does not take steps to keep up. Because of this she may feel pressured to return to work well before she is ready to do so. If she persists in pursuing her career as a mother she is likely to watch as her peers return to the paid workforce and to feel as though she is being left behind. Which, in a very real sense, she is. When a mother takes on a paid job she does leave behind those who choose to be full-time mothers. The working woman has little time to support and be with her mothering friends. As more and more women are steadily drawn back into the workforce the full-time mother finds her circle of friends shrinking until she, too, in search of social contact if nothing else, succumbs to the search for a job. Jeanie, who loves being a full-time mother to her four children, confided:

> It seems like all my friends are getting jobs. I am beginning to feel I will have to look for one myself. It gets lonely when everyone else is at work.

If a woman is in her thirties when she begins her family and she chooses to be a full-time mother until her children reach high school ages, she is then looking at perhaps having to undertake several years of training and study before being in a position to compete for a job. Then, in her mid-forties she finds herself trying to begin a new career alongside women twenty years her junior. Camille is battling with herself over this one.

> I want to have another child but I can see the workforce slipping away from me. I need to study and do a masters now. I worry about whether I am going to be able to cope, to write the essays, etc. But leaving it longer just means putting off my career even longer. I'll be fifty before I get started again!

While motherhood remains as undervalued as it currently is, it will seem that everything else in the world has more worth and more importance than mothering. It will seem that to spend time in the profession of motherhood is to be wasting time, rather like hanging out in a billabong instead of rushing headlong down the river, with everyone else, towards the ocean. Yet it is in the billabongs that life is generated and nurtured and raised, where the life force matures, ready to feed the river when it becomes old and depleted. Destroy the billabongs along our rivers and we destroy the rivers themselves.

WOMEN WHO DON'T WORK ... AND THOSE WHO DO

The United Nations acknowledges that around the world women do two-thirds of all work, both paid and unpaid, but receive only 10% of the world's salaries. It is 'semantic slavery' to refer to a woman whose primary role is to care for her children, her home and her partner as a 'woman who does not work'.[93]

Just as Australia's gross domestic product would rise dramatically if unpaid labour were taken into account, Kenneth Galbraith has calculated that if homemakers' labour were included in Canada's GDP it would rise by 40%. The Canadian Human Rights Commission estimates that if equal pay were to be

---
93 Gloria Steinem, *Moving Beyond Words*, London, 1994, p.239

awarded for equal work, a homemaker's worth would be equivalent to that of a middle level supervisor, a senior specialist, therapist, social worker[94]—and this without taking into account the massive overtime she inevitably invests in her occupation.

In the national census and in the calculation of the country's GDP there is no provision made for recording the work of unpaid child care or homemaking, thereby implying that this is not legitimate work. Indeed, breastfeeding does not add to the GDP—but bottle feeding does. What a woman purchases boosts the GDP—but what she makes in the home does not. If she grows her own food, sews the family's clothes, builds her own home, cares for her own children, a woman is deemed to be not working, not contributing to the collective GDP and therefore economically a nonentity.[95] By default she must be at leisure.

In addition to the social denial that the work a woman does in the home is work at all is the fact that success or failure in the role of mother can only be judged on the quality of the long-term relationships she builds. There are few clear guidelines as to how to perform well in this role and whatever feedback a mother receives varies according to the beliefs of those who evaluate her performance. Her rewards are, therefore, not always immediately obvious. They may well be outweighed by the censure she experiences on a daily basis and there is very little possibility that she will ever be promoted to a higher position within the role. In the absence of regular positive feedback in a role as nebulous as this, it is difficult to grasp and hold onto a solid sense of self. On the other hand, the role of a paid worker is usually well defined with clear parameters for success or failure. Feedback in a paid job is generally immediate, rewards are consistent and obvious, and there is normally an accepted pathway for promotion.

These factors contribute to the conflict surrounding the choices between mothering full-time or mothering *and* returning to the paid workforce and can affect any woman who finds herself grappling with an uncertain identity in the new territory of motherhood. After she has had her first child she may be shocked by the changes it has brought to her life. She may not have time to adjust to her new role or to understand her baby's particular personality quirks, or to readjust her relationship with her partner. The result can be an intense confusion regarding her roles and identity. As Catrina said:

---

94 G. Steinem, *ibid*, pp.214–215

95 G. Steinem, *ibid*, p.216

The women who are working feel guilty for not being with their kids and the ones who aren't working are made to feel guilty because they are not. It is crazy.

In 1991 Bittman found that women's unpaid work increases by 60% when they marry, and by 91% when they become mothers.[96]

Perhaps this increase in the thankless, unrecognised work is contributing to the rapid growth in the numbers of women re-entering the workforce after they become mothers. In 1965 in the United Kingdom only 14% of mothers with preschoolers worked. In 1989 that figure had risen to 50%.[97] One-third of women now expect to combine income earning and the duties of home and children by the time their first born is six months old and 97% by the time the child reaches eighteen years of age.[98]

Similarly, the Australian Bureau of Statistics reported that in 1992:

- 50% of women with children under five were in paid work[99]
- 80% of women with children in high school worked
- 59% of two-parent families with dependent children had both parents in the workforce
- 40% of women in the workforce had dependent children[100]

Some of the reasons women now so overwhelmingly feel they need to be a part of the paid workforce are:

- Economic necessity
- Not wishing to slide down the career ladder
- Lack of preparedness for the rigours of child raising
- Inability to find fulfilment in the role of mother and homemaker
- Rising insecurity in marriage
- Regaining personal power

---

96 Shelley Cooper, 'What organisations can do and why it makes good business sense' in *Marrying Work & Family Responsibilities*, University of New England, Armidale, 1995

97 D. Richardson, *op.cit.*, p.20

98 S. Feldman, *op.cit.*, p.15

99 Bettina Cass, 'Bringing equity to the balance of family responsibilities and employment; the roles of workplaces, industry partners and government' in *Marrying Work & Family Responsibilities*, UNE, Armidale 1995

100 Sue Walpole, 'Sex Discrimination, Work & Family Responsibilities' in *Marrying Work & Family Responsibilities*, UNE, Armidale, 1995, pp.1–2

- The desire for achievement and publicly recognised success rather than always serving others[101]

They also go back to work to escape the isolation of motherhood, to regain their self-esteem, autonomy, economic independence and to create something which is considered to be worthwhile. Increasingly mothers are returning to work because their friends are being drawn back, which leaves those who remain alone and minus their hard won support networks. It begins to look as though the workplace is the only venue for social interaction.

Given the escalating breakdown in marriages, it has been said that:

> Traditional motherhood is not a rational life choice unless a woman has a contingency plan for supporting herself and her children.[102]

The difficulties of returning to the workforce, however, are formidable. The lack of quality child care facilities, as already noted, is one. Waiting lists are often years long. Other obstacles are employers who do not comprehend that children, even if ill, should claim a higher priority than the work a woman (or indeed a man) is employed to do. It is estimated that, in Australia, 50% of absenteeism is a direct result of the conflicts of interest between paid work and the responsibilities of being an adult member of a family.[103] Since absenteeism costs the country approximately 60 million working days per year, family-based absenteeism accounts for 30 million of those days.

When a woman does return to the workforce she often finds that she is treated as though nothing has changed in her life, as if having a child were as incidental as taking a holiday. She is expected to forget that she is a mother during the time she spends at work and certainly is frowned upon if she allows her role as mother to interfere in her productivity in any way. Sandra, a doctor in a teaching hospital, wrote:

> I might just manage to be okay if I never ever discussed woolly woman stuff like babies. Liberal feminism, far from liberating women, played on this sort of thinking; if women want their place

---

[101] S. Feldman, *op.cit.*, p.15
[102] K.M. Baber & K.R. Allen, *op.cit.*, p.146
[103] B. Cass, *op.cit.*

> in the world of power they should think and act like men; if they must have babies they should never let it affect their career (or inconvenience their male colleagues), and it is oh, so unprofessional to discuss anything to do with babies during coffee-break at work ... you're supposed to talk about cars, cricket and how to make lots of money.

It is stressful to divide one's time and attention between two modes of being and thinking that are as different as those of mothering and working. The working world demands linear thinking which is goal-oriented. The mothering world demands that a woman be able to think of and focus on relationships and dozens of tasks at one time, achieving each in piecemeal fashion as and when the baby or child sleeps or is happily occupied. Switching from one to the other is not easy.

Paid work combined with home work leaves virtually no time for the working mother to invest in her children, let alone her own regeneration.[104] Hannah has worked as a full-time mother for 14 years. She recently worked in a paid job and was shocked at how quickly it affected her desire to provide the level of quality mothering she and her family have come to expect.

> By Wednesday my head was so full of what had happened all day and what I had to deal with tomorrow that I came home and found I did not want to know about the children or their homework or making dinner. Intellectually I knew that working women had to give up a lot but I did not realise how much.

Clearly the majority of women who return to paid work for any length of time do find some sort of balance as they readjust their priorities. However, I found only two who considered they had found an ideal balance between paid work, mothering and time for themselves. Betty, who was pregnant with her third child at the time of attending one of the forums, worked two days per week as a secretary, spent one day per week on her hobby of leadlighting and the other four she devoted to her family. She saw no reason to alter her lifestyle for more than a few weeks after the birth of her next baby. She told her group:

---

104 S. Kitzinger, *op.cit.*, 1992, p.213

> After the first six months my boss let me bring the [first] baby in a couple of hours a day here and there to get normal again. It worked well with the first two children and now the third one will be the same with a new boss. I found I enjoyed motherhood *and* my part-time work.

Similarly, Taylor had found a balance which suited her—she was able to dictate her own hours as an accountant and worked four full days per week. She also had her paid child-carer and the carer's grandparents to care for her two pre-school age children and her husband was involved and supportive in spite of his own busy career. Nevertheless, she still felt pulled by a powerful need to be with her children.

> I think I'm schizophrenic. At the end of the week I think, 'I've got a few days off with the kids—great!' And I can't wait. Then when I've had my time off I can't wait to go to work. Next year I'm reducing my hours so that after school I can be with my kids.

Betty's ability to successfully combine work, home and self life was not solely dependent upon having found a job which enabled her to bring her very young children to work. She also had a mother-in-law who lived close by who not only took care of the children regularly, but who complained that she did not see enough of them. And she had a husband who shared the housework, did the majority of the cooking and who fully supported her in taking time out for herself. Taylor's job, on the other hand, paid well enough to enable her to afford top-of-the-line child care.

It appears that the following three elements, at least, are essential for a woman to cope and feel comfortable with paid work and mothering:

- part-time work with flexible hours
- workplace child care or remuneration adequate to pay for excellent, near-to-hand child care
- close and supportive extended family and/or a partner who shares the responsibilities of home work and child care

In spite of the fact that the majority of mothers do not have these supports, they are returning to the world of paid work in unprecedented numbers. Not least amongst their reasons for so doing is to restore the balance of power in their relationships. A woman's power drops as soon as her first child is born and there ensues an inverse power relationship between mother and father according to the number of children in a family. Pam found that part-time work, for her, was essential.

> I go to work for the financial benefit. I like to work. To use my head.
> I function better, I am mentally more alert and more organised. This job is not mind-boggling at all but it is MY day and it is MY money and it is to get away from the kids. That money is MINE. Even if I spend it on the house I can spend it on what I want.

When a woman rejoins the workforce she gains more control over the combined income of the household. Her return to paid work not only legitimises her power[105] but raises her status, her sense of worth and helps her restore her competent and autonomous identity.[106]

When a woman is in paid work it is considered legitimate that she should expect assistance around the house and with the baby. As a full-time mother this is not necessarily so. When she is unable to obtain relief from the tedium of household chores and the emotional drain of full-time child care, paid work begins to look like an attractive escape hatch. Linda found she had to go back.

> I need to be working for my Self. I just love it. Now that I have gone back to my career my husband will help me a lot for some reason.
> But why wasn't being a mother career enough to get the sort of help I needed before?

In recent times those who control paid work are beginning to realise that when they lose women to motherhood they are losing valuable assets. The carrot of paid maternity leave is being dangled as an enticement to agree to come back to the paid job as little as six to twelve weeks after the baby is born. It is an attractive carrot and, for those who do not want to give up their careers, a valid support which needs to be applauded and extended. Adelle knew she had to return to paid work even before she had her first child.

---

105 M.R. Polatnik, *op.cit.*, in ed. J. Treblicot, *op.cit.*, pp.25–31
106 B. Wearing, *op.cit.*, p.139

> I knew at the time when I was pregnant that I HAD to go back to work and I did, six weeks later. I would have gone downhill at home.

Most women, however, do not know how motherhood is going to affect them. Six weeks after her baby is born her body will still not have fully recovered, especially if she is an older mother or one who has suffered complications during birth. She is likely to be extremely tired, if not exhausted. The baby is unlikely to have developed a routine sleeping pattern. She will have to wean her baby almost as soon as it is born and may be extremely surprised at how physically and emotionally painful that can be. Her wardrobe is as likely not to fit her properly yet, if it ever does again. Six weeks is not long enough to adjust her self-image, to embrace the role of mother, to reorganise her thinking. Above all, it is not long enough to get to know her baby well or to have developed a working relationship with him or her.

A woman who agrees to take maternity leave may find that as the date of her return to the workforce approaches she becomes seriously distressed at having to leave her baby. She may discover that she has fallen deeply in love with her child. As a result all her priorities will have changed radically with paid work shuffled to the bottom of the pack for the time being. Geraldine, just prior to returning to her job after twelve months maternity leave, said:

> It is breaking my heart having to go back to work, having to leave her. I cannot bear to think about it.

To feel compelled to return to a job at this most precious time in a baby and mother's life can leave her feeling torn in two, guilty and remorseful with an abiding sense that she is missing something she will never be able to recapture. A first-time mother often finds it surprisingly difficult to give up her child to the care of others and feels torn between her need to nurture and her need to succeed,[107] feeling as though she is somehow cheating her children and, sometimes, her husband if she goes back to the workforce.[108] This is something which a woman may not know until after she first holds her baby.

Many women said that their desire for success in the paid workforce altered dramatically as soon as they became mothers, even going so far as to say it

---

[107] J.F. Kuchner & J. Porcino, *op.cit.*, in eds. B. Birns & D.F. Hay, *op.cit.*, p.273
[108] M.R. Polatnik, *op.cit.*, in ed. J. Treblicot, *op.cit.*, p.27

'evaporated'. Marge, whose first child is three and who is soon to give birth to her second, was one such woman. She described her feelings to her discussion group with some passion, saying:

> My aspirations for the future changed absolutely. I wanted to be detective come hell or high water, that's all I wanted to do, and I did that. Then along came the baby and I wouldn't care if I never worked another day in my life. We need the money so I go to work purely for that. Apart from that I have no aspirations to apply for promotion, to try to attend any courses because that would take me away to the academy in Goulburn, away from my daughter. I'm just happy being mum.

Another woman whose desire for success deserted her as soon as she became a mother was Rosemary who was a PhD student on a scholarship when she became pregnant at the age of forty. She, too, had to return to her studies almost immediately after the birth of her baby because she and her husband needed her income. She said:

> I find it really hard some days to settle myself to studying because that seems unimportant in comparison to raising Zac. I'm too aware of the cost to him. It feels unfair because I have already done it once. I've had my time. Now what I should be doing is giving my time to him.
>
> I could probably still do well in my career but I've completely lost my ambition. Perhaps it's because I've already had one successful career and been around the world and done all that high flying stuff and know that that gave me very little enjoyment in the end. In retrospect, I know that I used that as a substitute because I couldn't have kids. I also know that having all those things didn't bring me the happiness that I thought it would. There was still this thing missing. I know now I've found that thing and that is more important to me than anything else.

Yet the decision to stay at home with a baby may carry equally painful and difficult consequences for the new mother. The unexpected isolation, work load, exhaustion and constant emotional giving can combine to make her feel as though she has entered a black hole from which she will never be able to escape.

Sarah, a mother of three who has worked part-time since her first was only a few months old, acknowledged that:

> The hardest thing is to decide to stay at home. It would be a lot easier to go back to work and let someone else mind your kids. It is so full on. There is no time to yourself. I cannot even go to the toilet alone. I sometimes run away and sit in the garden where they cannot find me.

Camille who has been a full-time mother for six years confirmed these sentiments, saying:

> I have never worked so hard in my life. I do feel like a slave.

Women are being given confused messages about their roles as mothers and workers. On the one hand we want our women to stay at home and look after the children, on the other we want them back in the workforce. We need and want their nurturing qualities and their relational abilities but we want them to join the competitive world of work where these talents have little or no place. We are told, as Eileen says:

> You are 100% responsible for this child but when are you going back to work? But when you go back to work you are not doing the right thing by your child. I get really angry that I am expected to separate from my daughter to do anything—work or study. I am expected to put her into day care. You are expected to bond with them at birth but then separate right afterwards.

Some women return to the workforce because this is what they think they should do or because it is what they think they want only to find that it is neither, for them. The realisation that they cannot do both jobs to their personal satisfaction causes them to feel as though they are less adequate than other women who, apparently, are able to make both roles work for them. Margaret could not make both roles work for her.

> I resigned from my teaching job because I found mothering and working to be incompatible roles. I am just not a very adequate person.

THE GREATER WORLD

> I knew I could not do it all. I knew I would be a pretty rotten mother if I worked.

The trouble is that when we compare ourselves to a woman who appears to be successfully mothering and working we do not question whether her support systems are strong, be they in the form of a supportive spouse, family, friends or paid help. Neither do we know the cost of her success to herself, to the members of her immediate and greater family, to her community. Instead, as Margaret did, we simply assume that there is something wrong with us—or we juggle the time balls faster.

Prior to having their son, Jessie and her partner had agreed to share the earning and parenting roles so both were working from home part-time. However, she found it difficult to cope with her toddler's constant interruptions, the lack of boundaries between home and work, and the fact that she could do neither job properly. She described the situation as 'maddening'. Ultimately she decided to move her business into an office away from the home but found the adjustment to be a bigger strain than she had imagined it would be. She explained:

> I wish I could be at home. It's been an enormous adjustment for my little boy. Being away from him a lot over the past few months has really taken its toll on him and me. I feel incredible sorrow about that *and* that I've made this decision which I can't really change now.
>
> I feel like my life is about juggling these big balls in the air all the time and I can't stop and rest or take time for myself because the time that I can stop I need to really connect with my little boy because he longs for that. He's disappointed when I go and so pleased to see me when I get back. He tantrums at the moment because he's frustrated about the lack of contact and I find that really sad. It really pulls on my heart to have to go away to work even though I'm leaving him with my partner. But he's with him more than I am and that doesn't feel right either.

In a similar reversal of roles, Kerry, who holds a senior position in a government organisation, went back to work full-time when her daughter was six weeks old. Her husband was on long-term leave from his profession after a serious workplace accident and was comfortable with his role as the primary caregiver.

At no stage did Kerry feel as though her daughter was 'missing out' on adequate nurturing, nor did she feel as though she was trying to combine two jobs since her husband also filled the role of home carer. Nevertheless, she had sorely felt the loss of her role as 'mother'. Her daughter had just turned three when she said:

> The only negative thing I've found about motherhood is that in the past twelve months I've really wanted to be a mother, I *really* want to be at home with Rebecca. Because of circumstances I'm feeling *really* deprived of that. I'm very jealous of Greg and at times I'm jealous of the relationship he has with her.

However, having given up work, it does not take long to realise there is a widespread attitude that a woman who is mothering is doing nothing. In general, the women who had elected to stay at home felt, as Jennifer did, that:

> Working women are not very supportive of women who stay at home.

Perhaps this phenomenon is caused not by disinterest in full-time mothers so much as by a lack of time in the working mother's life to meet even her own and her children's needs, let alone those of others. Jessie experienced the lack of time to express her creativity, for instance, as an enormous loss once she returned to paid work, as her words reflect:

> I just park it [my creativity] over there and try to get on with it; I put it over there again ... and again. That's what I do with those aspirations. In terms of creativity I feel envious and frustrated. I want to work with colour and design. There's this whole part of me that is so frustrated, that feels like I'm being strangled slowly. Because there isn't the time to fit that into the picture—there isn't enough time!

Many feel that the feminist movement bears much responsibility for this division within motherhood. Amongst the full-time mothers there were some women who expressed real bitterness that the needs and concerns of the full-time mother have been so completely ignored and dismissed as having no validity. Margaret wrote:

The feminist movement has to respect the choice of women who stay at home. I feel feminist thought to date has been a bit 'white collar'—women brought up in families of less socioeconomic opportunities may never have had the opportunity to look at career/mothering issues that our education has allowed us. Let's all respect the choices we made, I say, as our individual right; self-actualisation is surely the issue here and motherhood, which may be one woman's treasure chest, could well be another woman's Pandora's box of troubles!

Many women, whether they had returned to paid work or not, decried the fact that it was politically incorrect to believe that a woman may be more capable of nurturing her family than a man or that this may be an instinctive response to motherhood. This intellectual electric fence makes it difficult for women to discuss the issue, let alone how they might cope with it given the current social structures and taboos. Kerry, in spite of her belief that she was making an important contribution to her society in her career, said:

> What amazes me is that if I have a day off and Greg is going out of the house, I come down in my dressing gown, get breakfast and then I have a routine. I clean up downstairs and upstairs, I clean the bedrooms and tidy the place. It's like I have feathers fluffing behind my back and loving it! I love it! I just love those feather fluffing days. It's almost like this is a normal sort of life—you're tripping off to work and I'm staying home. I actually have a great anticipation of having a day like that.

Marge extended this concept. She, who had had great difficulty in breastfeeding (thinking, 'It was the weirdest thing I'd ever seen') and felt she knew nothing of how to do mothering (eg: feeding, bathing, changing a nappy, dressing a baby), nevertheless believed she was genetically programmed to *be* a mother. She said, 'I feel it's *in me* to take the Domestos and do the bathroom. It is *in me* to sweep the floors.' The ensuing discussion was echoed in every focus forum and interview, and Mary's comments summarise the opinions of both paid working mothers and full-time mothers:

> It's *such* a big issue. If you're a mother at home you feel like you are missing out, but if you're a mother working you feel like you're missing

out. We've come so far and we've got all these options, but we're still not happy.

There's still such a big difference between men and women, isn't there? Men can still focus on the career totally, and do it. I used to have a career and I earned a lot more than he did but now it's gone. I can't pick it up where I left off. That's the sacrifice I've made and it's a big sacrifice. I do feel regret. If we lived in Canberra still, I'd have gone back to work 12 months later. I don't regret being at home because I love it but yeah, sometimes I worry about what I'm going to do in the future. Because I do want that back.

Those who wanted to work as well as mother also experienced this seemingly irresolvable conflict of paradigms as they tried to find a balance. Even those women who desperately wanted to contribute in the paid workforce found the dilemma of mothering impacted significantly on their choices. Kylie has found that in spite of her enormous ambition, she cannot compromise the life circumstances (that is living on a small property near a large regional town) in which she has chosen to raise her child. She explained:

I was twenty-seven when I had Alex and I hadn't finished yet. It is like my life has been on hold and I find that difficult at times. I am very ambitious in the sense that I think I have possibilities of going a long way and making a difference in the world—and I've already got a lot of recognition—but right now I'm making choices and decisions that will potentially compromise my career. The logical place for me to be living is in Sydney as far as my career goes, but there is no way I'm going to subject my child to that lifestyle.

Now, with my son twelve, I'm seeing an end in sight of that intensive day-to-day child care and I'm starting to think about where do I go from here and what do I do next. I love my child desperately but I don't know that I'm going to suffer from the 'empty nest syndrome'.

The trouble is that nobody explains to women before they become mothers that they simply cannot be 100% good mothers and 100% good wives and 100% good housekeepers and 100% good workers all at the same time. Trying to produce excellence in every one of these jobs simultaneously can make a woman feel as though she is failing on all fronts. Alanna works full-time and has done so since her eldest child was six weeks old. She confided:

> I feel guilty that I cannot be there for my kids when they have a sports day, do a play at school, for education week, after school. I hate it when my youngest cries at the day care gate reaching through the bars, begging me to take him with me.

As well as struggling to achieve the impossible, the guilt which women feel for their perceived failures leads them to try to compensate their children and partners for the sacrifices each must inevitably make. Such compensation always comes at a cost to the mother until she can feel as though she is being torn apart.

As Moir and Jessel concluded in their book, *BrainSex*:

> To succeed on male terms, by male methods ... makes successful motherhood an impossibility; there simply are not enough hours in the day.[109]

The only way out of this dilemma is for women to become proactive in altering the base definition of success so that it encompasses and embraces their values as equal to those of males. If we cannot do this then success will continue to be defined by the doing paradigm where success is achieved via aggression, competitiveness and,

> ... a relative suspension of social and personal values, to which the female brain is simply not attuned.[110]

These unwritten rules make winning the game, or even achieving a sense of being a valid member of the team, extremely difficult for women—especially for mothers of small children.

The Australian Bureau of Statistics estimates that by 2005 the Australian workforce will be made up of 60.3% women and 39.7% men.[111] If this prediction becomes reality then surely it must be possible to construct the

---

[109] A. Moir & D. Jessel, *op.cit.*, p.166
[110] A. Moir & D. Jessel, *ibid*, p.166
[111] Office of the Director of Equal Opportunity in Public Employment, *op.cit.*, p.5

workplace in such a manner that women are able to mother whilst achieving work-related goals. This may mean rethinking the structure of paid work quite radically. What if a full-time job were defined as being 20 hours per week and training, leave and promotion were based on this definition? What if there were no tax penalties for those people who wanted to work the equivalent of two or more jobs? What if employers identified the number of hours required to fulfil the requirements of a particular job and then allowed their workers to divide that job amongst any number of people, provided the work was consistently of the standard required and completed on time? What if every worker had the right to take their job home whenever that was possible and was therefore, able to structure their working day around the needs of their family? What if child care were tax deductible in the same way any other work-related expense is deductible? What if excellent workplace child care were an integral part of the paid working world where a mother or father, whether single or partnered, could bring their preschool age children secure in the knowledge that if their children were hurt or became ill or upset at any time during the day they could comfort them almost immediately; where they could form a relationship with the carers and be assured of the quality of care their children were receiving and that their children's needs were being met; where they could be with their children during morning and afternoon tea breaks and lunch times if they wanted to; where their children were able to come before and after school if that were practical in terms of proximity to their schools; where they could bring their sick children and know they would be cared for well; where a parent did not have to leave home so much earlier in order to take her child to a child care centre which was at a distance from her place of work and to handle the upsets of separation for both mother and child which can be so distressing; where a parent arrived home earlier at the end of the day because she did not have to do this double shuffle in reverse? What if governments actively supported and promoted these initiatives? What if ...?

These are the suggestions made to me over and over again by women who have battled with the work/child care dilemma. No doubt there are others I have not yet encountered. However, when these, at least, are commonplace across our society women will not have to make so agonising a choice between motherhood and career.

Simultaneously, we simply must revalue motherhood so that raising our children well becomes a top priority in our country and, therefore, the profession of motherhood one which carries significantly higher status than it currently does. Only then will women be able to make truly meaningful and fulfilling choices.

As Phillipa told me:

> I work in child care, have done forever, training people to be professional child carers. I have to admit there are times when I think this is a strange thing to do. It is bizarre that women think that in order to be legitimate people they have to be 'out there' in the workforce as opposed to being valued for parenting their child. The reality that people are putting their children into child care for up to twelve hours a day is strange.

Whether we work at home or work in the paid workforce, the reality is that our children need us and have a right to receive both quantity and quality time with adults who are relaxed enough to hang out with them. This cannot happen as long as the paradigm of material achievement dominates the paradigm of relationships to the extent that it does today. The New South Wales Legislative Council Standing Committee on Social Issues recently conducted an inquiry into parenting. Its first recommendation supports the need to revalue the relational paradigm in stating (in part) that:

> A democratic society has a duty to ensure that every child is provided with a nurturing environment that will enable the realisation of that individual's potential [and that] the interests of the children must be paramount ... It is in the interests of the whole community to ensure that parents are adequately supported and assisted in this role, given the impact of parenting on the development of children.[112]

This report went on to say, 'The Council notes that the objective of a child-friendly society would be to promote the optimal wellbeing and development of children.'[113] Unfortunately, amongst their 89 recommendations not one addressed the issues of paid work whether full- or part-time, the dilemmas of child care, the time stress of paid working parents or the conflict between

---

[112] Standing Committee on Social Issues, *Working for Children: Communities Supporting Families—Inquiry into Parent Education and Support Programs*, Parliament of New South Wales Legislative Council, Report No.15, Sydney, 1998, p.xi

[113] Standing Committee on Social Issues, *op.cit.*, p.32

parenting and career. In other words, no recommendation was made that might impact on the foundations of the doing paradigm. In the face of such governmental reluctance to address the big issues of parenthood, it looks as though the only way meaningful change can come about is if those of us who feel strongly that the imbalance of values is detrimental to our children, parents and society, unite in numbers large enough to exert the degree of pressure necessary to bring about a more healthy balance of paradigms—no matter which side of the fence we have decided suits us best as individuals.

HELP FOR HANGING IN THERE

Your Mother is Still a Mother, Too

Grandmotherhood was supposed to be a time when a woman reaped the rewards of her hard work as she became the revered matriarch of the extended family. Today, she may never see any member of her family because they have moved away and all she is left with is her older age. I believe a great deal of the criticism grandmothers level at their daughters and daughters-in-law is a cry, in disguise, for acknowledgement. It is a plea to be taken seriously, to be included, to belong to the greater family; and a desperate attempt to prove that their lives were not wasted and the knowledge they gained as mothers still has significance. Motherhood was, after all, more often than not their central life role.

Next time your mother or mother-in-law appears to criticise you, hold back your reaction for a moment. Ask yourself whether she is being totally self-centred and uncaring, or is she perhaps asking you to recognise her as a woman of worth? Just as some women find motherhood easier than others, some grandmothers find grandmotherhood easier than others. Is yours asking for help? Explain to her the differences in being a mother in today's world compared with the way it was for her. Help her to understand that you are not rejecting her, as a person, but that you need to do things differently to meet different pressures.

Help the Rest of Your Family Understand

The rest of your family may not understand why you have transformed from a perfectly reasonable human being into a total ratbag. Explain to them, in as non-blaming a manner as you can, what your daily reality is like, how you feel and why. Admit to being exhausted. Do not try to hide it or to pretend you are coping if you are not. Ask for their help directly rather than beating around the bush.

If in becoming a mother you have triggered the release of denied or suppressed family issues or differences, this is not your fault and it is not your responsibility to fix them. Only those members of the family who have the problem can do anything about it. All you can do is learn what these issues mean for you and support others with love as they come to grips with what they mean for them—which could take a considerable amount of time. It is even possible that you will need to maintain a physical distance from them during this period in order to protect yourself from becoming emotionally caught up in problems that are not yours to resolve.

Mothers Need Friends

Do not expect your non-mothering friends to necessarily be understanding of your new circumstances. Since your relationship cannot remain unchanged, they may be experiencing your move into motherhood as the loss of a valued friendship. It is possible you will see less of each other over the next few years.

You may feel an urgent need to find like-minded women after your baby is born and you may feel devastated to realise they are not easy to come by. Good places to look are in the baby health clinics, playgroups, through Nursing Mothers and amongst your friends who became mothers ahead of you. There is a huge need for postnatal support groups where new parents can meet people in their own situation, talk about the problems of their transition to parenthood and develop friendships.

Often friendships which grow out of motherhood are deeply rewarding and extend across a lifetime. You share the joys and the pains of mothering with another mother who knows exactly what you are talking about. You watch and help each other's children develop. A bond then grows between you which can be bigger than a simple friendship involving only two adults.

Other People's Children

If you first meet a child as a baby you may bond with her instantly and thereafter find her easy to relate to. Meeting her for the first time at three years old may mean meeting her when she is in a seriously revolting phase, causing you to conclude you will dislike her for all time. The next time you meet, she may have progressed to angelic mode. Do not judge other children by your first meeting with them. Give them a chance over time.

If you find you are noise sensitive create play areas in and around your home which are safe and at a distance from where the adults gather. Alternatively, meet your friends at outdoor venues like parks or beaches so the noise of your collective children can dissipate into the atmosphere rather than penetrate your brain.

Your child's friends will almost inevitably infiltrate your life. It will deepen your relationship with your own child if they become important to you. The reward comes when they begin to treat you as a significant person in their lives. Then you feel a growing sense of your value and ability to contribute to the greater family of humankind—your own family expands.

Child Care

It is asking too much of yourself to expect you will be able to enjoy caring for your child all day, every day, without any relief. The sooner you can come to terms with leaving your baby with a trusted person, the easier you will find these early years of motherhood. If you have a friend with a baby of a similar age to yours, when you both feel ready, try leaving your babies with each other even if only for half an hour at first.

This reciprocal arrangement has many benefits. It gives you a guaranteed period of time out to look forward to each week. Your baby will learn to respond to another carer so that when she reaches the stage of being afraid of strangers, this person will not be part of that mindset. You will learn that you are not the only person in the world who is capable of looking after your child—and that is a very freeing discovery.

For women who live in rural areas, swapping children in this manner is not always possible because of the distances separating them. The need for more and affordable occasional child care places in the regional towns and cities is all the more crucial.

Child care centres and day care mothers can be a priceless source of relief from the continual demands of looking after an infant or toddler. If you have not returned to paid work it may be helpful to spend the first six months or so of motherhood seeking out a carer or a care centre that will meet your requirements when you do return to work or when you feel you need a day to yourself to regroup. Ask your community health worker, doctor or friends for referrals. Do not be afraid to go to the places they suggest and spend some time getting to know the people who may ultimately look after your child for you and the philosophy of the centre for which they work. If you know that you will be returning to paid work soon after your baby is born this research will need to be undertaken during your pregnancy. Once you have chosen a child care institution or carer, if you are not happy with the quality of care your child is receiving, do not feel embarrassed about removing him and finding another—nor should you feel guilty about having placed him in less than 'perfect' care in the first place. Truly, the infant human being is a resilient creature who can tolerate short periods of unhappiness without sustaining permanent damage. What your child will appreciate more than anything is having a mother who is not so stressed out that she cannot happily interact with him when you are together. It is much better to have some time away from each other if that is going to help you develop a more healthy relationship and if you do not have trusted family members or relatives nearby who can give you a break, paying a carer is a reasonable and viable alternative.

Holidays and Relaxation Change

One of the great pluses of becoming a parent is that it opens up new worlds of experience. Having children is the best excuse for going to fun parks, children's movies, children's theatre. It is the best way to lighten up, to rediscover the child inside you who is busting to get out and have fun. If you will allow yourself to become immersed in these activities rather than resisting them, you may be pleasantly surprised at how much you enjoy your children's enjoyment.

You will need to negotiate a balance of caring duties when on holiday, otherwise you may find your partner continues to look after the children at the same level he does when he is at home. If you do not split the caring time equally it is likely you will grow impatient with his attitude and arrive home more stressed than when you left.

It is best to give up all notion of sophisticated holidays until after your children can adequately entertain themselves. Caravan parks, motels and holiday resorts which cater for babies and young children will provide you with a more relaxing holiday and they will cost you less. There is no sense wasting good money on an expensive holiday when you cannot get clear of your toddler long enough to enjoy the facilities for which you are paying. Keep it simple.

No matter how you spend your relaxation time and holidays, as long as you have a baby or toddler their needs will dominate. There is no getting away from it.

Feeling Left Behind

If you are in a position to be there for your family, have no desire to have a paid job and love this work you do at home, do not, not for one minute, think you are wasting time, inadequate or being left behind. You are a dying species and our communities, whilst not yet realising it, desperately need you. Motherhood is special—never forget that.

If you are a woman who wants to be a full-time mother only until your children are in school, give yourself permission to take this time out from the workforce. Although in the early days of mothering you are unlikely to realise it, the training you are undergoing as a mother is infinitely more valuable than all the university courses you could possibly study. It may not be until you re-emerge into the workaday world that you understand just how much stronger, more organised, more compassionate you have become over those years.

After becoming a mother, many women find their true path for the first time in their lives. Occupations which seemed attractive before now seem trivial and those which she never considered draw her like a magnet. You may find motherhood triggers in you a deep desire to create, to teach, to study, to campaign for women and children's rights, to help the environment. If you do return to your original profession you may be surprised how passionate you become about aspects of it you never before considered important. You may find the courage you have gained enables you to stick your neck out where before you would have kept quiet.

It is true that the world is rushing ahead at an ever increasing pace. Whether one is in the workforce or not it is easy to feel afraid of not keeping up. In many ways this is an illusion. It is a matter of choice whether we plunge deeply into the raging river or whether we are content to play in the shallows where change happens more sedately. When you are ready there will be a course available to help you bridge the gap. Study is often more rewarding at an older age anyway, since you know what you want and why. Your time will be more precious to you as well and you will not easily waste it. This makes a mother returning to the workforce a very focussed being.

To Work or Not To Work?

Only each individual woman can decide whether paid work is for her or not. If you are desperate not to return to the workforce and can afford to stay home, do it. Provided you are happy in yourself with the decision, the benefits are enormous. You will be there for your children and they will not have to come home to an empty house after school or spend half their life in day care centres. You will have time to prepare meals for your family, to look after house and garden. It is less likely you will feel the pressures of time and you will be less stressed than if you were perpetually trying to meet deadlines. However, it is likely you will experience at least some loneliness and a sense that life is passing you by in the early days of motherhood unless you have an excellent support network available to you. When your children go to preschool or school, though, you will find you have the time to enrich the quality of the lives of all your family members—especially yours.

If you do not return immediately to the paid workforce you have an opportunity to develop a network of support and friendship amongst other full-time mothers. When one of your friends is in trouble, you will have the time to help. When your children are sick, you will be there to nurture them. If your friends, who are in paid work, find themselves torn between their paid and unpaid duties, you may be able to help. You are likely to do more for your community and the schools your children attend if you are a full-time mother. You, and your children, are unlikely to develop any of the manifestations of anxiety or stress which arise out of having too many inflexible deadlines which afford you too little time to just be with each other. You will be available to support your partner in his career. If you are a full-time mother, never feel inferior. Do, however, listen to and acknowledge the achievements of those who have returned to the paid workforce.

Should you be a mother who does not want to return to a paid job but feel you must for financial reasons, take a look at your options. We have become so hooked into being good little consumers that we do not question whether we need what we buy. There is a real need to weigh up the benefits of having more money to spend on 'stuff' and those of having more time to spend with our children. Money and possessions can come later. Children will not wait to grow up. You only have the opportunity to be with them for a very small percentage of your lifetime. Is it worth missing those years just to get ahead financially? Will they thank you in the long run? Sometimes we have more choices financially than it seems.

For the significant minority of mothers who really do not have these financial choices (50% of women with preschool age children choose not to work and not all those who do choose paid work do so out of financial necessity), for those who return to paid work for fear of losing their sanity at home and for those who thoroughly enjoy their careers get over the guilt of not being a full-time mother immediately. It is a wasted emotional effort and achieves nothing. If you must or want to work, for whatever reason, give yourself permission to enjoy what you do. To resist your situation or your choice will cause you to resent your children when they make demands on you which seem to say 'you should be here for us'. You will find you have much more time and energy for your family when you accept that aspects of your situation are beyond your control or when you own your choices and your right to them.

When a woman undertakes paid work whilst raising a family she needs to take care of herself and find ways to regenerate or she will burn out. Make sure you organise all members of the family to do their fair share of the household chores. Let your standards slip a little rather than driving yourself and everyone else nuts trying to keep up appearances. Develop a network amongst both working and full-time mothers so you have support when you need to be in two places at the one time. Do not allow your sense of humour to become buried under all your responsibilities.

If you need to take a young child to child care, especially if she cries at the gate every day, insist that your partner takes her half the time. Otherwise you will shoulder all the guilt and fear of damaging your child and he will accept none of the responsibility. Your child will learn to adjust all the more quickly if she knows both of you believe this to be good for her.

Should you not have the option of sharing this load with your partner either because he cannot or will not become involved at this level or because you are single, some of the heartache of leaving your child can be alleviated by making the time to develop a relationship with her carer/s. This can be done by joining the management committee of community based child care centres or simply sitting in on these meetings, or attending weekend activities at the centre (such as fetes, working bees, etc.) with your child. When she sees you enjoying the company of the adult carers it is likely she will all the more quickly accept them as part of her own world. The added bonus, especially if you are a single mother, is that you will begin to connect with other adults who may be willing to offer their support and ease your load just a little.

Be aware of hurry sickness. Mothers who are in the paid workforce experience a chronic shortage of time. Notice when you are short-tempered in the mornings how much you tell your children they must hurry, must rush. Notice how tense and tight you feel inside. It is not easy to let that go but if you can develop a more flowing relationship with time the entire family will be more relaxed and all the healthier for it.

Whether you are a full-time, paid-to-work mum or a full-time, at-home mum, do not judge each other to be selfish or lazy, unloving or brainless. Neither of you is any of these and you are both making your individual contribution to the society the best way you know how. You each need to be equally acknowledged for your ability to cope with the difficulties inherent in your decisions and for the achievements and successes you extract from your chosen roles. If we mothers cannot support each other in our individual choices, how can we expect the wider community to do so? As Colleen, now in her sixties, wrote with the wisdom of hindsight:

> In every generation women have been made to feel they are mentally inferior beings and most have been financially dependent on their spouses. It is only now it is acknowledged that women are mentally equal to men. It is, therefore, this generation of women who have the push/pull attitude towards mothering versus career, which must be very difficult. Our day was long and labour intensive, but we did not have the stressful pull between family and career.

Each of us must resolve this tension in our own way and in our own time. What every woman needs is more support for her personal resolution of this dilemma.

I have yet to meet a mother who is not doing her very best to raise her children as well as she can within the parameters of her particular circumstances and based on the knowledge and support she has at any given moment. If she is not doing as well as others might think she should it is pretty well certain that that is only because she needs something: help, money, education, time, sleep, love, acknowledgement, friends, community, meaningful paid work, a caring partner ...

Most of us love our children with a depth that cannot be duplicated anywhere else and most of us try extraordinarily hard to balance the needs of every member of our family. Certainly every one of us could do better—if only we knew how. If we were all willing to openly share our experiences as mothers, as women, as people, whatever they may be, the degree of emotional and practical support we could give to and receive from each other would help every one of us 'do it better'.

NAKED MOTHERHOOD

It makes no sense for women to be divided over the issue of motherhood. Time spent arguing amongst ourselves and justifying our individual choices is time that could far more profitably be spent focussed on changing the social structures that make it so difficult for us to mother our children whether we are in paid work or not. Many lone voices in the wilderness will change nothing; a united chant brought down even the Berlin Wall.

EIGHT
REMARKABLE REWARDS

Motherhood offers a dimension to being a woman unimaginable to one who has not lived with, raised and loved a child. It may be possible to imagine the kinds of changes a baby brings to her life but it is impossible to imagine the magnitude of those changes. Motherhood alters a person at such a fundamental level. It exerts influence on the way she relates to herself, other people, the world and on her very experience of existence.

A woman who has chosen not to have children may feel offended at being told she cannot fully comprehend what it is like to be a mother; but she cannot. She can never truly know what it is she may have had to give up or what her mother self may have been like. No matter how a woman relates to it, the state of motherhood is like no other on earth. Like pain and pleasure, there is no way one person can know completely another's experience or how one might be affected by similar circumstances.

On the other hand, a woman who once had a career and who becomes a mother at an older age is aware of what she gave up to enter this special sisterhood. She knows what it was like to have independence, autonomy, power and status, freedom. She knows what some of the possibilities for her life were. An older mother knows her non-mother self as well as her mother self. Beverley wrote:

> I was aware that the child would change my life to a degree but I think
> I really was unprepared for the realities of motherhood. This I found
> surprising as I was one of nine children (third eldest) and so was
> reasonably familiar with parenting (or so I thought).

Having spent so long writing about the dark side of motherhood, I am delighted now to be able to sit at my computer and contemplate its many wonders. For me, conceiving, carrying, giving birth to and raising my son have brought me a greater, more enduring joy than all the money, all the power, all the status and all the success in the world could ever have given me. There is nothing anyone could offer me that could begin to compare with being Daniel's mum.

Being a mother has caused me to tap into emotions I never knew were possible; strengths I did not know I could muster; endurance of which I did not know I was capable; a depth of friendships with other women I never expected; tolerance where previously I only saw reason to judge; patience where once there was anger; and a connectedness, a oneness with all life on the planet about which I had read but now experience almost continuously. And so very much more.

These are remarkable rewards. In spite of having experienced many of the darker aspects of motherhood contained in this book I still consider the cost to have been minimal in comparison with what I have gained.

Thirteen years ago I stood on the threshold of motherhood so innocent of what I was about to undertake, so naive of what it would mean for me as a person. Today, I look ahead to the rest of my life knowing that I will achieve things I would never have contemplated, be who I never would have been, give what I never could have given and age with purpose as I never would have aged—had I not been a mother. And I know in my heart that I am, and will always be a better person for it. Whatever sacrifices I may have made, they are naught compared with this.

During every interview I conducted, and every discussion group, once the women had got off their chests all their untold grouches about being a mother every single one of them turned to the pluses of motherhood. Even those who said that, if they had their time over again, they would choose to be childless believed they had gained more than they had anticipated in becoming a mother. These rewards are not obvious in the early days and often it is difficult to believe there ever will be any. In retrospect they are astounding. Here are what the women, who so freely gave of themselves to contribute to this book, considered to be those rewards.

MOTHERHOOD REFRESHES

The adult world is so sensible, politically correct, economically rational. An adult participating in this world is expected to find these attributes acceptable and to live a life of principles which reflect their central importance. Thank goodness for children or we would all be narrow, stuffy bores.

Babies and children wash away the strait-jacketed models we build for ourselves. They respond to their circumstances with an honesty we adults have either long since lost or become afraid to express. They see the truth clearly and do not hesitate to let us know what they think of it. They tell us when the emperor walks naked and make fools of we who think we saw him clothed because we are afraid to stand out from the herd's definition of correctness.

In entering motherhood we have the chance to re-experience the child within ourselves who has never died, but only been forgotten. Whether our childhood was fabulous or dreadful we have a new opportunity to enter a wonderful world of fantasy, mystery and discovery if we will allow ourselves to become as children once more.

To see the world through the eyes of a child is to feel washed clean of judgements. Colours and textures, shapes and sounds vibrate with a glow and a quality the jaded, faded eyes of adulthood have long forgotten. Miracles occur moment by moment. Birds and butterflies, clouds and trees once again become the magical creations they have always been but which we have taken for granted for so long.

Children inspire the ridiculous and remind us not to take ourselves too seriously. They make us play. Their laughter splashes us with joy from the fountain of life. And we are refreshed in our souls by their delight at being alive.

PHYSICALITY AND SENSUALITY REDISCOVERED

The physicality of pregnancy, birth and babies was a wonder to many mothers who regularly said they felt like beautiful, powerful goddesses while they were pregnant. Helen recalled:

> I had an extraordinary sense of power when I was pregnant, it really took me over. There was the issue of where was the boundary between me and the baby, and how confused that was, and how wonderful and frightening because I was *him* and *me* at the same time. I think that's part of what happens when we send them outside of ourselves—we know they are an extension of ourselves. We know that that's our body and that's what is so extraordinary when we see them as so beautiful and so lovely.

Because of a sense of having been the powerful creative agent of new life, the bond these women felt with their children was often greater than any other they had ever experienced and it highlighted the sensuous nature of babies. Helen continued:

> That's one of the pleasures I didn't expect about motherhood—the sensuousness of babies, the sensuousness of touch. It's almost frightening. It's electric sometimes. Lachlan [aged two] lies full on top of me and rubs his head on me and I find myself wanting to go with it but also wondering where the boundaries are. But this is touch, this is *really* touch, and it's confusing. I didn't expect that at all. It wasn't told to me. I can't remember any conversation with other mothers, and given that I read avidly pre-baby it wasn't mentioned except for baby massage. We're talking about the sensuous nature of the beast.

In spite of all the newly emerging taboos and fears about touch and sensuality, every mother understood Francis when she said:

> When you see them naked with their gorgeous little bums it is so delicious.

Not only was it the mothers' need to touch their babies, but the children's need to touch their mothers which brought both pleasure and confusion to these women. Jessie related how her son needs to touch her breast.

> My little boy fed till he was two and a half and now he's three and a half. I'd managed to get his hand out [of my shirt front] but because he's missing me a lot the hand is definitely, very firmly going back in

there. I've said that for one minute you can hold it [her breast], but now he's got it up to four minutes and he says, 'Mummy, I need to hold it for four minutes.'

Whilst these stories brought laughter from those listening there was not a mother present at this discussion group who did not understand the powerful draw to touch and be touched by their babies and children.

THERE IS NO BETTER EXCUSE

Today a child's world is one filled with marvellous activities, toys, books. Having a young child is the best excuse to let down our persona of 'adult person in control of her life' and to build sandcastles on the beach. Is there a better excuse to sit on the floor and while away whole hours building wonderful creations with blocks and Lego? How otherwise would you explain to your one-time colleagues that you spent half the day up to your elbows in playdough and paint and glue creating a delicious, useless, worthless pile of mess? That you did nothing of 'importance' for an entire day? Or that you secretly enjoy reading children's books with all their simple, uncluttered wisdom?

As children grow older their interests expand. Now you can look forward to camping and sport, children's movies, fun parks—and even more interesting books and toys.

APPRECIATION OF OTHER WOMEN

Upon crossing the Rubicon into motherhood a woman may find she develops an admiration for all of womankind for all time. In becoming a mother she suddenly understands the passion and the pain women have endured since the dawn of human evolution. She comprehends the risks we each take with our physical wellbeing and with our very lives every time we give birth. She knows other women across the planet have endured the unacceptable—and survived because they had to survive for their children.

Many women admitted that once they became mothers they understood and admired other parents in ways they had never before considered important. Clearly this is because they now know that parenting is not as easy as it seems.

Similarly, many a woman finds she comes to terms with her own childhood as she gradually understands why her mother did and said the things she did.

Suddenly her mother's behaviour does not seem to have been quite so uncaring and, seen in the light of her mother's life circumstances, it may even make sense. Even if she still wishes things had been different in her childhood, the compassionate mother soon realises that, in most cases, her mother did do the very best she knew how with what she had at her disposal. Out of motherhood women often develop friendships with their own mothers which had previously not been possible.

Sisters (and brothers) understand each other better. After leaving home they may have drifted apart, now they find value in being friends and aunts (and uncles) to each other's children. Sandra suffered prolonged and serious depression after having her first child. Her relationship with her partner went into decline and is now dissolved. In the struggle to put herself back together she discovered her family for the first time in her adult life. On the brink of having her second baby, she wrote:

> My sister is an absolute brick and we will always support each other through bad times and good. My mother is enlisted to come and help with the new baby—the fact that I invited her to do so is a telling example of how much our relationship has changed.

FRIENDSHIPS BECOME MORE MEANINGFUL

Friendships are built on shared experiences, beliefs and life directions. The more meaningful the shared experiences are to the people involved, the more meaningful will be their friendship. Since there is little a woman can do in her life which will have as much meaning as becoming a mother, it stands to reason that when she meets someone with whom she can share her mother-self, as well as her other self, the friendship will be a deep one.

So many of the experiences of motherhood are common to us all that they provide a firm foundation on which to build relationships. Natalie wrote to me:

> I made new friendships forged from common fears and desires and shared experiences. I made blunders as a mother which my friends made me laugh about.

As we fumble through our early years of parenting, it is our friends who help us see we are making progress, who point to the light at the end of the tunnel so we are not swamped by guilt and remorse. We, of course, do the same for them. We share our creative solutions to personal and relational problems and so we grow together. Adelle said during our interview:

> You build a better trust with friends who also have kids. It is a warm part to a relationship which grows as the children grow.

Friendships built on motherhood establish a strong network of support for the women involved and for their children. Before motherhood the friendship of women may never have been important. Now it is paramount. Motherhood is so hard and so special that only another mother can fully validate and reflect the on-going enormity of the experience and comprehend the impact it has on another woman's life. Support and understanding at this level are the essence of true companionship.

HUMILITY

Before motherhood, especially if we have enjoyed a successful career, women tend to be egocentric. We have conquered the obstacles of work and money and men. Directed our lives. Purchased our commodities of comfort. Come and gone as we pleased. It is easy to believe oneself to be a little above those who are less successful, who have achieved less in the way of material recognition, who have 'merely' been mothers and done 'nothing' with their lives.

What a shock it is to discover that as mothers we are all the same. We all fumble and fume. We all become 'just mothers', lose control over our lives for a time and realise we are far less powerful than we once thought we were.

Kylie is a psychologist whose areas of expertise are domestic violence, child abuse and sexual assault. She had her first child when she was twenty-eight. Of her initiation in the humility of motherhood she said:

> I was one of those young, arrogant things who knew everything about child abuse and how to handle babies. But my baby cried up to fifteen times every night. One night I couldn't take it anymore. I took him and threw him onto the bed next to my husband and told him I was leaving them both ... then I went outside onto the verandah and cried.

I doubt that Kylie experienced this episode as a gift at the time it occurred. Yet today, more than ten years later, she can look back on it and know that this was when she crossed the line which separates judgementalism and humility. This is when she, as have the rest of us who have discovered we cannot be all things to all people at all times, began to accept her own limitations and to judge others less harshly for theirs.

Motherhood is an opportunity to understand that underneath all the fizz and fuss of worldly success there lies a deeper world of life and death, relationships and survival. It is a world we cannot control, one we cannot always steer in the directions we might prefer and one which is always vulnerable to influences outside our understanding. No matter how much we know about our external world, none of us know for sure how the internal one will play itself out. It is a humbling experience to walk through the door of motherhood and find a world full of women who have had to face humility. Whether they have chosen to integrate it, or to fearfully shove it away, is quite another matter, though.

MOTHERHOOD IS CONNECTEDNESS

Once the early sense of isolation has passed, motherhood heralds an opportunity to appreciate the connectedness of all life on this planet. Many of us do not notice it is happening to us because this connectedness grows slowly, building upon itself day by day. Some of us never put a name to it and yet we feel it deeply.

Perhaps it begins with seeing another woman on the television screen pleading for help in finding her abducted child—or crying for her murdered child in Dunblane or Port Arthur. You, sitting in the safety of your lounge room, experience an upwelling of compassion for her; feel, for a moment, her fear and her pain. Maybe you shed a few tears on her behalf or feel compelled to switch off the television and turn away from an agony too big to face. You find yourself giving your baby an extra hug that night, reading just a little bit more than usual to your toddler or you stand at your child's doorway and watch him sleep. Quietly, in the recesses of your mind you pray that such a dreadful experience never enters your life. For an evening you feel an empathic connection with a total stranger.

As you first begin to move out into the world and circulate with other mothers you may well feel irritation at being stereotyped, at the baby–husband conversations and the patronisation. Then comes the day when you realise we are all in this together, that we are not alone. As Catrina said during a discussion forum:

REMARKABLE REWARDS

I used to imagine no-one else but I could feel that way ...

But we all feel 'that way', sometimes. The more women talk with each other the more they discover that their experiences are shared tens of thousands of times across the spectrum of motherhood.

As we are steadily drawn ever more deeply into motherhood we begin to realise how many gaps there are in this society which cannot be filled with government dollars. And we fill them with gifts of our time, our energy, our compassion, our talents. The holes in our social safety net, which we might never have noticed had we gone on treading the worn pathways of paid work, become glaring abysses through which we see members of our community falling. We feel compelled to help hold them up. We do this in our schools, in volunteer organisations and amongst our immediate network of friends and acquaintances.

We may be more or less educated than each other, more or less wealthy. We may rejoin the paid workforce or we may choose to mother full-time. We may agree or disagree with each other's methods of raising our children and the ways we all arrive at motherhood may be different. We may be single or happily, or not so happily, in a relationship. Our cultural backgrounds can vary widely. No matter all these differences, there are some fundamental commonalities in how we feel about our children and in the ways our lives have changed simply because we have transformed into mothers. These commonalities are what form a base web of connectedness between all mothers across the planet.

When a woman begins to tap into this web she comes to understand that every child is precious and that every one of them has a right to a safe, fulfilling and rewarding future. When you look out upon the world with the eyes of a new mother you may see, perhaps for the first time, how vulnerable the future for your child, for every child, really is. I found it normal for women to express, as Jennifer did, their realisation that they are not separate from anything which happens in our world.

Motherhood started me thinking about, not only my own future, but my child's future, and therefore the way the world is going. It scares me, for her.

When you begin to feel the ills of the planet as a direct threat to your own child's inheritance, it is frightening. The first time you find yourself crying for the children of the world and their mothers, their futures, you will know you have tapped into the world-wide web of motherhood.

In the doing paradigm the Internet is being heralded as a miracle for communication and learning, which undoubtedly it is. It is time women, mothers, understood their own web of connection and used it to halt the march of the forces across this planet which are steadily eating up our children's futures.

MOTHERS ARE TOUGH

There is no way a woman can survive the rigours of childbirth without being pretty strong both physically and mentally. When the going gets tough this can provide her with a foundation of assurance that she possesses a well of strength to draw on, even after she feels as though she can go on no more.

Birth, of course, is but the first test of strength. It is the most powerful testimony to the toughness of women that they are able to survive and rise above extreme sleep deprivation, extreme depression, battered bodies, chronic isolation and loneliness and endless physical and emotional demands—all against a backdrop of outrageous societal undervaluation of their lives. That so few of us crack under this pressure is proof positive that mothers are tough. Let alone when you consider that most of us, in spite of the hurdles, manage to go on giving and nurturing even when we feel we will die if we cannot lie down and sleep for days.

When I meet a woman who tells me she is sinking in her struggle to transform into a mother, I am able to assure her with absolute certainty that when she begins to rise above her feelings of worthlessness or depression she will discover she is infinitely stronger for the experience. It is cold comfort at the time but it is a hope to hang onto. Always women emerge from motherhood strong in ways they never suspected possible. Hundreds of times over women have told me how much stronger they are for having been a mother and how very much they value their strength.

MOTHERS ARE RESOURCEFUL

Motherhood is a world where the unexpected should always be expected. A baby or toddler knows no sense of timing and has no understanding of the impact of his actions upon those around him. He simply reacts to his own internal dictates. Therein lies the source of a mother's resourcefulness.

All plans are subject to alteration at a moment's notice when a baby enters the house. A mother quickly learns to devise a multitude of contingency plans and creative ways to get through even the most basic of tasks. Dinners are cooked one-handed. Creative distractions keep the toddler out of the cookie shelves in the supermarkets even as she reads the grocery labels, scanning them for unacceptable chemical additives. Conversations, which are carried out in short snatches between interruptions, require the ability to remember and synthesise meaning out of brief moments of shared information.

Time becomes a precious commodity, not to be squandered. Every task in the day is soon allocated an appropriate priority. The least important are relegated to the *manyana* file, the most important become the point of intensely focussed attention and activity. Organisation becomes paramount as does the ability to plan, with several back up alternatives, every moment and every movement of every day. Military precision and business planning have nothing on a mother determined to get through another day.

If a mother's baby's health or wellbeing is at stake her resourcefulness knows no bounds. Doctors may patronise her, nurses may try to side-track her, but nothing will halt a mother in the protection of her child. Even the most meek and mild of us, against all odds, will find answers to vital questions when they affect our children.

Until a woman becomes a mother she probably has very little idea about how resourceful she can truly be.

NECESSITY IS THE MOTHER OF INVENTION

If there is one thing mothers find essential it is a need to feel they can provide a safe, secure environment for their children. Deregulation and economic rationalism have steadily undermined economic security. Jobs do not last forever and when one ends there is no guarantee another will begin. Men have been adversely affected by these changes as their ability to provide for their families has been eaten away. The number of men in full-time employment is still shrinking. If they are working, their wages are falling and their hours are rising.

This structural change has caused women to re-enter the workforce in unprecedented numbers in an attempt to maintain the family's lifestyle and to help provide stability and security. Many have found they are unable to obtain work which is fulfilling, which offers opportunities for them to grow professionally and which allows them to maintain a satisfactory mothering role in the home. In response they are taking matters into their own hands and are quietly building their own economic revolution. In the United States, 43% of all small businesses are now owned by women. In Australia one-third are owned by women and by the year 2000 this figure will be 50%.[114] Women in small businesses contribute 10–15% of output in Australia, about half the private sector employment and 20% of net employment creation. Businesses owned by women have a higher survival rate than do men's.[115]

In the most positive way imaginable women are protesting against the very foundation on which our male counterparts base their economic rationale. They are building businesses which value people's time and relationships; which respect and honour the needs of children; which listen to the needs of the people who work for them; which place quality above quantity; which care for and respect the environment and our future.

Louise is but one example. She is a mother of three who established her secretarial service and employment agency in response to a family financial crisis caused by her husband's retrenchment and subsequent inability to find alternative work. She has built her business based on the premise that women need to have access to meaningful work which leaves them enough time to be with their children as and when they need to be. Louise stated:

> We have to help each other, we have to be strong together. We all need to do this together.

With their motherhood training in crisis management, forward planning, contingency design, time juggling, prioritising, delegation, empathy, endurance, identity clarification, interconnectedness (and so on), women make wonderful business managers. What could be so hard about business when you have been a mother!

COURAGE

It takes courage to be a mother. A woman must give up some of her most cherished beliefs and dreams in order to be a mother, at least for a while. She

---

[114] Jane Cadzow, 'Looking Towards the New Millennium', *Good Weekend, Sydney Morning Herald*, 16 March 1996, p.35

[115] The Federal Minister for Small Business, keynote address at the *Australian Businesswomen's Network Seminar and Expo*, Melbourne, 18 November 1995

must put another human being ahead of herself every day and in every way, and she must do it on faith that her methods of mothering will bring rewards for her child and herself uncountable years down the track.

As soon as she steps out into the world as a mother she is automatically treated as though she knows nothing. If she insists she has an intelligent contribution to make—especially if it contravenes the established hierarchy and their beliefs—she is deemed to be nothing but an hysterical woman. It takes courage to stand strong in the face of so entrenched a dismissal of her self and the whole section of our population to which she now belongs.

It takes courage to stand up to a partner who treats her as a possession with which he can do as he pleases because she no longer has economic value. It takes courage to survive his slings and arrows.

Above all, to love somebody with all your heart knowing full well that ultimately you will have to let them go, and still to go on loving them, is an act of total courage.

THE PRIVILEGE OF MOTHERHOOD

Is there anything more incredible than waking up to your newborn baby to discover that she changed overnight? Is there anything more wonderful than watching her grow and learn and unfold before your very eyes?

I consider that being given the chance to watch my son emerge as an independent person is the greatest honour life could ever have bestowed upon me. This is not to say that we do not argue, that I do not nag, that he does not refuse to do as I ask. It is to say that beneath the surface froth and bubble of my mother–son relationship, I know there is nothing in this world which could have opened my heart so wide that it sometimes feels it will burst. There is nothing this world could have entrusted to my care which could have held me so spellbound for so many years. Sandra wrote:

> I certainly wouldn't be without my children—what would I do instead? Drift around the world, live in a pretty but empty home, pile up money in the bank with only myself to enjoy it?

To watch a tiny life mature and develop her own personality and character, sense of humour, strengths and weaknesses, talents, friendships is, in many ways, to be an intimate voyeur of the unfurlment of life itself. And just as life moves ever onward, so too will she. Being a mother means bursting with pride when a child achieves her goals, when she learns something new, when she takes another stride towards independence. It is drinking in the joy of a toddler's hug and the honour of being told you are the best mum in the world.

To my great surprise, the awe and wonder I first felt the moment my son was born has grown over the years. I continue to marvel at the process which began with a seed and before my very eyes has blossomed into a young man. I look forward, for the rest of my days, to the knowing of him.

Sarah put the feelings of many mothers into a nutshell when she announced at the end of a discussion forum:

> I am glad I am a mother. I wouldn't give the experience up for anything in the world.

It is truly a privilege to be a mother, hard though it can be.

ASSERTIVENESS GROWS

Women quickly learn to be assertive if they will allow themselves to learn the lessons of motherhood. On the one hand they become more compassionate and empathic and, therefore, more understanding of other people's problems and behaviour. On the other, as they realise how undervalued motherhood is, they grow less able to accept this ignorance of their worth. Marie wrote to me:

> My placid nature became more assertive once I had a baby, especially towards doctors, people who gave advice and who treated me with condescension.

In the beginning we tend to believe that people in authority have our best interests at heart. It does not take long to see that many do not and are merely ensuring we take up only 'economically viable' periods of time in their offices. What they do not count on is the tigress inside every woman who no longer cares what authority figures think of her if it means she will get what she needs to care for her child.

Although tolerant assertiveness may take years to fully develop, there is nothing quite like the inequities of motherhood to fan the fires of a determination to be taken seriously.

CONFIDENCE RISES

When we first enter motherhood few of us know what to expect—even if we think we do. At first our confidence may be shattered in the slow (or sudden) realisation that we understand little of what it means to be a mother. As the years pass we grapple with life's little, and not so little, crises.

Our children fall down and hurt themselves. We feel fear and compassion and we wish we could wash away their pain. We hold them tightly to our chests and hope that some of their anguish transfers itself into our bigger bodies which are so much more easily able to cope with hurt. We nurse our children when they are sick. We pray that the gods will protect them for all time.

Then one day we wake up and realise that they, and we, have survived babyhood and toddlerhood and our children are walking, talking, laughing, loving, fun-loving little people. And we realise we have coped. Not only have we survived all the deprivations of motherhood, but we have raised children who are, by and large, good people. These are achievements of which every mother ought to be justly proud. As Charmaine said:

> I was desperate to have children. Even so, it is the hardest, most demanding job I have ever had. But I have become a more confident person because of it.

After motherhood any shock the world could throw at us pales into insignificance. Our abilities to survive and to rise above knockdowns and setbacks are finely honed against the grindstone of daily parenting. If we allow ourselves to experience our mothering as an achievement of enormous proportions, then our confidence in ourselves blossoms.

EMOTIONAL AND PERSONAL GROWTH

As adults we like to think we are able to give of ourselves when others need our support. However, it is a rare person who is able to give unconditional love to her partner, to her parents, her siblings, her friends. What we give to each other, in fact, is but a pittance of what we give to our babies and children. Yet we do not, indeed cannot, realise this until they come into our lives.

A baby has the ability to reach into the depths of its mother and pull forth a range of feelings she may never have known she had and emotions she did not know she was capable of feeling. As her life as a mother begins to become more balanced, less baby-centred and less inward-looking, she turns to gaze outward into a strange, new world. Events and people are still the same but she sees them differently. She now understands pain and fear, pleasure and joy with a clarity and an intensity which colour her feelings for other people differently. Her capacity for compassion opens wide. Her sense of the injustices of this world mushrooms.

In the process of becoming a mother a woman becomes less self-centred and more easily able to empathise with the needs and fears of others. She grows up emotionally and realises that others need and deserve help. Perhaps she finds herself drawn to supporting others in ways she would not have considered before.

For anybody interested in personal growth, motherhood can be a fast track to enlightenment. Many a mother has said to me, as Maureen did:

> Motherhood forced me to confront the issues in my life that I had put on the back burner. It is an accelerated growth process.

Seeing your own issues and neuroses mirrored in your child can be the greatest impetus to face and resolve them so they are not passed along to another generation.

A PERSON COMPLETE

Until a woman becomes a mother there is a side of her personality which is not activated. She may think she is being all of who she could be in her chosen profession yet after motherhood she realises she had hardly scratched the surface of her self. Adelle felt this strongly when she said:

> A mother becomes a complete person. Work identity is very false and superficial. It is based on control and power. Once you become a mother your identity is based on the emotional and spiritual aspects of self. Work uses only part of your identity.

Motherhood offers a woman the opportunity to explore all aspects of herself and to bring them into balance. Before she has a child her focus may have been on what she could achieve, what accolades she could win, how equal she could be to the men in her life. Afterwards she learns that her nurturing, caring, empathic self has value too. As her children grow up she begins to see that these qualities have a purpose and are essential in every other area of her life. Whether or not she re-enters the paid workforce, if she will allow this balance to permeate all aspects of her life she will feel forever more complete as a woman and as a person.

Sandra's letter, after pouring out the soulsearching she has done over the past four years since the birth of her first child, concluded with a PS which said:

> Thank God I did have Bettina! Otherwise I never would have found my identity, never would have discovered the support I do have from my family, would probably still be drifting around the world feeling cut-off and adrift.

THE DAILY HERO

Every day of the week mothers perform heroic acts of loyalty and endurance and love. They fall, virtually overnight, from a position of equality into the patronised world of motherhood. Here their old identity is meaningless and sooner or later they must let it go and begin the process of building a new one. In so doing they must eventually face their internal demons and lay them to rest or they will be consumed by them.

Margaret struggled with a deteriorating relationship after her first child was born and not surprisingly, with depression. She has since remarried and gone on to have two more children, the birth of whom did not cause her to feel depressed again. Here is her summation of her personal hero's journey through motherhood.

> With a lot of effort I now see myself progressing through the 'earth mother' phase. I've breastfed for three-and-a-half years in total, went to NMAA [Nursing Mothers] meetings, climbed mountains when pregnant, had my babies a) in a beanchair, b) at home, c) underwater. I now see these things in my life as achievements.
>
> I feel there is a possibility of daily heroism in the sacrifices involved in motherhood. The intelligences, abilities and zest of my three kids are indeed achievements. Somehow it has developed that I don't need the outside world to pat me on the back anymore. I realise that a loving

family which is relatively functional is the basis of world peace and harmony!

I have made the quantum leap to defining my achievements in terms of my relationships, not just my occupation. I hope a lot of males in the next generation will get this opportunity.

Every mother is a hero. Too few of us know this.

FAITH AND SPIRITUALITY

Many women find that after they become mothers their relationship with their God, their religion and their spirituality blossoms. Breathing life into another human being is such an awe-inspiring event and the responsibility so humbling that many of us want to give thanks to whomever we feel has laid this opportunity at our doorstep.

In giving birth we often find ourselves having to come to terms with the fact that life is something bigger than all of us put together, something quite outside our control and something we may never understand in its fullness. At the time our first children are given to us some of us are also given a stronger, deeper and more meaningful connection to our spiritual selves, our spiritual paths and whomever we consider to be our spiritual teachers and guides. Marie wrote:

Since becoming a mother I am more in tune with God, my adviser.

In a sense, the combination of the overwhelming love for a baby and the impact of its absolute vulnerability almost forces a woman to call upon a higher, omnipotent being to help her protect this precious, new life.

THE LOVE IS UNBELIEVABLE

In my opinion there is nothing more incredible than to love and be loved by a child. There is no experience more untainted by judgements, demands and thwarted expectations. There is no experience on earth more pure.

When your toddler runs to greet you with his arms spread as wide as they can go, screaming with delight and throws himself into your arms; when she snuggles into your neck and hugs you with clear, clean, unblemished love it is difficult not to feel as though your heart will explode with the love you share. To be taken by the hand and led proudly through the kindergarten to be shown her paintings and drawings is to know that there is no-one in the world more important to her than you. And no matter how dreadful her creations may be, you know there is not a chance you will tell her anything other than how beautiful they are. The trust that a child offers her mother is so complete, so intensely innocent that to betray this vulnerability is to betray one's self.

Babies and young children love unconditionally. When we are honoured by one of them coming to join us in our lives we are given a template on which to recreate our own ability to give and receive unconditional love. If we do not feel we are worthy to receive it, we will never learn to give it. In becoming a mother we have the chance of a lifetime to choose the path of love. If we can all do this we will find that the pebble of love, which our children drop so innocently into the lake of life, ripples outward to touch every corner of the earth.

EPILOGUE

It is still not recognised that any woman who steps into the role of 'mother'—regardless of whether she does so full-time, juggles it with paid work, shares it with a partner, copes with it on her own, or even undertakes it in the capacity of step-mother—is a person who:

- Works
- Works in a valid profession or career
- Works unfriendly shifts and on every public holiday
- Works a massive number of hours overtime
- Works 365 days per year without a single day off
- Works virtually unpaid
- Works even when she is ill
- Works often without any support or assistance
- Works without provision for superannuation and future security

Sandra expressed the feelings of the majority of women to whom I have spoken when she wrote:

> There seems to be a cultural denial that caring for a baby is work at all, let alone harder work than many paid jobs. And that there is a *craft* involved in mothering and parenting.

EPILOGUE

Researching and writing this book has turned me into, not so much a feminist, as a rabid humanist. Every time I have sat down to write I have felt an increasing sense of outrage at the endemic dismissal of the worth of a mother, of a parent, and subsequently of our children. This is the background against which we all struggle to raise our precious children even as the paradigm of achievement sucks us in and robs us of our ability to parent as well as we would like. The pages of this book are the cries of mothers to be heard, to have their needs taken seriously, to see proof that their children are valued by their society.

Anybody with only half an eye and ear open to the world at large has to know by now that 'economic rationalism' is not just a contradiction in terms, but an insanity. To place more value on the ability to earn a dollar than the ability to create supportive communities and families is crazy. It is causing people in their thousands to fall through the gaping holes in our underfunded social safety net and they are taking with them our children and their future.

The generation who are now becoming parents lament the distant relationships they had with their fathers because fathers were perpetually away from the home chasing their careers and the dollars. Many a woman has told me that she has either never developed a decent relationship with her father or is only beginning to do so in her thirties or forties. Now our mothers are being told that they must invest more hours per week in a paid job than they invest in their own children.

Professional child care clearly supports a mother who needs to obtain paid work in order to break free of the poverty trap. It also gives her time to explore her talents and potential, offers her a safe place where her children can experience a wider variety of input than she alone can offer, or provides her with respite from the constancy of child care. For those who need and want these options, this is a valuable social development which must be made universally accessible and affordable. However much we may applaud professional child care, though, is it right that a woman should feel compelled to give up much of the care of her children in order to survive physically and emotionally in our society if her first choice would be to work as a full-time mother?

As the dominance of the paradigm of material achievement gathers pace it is crushing the paradigm of relationships as inexorably as an avalanche crushes granite boulders into dust. Because it is founded on the principles of productivity, economic rationalism and eternally escalating consumerism it is steadily causing the gap between the very rich and everybody else to widen. It is taking greater and greater bites out of the majority of paid workers' private lives and undermining their sense of job security. As the number of people who are unemployed or underemployed grows, their underutilisation becomes ever more entrenched and accepted as the norm. It is becoming increasingly difficult for the majority of the population to plan confidently for the future and, almost without exception, every member of the society is experiencing a growing sense that there is not enough time for anything other than the functions necessary to get through another day. These pressures are creating a society full of people who cannot carve out enough time to develop and maintain healthy relationships with their spouses, children, extended family or greater community and the results are rapidly being made clear to us.

The overwhelmingly obvious effect on a society that tries to blindly outrun the avalanche of demands made by the doing paradigm, rather than standing to one side and letting it pass by, is an epidemic of relational breakdown. Parents are chronically preoccupied and stressed by lack of time, security, money, control, support, connectedness and meaning. Many fear for their own future, their children's futures, and the future of the planet their children are to inherit, and feel helpless in the face of these enormously difficult issues. Marching across all social boundaries, hand in hand with rising levels of poverty, isolation, powerlessness and stress, is an epidemic of drug, alcohol, gambling and work-related addictions, domestic violence, child abuse, violent crime and suicide. These gathering pressures have reduced the survival rate of the average marriage to just over seven years. As a result Australia now has over half a million parents trying to cope with these difficulties on their own, many of them on low incomes. There are almost as many parents and grandparents who are, to one degree or another, estranged from their children or grandchildren—and children who are estranged from them.

The questions that must be asked are these: When parents can no longer cope with their own lives, how can they be expected to cope with their children's? Who is suffering most from this breakdown in relationships? And is this OK with us? When 90,000 Australian children are beaten, raped, burnt or neglected in a single year and 100,000 have nowhere to live other than on our streets, when the suicide rate amongst 15–24-year-old males has trebled in the past thirty years,[116] and when these figures do not begin to reflect the growing numbers of children who would just plain appreciate more time with

---

116 Michael J. Dudley, Norman J. Kelk, Tony M. Florio, John P. Howard & Brent G.H. Waters, 'Suicide among young Australians, 1964–1993: an interstate comparison of metropolitan and rural trends' in *The Medical Journal of Australia*, Vol.169, no.2, July 1998, p.77

EPILOGUE

and support from their parents and community, it is clear that the imbalance of paradigms is taking too high a toll on these most vulnerable members of our society.

To whom do children turn for guidance and role models when their own parents are too busy or too stressed to be able to help them? In whom do they confide their fears and their triumphs? In whom do they trust? On whose template do they build their own relationships? It is becoming all too obvious that many of our children are growing into young adults who are lost, hurt, damaged, angry. They are beginning to cost us all serious dollars as they understandably exact revenge on a society which valued economic rationalism over life quality and the nurturance of its children. Ultimately the greatest costs are in *their* broken health—physical, mental, emotional and psychological—and in their lost potential, in their suicides and drug addictions. They pass along dysfunctional family dynamics which they learned from their earliest days and generation by generation the cost of providing social support skyrockets.

It is not economically rational to sacrifice our mothers, and therefore their children, on the altar of a GNP which excludes all acknowledgement of the millions upon millions of productive, developmentally sustainable, life-giving, quality hours mothers invest in nurturing and raising our children. In teaching our children they are worthwhile human beings with worthwhile futures. In imbuing them with love and self-esteem and self-respect and self-discipline. In educating them. In helping them develop supportive relationships. In providing a stable foundation of trust on which they build for the rest of their lives. To deny the value of the hours we invest in raising our children is a supreme act of economic insanity. ***And it is not OK.***

Motherhood must be recognised as a valid and valued profession. Equal Employment Opportunity must include an equal right to choose the employment option of professional mother. Affirmative Action must include equal support for those who aspire to the profession of motherhood as those who choose any other profession. A woman must be able to become a mother without fear of being denigrated for her choice and with the expectation that she will be accorded the same level of respect she would expect to receive were the job a paid one. Antidiscrimination Acts must insist that mothers are afforded the same social and economic rights now expected by indigenous people, ethnic minorities, the disabled and the elderly.

The economic contribution of women must be acknowledged in the gross *domestic* product of the nation and their work must be acknowledged in the national census. Work needs to be redefined in such a manner that parents who choose to work part-time are considered to be relationally responsible, not economically irresponsible. It must be understood that they make as valuable and as valid a contribution as any full-time worker. They are entitled to equally meaningful work which offers equal benefits, security, access to training and promotion, and a flexibility which allows them to adequately care for, nurture and support their children. Businesses must cease dividing parents from their families and begin to take responsibility for supporting the relationships between their employees and their children by providing day care and after school care in close proximity to the workplace. Governing bodies must support the business community in taking these steps towards revaluing relationships.

It is time to work towards restructuring our priorities such that sustainable life quality is the cornerstone on which we base all economic, social and political policies. Mothers are the people who are most clearly able to see this need because it is they who can most clearly foresee the consequences of continuing in a world which is not only dominated by the paradigm of material achievement but which denies the very existence of and need for the paradigm of relationships. These *have to* stand side by side in *equality*.

The network between mothers is a powerful but still dormant tigress. It is one which is strong enough to change the destructive social structures which are wreaking such havoc on our children. Let us not wait to awaken her until one by one we have all found ourselves standing alone on the playing field of achievement, having tried to win by those rules and having found the cost too high. To face this problem of inequality as individuals, alone, is to invite personal stress, even peril. To face it together is to strongly increase our chances of bringing about a more equitable balance of paradigms. We could, between us, change the rationale on which our world is built if we would but dare step into and own our collective power as women who value, appreciate and honour the paradigm of relationships.

You can begin to make a contribution today by speaking out your truth. If you have been affected by any of the issues in this book—or others I have missed—talk amongst yourselves, tell your story with honesty. Pass along your wisdom and your learning. Hold out your hand to a struggling mother and know that she is but one of many thousands. Do not judge her. Reach out for help if you are sinking and know that you are not alone. Do not judge yourself. One day, when enough of us are talking, the collective tigress will roar into life with the power to create true equality. But we had better do it soon.

APPENDIX I

EFFECTS OF MOTHERHOOD ON COPING MECHANISMS: DIFFICULT, SEVERE OR EXTREME IMPACT ON A MINIMUM OF 70% OF RESPONDENTS

Effect	% Affected
Exhaustion	90
Increased emotionalism	88
Altered relationship to partner: Spontaneity	85
Altered relationship to partner: Disharmony	85
Interrupted sleep	84
Body changes	84
Frustration: unable to meet baby's needs	84
Feeling out of control	82
Late nights	80
Altered relationship to partner: Lovemaking	79
Difficulty completing conversations	78
Altered relationship to partner: Roles	77
Loss of freedom	76
Baby's interruption to tasks and hobbies	76

Altered relationship to partner: Intimacy	76
Personal interests suffer	76
Isolation	75
Reduced financial resources	75
Altered relationship to partner: Conversations	74
Lack of spontaneity	73
Emotional pain when baby is in pain	73
Feeling a phase in baby's life will go on forever	73
Loneliness	72
Muddled thinking	71
Feeling unable to 'achieve'	71
Feeling conned by the public face of motherhood	71
Decline in feelings of self-worth/esteem	71
Dependency on partner: Financially	70
Dependency on partner: Emotionally	70
Fear of baby's death	70

APPENDIX II

EFFECTS OF MOTHERHOOD ON INTRAPERSONAL CONFLICT: DIFFICULT, SEVERE OR EXTREME IMPACT ON A MINIMUM OF 57% OF RESPONDENTS

Effect	% Affected
Increased emotionalism	78
Feeling out of control	76
Isolation	72
Frustration: unable to meet baby's needs	72
Altered relationship to partner: Disharmony	69
Loss of freedom	67
Experience of guilt if baby is hurt	67
Altered relationship to partner: Household support	66
Altered relationship to partner: Lovemaking	65
Exhaustion	64
Inability to halt baby's crying	63
Body changes	63
Altered relationship to partner: Intimacy	63
Loneliness	63

Decline in feelings of self-worth/esteem	63
Dependency on partner: Financially	61
Fear of baby's death	61
Interrupted sleep	60
Feeling unable to 'achieve'	60
Dependency on partner: Emotionally	60
Reduced financial resources	60
Feeling a phase in baby's life will go on forever	60
Emotional pain when baby is in pain	59
Fear of damaging baby	59
Being confronted with own unresolved issues	59
Onset of advice from others	58
Loss of or confusion over identity	57
Feeling trapped by motherhood	57
Baby's interruptions to tasks and hobbies	57
Altered relationship to partner: Roles	57
Grief over loss of pre-mother lifestyle	57

APPENDIX III

EFFECTS OF MOTHERHOOD ON INTERPERSONAL CONFLICT: DIFFICULT, SEVERE OR EXTREME IMPACT ON A MINIMUM OF 50% OF RESPONDENTS

Effect	% Affected
Exhaustion	81
Increased emotionalism	78
Altered relationship to partner: Disharmony	73
Loss of freedom	72
Altered relationship to partner: Lovemaking	69
Interrupted sleep	66
Inability to halt baby's crying	66
Altered relationship to partner: Household support	65
Isolation	65
Altered relationship to partner: Spontaneity	64
Feeling out of control	64
Altered relationship to partner: Intimacy	63
Drop in desire for sex	63
Altered relationship to partner: Roles	60

Personal interests suffer	59
Loneliness	58
Dependency on partner: Emotionally	57
Envy of partner's acclaim in the world 'out there'	57
Altered relationship to partner: Conversation	56
Loss of or confusion over identity	55
Feeling trapped by motherhood	55
Manic need to get things done	55
Altered relationship with first family	53
Being confronted by own unresolved issues	53
Loss of recognition or acclaim for successes	52
Reduced financial resources	52
Decline in feelings of self-worth/esteem	52
Muddled thinking	51
Lack of spontaneity	51
Feeling unable to 'achieve'	51
Baby's interruptions to tasks and hobbies	51
Altered relationship to partner: Outings	51
Frustration: unable to meet baby's needs	50

WHO TO CALL FOR HELP

NATIONAL

Child Care (Commonwealth Child Care Cash Rebate Scheme) 13 2124
Child Support Agency 13 1272
Family Counselling Legal Advice 13 1384

NEW SOUTH WALES (AREA CODE 02)

Family Services and Parenting Assistance and Advice

Aunties and Uncles Co-operative Family Project Ltd 9638 2480
Family Crisis Service (6pm-11pm) 9622 0522
Family Support Services Association of NSW Inc 9743 6565
Interrelate, Family Life Movement (family and relationship counselling) 9747 3988
Lone Parent Family Support Service 9251 5622
Parent Line 13 2055
Relationships Australia 9418 8800
Unifam Marriage Reconciliation, Separation and Family Counselling and Mediation 9261 4077

Pregnancy, Childbirth and Infant Assistance and Advice

Karitane Mothercraft (parent infant counselling) 9794 1852
NSW Baby Health Centres (NSW Health Department) 9391 9000

Nursing Mother's Association of Australia 9639 8686
Pregnancy Counselling Service 9489 7911
SANDS NSW (Stillbirth, Neonatal Death and Miscarriage
   Support) 9721 0124
Tresillian 24 Hour Parent Help Line 9787 5255 or 1800 637 357

Child and Youth Services including Child Care
Association of Child Care Centres of NSW, The 9687 9055
Child Abuse Prevention Service (24hr) 9716 8000 or 1800 688 009
Child Care Assistance Hotline (Centrelink) 13 1524 or 13 1525
Child Protection and Family Crisis Service 1800 066 777
Department of Community Services: Child Protection and Family Crisis
   Service (24hr) 1800 066 777
Families at Work—Work and Families Specialists 9261 1855
Network of Community Activities (Out of School Hours/Vacation
   Care) 9212 3244
NSW Child Protection Council 9286 7276

Domestic Violence
Domestic Violence Line (Department of Community Services) 1800 656 463

Other Organisations
Association of Self Help Organisations and Groups 9558 3256
Men's Phone Line (information and referral) 9979 9909
NSW Department for Women 9334 1160/Information and Referral
   Service 1800 817 227
Women's and Girl's Emergency Centre 9281 1277
Women's Legal Resource Centre 9637 4597 or 1800 801 501
Women's Resource Centre 9607 7536
Working Women's Centre NSW 9689 2233 or 1800 062 166

ACT (AREA CODE 02)

Family Services and Parenting Assistance and Advice
Canberra Family Support Service 6239 7700
Canberra One-Parent Family Support-Birthright 6247 4282
Compassionate Friends (bereaved parents) 6286 6134 or 6291 9029

WHO TO CALL FOR HELP

Family & Adolescent Centre 6239 5588
Lone Fathers Association 6258 4216
Marriage Relationship Guidance 6281 3600
Parent Support Service 6278 3995
Parents Without Partners 6248 6333
Relationships Australia 6281 3600

Pregnancy, Childbirth and Infant Assistance and Advice
EXPAND (Post and Antenatal Depression) 6247 1386
Karinya House for Mothers and Babies 6259 8998
Nursing Mothers Association of Australia 6258 8928
Post Natal Depression Support Group ACT Inc 6288 83337 or 6237 5108
Pregnancy Information and Counselling Services 6248 6222
SANDS (Stillbirth, Neonatal Death and Miscarriage Support)
   ACT 6294 6727

Child and Youth Services including Child Care
Child Abuse Prevention Service (24hr) 1800 688 009
Child Protection:
   Family Services Northern Region Office 6207 1069
   Family Services Southern Region Office 6207 1466
Child Protection & Family Crisis Service (DOCS) 1800 066 777
Children's Services Resource and Advisory Program 6295 3800
Open Family Australia Inc (24hr for children and adolescents) 6260 3812

Domestic Violence
Domestic Violence Crisis Service (24hr) 6248 7800

Other Organisations
NSW Department of Community Services (Queanbeyan) 6299 1111
Women's Centre for Health Matters Information Line 6290 2166
Women's Health Information Line 6286 2043
Women's Information and Referral Centre 6205 1076 or 6205 1075
Women's Legal Centre (advice, 9.30am-12pm) 1800 634 669 or 6257 4499

VICTORIA (AREA CODE 03)

Family Services and Parenting Assistance and Advice
Care Ring 13 6169
Family Support Program and Counselling Service Crisis Line 9830 5597
Lone Fathers Association of Victoria 9878 6588
Parent Effectiveness Training 9696 4714
Parent Training Australia (marriage, family and personal
  counselling) 9879 7257
Parents Support Network 9830 0412
Parents Without Partners 9836 3211 or 9836 3554

Pregnancy, Childbirth and Infant Assistance and Advice
Maternal and Child Health Service:
  Metropolitan 9853 0844
  North West 9387 4955
Mothercraft Home Support 9534 5209
Nursing Mothers Association of Australia 9885 0855 or 9885 0653
SANDS (Stillbirth, Neanatal Death and Miscarriage Support) 9773 0221

Child and Youth Services including Child Care
Child Abuse Advice After Hours Crisis Line 13 1278
Child Accident Prevention Foundation of Australia 9427 1008
Child and Adolescent Mental Health Service 9770 1050
Child Care Centres Association of Victoria 9859 6831
Child Care Consulting Service 9882 8344
Department of Human Services-Children's Services Program 9616 7777
Youth & Family Services 9616 8027

Domestic Violence
Domestic Violence and Incest Resource Centre 9380 4343

Other Organisations
Women's Clinic on Richmond Hill 9427 0399
Women's Health Information Centre 9344 2007
Women's Health of Victoria Inc (information service) 9662 3755
  or 9662 3742 or 1800 133 321

Women's Information and Referral Exchange 9654 6844 or 1800 136 570
Women's Legal Resource Group (advice) 1800 133 302 or 9642 0343

TASMANIA (LAUNCESTON & NORTH EAST TASMANIA, AREA CODE 03)

Family Services and Parenting Assistance and Advice
Family, Child and Youth Support 6336 2376
Family, Child and Youth Health Service 6337 2850
Family Resource Centre 6334 0895
Marriage Counselling (Centacare) 6331 6811
Relationships Australia 6331 9157

Pregnancy, Childbirth and Infant Assistance and Advice
Nursing Mothers Association of Australia 6331 2799
Pregnancy Support Service 6334 4291
Pregnancy Support Service (Centacare) 6331 6811
Pregnant and Young Parents Support Group 6334 4249 or 0412 906 526

Child and Youth Service including Child Care
Child Protection Assessment Board 6336 2376 or 1800 001 219
Hassles Conflict Resolution Centre for Young People and Parents (Anglicare) 6334 6060

Domestic Violence
Domestic Violence Crisis Service 6233 2529 or 1800 633 937

Other Organisations
Hobart Women's Health Centre 6231 3212 or 1800 353 212
Office of the Status of Women 6233 2208
Women's Legal Service (advice and referral) 6224 0774
Women's Health Information Service 1800 675 028
Working Women's Centre 6234 7007 or 1800 644 589

TASMANIA (NORTH WEST AND WEST COAST, AREA CODE 03)

Family Services and Parenting Assistance and Advice
Parent Information Telephone Assistance Service 1800 808 178
Parenting Centre 6434 6201
Relationships Australia 6424 8064 or 1800 002 222

Pregnancy, Childbirth and Infant Assistance and Advice
SANDS (Stillbirth, Neonatal Death and Miscarriage Support) 6431 2731

Child and Youth Services including Child Care
Child Adolescent Mental Health Service 6434 7280
Child Protection Board 6434 6246 or 1800 001 219

Domestic Violence
Domestic Violence Unit 6434 6246 or 1800 633 937

SOUTH AUSTRALIA (AREA CODE 08)

Family Services and Parenting Assistance and Advice
Family and Youth Services 8226 7000
Relationships Australia 8223 4144

Pregnancy, Childbirth and Infant Assistance and Advice
Nursing Mothers Association of Australia 8411 0050
Pregnancy Advisory Centre 8347 4955 or 1800 672 966

Child and Youth Services including Childcare
Child Abuse Report Line 13 1478
Child and Youth Parent Helpline 1300 364 100
Child Protection Services (Women's and Children's Hospital) 8204 7346
Children's Services (DEET) 8226 0044 or 1800 088 873
Friends of Child and Youth Health 8303 1544

Domestic Violence
Domestic Violence Helpline 1800 800 098
Emergency After Hours Crisis Care Unit 13 1611

WHO TO CALL FOR HELP

Other Organisations
Commonwealth Department of Health and Family Services 8237 8111
Men's Contact and Resource Centre 8212 0331
Office of the Commissioner for Equal Opportunity 1800 188 163 or 8207 1977
Office of Minister for Education, Children's Service and Training 8226 1205
Office for the Status of Women 8303 0961
Women and Children's Health Clinic 8263 6977 or 1800 249 777
Women's and Children's Hospital Health Information Centre 8204 6875
Women's Community Centre 8362 6571
Women's Health Information and Counselling Line 8267 5366
Women's Health Statewide 8267 5366
Women's Information Service 8303 0590 or 1800 188 158
Women's Legal Service 8221 5553 or 1800 816 349
Women's Shelter 1300 362 700

WESTERN AUSTRALIA (AREA CODE 08)

Family Services and Parenting Assistance and Advice
Crisis Care Unit 1800 199 008 or 9223 1111
Family and Children's Services 9222 2555 or 1800 622 258
Family Helpline 24hr Counselling and Information 9220 1300
Family Helpline (law service) 9220 1300
Family Skills Training 9440 0400
Parent Help Centre 9272 1466
Parent Link 9440 0400
Parent Link Home Visiting Services:
   Thornlie 9493 6616
   Belmont/Canning 9472 9144
   Fremantle 9336 7778
   Joondalup 9349 3440
   Scarborough 9440 5170
Parents Without Partners 9389 8350
Parenting Information Centres 9272 1466 or 1800 654 432
Parenting Line 9272 1466 or 1800 654 432
Relationships Australia 9362 0362

Pregnancy, Childbirth and Infant Assistance and Advice
Nursing Mothers Association of Australia 9309 5393

Child and Youth Service including Child Care
Child Abuse, Advice and Information 9222 2555
Family Day Care Scheme (Cockburn) 9337 7177
Kidsafe WA 9340 8509

Domestic Violence
Domestic Violence Prevention Unit 9264 1920
Men's Domestic Violence Helpline 1800 000 599 or 9223 1199

Other
Minister for Family and Children's Services 9481 7810
Women's Advisory Council 9264 1920 or 1800 199 246
Women's Health (Rosalie Gollan Centre) 9346 4014
Women's Health Care House 9227 8122 or 1800 998 399
Women's Information Service 9264 1900 or 1800 199 174
Women's Policy Development Office 9246 1920
Women's Refuge Group of WA 9227 1642
Women's Refuges Multicultural Service 9325 7716

NORTHERN TERRITORY (AREA CODE 08)

Family Services and Parenting Assistance and Advice
Anglicare Resolve (Family Counselling) 8985 0040 or 1800 898 500
Family, Youth and Children's Services 8951 5170
Relationships Australia:
   Alice Springs 1800 634 405
   Darwin 1800 652 404

Pregnancy, Childbirth and Infant Assistance and Advice
Childbirth Education Association Darwin Inc 8927 2575
Pregnancy Helpline 8981 8526 or 8941 0022

WHO TO CALL FOR HELP

Childrens and Youth Services including Child Care
Association for the Welfare of Child Health 1800 244 396
Children's Services Community Counsellor 8953 0785
Children's Services Unit 1800 019 161
Family, Youth and Child Services:
  Alice Springs 8951 5170 or 8951 7808 or 8951 7777 (a/h)
  Darwin 8922 7268 or 8922 8084
  Katherine 8973 8600 or 8973 9211 (a/h)
  Nhulunbuy 8987 0400 or 8987 0408 (a/h)
  Tennant Creek 8962 4334 or 8962 4399 (a/h)
Nursing Mothers Association of Australia:
  Alice Springs 8955 0187
  Darwin 8981 7086 or 8945 6886
  Katherine 8972 3531
  Palmerston (rural) 8988 4616 or 8983 2380

Domestic Violence
Domestic Violence Crisis Line 24hr Telephone Counselling 8981 9227 or 1800 019 116
Domestic Violence Legal Help 8981 9726

Other Organisations
Territory Health Services 8999 2400
Women's Advisory Council to the Chief Minister 8999 6107
Women's Crisis Centre (Catherine House) 8981 5928
Women's Information Service 8951 5880 or 1800 813 631
Women's Resource Centre 8979 3013

QUEENSLAND (AREA CODE 07)

Family Services and Parenting Assistance and Advice
Department of Families, Youth and Community Care 3224 8045 or 1800 811 810
Family and Kids Care Foundation Inc 3341 8933
Family Life (counselling) 3396 2540
Parentline 1300 301 300
Parents Without Partners 3275 3290

Queensland Lone Parent Club 3252 7003
Relationship Breakdown Advice 1800 803 285
Relationships Australia 3217 2900 or 1300 364 277

Pregnancy, Childbirth and Infant Assistance and Advice
Nursing Mothers Association of Australia 3844 8166 or 3844 8977
Pregnancy Counselling Link 3831 6161 or 1800 777 690

Children's and Youth Services including Child Care
Child Care Information Service 3224 4225 or 1800 637 711
Royal Children's Hospital (telephone support) 3862 2333 or 1800 177 279

Domestic Violence
Domestic Violence Resource Centre 3217 2311
Domestic Violence Telephone Service (24hr) 1800 811 811
Men's Domestic Violence Telephone Counselling Service 1800 246 346

Other Organisations
Brisbane's Health Service Information Line 3852 2995 or 1800 005 998
Men's Helpline 3830 0055
Minister for Families, Youth and Community Care 3224 7477
Minister for Women's Policy 3227 8819
Office of Women's Affairs 3224 4062
Women's Health Information and Referral Service 1800 017 382
Women's Health Centre (Ipswich) 3812 0138 or 1800 065 454
Women's Infolink 3224 2211 or 1800 177 577

If your organisation would like to be included in this list please write to Wendy LeBlanc at P.O. Box 964, Armidale, NSW 2350 or email wendyl@northnet.com.au.

BIBLIOGRAPHY

Adelaide, D. ed. *Mother Love*, Random House Australia Pty Ltd, Milsons Point, 1996
Adelaide, D. ed. *Mother Love 2*, Random House Australia Pty Ltd, Milsons Point, 1997
Apter, T. *Why Women Don't Have Wives*, The Macmillan Press Ltd, London, 1985
Asimov, I. *The Human Brain*, The New American Library, Inc., New York, 1965
Aspin, L.J. *The Family: An Australian Focus*, Third Edition, Longman Cheshire Pty Ltd, Melbourne, 1994
Baber, K.M. & Allen, K.R *Women and Families*, The Guilford Press, New York, 1992.
Badinter, E. *The Myth of Motherhood: An Historical View of the Maternal Instinct*, Souvenir Press (Educational & Academic) Ltd, London, 1981
Ball, J.A. *Reactions to Motherhood: The Role of Post-Natal Care*, Cambridge University Press, Cambridge, 1987
Belsky, J. and Kelly, J. *The Transition to Parenthood*, Delacorte Press, New York, 1994
Bepko, C. and Krestan, J. *Too Good For Her Own Good*, HarperCollins Publishers, New York, 1991
Berryman, J., Thorpe, K. and Windridge, K. *Older Mothers*, HarperCollins, Publishers, London, 1995
Birns, B. and Hay, D.F. *The Different Faces of Motherhood*, Plenum Press, New York, 1988
Bittman 1991 as quoted by Office of the Director of Equal Opportunity in Public Employment in *Success With Flexible Work Practices*, Sydney, 9/1994
Blackie, P. *Becoming a Mother After Thirty*, Basil Blackwell Ltd, Oxford, 1986
Boukydis, C.F.Z. ed. *Research on Support for Parents and Infants in the Postnatal Period*, Ablex Publishing Corporation, Norwood, 1987
Boulton, M.G. *On Being a Mother*, Tavistock Publications, London, 1983
Bradman, T. *The Essential Father*, Unwin Paperbacks, London, 1985
Briggs, F. ed. *Children and Families: Australian Perspectives*, Allen & Unwin Pty Ltd, St Leonards, 1994
Brockner, J. and Rubin, J.Z. *Entrapment in Escalating Conflicts: A Social Psychological Analysis*, Springer-Verlag New York Inc., New York, 1985
Brombeck, E. *The Second Oldest Profession*, Macdonald & Co. (Publishers) Ltd, London, 1984
Brown, S., Lumley, J., Small, R. and Astbury, J. *Missing Voices, The Experience of Motherhood*, Oxford University Press, Melbourne, 1994
Burton, J. ed. *Conflict: Human Needs Theory*, St Martin's Press, Inc., New York, 1990
Burton, J. *Conflict: Resolution and Prevention*, St Martin's Press, New York, 1990
Capra, F. *The Web of Life: A New Synthesis of Mind and Matter*, HarperCollins Publishers, London, 1997
Cook, P. *Early Child-care: Infants and Nations at Risk*, News Weekly Books, North Melbourne, 1996
Corea, G. *The Hidden Malpractice; How American Medicine Mistreats Women*, updated edition, Harper Colophon, New York, 1985

Davies, C. *Success with flexible work practices*, Office of the Director of Equal Opportunity in Public Employment, Sydney, September 1994
Davis, E.G. *The First Sex*, Penguin Books Inc., New York, 1972
DeFrain, John *Life Matters*, ABC Radio National, 10.8.1998
Department of Social Security *Annual Report 1993–1994*, Sydney
Deutsch, M. *The Resolution of Conflict: Constructive and Destructive Processes*, Yale University Press, Ltd, London, 1973
Deutsch, M. *Distributive Justice: A Social-Psychological Perspective*, Yale University Press, Ltd, London, 1985
deVaus, J.E. *Mothers Growing Up*, Allen & Unwin Pty Ltd, North Sydney, 1992
Dickens, P. *Urban Sociology: Society, Locality and Human Nature*, Harvester Wheatsheaf, Hemel Hempstead, 1990
Dix, C. *The New Mother Syndrome: Coping with post natal stress and depression*, Allen & Unwin (Publishers) Ltd, North Sydney, 1986
Dunnewold, A. and Sanford, D.G. *Postpartum Survival Guide*, New Harbinger Publications, Inc., Oakland, 1994
Elkind, D. *Ties That Stress: The New Family Imbalance*, Harvard University Press, Cambridge, 1994
Everingham, C. *Motherhood and Modernity*, Allen & Unwin, St Leonards, 1994
Eyre, L. and R. *Three Steps to a Strong Family*, Simon and Schuster, New York, 1994
Feldman, S. *Making Up Your Mind About Motherhood*, Bantam Books Inc., New York, 1985
Fineman, S. ed. *Unemployment: Personal and Social Consequences*, Tavistock Publications, London, 1987
Forman, F.J. with Sowton, C. eds *Taking Our Time: Feminist Perspectives on Temporality*, Pergamon Press plc, Oxford, 1989
Forward, S. *Toxic Parents*, Bantam Doubleday Dell Publishing Group, New York, 1990
French A. and Berlin, I.N. eds *Depression in Children and Adolescents*, Human Sciences Press, New York, 1979
Friedan, B. *The Feminine Mystique*, Penguin Books Ltd, London, 1963
Galbraith, J.K. *The Anatomy of Power*, Hamish Hamilton Ltd, London, 1984
Gansberg, J.M. *The Second Nine Months*, Thorsons Mostel, A.P. Publishers Limited, Wellingborough, 1985
Gardner, F.E.M. 'The quality of joint activity between mother and their children with behavioural problems' in *Journal of Child Psychology and Psychiatry and Allied Disciplines*, Vol.35(5), July 1994, 935–948
Gardner, H. *Frames of Mind*, Fontana Press, London, 1993
Gelles, R.J. and Cornell, C.P. *Intimate Violence in Families*, 2nd ed., Sage Publications, Inc., Newbury Park, 1990
Gerstel, N. and Gallagher, S. 'Caring for Kith and Kin: Gender, Employment, and the Privatization of Care' in *Social Problems*, Vol.41, No.4, November 1994, 519–539
Gilding, M. *The making and breaking of the Australian family*, Allen & Unwin Pty Ltd, St Leonards, 1991
Glasser, W. *Control Theory*, Harper & Row, Publishers, Inc., New York, 1984
Glenn, E.N., Chang, G. and Forcey, L.R. *Mothering; Ideology, Experience and Agency*, Routledge, New York, 1994
Goldberg, W.A., Greenberger, D., Hamill, S. and O'Neil, R. 'Role demands in the lives of employed single mothers with preschoolers' in *Journal of Family Issues*, Vol.13, September 1992, 312–333
Goleman, D. *Emotional Intelligence, Why It Can Matter More Than IQ*, Bantam Books, New York, 1995
Golombok, S. and Fivush, R. *Gender Development*, Cambridge University Press, Melbourne, 1994
Gray, J. *What Your Mother Couldn't Tell You and Your Father Didn't Know*, Hodder Headline Australia Pty Ltd, Rydalmere, 1994
Graycar, A. 'Poverty, Parenting, Peers and Crime-Prone Neighbourhoods', in *Trends and issues in crime and criminal justice*, Australian Institute of Criminology, No.85, April 1998, 1–6
Green, C. *Toddler Taming*, Doubleday Australia Pty Limited, Lane Cove, 1984
Grizzle A.F. *Mothers Who Love Too Much*, Ballantine Books, New York, 1988
Grof, S. *Healing Potential of Non-Ordinary States of Consciousness: Observations from Psychedelic Therapy and Holotropic Breathwork*, Portiuncula Centre for Spiritual Growth, Toowoomba, February, 1996
Hampshire, S. *The Maternal Instinct*, Sidgwick & Jackson Limited, London, 1984
Harper, J. and Richards, L. *Mothers and Working Mothers*, Penguin Books Australia Ltd, Ringwood, revised ed. 1986

BIBLIOGRAPHY

Hawkins, A.J., Marshall, C.M. and Meiners, K.M. 'Exploring Wives' Sense of Fairness About Family Work: An Initial Test of the Distributive Justice Framework' in *Journal of Family Issues*, Vol.16(6), November 1995, 693–721

Henwood, B. *The How To Of Being A Working Mother*, HarperCollins Publishers Australia, Pymble, 1995

Hills, C. *Creative Conflict*, University of the Trees Press, Boulder Creek, 1980

Hite, S. *Women and Love: The Hite Report*, Viking, London, 1988

Hite, S. *The New Hite Report: Women and Love*, revised edition, St Martin's Press, New York, 1989

Hite, S. *The Hite Report On the Family: Growing Up Under Patriarchy*, Bloomsbury Publishing Ltd, London, 1994

Hochschild, A. *The Second Shift*, Viking, London, 1989

Hollis, C. 'Depression, family environment, and adolescent suicidal behaviour' in *Journal of the American Academy of Child and Adolescent Psychiatry*, Vol.35(5), May 1996, 622–630

Horan, Wall & Walker, 'Statistics: Facts of the Matter', *Good Weekend, The Sydney Morning Herald*, 6 March 1993

Horsfall, J. *The Presence of the Past: male violence in the family*, Allen & Unwin Pty Ltd, North Sydney, 1991

Ironmonger, D. 'Bringing Up Betty and Bobby: The Macro Time Dimensions of Investment in the Care and Nurture of Children' in *Investing in Children: Primary Prevention Strategies*, The Inaugural Child and Family Policy Conference, University of Otago, 10–13 July 1996

Janov, A. *The Feeling Child*, Abacus, London, 1977

Janov, A. *Prisoners of Pain*, Abacus, London, 1988

Janov, A. *The Primal Scream*, Abacus, London, 1992

Janov, A. *The New Primal Scream*, Abacus, London, 1993

Joseph, J.M. *The Resilient Child: Parenting Today's Youth for Tomorrow's World*, Plenum Press, New York, 1994

Jung, C.G. *Four Archetypes: Mother, Rebirth, Spirit, Trickster*, Ark Paperbacks, London, 1986 (1972)

Kagan, J. *The Nature of the Child*, Basic Books, Inc., Publishers, New York, 1984

Karen, R. *Becoming Attached: Unfolding the Mystery of the Infant–Mother Bond and Its Impact on Later Life*, Warner Books, Inc., New York, 1994

Kashani, J.H., Burbach, D.J. and Rosenberg, T.K. 'Perception of Family Conflict Resolution and Depressive Symptomatology in Adolescents', in *Journal of American Academy of Child and Adolescent Psychiatry*, Vol.27, January 1988, 42–48

Kempe, C.H. and Helfer, R.E. *The battered child*, third edition, The University of Chicago Press, Chicago, 1980

Kilpatrick, K. *Post Traumatic Stress Disorder, Anxiety and the Child Witness to Domestic Violence: The 'Forgotten' Victims*, Master of Letters, University of New England, Armidale, November 1993

Kitzinger, S. *Giving Birth—how it really feels*, Victor Gollancz Ltd, London, 1971

Kitzinger, S. *Pregnancy and Childbirth*, Doubleday Australia Pty Ltd, Lane Cove, 1982

Kitzinger, S. *Ourselves As Mothers*, Doubleday, Toronto, 1992

Kitzinger, S. and Lees, B. *The Year After Childbirth*, Oxford University Press, India, 1994

Klaus, M.H. and Klaus, P.H. *The Amazing Newborn: Making the Most of the First Weeks of Life*, Addison–Wesley Publishing Company, Inc., Reading, 1985

Klaus, M.H. and Kennell, J.H. *Parent–Infant Bonding*, second edition, The V.C. Mosby Company, St Louis, 1982

Klaus, M.H., Kennell, J.H. and Klaus, P.H. *Bonding: Building the Foundations of Secure Attachment and Independence*, Addison–Wesley Publishing Company, Reading, 1995

Knudtson, P. and Suzuki, D. *Wisdom of the Elders*, Allen & Unwin Pty Ltd, North Sydney, 1992

Lancaster, J.B. *Primate Behaviour and the Emergence of Human Culture*, Holt, Rinehart and Winston, New York, 1975

Lane, A.R. and Wilcoxon, S.A. 'Dyadic Adjustment During the Transition to Parenthood: A Look at Perceived Similarity of Spouses' Family-of-Origin Experiences', in *Australian Journal of Sex, Marriage and Family*, Vol.10, No.4, November 1989, 165–171

LaRossa, R. *Conflict and Power in Marriage: Expecting the First Child*, Sage Publications Inc., Beverly Hills, 1977

Lavee, Y., Sharlin, S. and Katz, R. 'The Effect of Parenting Stress on Marital Quality: An Integrated Mother-Father Model', in *Journal of Family Issues*, Vol.17, No.1, January 1996, 114–135

Leach, P. *Children First*, Michael Joseph, London, 1994

Leboyer, F. *Birth Without Violence*, Rigby, Australia, 1975

Lerner, H.G. *The Dance of Anger*, Harper & Row, Publishers, Inc., New York, 1985

Lerner, H.G. *The Dance of Intimacy*, Harper & Row, Publishers, Inc., New York, 1989

Lewin, K., Lewin, G.W. ed. *Resolving Social Conflicts*, Souvenir Press (Educational and Academic) Ltd, London, 1973

Liedloff, J. *The Continuum Concept*, revised edition, Warner Books, Inc., New York, 1977

Loane, S. *Who Cares? Guilt, hope and the childcare debate*, Reed Books Australia, Kew, 1997

Lucas, A., Morley, R., Cole, T.J., Lister, G. and Leson-Payne, C. 'Breast milk and subsequent intelligence quotient in children born preterm' in *Lancet*, Vol.339 (8788), 1992, 261–264

McConville, B. *Mad to Be A Mother: Is there life after birth for women today?* Century Hutchinson Ltd, London, 1987

McGinnis, J. and McGinnis, K. *Parenting for Peace and Justice*, Orbis Books, 9th printing, Maryknoll, 1988

McGinnis, K. and Oehlberg, B. *Starting Out Right: Nurturing Young Children as Peacemakers*, The Institute for Peace and Justice and The Crossroad Publishing Company, New York, 1991

McKenna, E.P. *When Work Doesn't Work Anymore: Women, Work, and Identity*, Hodder Headline Australia Pty Ltd, Rydalmere, 1997

Maushart, S. *The Mask of Motherhood: How mothering changes everything and why we pretend it doesn't*, Random House Australia Pty Ltd, Milsons Point, 1997

Mendelson, W.B. *Human Sleep: Research and Clinical Care*, Plenum Publishing Corporation, New York, 1987

Micchelli, M. 'Managing Motherhood: Work, Family and Mental Health', in *The Humanities and Social Sciences*, 1995, 55, 7, Jan, 2143–A

Miedzian, M. *Boys Will Be Boys: Breaking the Link Between Masculinity and Violence*, Virago Press Limited, London, 1992

Miller, A. *For Your Own Good: The Roots of Violence in Child-rearing*, Virago Press Limited, London, 1987

Miller, A. *Banished Knowledge; Facing Childhood Injuries*, Virago Press Limited, London, 1991

Minturn, L. and Lambert, W.W. *Mothers of Six Cultures*, John Wiley & Sons, Inc., New York, 1964

Mitchell, E.A. 'Post Natal Depression and SIDS: a prospective study' in N. George, *PND, Culture and Alternative Birth*, Social Sciences in Public Health, Auckland, 1992

Moir, A. and Jessel, D. *BrainSex*, Michael Joseph Limited, London, 1991

Molnar, A. ed. *The Construction of Children's Character*, Part II, The National Society for the Study of Education, Chicago, 1977

Montagu A. *Touching: The Human Significance of the Skin*, Harper & Row, Publishers Inc., New York, 1986

Myers-Walls, J.A. 'Balancing multiple role responsibilities during the transition to parenthood' in *Family Relations*, Vol.33, April 1984, 267–271

New South Wales Women's Advisory Council *Occupation: Housewife—a discussion paper*, sixth printing with revisions, Sydney, June 1988

New South Wales Women's Advisory Council *Women and Work: An Overview*, Sydney, 1991

New South Wales Women's Consultative Committee *If Motherhood is Bliss Why Do I Feel So Awful?*, NSW Ministry for the Status and Advancement of Women, Woolloomooloo, 1994

Nicholson, P. 'A brief report of women's expectations of men's behaviour in the transition to parenthood: Contradictions and conflicts for counselling psychology practice' in *Counselling Psychology Quarterly*, Vol.3(4), 1990, 353–361

Noble, E. *Primal Connections*, Fireside, New York, 1993

Oakley A. *Becoming a Mother*, Martin Robertson & Company Ltd, Oxford, 1979

Oakley, A. *From Here to Maternity: Becoming a Mother*, Penguin Books Ltd, Harmondsworth, 1981

Oakley, A. *Subject Women*, Fontana Paperbacks, Glasgow, 1982

Oakley, A. *Social Support and Motherhood*, Blackwell Publishers, Oxford, 1992

Office of the Status of Women *Juggling Time: How Australian Families Use Time*, Department of Prime Minister and Cabinet, Commonwealth of Australia, 1991

BIBLIOGRAPHY

Office of the Status of Women *National Agenda for Women: Implementation Report*, Department of Prime Minister and Cabinet, Australian Government Publishing Service, Canberra, August 1991

Ogley, R.C. *Conflict Under the Microscope*, Avebury Gower Publishing Company Limited, Aldershot, 1991

Ohehir, W. *Men's Health: Uncovering the Mystery—A Working Manual*, Openbook Publishers, Adelaide, 1996

Oliker, S.J. 'The proximate contexts of workfare and work: a framework for studying poor women's economic choices' in *Sociology Quarterly*, Vol. 36, Spring 1995, 251–272

Osherson, S. *The Passions of Fatherhood*, HarperCollins, Publishers, Pymble, 1996

Parke, R.D. ed. *Review of Child Development Research*, The University of Chicago Press, Chicago, 1984

Paul, J. and Paul, M. *From Conflict to Caring*, CompCare Publishers, Minneapolis, 1988

Pearce, C.J. *Magical Child*, Bantam Books, Inc., New York, 1977

Pearce, C.J. *Magical Child Matures*, Bantam Books, Inc., New York, 1986

Phillips, A. ed. *Feminism and Equality*, Basil Blackwell Ltd, Oxford, 1987

Phillips, J. *Mothers Matter Too!* Thomas Nelson Australia Ltd, Melbourne, 1985

Phoenix, A., Woollett, A. and Lloyd, E. *Motherhood: Meanings, Practices and Ideologies*, Sage Publications, London, 1991

Power, T.G. and Parke, R.D. 'Social Network Factors and the Transition to Parenthood' in *Sex Roles*, 10, 11–12, June 1984, 949–972

Radojevic, M. 'The Developmental Needs of Children and the Impact of Parenting on Developmental Outcomes: A review of the research', in Standing Committee On Social Issues, *Working for Children: Communities Supporting Families—Inquiry into Parent Education and Support Programs*, Parliament of New South Wales Legislative Council, Report No.15, September 1998, Attachment A, 1–18

Ribbens, J. *Mothers and Their Children: A Feminist Sociology of Childrearing*, Sage Publications Ltd, London, 1994

Rich, A. *Of Woman Born*, W.W. Norton & Company Inc., New York, 1976

Richards, L. *Having Families: Marriage, Parenthood and Social Pressures in Australia*, revised edition, Penguin Books Australia Ltd, Ringwood, 1985

Richardson, D. *Women, Motherhood and Childrearing*, The Macmillan Press Ltd, London, 1993

Ridgeway, R. and D. *Preparing for Parenthood*, Penguin Books, London, 1990

Rix, J. *Is There Sex After Childbirth?* HarperCollins, Publishers, London, 1995

Rodd, J. 'I love them but they're driving me crazy: Stress in Mothers of Young Children' in *Children Australia*, Vol.17, No.4, 1992, 24–26

Rossi, A. ed. *Gender and the Life Course*, Aldine Publishing Company, New York, 1985

Rothman, B.K. *Recreating Motherhood: Ideology and Technology in a Patriarchal Society*, W.W. Norton & Company, New York, 1990

Rubin, L.B. *Families on the Fault Line: America's Working Class Speaks About the Family, the Economy, Race, and Ethnicity*, HarperCollins Publishers, Inc., New York, 1994

Saul, J.R. *The Unconscious Civilization*, Penguin Books Australia Ltd, Ringwood, 1997

Schaef, A.W. *Co-Dependence: Misunderstood–Mistreated*, HarperCollins Publishers, New York, 1986

Schaef, A.W. *Escape from Intimacy: Untangling the 'Love' Addictions: Sex, Romance, Relationships*, HarperCollins Publishers, New York, 1989

Scheper-Hughes, N. 'Infant Mortality and Infant Care: Cultural and Economic Constraints on Nurturing in Northeast Brazil' in *Social Science and Medicine*, Volume 19, 1984, 535–546

Seligman, M.E.P. *Learned Optimism*, Random House Australia Pty Ltd, Milsons Point, 1991

Seligman, M.E.P. *What You Can Change and What You Can't*, Random House Australia Pty Ltd, Milsons Point, 1994

Seuss, G.J., Grossman, K.E. and Sroufe, A.L. 'Effects of infant attachment to mother and father on quality of adaptation in preschool: From dyadic to individual organisation of self' in *International Journal of Behavioural Development*, Vol.15(1), March 1992, 43–65

Sharp, R. and Broomhill, R. *Short Changed: Woman and Economic Policies*, Allen & Unwin Australia Pty Ltd, North Sydney, 1988

Sheldrake, R. *A New Science of Life: The Hypothesis of Formative Causation*, J.P. Tarcher, Inc., Los Angeles, 1981

Sheldrake, R. *The Presence of the Past: Morphic Resonance and the Habits of Nature*, Vintage Books, New York, 1988

Sheldrake, R. and Fox, M. *Natural Grace: Dialogues on Science and Spirituality*, Bloomsbury Publishing Plc, London, 1997
Sidoti, C. 'Keynote Address' in *Giving Children a Voice*, State Conference NSW Child Protection Council, Newcastle, February 17–18 1997
Small, M.F. *Female Primates: Studies by Women Primatologists*, Alan R. Liss, Inc., New York, 1984
Small, R., Astbury, J., Brown, S. and Lumley, J. 'Depression after childbirth: does context matter?' in *Medical Journal of Australia*, Vol.161, No.8, October 1994
Smith, J. 'Conceiving Selves: A Case Study of Changing Identities During the Transition to Motherhood' in *Journal of Language and Social Psychology*, Vol.10(4), 1991, 225–243
Smith, J.A. 'Reconstructing Selves: An Analysis of Discrepancies Between Women's Contemporaneous and Retrospective Accounts of the Transition to Motherhood' in *British Journal of Psychology*, Vol.85(3), August 1994, 371–392
Smoker, P., Davies, R. and Munske, B. eds *A Reader in Peace Studies*, Pergamon Press Australia Pty Ltd, Potts Point, 1990
Solomon, M.F. *Narcissism and Intimacy*, W.W. Norton & Co, Inc., New York, 1992
Spelman, E.V. *Inessential Woman: Problems of exclusion in feminist thought*, The Women's Press Limited, London, 1990
Standing Committee On Social Issues *Working for Children: Communities Supporting Families—Inquiry into Parent Education and Support Programs*, Parliament of New South Wales Legislative Council, Report No. 15, September 1998
Stein, A., Gath, D.H., Bucher, J., Bond, A. and Cooper, P.J. 'The relationship between post-natal depression and mother–child interaction' in *British Journal of Psychiatry*, Vol.158, January 1991, 46–52
Steinem, G. *Moving Beyond Words*, Bloomsbury Publishing Ltd, London, 1994
Stettbacher, J.K. *Making Sense of Suffering*, Penguin Books Australia Ltd, Ringwood, 1991
Stevens, A. 'A Basic Need', in *Resurgence*, No.174, January–February 1996, 42–43
Stigler, J.W., Shweder, R.A. and Herdt, G. eds *Cultural Psychology: Essays on Comparative Human Development*, The Press Syndicate of the University of Cambridge, Cambridge, 1990
Stockard, J. and Johnson, M.M. *Sex Role Development*, Prentice–Hall, Inc., Englewood Cliffs, 1980
Swigart, J. *The Myth of the Bad Mother*, Doubleday, New York, 1991
Taitz, L.S., King, J.M., Nicholson, J. and Kessel, M. 'Unemployment and child abuse' in *British Medical Journal: Clinical Research Edition*, Vol.294, April 1987, 1074–1076
Taylor, V. and Spears, S. 'Breaking the Emotional Rules of Motherhood: The Experience of Postpartum Depression' in *North Central Sociological Association (NCSA)*, Association Paper, 1988
Theobald, R. *Reworking Success: new communities at the millennium*, New Society Publishers, Gabriola Island, 1997
Thompson, P.J. 'Day care for ill children: An employed mother's dilemma' in *Issues in Comprehensive Pediatric Nursing*, Vol.35, No.16, April–June 1993, 77–89
Thurer, S.L. *The Myths of Motherhood*, Houghton Mifflin Company, New York, 1994
Tominson, A.M. 'Child Abuse and other Family Violence' in *Family Matters*, No.41, Winter, 1995, 33–38
Tominson, A.M. and Tucci, J. 'Emotional Abuse the hidden form of maltreatment', in *Issues in Child Abuse Prevention*, The Australian Institute of Family Studies, Melbourne, No.8, Spring 1997
Tong, R. *Feminist Thought: A Comprehensive Introduction*, Allen & Unwin (Australia) Ltd, North Sydney, 1989
Treblicot, J. *Mothering*, Rowman & Allanhead, Totowa, 1983
University of New England, Dr Meredith Burgman, 'Workplace Change: What Women Want and How Some Men Will Try to Stop It'; Professor Bettina Cass, 'Bringing Equity to the Balance of Family Responsibilities and Employment'; Shelley Cooper; 'What Organisations Can Do and Why It Makes Good Business Sense'; Sue Walpole, 'Sex Discrimination, Work and Family Responsibilities', in *Marrying Work and Family Responsibilities: New Workplace Flexibility Forum*, Armidale, March 1995
Verny, T. and Kelly, J. *The Secret Life of the Unborn Child*, Sphere Books Limited, London, 1982
Vinson, T., Baldry, E. and Hargreaves, J. 'Neighbourhoods, Networks and Child Abuse', in *British Journal of Social Work*, Vol.26, No.4, 1996, 523–543
Wallerstein, J.S. and Blakeslee, S. *Second Chances*, Transworld Publishers Ltd, Moorebank, 1990

BIBLIOGRAPHY

Walmsley, D.J. and Weinand, H.C. 'Is Australia Becoming More Unequal?' in *Australian Geographer*, Vol.28, No.1, 1997, 69–88

Walsh, F. 'The Concept of Family Resilience: Crisis and Challenge', in *Family Process*, Vol.35, No.3, September 1996, 261–281

Waring, M. *Counting for Nothing*, Allen & Unwin, North Sydney, 1990

Wartner, W.G., Grossman, K., Fremmer-Bombik, E. and Suess, G. 'Attachment patterns at age six in south Germany: Predictability from infancy and implications for preschool behaviour' in *Child Development*, Vol.65(4), August 1994, 1014–1027

Wearing, B. *The Ideology of Motherhood*, George Allen & Unwin Australia Pty Ltd, North Sydney, 1984

Wearing, B. 'Leisure, unpaid labour, lifestyles and the mental and general health of suburban mothers in Sydney, Australia' in *Australian Journal of Sex, Marriage and Family*, Vol.10, No.3, August 1989, 118–132

Wearing, B. *Gender: The Pain and Pleasure of Difference*, Addison Wesley Longman Pty Ltd, Melbourne, 1996

Webster, J., Sweett, S. and Stolz, T.A. 'Domestic violence in pregnancy: A prevalence study' in *The Medical Journal of Australia*, Vol.161, 17 October 1994, 466–470

Webster, J., Chandler, J. and Battistutta, D. 'Pregnancy outcomes and health care use: Effects of abuse' in *American Journal of Obstetrics and Gynecology*, Vol.174, No. 2, February 1996, 760–767

Wilber, K. ed. *The Holographic Paradigm and other paradoxes*, Shambhala Publications, Inc., Boulder, 1982

Williamson, M. *A Woman's Worth*, Random House, Inc., New York, 1993

Wilson, E.O. *On Human Nature*, Harvard University Press, Cambridge, 1978

Wilson-Schaef, A. *Beyond Therapy, Beyond Science: A New Model For Healing the Whole Person*, HarperCollins Publishers, New York, 1992

Wolf, N. *Fire with Fire*, Chatto and Windus Limited, London, 1993

INDEX

A
abandonment, feelings of 53–6
abdomen, changes 96–7
abusive behaviour *see* violence
access visits 246–7
acclaim 73–5
achievement
   failure 126–7
   loss of 71–3
   sense of 349–50
adjustment 31–2, 44
age of mothers 3, 122–3
ageing 95
anaemia 101
anger 144–6, 171–2, 175, 208
ankles 97
appreciation of other women 337–8
assertiveness 225, 346
autonomy, loss of 68–9
B
babies
   bonding 22–30, 45–6
   breastfeeding 38–41, 47
   changes 66, 68, 345–6
   crying 43, 64–5, 87–8
   disruption to conversation 112
   empathy for 153
   failure to relate to 125–6
   health 105–6
   instinct to protect 50–3
   sleep 36–8, 47
   temperament 106
   time consuming 63–4
behaviour modification 172
behavioural problems 119
birth
   difficult 27, 28
   discussion with other mothers 113–14
   emotional impact 12–14
   expectations 44–5
   experiences 19–22
   health effects of 100–3

physical effects 94–100
single mothers 230–2
support organisations 363–4, 365, 366, 367, 368, 370, 372
bladder 99
blame 232–3, 272. *see also* judgementalism
blood pressure, high 17
blues 161–6
body changes 94–8
body image 103–5
bonding
   difficulties 24–30, 168
   ensuring 45–6
   successful 22–4
bottle feedings 40
bottom 97–8
bowels 98
breastfeeding 38–41, 47, 132
breasts
   changes 96
   during feeding 39–40
business management, women in 343–4
C
caesarean section 19–20
calves 97–8
career 3, 29. *see also* workforce, mothers in
changes
   partner's adjustment to 181
   result of motherhood 306–7, 328
child abuse 145–6, 171, 174, 300–1
child care
   benefits 326–7, 353
   experiences 298–304
   reluctance to use 52
   single mothers 244–5
   support organisations 364, 365, 366, 367, 368, 370, 371, 372
   working mothers 330
child welfare authorities 172
childbirth *see* birth
childhood issues 155–9, 175
childless women

INDEX

friends 285–6
judgements 118
children, other people's 289–90, 325–6
cinemas 130
clothes 104–5
colic 39, 43, 87
communication
   conversation 63, 112–14, 133
   with other mothers 340–2
   with partner 192–3, 219–20
compassion 340
competitive mothering 286–8
completeness 348–9
confidence 347
conflict
   effects of motherhood 359–62
   resolution 225–6
   result of exhaustion 35
connectedness 340–2
conspiracy of silence 79–84, 91–2
constipation 98
control 138–42, 242–3
conversation 63, 112–14, 133, 192–3
cooking 48
coping
   breakdown 206–9
   effects of motherhood 357–8
   failure 124
   loss of control 138–42
courage 344–5
crying baby 43, 64–5, 87–8
D
death, fear of 151–2, 173
debriefing 113
decision-making 241–3
dependency 183–7, 216–19
depression
   cause 141
   experiences 161–6
   help 176–7
   men 188
   postnatal 9, 141
diabetes 101
disabled child 105–6, 132
discipline 244
divorce and separation 191, 214–15, 241, 243, 246–9
'doing' paradigm 9–11, 23, 354
E
economic imperative 4–5
   single mothers 237–40
EIQ (emotional intelligence quotient) 170–1

emotional abuse 211–12
emotional dependency 186, 218
emotional growth 347–8
emotional intelligence quotient (EIQ) 170–1, 174
emotionalism 142–3
emotions 138–78
   anger and rage 144–6, 171–2
   blues, stress and depression 161–6, 176–7
   childhood issues 155–9
   control and coping 138–42
   emotionalism 142–3
   empathy 152–5, 174
   envy 202–3
   fear 148–52, 173–4
   frustration 143–4, 171–2
   grief 160–1, 175–6
   guilt 146–7, 172
   joy 143
   love 168–70, 178
   post traumatic stress 167–8, 177–8
   responsibility 147–8
empathy
   benefits 174–5
   experiences 152–5
   with other mothers 340
   partner's lack of 190–2
   quality of family life 225
energy, loss of 103
entertainments 70, 130
envy 202–3
episiotomies 101
equality
   definition 9–11
   experiences 198–9
   gender roles 220
   insistence on 223
   limitations 49–50
   loss of 3–4
   mother's role 201
   single mothers 266
ex-partners 245–9, 274–5
exhaustion
   effect on mental ability 42, 48
   effect on recovery from labour 101–2
   experiences 32–6
   prevention 46–7
   single mothers 237
expressing milk 40

extended family
  breakdown 294–7
  support systems 54
eye contact 45–6
F
face, changes in 94–5
facilities 69–71
failure 124–7, 134–6
faith 350
family
  appreciation 338–9
  breakdown 294–7
  feeling of 205–6, 224–5
  relationships 283–5, 324–5
family services 363, 364–5, 366, 367, 368, 369, 370, 371
father, one's own 283
fatherhood 188
fathers *see* partners
fatigue *see* exhaustion
fear 148–52, 173–4
feedback 93
feminism 49–50, 127, 208, 318–19
fetus, parents' attitude to 18
financial dependency 184–5, 216–17
financial independence 242–3
fitness 100–3, 131–2
flexibility 86–7
freedom
  loss of 56–9
  reclaiming 85–6
friendship
  experiences 285–6
  meaningful 338–9
  need for 325
  search for 60–1
  single mothers 255–8
  working mothers 306–7
frustration 143–4, 171–2, 208
G
genetic programming 179
'glow' of pregnancy 94
goal-setting 275–6
grandmothers 278–83, 295–6, 324
grief 160–1, 175–6
growth, personal 175
guilt
  experiences 146–7
  failure to bond 25–6
  lack of time 64
  purpose 171–2
  single mothers 232–3, 243–5

H
haemorrhoids 16, 98–9
hair changes 95–6
handicaps 28
health
  baby's 105–6
  mother's 100–3, 131–2
  during pregnancy 16–17, 28
  single mothers 234
help, asking for 78–9, 90–1, 110
high blood pressure 17
hips 97–8
holidays 304–6, 327
homoeopathy 132
hormones 41, 50, 160
horror hours 43, 48
hospitals
  birth 20–1
  mother-child bonding 23–4, 28
  single mothers 230–1
humiliation 237–40, 273–4
humility 339–40
humour, sense of 85
husbands *see* partners
hyperemesis 16
I
identity 107–8, 132–3
immersion-mania continuum 67
imprinting 157–8
in-laws 280–2
income 4, 184–5
independence 262
instinct 50–3, 84
interdependence 216–19, 225
interests, personal, interruptions to 62–4
interruptions 86
intimacy 194–5, 222–3
IQ 170–1
iron deficiency 101
isolation
  cause 3
  effects 110, 290–8
  experiences 59–62
  feelings of abandonment 54
  need for child care 304
  single mothers 265
J
journal 44
joy 143
judgementalism
  avoiding 134
  childless women 154

INDEX

effect on self-esteem 109
experiences 118–24
single mothers 232–3, 254, 267

L

labour
  difficult 119
  reactions to 19
leisure *see* time out
letting go 170
Local Exchange Trading System (LETS) 274
loneliness 59–62
losses 160
love 168–70, 178, 350–1
lovemaking 116, 134, 195–8, 221–2

M

madness 145–6
mania 65–8, 88
marriage *see* partners
masculinity 211
mastitis 40
maternity leave 313–14
memory of motherhood 123–4
men *see* partners
mental abuse 211–12
mental dependency 185–6, 218
mental effects
  of exhaustion 34–5, 42, 48
  of pregnancy 41
milk 39, 50
mobile society 3
mortality, fear of 151–2, 173
mother, one's own 155–9, 278–83, 295–6, 324
mother-child relationships 157–8, 262–4
mothers-in-law 280–2
mothers, other
  appreciation of 337–8
  communication with 113–14
  empathy for 153–4
  isolation from 60–1
  relationships with 286–90
  single mothers' relationships with 236, 272–3

N

needs, failure to meet 124–5
networking 272–3
nipples
  changes 96
  sore 39
nuclear family, rise of 165
Nursing Mothers Association of Australia 47, 132
nurturing instinct 50–1, 84

O

obsession 65–8, 70
obstetricians 45
organisations 363–72

P

paid work *see* workforce, mothers in
pain during labour 19
panic attacks 167
parenting
  assistance and advice 363, 364–5, 366, 367, 368, 369, 370, 371
  conflict with partner 204–5, 224
  single mothers 270
  style 279
parents, one's own 155–9, 278–83, 295–6, 324
partners 179–228
  abuse of 213–15
  during birth 45
  breakdown of coping mechanisms 206–9
  changes in 187–9, 220
  communication with 192–3, 219–20
  dependency on 183–7, 216–19
  effect on bonding 29
  envy towards 202–3
  equality 198–9, 223
  exhaustion 46
  feedback 90
  feeling of 'family' 205–6, 224–5
  financial power 184
  intimacy 194–5, 222–3
  lack of empathy 190–2
  in mother's gossip 114
  mother's ill-health 103
  needs 125
  postnatal reactions 114
  power balance 199–201, 224
  raising the children 204–5
  resentment of new baby 180, 200
  response to single motherhood 232–3
  roles 201–2, 220–1
  security 182–3, 215–16
  selfish 189–90
  separated 191, 214–15, 241, 245–9, 246–9, 274–5
  sex 115–16, 133, 195–8, 221–2
  subject of mother's gossip 214–15
  unsupportive 17–18, 42–3
  violent 209–13
  woman's changes 220
  women without *see* single mothers
  women's changes 181
pension 238–9, 273

personal growth 175, 347–8
personal interests, interruptions to 62–4
personality changes 108
physical changes 94–100, 131
physical contact 87, 336–7
physical dependency 185, 217–18
physicality 335–7
planning ahead 58
playgroup 290
post traumatic stress 167–8, 177–8
postnatal depression (PND)
    cause 9, 141
    men 188
    support groups 176
postnatal psychosis 168
postnatal stress (PNS) 9, 161–6
poverty 128, 136, 237–40
power
    exercising 224
    relationship with partner 199–201
    return to work 312
    right to 217
pregnancy
    benefits 335–6
    body changes 94–6
    difficult 16–18, 28
    mental effects 41
    successful 15
    support organisations 363–4, 365, 366, 367, 368, 370
    unplanned 18
premature birth, effect on bonding 28
premature labour 17
priorities 221
productivity 10
protective instinct 52
psychosis 168
public facilities 69–71
public transport 136
Q
quality time 205–6, 224–5
questionnaire 7
R
rage 144–6, 171–2, 208
raising children see parenting
reasoning impaired due to exhaustion 34–5, 42, 48
recognition 73–5, 89–90
'relating' paradigm 10–11
relationships 277–332
    with child 135
    conversation 112–14

extended family 283–5, 324–5
failure 125–6
friends 285–6, 325
isolation 290–8
mother-child 157–8, 262–4
one's own mother 278–83, 324
other mothers 286–90
partners see partners
relaxation 75–8, 90, 304–6, 327
remarriage 261
resourcefulness 342–3
responsibility
    experiences 147–8
    moderating 172–3
    single mothers 241–3, 272
restaurants 305
rewards of motherhood 333–56
rites of passage 13–14
rituals 44
roles
    changes in 220–1
    models 158
    relations with partner 201–2
rural mothers 61, 326
S
school system 267–8
security 182–3, 215–16, 343–4
self-esteem 109–11, 232, 278
self-image 93–137
    baby's health 105–6
    conversation 112–14, 133
    failure 124–7, 134–6
    health and fitness 100–3, 131–2
    identity 107–8, 132–3
    others' judgements 118–24, 134
    physical changes 94–100, 131
    self-esteem 109–11
    self-perception 103–5
    sex appeal 114–16, 133–4
    social attitudes 127–33
    status 116–18
self-perception 103–5
selfish partners 189–90
sense of humour 85
sensuality 335–7
separation after birth 23–4, 28
separation, marital see divorce and separation
sex appeal 114–16, 133–4
sex life 116, 134, 195–8, 221–2
sex of baby 29
shop design 129, 130, 136
single mothers 229–76

INDEX

benefits 269–71
birth experience 230–2
blame 232–3, 272
decisions and responsibility 241–3
ex-partners 245–9, 274–5
guilt 243–5
lack of support for 264–9
mother-child relationships 262–4
paths to 229–30
poverty and humiliation 237–40, 273–4
relationships with men 250–1, 258–62
schedule 252–4
social attitudes to 268–9, 271
social life 255–8
stress 233–7
vulnerability 250–2
sleep
  babies 36–8, 47
  deprivation 32–6
social life 29, 255–8
social security 238–9, 273
social status 116–18
society's attitudes 127–33, 136–7
sole mothers *see* single mothers
spiritual dependency 186–7, 218
spirituality 350
spontaneity 56–9, 86
status 116–18
step-fathers 260
stimulation 106
stress
  experiences 41–3, 161–6
  mitigating 48, 176–7
  post traumatic 167–8, 177–8
  postnatal 9, 161–6
  during pregnancy 16
  single mothers 233–7
stretch marks 97
study 70
support
  lack of 291–2
  network 84–5
  organisations 363–72
  search for 54–5
  for single mothers 264–9
survey 6–9

T
tears (during birth) 101
television 129, 136–7
temperament
  baby's 106, 132
  disparity in 126
  mother-child relationship 263–4
thighs 97–8
time out
  ensuring 90
  experiences 75–8
  lack of 62–4
  single mothers 234, 276
toddlers 63–4
touch 336–7
toughness 342
toxaemia 17
transport 136
trapped feeling 68–71
travel 305
tribal societies 13, 164, 218, 290
trust 298–9

U
unplanned pregnancy 18
unresolved personal issues 155–9
unsupportive partners 17–18
urban mothers 61–2
urinary problems 99
uselessness, feeling of 72
uterus, prolapsed 99

V
vagina 99–100
vaginal bleeding 17
varicose veins 16, 97
violence
  against children 145–6, 171, 174, 300–1
  against men 213–15
  poverty 240
  against separated mothers 248
  by step-fathers 260
  support organisations 364, 365, 366, 367, 368, 370, 371, 372
  against women 209–13, 226–8

W
weaning 41, 47
work community 60
workforce, mothers in 307–24
  choosing to return 328–32
  conflict with instinct 51–2
  guilt 147
  judgementalism 119–22, 119–22
  reasons for 4
  rejoining 306–7
  security 343–4
  single mothers 252–3, 266–7
wrinkles 95